# NICK GREINER

## A Political Biography

By the same author:

*White Liberals, Moderates and Radicals in Rhodesia, 1953-1980*
and with Peter Godwin,
*Rhodesians Never Die: White Reactions to War
and Political Change, 1970-1980*

*National and Permanent?: The Federal Organisation
of the Liberal Party of Australia, 1944-1965*

*John Gorton: He Did It His Way*

*The Liberals: A History of the NSW Division
of the Liberal Party of Australia 1945-2000*

# Nick Greiner

*A Political Biography*

## Ian Hancock

ppi public policy institute

connorcourt PUBLISHING

✛ACU AUSTRALIAN CATHOLIC UNIVERSITY

Published in 2013 by Connor Court Publishing Pty Ltd

Connor Court Publishing Pty Ltd.

PO Box 1

Ballan VIC 3342

sales@connorcourt.com

www.connorcourt.com


ISBN: 9781922168542 (pbk.)

Cover design by Ian James

Printed in Australia

# CONTENTS

# Government, Policy and Politics Series

## A partnership between Connor Court Publishing and Public Policy Institute, Australian Catholic University

*Greiner: A Political Biography* by Ian Hancock is part of the **Government, Policy and Politics Series**, a joint initiative of Connor Court Publishing and the Public Policy Institute (PPI), Australian Catholic University (ACU). The series seeks to explore past, present and future developments in Australian government, policy and politics.

Ian Hancock is a distinguished historian and biographer, for three decades based at the Department of History at the Australian National University, and, for a period, head of the department. He is now a Visiting Fellow at the Public Policy Institute, ACU, Editorial Fellow at the Australian Dictionary of Biography and author of numerous books about Australian and African history.

The Public Policy Institute is an academic unit within the ACU involved in research, analysis and commentary on a range of public policy issues. The PPI undertakes policy-relevant research, provides analysis and commentary on important issues on the public agenda and seeks active engagement with the broad policy community.

**Series Editor: Professor Scott Prasser, Executive Director, Public Policy Institute, Australian Catholic University.**

**Books in the Series:**

Gary Johns, *Right Social Justice – Better Ways to Help the Poor* (2012)

Graeme Starr, *Carrick: Principles, Policy and Politics* (2012)

Scott Prasser & Helen Tracey, *Royal Commissions and Public Inquiries – A Citizen's Guide* (2013)

Scott Prasser & Helen Tracey (eds), *The What, How and Why of Royal Commissions and Public Inquiries* (2013)

John Nethercote, Scott Prasser & Nicholas Aroney (eds), *Her Majesty's Loyal Oppositions* (2013)

# Abbreviations

| | |
|---|---|
| ABC | Australian Broadcasting Corporation |
| *ADB* | *Australian Dictionary of Biography* |
| *AFR* | *Australian Financial Review* |
| ASX | Australian Securities Exchange |
| CAC | Corporate Affairs Commission |
| *DT* | *Daily Telegraph* |
| *DTM* | *Daily Telegraph Mirror* |
| Elcom | Electricity Commission |
| EPA | Environmental Protection Authority |
| FIM | Fédération de Internationale Motorcyclisme |
| GTE | Government Trading Enterprise |
| ICAC | Independent Commission Against Corruption |
| INSW | Infrastructure NSW |
| IPA | Institute of Public Affairs |
| LPA | Liberal Party of Australia |
| ML | Mitchell Library |
| NAA | National Archives of Australia |
| NLA | National Library of Australia |
| NCP | National Country Party |
| NP | National Party |
| *NSWPD* | *New South Wales Parliamentary Debates* |
| PJC | Parliamentary Joint Committee |
| *SMH* | *Sydney Morning Herald* |

# Preface

Nick Greiner, Premier of NSW from 1988 to 1992, set out to be a better manager and a reformer of what he called the largest business in the State, namely, the government.

Unlike other post-war Premiers of NSW he came into office with a wide-ranging program most of which, at considerable political cost, he implemented with speed. Greiner made "NSW Inc." more accountable, efficient and honest. He initiated or presided over significant and lasting changes to financial management, to the structure and culture of the Public Service, and to industrial relations, education, and transport. He promoted the corporatisation and, in a few cases, the privatisation of government trading enterprises, advanced the cause of open government and budget honesty, and attacked corruption. A leader in Australia in pursuing micro-economic reform, and never parochial in outlook, Greiner supported Bob Hawke's "New Federalism" as a means of improving Australia's competitive position in world markets, and was instrumental in the formation of the Council of Australian Governments.

It is a quarter of a century since Greiner became Premier. Sufficient time has passed to allow a study of the man who changed how NSW is governed, influenced methods of governance throughout Australia and who, through Infrastructure NSW and informal advice to the O'Farrell Government, continues to press the case for reform.

This book explores Greiner's life and political career. It examines his family background and education, his entry into politics and rise to the leadership of the Liberal Party in NSW, his actions, achievements and failings as Leader of the Opposition and as Premier, his forced departure from government and, briefly, his subsequent career in business to which he brought approaches he once used in politics. It describes and explains his motivations and habits of mind and considers the conventional wisdoms about "Greinerism" and about Greiner himself. The objective is to explore a political life, albeit one undertaken because his original, preferred career was obstructed. It is not a story about the Greiner Government but about the man who led it.

Several themes are woven into this narrative. There is the question of assimilation. Greiner's Hungarian father and Slovak mother, both wartime refugees, wanted their elder son to embrace what they regarded as the "quintessential" Australian culture. Greiner did not, until his early thirties, become fully conscious of his European and part-Jewish inheritance, and of his parents' experience of hardship and persecution. Protected from "Hungarianism" as a boy, Greiner identified with, and supported, ethnic communities throughout the 1980s and the 1990s, even as he sounded and acted like a cultivated "Anglo" Australian.

Greiner's life has been shaped by various personal and intellectual influences. Four individuals stand out: Miklós, the driven father he tried so hard to impress, expected his son to join him in business and made it impossible for him to stay; Clare, his mother, who was a great encourager and promoted his adaptation; Kathryn, his wife, who provided the missing social skills, captivated those with whom he had to deal, stood by him in every crisis, and accepted him back after he took what she called his "sabbatical" from their marriage; and Gary Sturgess, the adviser who joined his staff in 1983, headed the Cabinet Office during Greiner's premiership, and who was an inexhaustible source of ideas, delivered many of the arguments and the words of what became "Greinerism", and was at once Greiner's closest confidante and someone he could not afford – politically – to follow all of the time.

Two of the major influences were his drive to excel, and his experience of the Harvard Business School (1968-70). Greiner openly admits that modesty is not one of his virtues, and he has little reason for thinking it should be. From his arrival in prep school, he did not need any prompting to strive to be the best; it was rare for him not to come top academically and in debating; and he was always highly competitive in sport. At Harvard he was perhaps the youngest and certainly among the least prepared of the 700 students in his class. He nevertheless finished in the top 19. Harvard confirmed and expanded habits of mind: the emphasis on evidence-based, rational approaches to decision-making; the ready acceptance of change and risk; the focus on outcomes rather than processes; the preference for practical solutions over ideological consistency.

Greiner's political and personal life has been marked by paradox and contradiction. Apparently shy, remote, and even awkward, he has boundless self-confidence. He could seek advice but usually preferred his own. In politics he was conscious of, and reacted to, new ideas and worlds outside his own. At the same time, he was sometimes narrow in appreciating what was important, and remained almost impervious to emotional influences until later in his life. Seeing himself as a "non-politician", he was almost alarmingly frank and honest, and readily agrees with those who thought he had "unbelievably bad political instincts". Senior public servants liked him because they saw him acting on the basis of what seemed "right" rather than what was popular. Yet Bob Carr thought he was a "textbook" Leader of the Opposition and an astute "political" Premier. Supposedly uncompromising, and accused of being "ideological", Greiner could make populist decisions and retreat from preferred actions in the face of political fall-out. For all the appearance of toughness, he was not a Paul Keating or a Jeff Kennett.

He was always a Liberal but remained a non-conformist and an outsider within a Party of which he was the unchallenged Leader for nine years whilst often repudiating or ignoring its beliefs and conventions. He was always relaxed and appeared supremely rational, was not a good "hater", and quickly forgave his enemies in politics, if he ever actually thought about them. Even so, he carries a simmering resentment towards Ian Temby, the ICAC Commissioner, whose finding of "corrupt conduct" led to his political demise and obliged him to become a wealthy businessman earlier than planned.

The book draws attention to many of Greiner's qualities which

xi

help explain his actions: his self-belief, integrity, work ethic, intelligence and first-class debating skills; an ability to go quickly to the heart of any matter; an innate rationality, common sense and calmness under pressure. One of his great virtues and defining characteristics, however, contributed to what many at the time saw as his "tragic" downfall in June 1992 at the hands of his creation, ICAC, and of three non-aligned Independents. Nick Greiner has always been a strategic thinker, an unusual phenomenon in NSW and, indeed, in Australian politics. He was not a micro-manager. He left the details to others. In April 1992 he sought to bolster his numbers in the Legislative Assembly by securing the appointment of another Independent, the former Liberal Terry Metherell, to a senior position in the Public Service. Greiner reasoned that such an appointment was good politics but did not give sufficient attention to the method of securing his objective and to the pitfalls entailed.

On the day after his coerced resignation, Paddy McGuinness described Greiner as "the best failed Premier NSW has ever had, and a far better Premier than any of those who retired voluntarily". It is a judgment that probably still stands.

In writing this book I have made extensive use of what is on the public record. I have had access to Greiner's considerable personal records and to other family material, including extended recorded interviews with Greiner's late father, and to the private papers of Peter Collins, Rosemary Foot, Chris Puplick, Terry Metherell, Peta Seaton and Graeme Starr, and to Gary Sturgess' diary as well as to the Liberal Party's papers held in Canberra and Sydney. I have had many interviews with Greiner himself, as well as with Kathryn, the two Greiner children and Nick's brother, and with several former parliamentary and cabinet colleagues, Liberal Party officials, Greiner's key staff and many of his senior public service advisers and, among others, with Bob Carr, John Howard and Ian Temby.

A number of people helped me along the way. The Greiner family members were always very co-operative and forthcoming. Nick read two separate versions of the manuscript, and gently pointed out errors of fact or added more information. Instead, however, of reacting as former politicians often do – by rejecting even the mildest of criticism – he offered his own frank and often unfavourable assessments of his record. At no stage was I under pressure to modify judgments, or to by-pass sensitive issues.

I am very grateful to Lyn Jarrett in Nick's office who organised meetings and provided me with the space to read the Greiner papers. The librarians at the Mitchell Library in Sydney and at the National Library in Canberra were, as always, very professional, and Gareth Griffith of the State Parliamentary Library gave me access to the transcript of the Metherell inquiry.

Ainsley Gotto, with whom I worked in writing a biography of Sir John Gorton, suggested I approach Nick Greiner with the idea of writing his biography, and has since been encouraging while demanding I finish the job. She, along with Glenda Jones, Alastair McKenzie, Chris Puplick and Sebastian Hancock, commented on earlier drafts. Frank Bongiorno, David Clune and Ken Turner read the entire manuscript, and dealt with solecisms or questioned interpretations in their customarily informed and incisive manner.

John Nethercote, as ever, has given generously of his editorial experience and skills, and of his knowledge and understanding of Australian politics and government. My gratitude to him extends even further on this occasion; he helped me to obtain a publisher and assisted throughout the publication process.

I should also like to thank Michael Gilchrist for his forbearance and for his prompt and highly professional editing.

My greatest debt is to Susan Sharpe. It was difficult enough changing course from spending 15 years farming wild boar in Suffolk, England, to take on a new lifestyle in Canberra. Adjusting to a partner absorbed in the life of a former NSW Premier added to the challenge. But, like Nick Greiner, she is not "risk averse". Like him, too, she is also an "outsider", able to point out in her meticulous reading of the manuscript that what to the author looked to be clear and obvious was actually neither. More importantly, this book would not have been completed without her being there.

The errors, the choice of emphasis and the interpretations remain my responsibility.

# 1

# Three "New Australians"

Nicholas ("Nick") Frank Hugo Greiner was born on 27 April 1947 in Budapest, Hungary, the son of a Hungarian father and a Slovak mother. He arrived in Sydney with his parents in 1951 when he was not yet four years old. His mother had barely survived a Nazi concentration camp. His father, an enterprising and successful timber merchant, had witnessed and experienced two world wars, a depression and two communist takeovers which had severely reduced the Greiner family's worldly possessions. It was not until his early thirties that the son of two refugees, who had wanted to leave central Europe and its turbulence behind them, became fully aware of his cultural and ethnic inheritance and parental background.

## Hungary

Miklós Greiner was born in Budapest in 1908 in a country which, after a thousand years of shifts and turns, appeared to be achieving a measure of stability. The Magyars, the largest tribe to occupy what became Hungary (Magyarország), had moved there from an area lying between the Volga River and the Ural Mountains.[1] They established their state in 895 AD and proceeded to raid western and central Europe. Defeated in 955 by the forces of the Holy Roman Empire, their leaders converted to Christianity. King Stephen I was crowned by one Pope and canonised by another. "Historic Hungary", sometimes known as "Greater Hungary", consisted then of the vast lands of the Carpathian Basin. Strong kings proceeded to build a strong state; weak kings would preside over a weakened one; peasants and serfs and noble families and lesser gentry forever competed for rights or asserted claims; minority peoples sought rights, formed alliances and broke away; and the boundaries of the state periodically retreated or expanded. The peoples of Hungary always seemed to be at war with someone, and the winners tended to brutalise and butcher the losers, especially if those they vanquished shared their language and culture.

For three centuries Hungary withstood attacks from several neighbouring sources but the Mongol invasions of the 13th century temporarily subjugated a large proportion of the population. More seriously, the Ottoman Turks conquered much of Historic Hungary early in the 16th century, and the country was divided into three parts in 1541 following the capture of the city of Buda. The Austrian-centred Hapsburg empire took over the north-west, the independent Principality of Transylvania under Ottoman suzerainty assumed control in the east, and the Ottomans established the Pashalik of Buda. Following the expulsion of the Ottomans at the end of the 17th century the Hapsburgs remained as occupiers and proceeded to leech the occupied.

Inspired in part by the French Revolution, a revolt against the Hapsburgs united most classes among the Magyar speakers and continued into the mid-19th century. It culminated in attacks on the feudal land tenure system and serfdom and in a movement for democracy and industrialisation. On 15 March 1848 – the Ides of March – a group of young radicals issued a series of demands for the nobility to renounce their privileges, for the introduction of direct elections to parliament, and for guarantees of the freedom of religion, speech and the press. They initially made some progress in what also became a struggle for independence. But the Hapsburgs, supported by the Czar of Russia, reacting like other rulers to the revolutions in Europe in 1848, moved in to suppress the rebels. Inevitably, there was another brutal round of retribution before a compromise was reached in 1867: the emperor became the king of Hungary which was united with Austria while

Hungary retained its own government and full control over the non-Magyar nationalities. The period until the Great War became the halcyon if belated years of economic progress and a vibrant cultural life, and Budapest – the cities of Buda and Pest were united in 1873 – became the new centre of modernity.

Miklós Greiner began his life in a well-to-do Catholic family which had been involved in the saw milling industry for three generations.[2] His great grandfather had started the business in northern Hungary in 1822. The company's headquarters moved to Buda in the mid-19th century. Hugo, Miklós' father, a Doctor of Law and a solicitor who never practised, joined with his two younger brothers in taking over around 1890. With Hugo acting, in effect, as chairman, the brothers exploited the economic prosperity at the end of the century, bought church and state-owned forests, and converted their company into one of the three largest saw millers in the country. It would seem that Hugo presided over a civilised household where Gustav Mahler and several opera singers and musicians were among the visitors.

The Government enthusiastically joined the Germans and the Austrians in 1914 and entered the Great War by invading Serbia. The timber industry prospered in the short term because of the need for war materials and because the brothers were too old to go to the front. Miklós remembered going to the main railway station to meet the wounded as they returned to Budapest and spoke of a cousin joining the fighting in a war which had little personal impact on the Greiner family. But the aftermath was critical. By 1918 the Austro-Hungarian Empire had collapsed and some two million Hungarian soldiers were prisoners of war. There had been a major devaluation of the currency, a liberal-socialist revolution in October was followed by the declaration of a republic in November, and the neighbouring peoples were demanding their own nation states. The communists, headed by Béla Kun, established the Hungarian Soviet Republic in March 1919 which succeeded in alienating almost every class and grouping among the Magyars by trying to do too much too soon. The communist interregnum lasted just 133 days and Kun was later executed in the Soviet Union after another Stalinist purge. Though short-lived, the world's second communist government put pressure on the Greiners. The youngest of the three brothers was arrested and detained for a few months while Hugo, his wife and only son fled to Vienna. As they waited for a boat to cross the Danube a terrified Miklós recalled how he cried out, "I don't want to die yet".

Hugo's family returned to Budapest soon after the communists themselves took flight, victims on 1 August of an Allied-supported counter-revolution which outmatched the communists in imposing a reign of terror. By then the brothers had lost 90 per cent of their considerable wealth. Miklós recalled how his father's war bonds were "not worth a packet of cigarettes". The peace conditions of the Treaty of Trianon (1920) approved a drastic carve-up of Hungary: it lost two-thirds of its territory and three-fifths of its inhabitants. The Czechs, Slovaks, Serbs, Croatians, Slovenians and Transylvanian Romanians took over long-coveted lands. Following elections in 1921 the National Assembly appointed Miklós Horthy, a former aide-de-camp of Emperor Franz Joseph, as the regent of what was left of Hungary. Hampered by its delayed entry into the 19th century economic take-off, and hurt by the First World War and the Great Depression of the 1930s, Hungary remained primarily an agrarian, semi-feudal society with only a small secondary industry, mostly located in Budapest.

Hugo started again and gradually prospered, though on a relatively modest scale. The brothers had at least retained their physical assets though they now had "only a shadow of their previous standing". Meanwhile, Miklós resumed his lessons at the leading Catholic school in Budapest, his first four years having been spent with a private tutor. He excelled more at games than in the class room, happy enough to obtain middle-level marks while proving to be highly competitive in athletics and ice hockey. He wanted to enter the timber industry as soon as possible rather than go to university. Leaving school in 1926 he went to Transylvania to gain experience in a saw mill which the brothers had recently acquired. Miklós did not get on well with his uncles. Nevertheless, his on-the-job experience at all levels of the industry gave him the confidence and understanding to set himself up in Australia in the 1950s. By the outbreak of the Second World War in 1939 he was in charge of the family's White River Company.

"With faultless consistency", according to Volgyes, "Hungary has always chosen the losing side in war." Allied to the Axis Powers, it successfully reclaimed some neighbouring territory before formally entering the Second World War in support of the German invasion of the Soviet Union. But some serious military reverses in 1943-4 prompted Horthy to pursue terms with the Allies. In response, the Germans occupied the country, installed a puppet government and, with the assistance of local Nazis, deported thousands of Jews for extermination. The Germans, and then the Soviets (who took Budapest in February 1945), along with the Czechs and Serbian partisans, proceeded to murder, rape, execute and deport at will. More than 400,000 Hungarians were killed in the Second World War, property damage probably took 40 per cent of the country's wealth, and all the bridges over the Danube and the Tisza, 35 per cent of the country's railway installations, 80 per cent of its rolling stock and the entire Danube fleet were destroyed.

Although he was called up and served for a time in Poland, Miklós Greiner followed his father's footsteps during the Great War by supplying material for Hungary's war effort. The White River Company prospered. One night in Budapest, in 1943, he invited a woman to dinner. She asked if she could bring a friend. The host was not at all pleased, though he felt obliged to agree. Clare Redlinger was the "blind date".

## Slovakia

Born in 1907 in what has been known as Bratislava since 1919, Clare grew up in a non-observant Jewish family and followed her mother in becoming a Catholic. Her father was a jeweller. Trained as a teacher, Clare was fluent in several languages: Slovak, Hungarian, German, French and Italian. She married before war broke out but lost her husband who, along with other members of his family, was shot by the Nazis on the banks of the Danube. Clare had moved to Budapest with a younger sister who, towards the end of the War, persuaded her to return to Bratislava. She agreed to go despite the welcome attentions of the Budapest timber merchant.

The non-Jewish Slovaks had managed to avoid the Second World War until 1944, although the Treaty of Protection provided for free passage of German forces through the country and Slovakian troops initially fought with the Germans inside the Soviet Union.[3] The Nazis had given Slovakia the illusion of being a nation state. From the tenth century until the dismemberment of the Austro-Hungarian Empire at the end of the Great War it had been part of Historic Hungary. Thereafter the Slovaks were linked to the Czechs, their ethnic-linguistic brethren, and obtained a measure of local autonomy to complement their rising national consciousness. Czechoslovakia was dismembered after Munich in 1938, resulting in the formation of the first Slovak Republic under the leadership of Monsignor Joseph Tiso. But the Republic was just a German vassal state. Restrictions were placed on Slovakian Jews. They were forbidden to own agricultural land; shops and other property were seized; and more than 57,000 were deported to Poland between March and October 1942. An opposition alliance emerged in 1943 between the Slovak communists and those Slovaks who supported the Czech government-in-exile, although the real objective of many among the latter was the creation of a genuinely independent Slovak state. The alliance launched a military uprising against the Slovak Government in August 1944 which was smashed after two months with the arrival of German reinforcements brought in with Tiso's backing.

Tiso's administration had probably protected about 35,000 Jews from deportation in 1942 but there were few exceptions after the 1944 uprising was suppressed. Some 11,500 Jews were subsequently deported to labour and death camps in Germany and Poland. Clare Redlinger was among them. Denounced as a Jew by one of her father's former employees, she was transported to the Ravensbrück labour camp in northern Germany. Ravensbrück was established by the SS as the largest women's concentration camp in the Third Reich. It was later expanded to include males and held just over 150,000 inmates of various nationalities during the War, of whom tens of thousands were either murdered or died of hunger or disease or as a result of medical experiments. Although not originally a death camp, gas chambers were constructed around the time Clare arrived at the end of 1944. Between 5,000 and 6,000 prisoners were gassed by April 1945. The Greiner family attributed Clare's survival to her ability to speak German, and she may well have protected a younger cousin and some others.[4]

After the Red Army liberated the camp on 30 April 1945, Clare returned to Budapest where she renewed her relationship with Miklós. Writing to her uncle Edy on 1 June 1946, she spoke of having been in Prague for a few days and was about to leave for Paris to join her sisters. She had not seen one of them – Camilla (who appears later in this book) – since before the outbreak of war. In this letter Clare referred to negotiations she had undertaken to link her uncle to a company dealing with products such as bijouterie, leather belts and pearls. The letter then mentioned "something personal". She had "fallen in love with a Budapest timber merchant". He came from "a first class family, solid, full of character, very smart and presents well, a first class business man". Clare had known him for three years and thought it "(m)ost likely" they would marry towards the end of 1946. "We love each other very, very much."[5]

They in fact married soon after this letter was written, starting their life together as Miklós sought to restore the family business, much as his father had been forced to do after the Great War. His home had been destroyed, bombed by the invading Soviets. Only a green hat and his formal dinner wear had survived. Unable to have children by her first husband, on 27 April 1947, almost two years to the day after she left Ravensbrück, Clare gave birth to a son, Nick, in a Budapest hospital. The father, who was present, was "horrified" because the baby emerged with a head "like an egg". It was not a complicated birth, although Clare had been sedated. She was aged 39.

## A communist state

Hungary had once again become a republic. Following democratic elections, a broad-based coalition government took office. The Soviet Union, however, helped the small Hungarian Communist Party apply the "salami tactic" of slicing off rival parties to take control of the coalition. Seizing power in 1947, the Party quickly collectivised agriculture, forced the development of heavy industry, imposed central planning and eliminated or incarcerated real and suspected opponents or deported them to Soviet labour camps. The "Political Police Section" became one of the state's instruments, with its "Economical Section" hounding the "class enemy". Yet, unlike his treatment of Bulgaria, Poland and Romania, Stalin was in no hurry to convert Hungary into a satellite state. Historians have as a consequence argued about the formal beginning of communist rule which occurred somewhere between 1947 and 1949, by which time the communists were in complete control and Hungary was firmly placed within the Soviet bloc.

The communists took over the Greiner timber company and all its assets in the year Nick was born. At the end of October 1947, when leading industry figures were being arrested, the Greiner's butler, who was also the cook, announced during dinner that "two gentlemen" were at the door. They had come with a search warrant. Discovering a substantial quantity of cash – Miklós did not believe in keeping money in banks – they asked why he had so much, and why so much of it consisted of foreign currency. They departed soon after, whereupon Miklós burnt a book he described as listing "illegal expenses". It would be "detrimental" if found. He had made the right move. The secret police returned within

90 minutes and arrested both parents, leaving Nick in the care of his nanny. Miklós and Clare were taken to the secret police headquarters in Budapest and placed in the "Economical Section". Clare was released the next day but her husband was detained for nearly six weeks.

At first, Miklós was kept in a room measuring 4 x 6 metres with about a dozen others. After three days he was moved to a "comfortable" cell by himself that "wasn't too bad". Besides, a Norwegian merchant was allowed to visit him to conduct business. He was interrogated about aspects of his financial activities but his interrogators had nothing concrete on him, although they did recall seeing the book in the apartment before it had been destroyed. Miklós believed, no doubt correctly, that an instruction had been issued to find some evidence. To assist the process, he was moved to a two-man cell where it was impossible to stand up, and it was difficult even to breathe. Yet his interrogator was "a decent fellow" and, unlike many others in the same building, he was not beaten and felt he looked so much better than his distraught wife when she visited him.

The authorities did, however, find an excuse to hold him. Miklós had maintained a significant bartering business with suppliers in Romania delivering rails and small trucks in return for their timber. He was accused of tax evasion because, whilst the assets held in Romania had been declared, he had not paid tax on them. At Miklós' insistence, his "top book-keeper" was brought into police headquarters to confirm that all his actions were within the law. He had not paid tax because the assets had been confiscated by the Romanian authorities. After further interrogation some of his personal funds in Budapest were seized and he was released.

Miklós approached a friend in the finance area of the Hungarian Government who promised to help him to obtain restitution. Weeks passed, but nothing happened. After the friend's secretary told him on the telephone that nothing could be done, Miklós decided it was time to leave Hungary. The first step was to get Clare and the baby out of the country. She had a Czech passport, to which Nick's name was added illegally, enabling them both to secure an Austrian visa. To avoid the attention of the secret police who attended the main railway stations in force, Miklós stayed at home while the two boarded a train in Budapest for the journey to the Austrian border. He sent his butler to see whether his family left safely. Instead of returning immediately with the news of their successful departure, the butler spent the afternoon drinking. An agitated husband and father was not well pleased when his servant arrived home drunk in the evening.

Hoping to join his family in Vienna, Miklós paid to be smuggled out of the country. He was caught in the attempt. He had gone to a place near the frontier where he had previously done some business. Hearing of Red Army soldiers being prepared to take people into Austria, he dressed "like a proper gentleman", which included wearing a bowler hat, and joined a lorry with other would-be escapers. Shots were fired by some Soviet troops and a fellow sitting opposite him started bleeding and soon died. Miklós jumped out of the truck straight into the arms of the secret police. He heard afterwards that the case became complicated because the Soviets had killed a Hungarian and a court appearance could create embarrassing publicity. Miklós was returned to Budapest for interrogation where one of his interrogators, a White River customer, promised to help. Transferred to a prison camp just outside Budapest, Miklós remained there for two months until his customer was able to arrange some false documents and his release. In the meantime, he was required to report daily to the local police station where one of the officers, another acquaintance, came to the rescue when he missed an appointment.

Miklós tried once again to leave the country. One of his former employees arranged for him to cross the Czech border into Bratislava, carrying forged Austrian documents sent ahead by Clare. The ruse almost failed because the professional smuggler who had been engaged for the enterprise fell asleep and missed collecting him for the midnight crossing. Fortunately, the Soviet guards at the border accepted his documents. He entered Bratislava assisted by relatives of his former employee and then travelled by car to Vienna. There was one more unpleasant surprise. It was now May 1949. His son, who had not seen his father for more than 18 months, cried on meeting a stranger.[6] It took some time for Nick to accept the man who seemed to have appropriated the attentions of his mother.

A shrewd, bartering businessman, with contacts in many parts of Europe, could lose money and fixed assets yet not become impoverished. Miklós had already exported cash illegally to Vienna. He also had funds in other countries where he had previously done business, and had useful contacts in high places. One of them was the second-in-charge of the Vienna office of the post-war Marshall Plan who advised him on emigration to the United States. It also helped to be adept when confronting minor obstacles. After he went to Switzerland to reclaim some funds Miklós found, on returning to Vienna, that the Swiss authorities had denied him a re-entry permit. Two businessmen, who owed him money and wished to avoid payment, had informed Immigration that Miklós was using a forged passport. But he was able to obtain a transit visa from a Swiss Government representative in the Baltic States which he visited in pursuit of other business. Returning to Switzerland, he persuaded the two defaulters to pay up.

Life in Vienna was not normal for someone used to managing his own timber company in Budapest. The Greiners decided to leave Europe. So far as Miklós was concerned it really was a matter of collecting a map, closing his eyes and stabbing a finger on the page. But not quite: although he had visas for Chile and Argentina he wanted to go to an Anglo-Saxon country. So the family moved first to London where a man with whom he had skied in Austria in 1933 – the English friend was nicknamed "Bobby" and Miklós was "Paprika" – booked the Greiners a sea passage with the P&O line to Australia where some relatives were already living. Unfortunately, as they were about to board, young Nick was sick with influenza, and his father followed suit. Their landing permits as displaced persons apparently expired and the Marshall Plan contact was enlisted to secure an extension. Jack Tully, the NSW Agent-General in London and a former Secretary for Lands (1941-6) in the McKell Labor Government, provided the necessary visas. The ship had already left so the Greiners flew to New York where they stayed for a few days, resisting suggestions that they might apply to settle permanently. Instead, they flew on to San Francisco and then to Sydney where they arrived on 10 March 1951, the day after the High Court declared the Menzies Government's *Communist Party Dissolution Act* invalid.

## New arrivals

In 1949-50 more than 11,000 Hungarian-born refugees arrived in Australia; another 2,000 landed in 1950-1. The 1954 census recorded 14,602 Hungarian-born persons living in Australia; 9,054 were males. Hungarians had in fact been arriving in very small numbers since the 1830s. Some were Jews who found life in Europe unsettling. Others left because of the counter-revolution of 1848 or had heard exciting stories about rivers of gold in the Australian colonies. The numbers rose sharply from the mid-1930s as Hungarian Jews sensed an approaching crisis. Subsequent waves began with the so-called "westwarders" (some of them pro-Nazis and all of them fearing the invading Soviet forces), and were followed by those (usually Jewish) who saw what happened in 1944-5, the "border jumpers" who wanted to escape communist rule, and refugees who qualified as "displaced persons".

A striking feature of the post-war Hungarian intake was that many were young, single adults with tertiary qualifications. There were no peasants or workers among them. The older ones tended to be professional middle-class types or merchants or tradespeople.[7] In 1961 first-generation Hungarian migrants might have constituted just 0.314 per cent of the Australian population, and Hungarians might have accounted for only two per cent of the migrant intake between and 1945 and 1961. Yet many made a significant mark in Australian life. They included some who would cross the path of the young boy who arrived with the Greiner family in 1951. Four of them – (Sir) Peter Abeles, Joseph Brender, Frank Lowy and Larry Adler – contributed financially to Nick Greiner's political career. Ervin Graf would start the former Premier on his very successful, post-politics business career.

In 1951, however, the task for the Greiners was a basic one: to find a place to live and to establish a living. On arrival, the family moved into a very pleasant guest house in Cremorne. They could not stay there beyond one day because other families had prior bookings. Miklós went to see John Tully who happened to be in Sydney at the time. Tully found the Greiners a place to stay in Manly, a "horrible" flat – dirty and old and dusty – which made Clare "very unhappy". The real estate agency, Raine and Horne, subsequently found them a rental house in Greenwich where they remained for six years. Miklós had already acted on Tully's further advice. Within a fortnight of arriving in Sydney he visited a timber yard in Kempsey. He offered to buy some timber and then obtained an order from a "Scottish fellow" to supply material to the NSW Railways. His ability to meet the order within a week for what was then scarce material gave him a good reputation. With further assistance from Raine and Horne, Miklós soon acquired a timber yard at Guildford (he moved the operation to Greenacre in 1962), and he employed two Hungarians from Budapest as well as an Englishman. The White River Company was once again open for business.

In his history of the country he left after the Soviet Union crushed the uprising of 1956, Ivan Volgyes reproduced an oft-repeated "definition" of a Hungarian: "Someone who goes in the revolving door after you and comes out ahead of you."[8] The joke is said to reflect the national character: the caustic and dark humour and an acute self-awareness, along with an eye for the main chance. Nick Greiner's father was the perfect example of someone who, often against heavy odds, usually managed to come out of the door first. He was also the ideal "New Australian": he knew how to overcome adversity, was prepared to work hard and had arrived with portable skills. One of these skills was an instinct to recognise and to seize an opportunity; another – which was to annoy his Harvard-educated son – was how to barter and implement deals which advanced his business interests. Clare Greiner was also a perfect migrant. She ensured that her children assimilated into Australian society, and kept a careful eye on their progress by involving herself in their schools. Nick Greiner had clearly followed the advice sometimes attributed to Sir Robert Menzies; to do well, a man must first choose his parents wisely.

## Endnotes

1   This brief account draws principally on five texts: Jörge Hoensch, *A History of Modern Hungary – 1986*, translated by Kim Traynor, Longman, London, 1988; Miklós Molnár, *A Concise History of Hungary*, translated by Anna Magyar, Cambridge University Press, Cambridge, 2001; Steven Vardy, *Historical Dictionary of Hungary*, Scarecrow Press, London, 1997; Ivan Volgyes (ed.), *Hungary in Revolution 1918-19: Nine Essays*, University of Nebraska, Lincoln, 1971; and Volgyes, *Hungary: A Nation of Contradictions*, Westview Press, Colorado, 1982.

2   The following account of Miklós Greiner's life draws upon extended interviews with his grandson, Justin Greiner, conducted in 1991. The recordings are kept in the Greiner Papers. Unless otherwise identified, the direct quotations which follow are taken from those interviews.

3   The following account draws upon Stanislav J. Kirschbaum, *A History of Slovakia: the Struggle for Survival*, St Martin's Press, New York 1995, chs. 9-10 and Kirschbaum, *Historical Dictionary of Slovakia*, 2nd ed., Scarecrow Press, Maryland, 2007.

4   Nick and Kathryn Greiner visited the cousin in Melbourne in the hope of learning more about Clare's time in Ravensbrück but the cousin was not willing to discuss the subject.

5   Translated version, Greiner Papers.

6   See the article by Tony Stephens in *SMH*, 3 August 2004.

7   Egon Kunz, *Blood and Gold: Hungarians in Australia*, F. W. Cheshire, Melbourne, 1969, pp. 190-3, and *The Hungarians in Australia*, AE Press, Melbourne, 1985, ch. 6.

8   Ivan Volgyes, *Hungary, A Nation of Contradictions*, Westview Press, Colorado, 1982, p. 101.

# 2

# School: "a diligent achiever
# of exam results"

In 1952, a few months before his fifth birthday, Nick began attending the Woodley Preparatory School at Lane Cove. Miss Ethel Sydney Watson had rented part of a large house during the Second World War and established a private non-denominational school for children in their kindergarten, first and second years. It was a strict, conservative school. The boy, who had arrived in Australia with a smattering of words from other languages, was best at the German he had learnt from his nanny in Vienna. Now he had to master English in order to fit in. He soon did well enough at Woodley to collect the first of what would become a barrow load of school prizes. He recalls choosing a book about aeroplanes and also remembers making "abortive" stage appearances, including one where he played a king who wanted jam on his bread.[1]

Leaving Woodley, Nick was enrolled in Class Two at Loreto Convent, Kirribilli, at the beginning of 1954. Wearing a tie, a pressed shirt and shorts, he was one of eight boys in a class of 22 girls. A story to survive from that year was of young Nick (on his reckoning, "a little fat kid") going through an entire season of athletics always winning as the "blindfold" half in races with a lifelong friend, John Flynn, a future specialist physician. Tom Bathurst, appointed Chief Justice of the Supreme Court of NSW in 2011, was another friend. Little else survives in the memory except the occasion when, for a dare, he touched a red light on a statue of Jesus. "Dobbed in" by the other seven boys to Mother Anthony, who was "a bit of a dragon", he received a sharp rap over the knuckles.

15

Next year Nick went to St Aloysius' College, Milsons Point. Founded in 1879 at Woolloomooloo by the Jesuits, the school moved to Darlinghurst in 1883 and to Milsons Point in 1903. Nick soon established his record for coming first or very close to the top in all subjects. In his second year, for example, he came top on aggregate in the Elements I class of 36 boys, well ahead of Tom Bathurst, and top or equal top in six subjects. He won a prize for coming first in his class and prizes for Religious Knowledge, Junior English and Arithmetic. He came sixth in each of two other subjects – Writing, and Spelling and Dictation. His father commented solely about the result in Writing.

Doing well academically was important, but sport had become a fixation. In 1957, his final year at St Aloysius, Nick was a member of the undefeated Under-10 A rugby union team. The school magazine reported that the props "Nicky Greiner and Andrew Lukas contributed great weight to the scrums and were responsible for the start of many quick rucks". He was also a member of the Under-10 A cricket team which won seven of their nine games earning the following comment: "Wicket-keeper Nicky Greiner was always on the alert." Athletics were not neglected. Nick came third in both the 75 yard (Division F) and 100 yard (Division E) races for the Under-11 age group.[2] He might not have been "a natural" but he was forever competitive.

Nick had been joined at St Aloysius' by a special friend he had made in Greenwich. Robert Stewart was one of the very few children living in Robertson Street and the one with whom he could play. (Nick's brother – Chris – did not count. Born in 1952, he was much too young to be a childhood companion). The Stewart family was "quintessentially Australian", except that Robert's father was a Protestant and his mother came from a very conservative Catholic background while the two grandmothers – one a Protestant and the other a Catholic – also lived in the house. The two boys, separated in age by a few weeks, together did "Australian things" like cracker night and challenging each other to be more daring in riding billy carts down the sharp incline of their street. Robert and Nick became very close: "[H]e was my gateway into Australia". Robert also introduced Nick to rugby league. The boys went to watch Newtown play South Sydney. Robert declared for Newtown so Nick became a lifelong supporter of the Rabbitohs. But there was one hitch in their relationship. When his friend came to the Greiners for a meal, and was presented with Nick's favourite dish of Wiener Schnitzel, Robert announced that he did not like "dago food". The young host burst into tears.[3]

In 1958 Nick went as a day boy to St Ignatius' College, Riverview, one of Sydney's two most prestigious Catholic secondary schools for boys which took pupils from Year Six through to the then Leaving Certificate. The Greiner parents probably did not even consider the obvious alternative, St Joseph's College at Hunters Hill, founded by the Marist Brothers. Riverview was the logical step up from St Aloysius because Nick could complete his education at a Jesuit school. Since fairly humble beginnings in 1880, Riverview had developed a good reputation and a long list of distinguished *alumni*. Whether, in choosing Riverview, the parents took notice of the school's motto – *Quantum Potes Tantum Aude* ("as much as you can do, so much dare to do") – it encapsulated much of their own, and their elder son's, approach to life.

The school itself in 1958 was undergoing a major physical expansion but the Rector, Frank Wallace SJ, was preoccupied with even greater challenges. He wondered if there would be a sufficient supply of "vocations" to the priesthood to meet the demands of an increased number of classrooms. He used the school magazine of 1958 to admonish parents who tried to disguise opposition to their child's vocation by remaining "loftily indifferent" or talking of delay until the boy could be "sure". The "right attitude", Wallace wrote, was to consider there to be "no greater honour" than a call to follow Christ "in a special way". Parents should welcome the "call" and pray for it, though not force it.[4]

Young Nick was unlikely to test whether his parents had the "right attitude". He was not especially devout. There were some religious icons in his bedroom, he went with his family to church every week and did not eat meat on Fridays. He was briefly an altar boy but rang the bell so loudly he was banned. In his third year at Riverview he joined the Third Division of the Sodality of Our Lady and St Ignatius where he was the secretary and Robert Stewart was the treasurer. In 1961-2 he was a member of the Second Division and in his final year of the First Division. It was a normal progression for a Riverview boy who wanted to belong.

Nor should too much be made of the fact that Religious Knowledge proved to be one of his best subjects. According to Gerard Windsor, the subject was taught in "a very rationalistical and apologetical manner, readying one for the big defence of Catholicism in the world outside".[5] The subject was considered so important a boy could not win a prize in another subject unless he passed Religious Knowledge, while the winner of the Cardinal's Prize for Religious Knowledge had his name placed at the top of the prize list ahead of the Dux of School. Yet, for Nick, Religious Knowledge was just another subject, and he wanted to do well in every one he took. It did, however, appeal to him for embracing "broad and interesting history" with its emphasis on the Jesuits and by-passing the Popes. Perhaps he was also influenced by what Windsor himself noticed: "[I]n the days at Riverview when Economics was done only by those who couldn't do Latin, and history was an unimaginative dictation from a single book or set of notes, . . . Religious Knowledge was the only really intellectual, argumentative subject taught."[6]

Nick's parents did not have to drive him to succeed, nor did they attempt to do so. Perhaps their example acted on his sub-conscious. His motivation, which he admits was "not particularly flattering", was simple: "I was never a diligent student but I was a diligent achiever of exam results." He never studied hard during term and did so only when required. His methods worked. As he had done in his final three years at St Aloysius', Nick came top or close to the top in every subject in every year he was at Riverview. The exam system suited him perfectly and, while he believes he might not have done so well under a regime of continuous assessment, he assuredly would have adapted to it.

Sport was important for him, as it was to St Ignatius'. Nick was selected in the A teams for football – by which Riverview meant rugby union – in each of his years at the school, except for his final one, and generally as a front row forward.[7] He also did well at cricket, liked the game, and felt he understood it having spent many days with friends at the Sydney Cricket Ground watching Sheffield Shield matches. When not wicket keeping, he was a close-in fieldsman, a "glass arm" restricting his value in the outfield, and a right-hand opening batsman in the mode of the left-handed Bill Lawry, unspectacular but difficult to remove. There were some triumphs. He made 72 runs out of total of 169 for the 15C team against Newington in 1962, a match Riverview won by an innings and 32 runs. Above all, he was an eager participant and a competitor, whether in his final year at school playing for the Second or Third Eleven or coming second in the E Grade of the Under-17's 400 yards.

Perhaps the most revealing comment about his sporting activity was unrelated to achievement or prowess. A trainee Jesuit took him to the nets one day, made him stand behind the stumps and pelted the ball at him – saying that "modesty is a virtue Mr Greiner and you must strive to acquire it". His parliamentary colleagues and Nick himself, who reported this remark, would agree he did not always succeed.

While "interested in most things" at school, he was not always a participant. Attracted to the "product" rather than the means of getting there, he was "hopeless" at music and art yet later enjoyed the opera and frequently attended gallery openings. If the visual arts had been a compulsory subject for the Leaving Certificate he would have worked at it. Unlike his brother, who figured prominently in Riverview plays, Nick does not remember trying for anything on the stage after attending Woodley. Membership of the school Cadet Corps was compulsory but Nick Greiner could not be forced to revel in soldiering, let alone to seek advancement through the ranks. While friends became cadet under-officers, his letter home from a camp on 21 September 1962 set out his own priorities: "the tent is quite dry", the food "is not bad in parts" and the saving grace was a tuck-shop with a television set; and he wanted his parents to bring "a lot of food" when they came to see him on Sunday, notably, cold meat, cakes and biscuits. The postscript consisted of three words: "Food! Food! Food!"[8]

One of Riverview's offerings appealed to his competitive outlook and desire to succeed, and prepared him for the career in politics he had not so far contemplated. The College had long encouraged boys to take up debating. Father McDonald, SJ, who coached the senior boys in Nick's final year, best expressed the underlying assumption. He saw debating as "helping a young man find himself, and to mature with the true fullness of his personality, in a way that enables him to help and influence others".[9] The school liked to boast of its record in reaching and winning the final of the Great Public Schools (GPS) debating competition and in producing winners of the Lawrence Campbell Oratory Competition. When Nick arrived at Riverview the juniors had their own debating societies which held debates at night, thereby catering mainly for boarders. The junior societies were gradually replaced after Father Gerald Jones SJ began organising debates after classes and expanded the activity to include debates against outsiders. Nick first debated in 1959, teaming with John Flynn and Chris Rogers (another school friend he first met at St Aloysius) and agreeing to "Buy British". He came to notice in his second last year at school. As the second speaker and representing the Riverview Second Division against St Joseph's, Nick affirmed the proposition that "A Bird in the Hand is worth Two in the Bush". His team won easily and he took the Junior (Second Division) prize for debating.

In 1963 Father McDonald appointed him leader of the three-member Riverview team. The other members were Chris Hartcher, later a Liberal backbench MP during the Greiner Government and a minister in the O'Farrell Government, and Clifton Hoeben who, as a Major General, commanded the Second Division of the Australian Reserve, and who became a judge of the NSW Supreme Court. Considered inexperienced at the highest level, the Riverview team nevertheless won all three debates in its appointed zone of the GPS competition. Against St Joseph's it affirmed, "There will be peace in our time", and, against The King's School, "The Dead rule the World", while denying the proposition against Sydney High School that "Democracy is a fraud". The school magazine reported how Nicholas Greiner's "penetrating reply and summing-up became a feature of every debate". He liked to lead but especially enjoyed the role of demolishing the arguments of his opponents.

On 12 July 1963, in between the second and third zone debates, Nick went to Sydney Grammar to participate in the Lawrence Campbell Oratory Competition. Established in 1935 and named after a Sydney elocution teacher, the competition was open to representatives of the GPS and Associated Grammar Schools. Each competitor had to choose one of three topics revealed just fifteen minutes before being required to speak for ten minutes. Advance preparation was impossible though "manner" was as important as "matter". In 1963 the popular choice proved to be "Scientists should take a Ten Years' Holiday" and one boy spoke on the subject of "China and the USSR". Nick selected the third option consisting of Prospero's lines in Shakespeare's *The Tempest* which, coincidentally, was Riverview's school play which had been performed at the end of June:

> We are such stuff
> As dreams are made on; and our little life
> Is rounded with a sleep.

He won the competition. Hartcher described his speech as "of a very high standard".[10]

Early in August the Riverview team faced Sydney Grammar at Grammar in the final. They argued that "The individual no longer matters"; individuals had been submerged in the masses and had lost real influence on society. Their opponents entered the final "with a mixture of apprehension and philosophical acceptance". After all, Riverview had beaten them in a debate earlier in the year and Grammar's teamwork problems were not helped by age differences.[11] Nevertheless, after an unusually long interval the adjudicators awarded victory by a vote of 2:1 to Sydney Grammar, possibly persuaded by what Hoeben described in *Our Alma Mater* as a "very effective and witty speech" by the Grammar whip, Ross Clark, the runner-up to Nick in the Lawrence Campbell Oratory Competition. Hoeben did, however, add that "Nicholas Greiner rose to the occasion and gave perhaps the most devastating summing-up we have heard from him". Despite the disappointment, which still rankles, Nick was chosen to head the Combined GPS debating team against the Combined High Schools. He led them to victory in opposing the motion, "We should live only for today". Hartcher reported that Greiner and the Grammar whip – now on the same side – were "the two outstanding speakers".

Nick "wasn't particularly social" outside school. Many of his contemporaries would go with girls to the beach but he was not keen on the idea. His father would have disapproved. Beaches, Miklós said, "were for Aborigines", and identified walking about in bare feet as something "they" did. Nick did attend a local dance school opposite the Killara station because he was expected to do so: "I was hopeless." He did not go to many mixed tennis parties or dances until he was at university. His preference was to play or watch sport, always in the company of school friends and not with outsiders. Tennis on the family's court was a common activity, often involving Tom Bathurst who had an exceptional pedigree: his mother, Joan Hartigan, had won the Australian women's singles final three times and was twice a Wimbledon semi-finalist in the 1930s.

At Riverview itself Nick set out to make friends with the country boarders and mix with the "rugger buggers". Chris Rogers recalled how the country boys used to disparage Nick, possibly out of envy or because he seemed different. They never got a reaction and, in time, Nick won them over and they came to admire him.[12] He was particularly friendly with Dennis O'Brien from Walgett who was a member of the First Eleven and the First Fifteen in Nick's final year at school and School Captain in 1964. Harry Woods, another country boy, was Nick's captain in the 15A cricket team. A publican and a bookmaker, Woods later held the Federal seat of Page and then the State seat of Clarence for the Labor Party, and served as a minister in the Carr Government. At the same time, while Nick liked to mix with sporting types, if he had held a party when he was about 14 or 15 those invited would mostly have been drawn from his "natural group", the more academically-inclined.

Importantly, he never felt his background made him "different". For a start, although his parents were mostly older than those of his friends, the Greiner parents "never acted older". Moreover, they encouraged their boys to "fit in" with Anglo-Celt Australia: "their whole mindset was to leave Hungary and their lives there behind." At first, the family had contact with a Hungarian priest. They occasionally attended the church where he said Mass, and he sometimes visited their house in Greenwich. The parents retained a "Hungarian-ness" between themselves and among their Hungarian friends but they did not talk about the past nor make any effort to make "us" Hungarian. Nor did the boys "go to Hungarian children's things". Whereas some migrant families in the 1950s wore their experience on their sleeves, the Greiner parents hid theirs in the past and looked forward. And Nick's father went far enough forward to express road rage in the idiom locally-born motorists would easily understand. It was nothing for him to wind down a window and shout, "Lights, you mug", or "Sunday driver". Miklós Greiner also recognised the importance of actively supporting his son's school. He was one of the top group of subscribers who in 1961 gave or promised a sum in excess of £125 to the Riverview Building Fund.

Clare Greiner was critical to the process of assimilation. Not surprisingly, she picked up English very quickly. Although she might describe a "down pour" as a "pour down", she was never reticent nor self-conscious about anything said or done. It seemed a natural as well as a good idea to hire an elephant to provide rides for the children attending one of Nick's birthday parties (his daughter later referred to him as "the Elephant Boy"). "Mrs Greiner" became a distinct presence at both St Aloysius and Riverview, working in the canteen at the one and in the tuck-shop at the other. The woman who introduced iced donuts to a school was not one to be inhibited. She was "quite unconstrained", always ready to try something different, an approach which "rubbed off" on her elder boy. In 1960, with Chris starting his first year at St Aloysius, "Mrs Greiner" held a party at her home for the Ladies Committee. In 1961, when Nick was in his third year at Riverview, she hosted the annual Christmas party of the Parents and Friends Association. In the same year and in the following one she was an Association vice-president and in 1963 was one of the two honorary secretaries. By then she had branched out to be a volunteer for Meals on Wheels and was a member of the ladies' committees of the Mater Hospital and Sancta Sophia College. She set before both her sons a shining example of performing good works and caring for others.

The Greiner family had moved into their own home in Lyndhurst Avenue, Killara, by the time Nick went to Riverview. Edward Redlinger, Clare Greiner's nephew and closer in age to her younger son, joined the household for a few years. He had a troubled adolescence and, despite the best efforts of the Greiner family and of Riverview, never really settled into Sydney or Australian life. He was, however, the only discordant element in a pleasant family existence in Killara. The *Sunday Mirror* published a page-long piece on the house and garden on 22 March 1964 which conveyed two distinct images. One was of a migrant family which had prospered and assimilated; the other was of the little oddities about migrants which perplexed or amused Old Australia. The visiting journalist thought the house was notable for its "beautiful collection of Continental furniture" brought to Australia some 13 years earlier: a 17th century bureau from Austria, pieces made in the time of Louis XV of France; a delicately carved 18th century Italian suite; Bukhara, Persian and Chinese rugs, and Hungarian and Meissen china; and "unusual paintings from Hungary". But there was also a local influence: a spacious paved barbecue area. The journalist noted how Mrs Greiner employed an "interesting Continental idea". She stored bedclothes during the day in drawers beneath the beds. The mattresses and the platforms holding up the beds were upholstered, thus leaving everything looking tidy during the day.

Miklós Greiner was not interested in sport and, because he worked on Saturdays, could not in any case have watched his son play rugby union. Nick has no recollection of his father even kicking a ball with him. His mother, however, never missed one of his Saturday games. Although "she had no idea" about rugby she gave Nick threepence or sixpence when he was very young for every goal he kicked, and he would run to the sideline to remind her just how much he was owed. Ignorance did not render her reticent. She once complained to two young trainee Jesuits that the field at Cranbrook was too wet to play, and had to be told that the boys needed to learn to be tough. The important thing for both parents was for their boys to be accepted. Knowing or caring nothing about cricket did not stop them being immensely proud when Nick, like Robert Stewart, became a junior member of the Sydney Cricket Ground Trust (and remains a member to this day). That is, he had been "admitted to something quintessentially Australian".

But the Greiner parents did introduce their sons to wider horizons than those bounded by the North Shore and the other side of the Harbour Bridge. Business success in the timber industry, and contacts and funds overseas, opened the way for travel abroad during school holidays. The trips began in 1954 when Nick was aged seven. He recalls translating German for a Swiss ski instructor at St Moritz, and was so excited at a game of ice hockey he chewed through his gloves. In 1958 he went to Hong Kong and Japan where his school uniform, his short grey pants and boater fascinated the local children. In 1959 the family travelled more widely and the young Riverview boy decided to give awards for hotels and cities they visited: Istanbul came top, ahead – in no order – of Lisbon, London, New York, Chicago and San Francisco. Europe was the destination in 1963. In Budapest he met his father's friends and visited a church where the Greiner family had their own small "altar", but he did not then see the apartment in the middle of the city where he was born. The trip did not include his mother's Bratislava. Nick first visited the city when lobbying to win the Olympics for Sydney.

Travel was an enriching experience and of a kind not available to many young Australians of Nick's age group. Significantly, too, "overseas" did not mean "the Mother Country". Yet Nick was not then at all curious to find out about his family's history. His father had portraits of ancestors hanging in his office but his elder son was not disposed to ask about them, though he does not doubt answers would have been given to most questions asked. By not exploring the past, all he really knew at about the time he left Riverview was that he came from Hungary and his father was in the timber business.

In 1963 Nick was one of 24 prefects and this, his final year at Riverview, was his most successful academically. He carried off the Cardinal's Prize for Religious Knowledge and won prizes for English, French and History (Pass and Honours), and a prize each for debating and oratory. To his chagrin, however, he was not made Dux of the School and had to settle for the runner-up prize. It did not seem fair that the winner was repeating the Leaving Certificate as well as taking higher level Maths, Physics and Chemistry. The Leaving Certificate results, published early in January 1964, helped to right the "wrong". Nick was awarded first class honours in Latin and Modern History and an A in each of Chemistry (having no "feel" for the subject and, "knowing nothing", he learnt everything by heart), English, French and Maths III. Placed equal 39th in the State, he came top of the Riverview contingent, well ahead of the school Dux, and was one of only two boys from his school to obtain a maximum pass. Nick finished equal 17th in the State in Modern History, an exam for which he was very well prepared; he had written out answers to questions asked over a period of ten years.[13] The History result was gratifying but the Latin result pleased Nick more. His equal 19th place put him ahead of Riverview's favoured Latin scholar, Mark Armstrong, a future chairman of the ABC, who came 24th. Nick was also one of 22 Riverview boys to win a Commonwealth Scholarship for a university course, along with his friends Flynn, Rogers and Stewart, and Andrew Kaldor, another son of Hungarian parents and who later figured prominently in his rise to the premiership of NSW.

Friends are important to him, and one of Nick's striking characteristics is that he has kept in contact with so many of those he first met as a school boy. How far the schools themselves, and especially Riverview, influenced him is another matter. He was happy to be married in the College chapel and to send his only son to Riverview. When at university, he kept up the Riverview connection in the mid-1960s by attending one annual general meeting and two dinners held by the Old Ignatians' Union. He also returned to the school to assist with advice for the debating teams. In the mid-1970s he lectured the senior boys at St Ignatius' on business management for Careers Day and acted on many occasions as a school and GPS debating adjudicator. He helped to organise a centenary dinner in 1980. After his election to the NSW Parliament he received a congratulatory letter from Father Casey, SJ, a former Rector of St Ignatius' who was the Rector of St Aloysius' when Nick was enrolled there. Nick replied: "[M]uch of what I have achieved in my career in business and politics to date is based on the foundation that I developed at St. Aloysius' and St. Ignatius". He was "very conscious" of his debt to the Jesuits and his "earnest desire" was to be of assistance in any matter relating to the State Government.[14] The politician may have just been saying the right thing. He certainly applied a different emphasis when he returned to the College as Premier in May 1988 and answered a priest's question at a meeting by saying he learnt about life not during but after leaving the school.[15]

The school could well argue that its aim was to prepare a boy for handling life, not to expose him to all its vicissitudes. No school, and certainly no single sex school, could perform the latter role. Riverview's principal contribution to his career, other than allowing full rein to his competitive nature, may have been to reinforce his self-confidence. Riverview also contributed to the process whereby a potential outsider came to "belong" in Australia, albeit within a narrow and exclusive social circle. It may well have impressed upon him a sense of social justice, of a moral responsibility to assist others in need, and of the importance of personal integrity. Nevertheless, the school failed him in one respect. He left with a knowledge of religious history but none of Australian history or even of general political history. He was probably well versed in English history, though perhaps not to the extent of boys who attended the leading Protestant independent schools. Gerard Windsor is no doubt right: there was probably limited scope at Riverview in the early 1960s to contest interpretations. Either way, it hardly mattered. The young man who left school at the end of 1963 was more than bright enough to work things out for himself.

# Endnotes

1   Unless otherwise stated, the quotations in this chapter are taken from several interviews with Greiner recorded in 2010-11.

2   *The Aloysian*, 1957, pp. 77, 80.

3   *SMH*, 20 Aug. 1988.

4   *Our Alma Mater* (the College Magazine), 1958.

5   Gerard Windsor, Friends and sometime scholars: a history of St Ignatius' College, Riverview, 1977, National Library of Australia (NLA), MS 6920, esp. folders 5-6. Windsor was twice Dux of Riverview which he left in 1962. He trained at one stage to be a Jesuit, and now is a well-published author and literary critic.

6   Windsor, Friends and sometime scholars, p. 434.

7   He later played union for Chatswood and Hornsby but wisely moved on when finding himself lined up against some massive Islanders.

8   Family letters, Greiner Papers.

9   Windsor, Friends and sometime scholars, p. 401A.

10  *Our Alma Mater*, 1963. Previous winners included Murray Gleeson (twice), Lloyd Waddy, Mungo MacCallum and Gerard Windsor. Future winners included Nick Enright, Malcolm Turnbull, Adam Spencer of the ABC and Charles Firth of "The Chaser". Justin Greiner won it in 1990, and the Greiners, so far, are the only father and son success story.

11  *The Sydneian*, December 1963, p. 44.

12  Interview: Chris Rogers, 7 Jan. 2013. Rogers himself was a member of the Riverview First XI for two years and captained the team in Nick's final year of 1963.

13  Interview: Rogers, 7 January 2013.

14  Ku-ring-gai file, Greiner Papers.

15  Errol Lea-Scarlett, *Riverview: aspects of the story of Saint Ignatius' College & its peninsula 1836-1988*, Hale & Iremonger, Sydney 1989, p. 251.

# 3

# University: "just an extension of school"?

Carrying his prizes and leaving Riverview for the last time as a school boy, Nick Greiner encountered an elderly Jesuit who asked him whether he intended to take law or medicine at university. The priest expressed delight when Nick said he planned to do neither. Clearly, the young man had decided to become a Jesuit. It had never occurred to the priest that Nick would enrol in the Faculty of Economics at the University of Sydney. Nick himself believed you did not do economics if you were in the top 10 ten per cent of the class. His excuse, or explanation, was that his father saw economics as a useful subject for a son who would probably take over the family business.

## First Year

In 1964 Nick, not yet 17 years of age, arrived at Australia's oldest university. Considered by some to be conservative in outlook and slow to innovate, the University of Sydney had to embrace the changes forced on Australian universities caused by an explosion of knowledge, the increasing numbers leaving secondary schools, and the intervention of the Federal Government. In the 1960s it joined other tertiary institutions in accepting a significant expansion of staff and student numbers, new specialist and vocational courses, and revised directions for research and teaching.

Greiner enrolled in a Faculty whose undergraduate numbers had stabilised to around 1,000 following the imposition of quotas in 1963.

Postgraduate enrolments remained in single figures although the numbers were about to rise while evening classes for part-time students would soon be phased out. Economics constituted the largest department in the Faculty. There were three other departments: Government and Public Administration, Accounting and Economic Statistics. The legendary Professor Syd Butlin was the long-serving Dean (1946-56, 1959-67, 1969-71). Other luminaries included H.D. Black, a future Chancellor of the University, E.L. ("Ted") Wheelwright, the controversial and magnetic socialist economist, and Harry Edwards, later a Federal Liberal MP. For all the changes under way, the basic course structure would have been recognisable to a student who had enrolled at the end of the Second World War. Choice was strictly limited, and the underlying values had been implanted by Professor R.C. Mills (Dean, 1922-45) and built on by Butlin. They were "founded . . . on uncompromising intellectual discipline, a taste for scientific method, a distaste for ideal theorising, and an emphasis on academic understanding rather than vocational training".[1] Butlin, an economic historian, had the greatest respect for the study of history and for an empirical approach to understanding the past. Hence the Faculty laid emphasis on economic history and on the history of economic thought.

First year students in Economics took two compulsory subjects – Economics I and Descriptive Economics – and two more subjects selected from a limited range. The 1964 Handbook described Economics I as "a survey of the whole range of modern economic study (analysis and policy)". Descriptive Economics was designed to introduce students to the broad outlines and the detailed working of the Australian economy. Greiner chose Law I and Economic History I as his two options. The former, offered within the Department of Accounting, involved a study of the development of law in England and Australia pertaining to constitutional and administrative matters, contracts and regulatory laws. The latter covered the economic history of Western Europe from the Middle Ages to the 20th century.

Some freshers who bothered to read the Student's Handbook for 1964, and reached p. 35, might soon have become disillusioned. Michael Kirby, the President of the Students' Representative Council (SRC) and a future judge of the High Court, warned that "if you have come here on a quest for independent thought, you're bound to be disappointed. It is rarely achieved – almost never at the undergraduate level – and not encouraged." Kirby, an Arts and Law graduate enrolled in Economics, told new students that university was "not so much unlike school": be diligent, hand in your work on time, pass all the tests, meet the examiners' requirements, and "you will get through". Nick Greiner probably had those very intentions and expectations, and the Economics Department would not be tempting him in 1964 to think independently.

He adjusted quickly to the transition from school to university, partly because – as Kirby had warned – he found university to be "just an extension of school". He started well. Nick distinguished himself at table tennis in Orientation Week and was selected in the University's team; unfortunately "I was completely out of my depth".[2] He travelled every week day on the same train he had caught to Riverview, the journey now taking just a little longer. He often met up with the same people and, while his circle of contacts widened, continued to see friends he had made at school. His approach to study followed his practice as a school boy: work hard in the lead-up to exams, and, in the meantime, play sport and socialise. Nick did not have to worry about money or take vacation jobs, though occasionally he did work for his father. There was no possibility of his falling into any of the three traps which caught many young players in the mid-1960s: he was not interested in pub crawls; he had neither the talent nor the inclination to take up the theatre; and he was too level-headed to allow "love" to become diverting, let alone all-consuming.

Wise teachers say that the important thing about first year at university is to survive it. Nick did better than that. He soon discovered a liking for Economic History and obtained a Pass with Credit in each of his four subjects.[3] Awarded the Frank Albert Prize for General Proficiency valued at £7-10-0, and admitted to Honours, he could look back on 1964 with some satisfaction.

## A significant encounter

He was not a hermit. Nick escorted Clare Petre, the future Energy & Water Ombudsman NSW, to formal Balls where in turn she was chosen "Miss Newman Society" and "Miss University". The key meeting, however, occurred just months into his first university year. On 21 May 1964 Nick went to a tennis party at the Tancred family house in Drummoyne. John Tancred had been in his cohort at Riverview but had to repeat a year. By now a prefect, Tancred invited the head prefect of Loreto Convent, Kirribilli, to join the party.

Kathryn Callaghan, four months older than Nick, was one of three daughters of Bede and Mollie Callaghan. Bede Callaghan had started his working life as an errand boy for the Commonwealth Bank. By 1964 he was the General Manager of the Commonwealth Development Bank and from 1965 until 1976 (when he was knighted) was Managing Director of the Commonwealth Banking Corporation. Kathryn had grown up in a devout Irish Catholic family ruled by an authoritarian father and where Catholicism was a highly formative influence. One of her sisters became a nun. It was also a large family: her own father was one of four children and her mother one of six. Kathryn could claim 54 "first" relations. Bede Callaghan's work had taken the family to London and Washington so Kathryn had attended schools in three countries and, a year older than other girls in her year, was not shy.

Kathryn met Nick for the first time at the Tancred tennis party. She remembered him wearing white tennis shorts. Otherwise, she took no notice of him, or much notice of his female companion. There was "no great clashing of cymbals or crashing of drums".[4] But during the ensuing months Kathryn and Nick, with their respective partners, went on double dates. Convenience and the cost of petrol soon became factors. Kathryn lived in Gordon, much closer to the Greiner home in Killara than Drummoyne where Nick's girlfriend lived. The four of them travelled in the car Nick's parents had given him to a cafe in New South Head Road to listen to folk music. Nick would then drop off Kathryn's boyfriend and his own girlfriend home before returning Kathryn to her place. According to one version, their relationship started after they met by chance at the Town Hall station, travelled together to the North Shore and Nick later telephoned to invite her to a car rally and a barbecue. In another version their first date was a game of rugby league, firm proof – if any were still needed – that the son of a migrant family had fully absorbed the culture and priorities of a Sydney-based Australian Catholic male in the mid-1960s.

Relations between them had become sufficiently important for Nick to accompany Kathryn to the Fairfax Building early in January 1965 to find out that she had obtained two A Passes and three B Passes for her Leaving Certificate. The two were, by then, regarded as "an item". Nick was in his second year at university and Kathryn began a course in Social Work at the University of New South Wales. She was soon a regular visitor to the Greiner household. Accustomed to the society of Anglo-Celts, she now found herself in the very different world of European food and where the father, who was served first, would start eating immediately. Kathryn knew Miklós Greiner to be hard driving at the office but found him charming outside of work, urbane and always welcoming. Like her own father, he did not bring work home. She sensed, too, he understood that his wife was in charge of the home front. Kathryn found Clare to be an "amazing" woman, "steely" and "formidable" who, in another generation, would have been running BHP.[5]

## On being a well-dressed university student in the mid-1960s

In common with those attending other Australian universities, many students at Sydney in the immediate post-war years were caught up in the tensions and excitement which accompanied the influx of returned service personnel and the ideological jousting between Left and Right and between Left and Leftist. The 1950s were perhaps better remembered for the "Sydney Push" and a succession of student pranks. There was more of a stirring from the end of that decade over issues such as nuclear power, the White Australia Policy, apartheid in South Africa, and censorship. Public demonstrations were certainly not uncommon in the city of Sydney. A notable one occurred soon after Greiner arrived at the University when, on the annual "Commem Day", some 2,000 students gathered outside the US Consulate in support of civil rights. In the ensuing melee the police arrested 25 students. Three developments – the reintroduction of conscription at the end of 1964, the "Freedom Ride" of February 1965 into northern NSW in support of Aboriginal people, and the decision of the Menzies Government to send an Australian battalion to South Vietnam – created more ferment. Indeed, the student newspaper, *Honi Soit,* reported on 14 July 1965 that the University "is currently seething about Vietnam".

The Economics student from Killara, who arrived each day at university wearing a jacket and tie, looking well groomed and conservative, was not especially moved, let alone seething. He had left school without any real interest in politics. He is not sure now whether he could then name the Premier of NSW, and believes his lack of concern and knowledge was probably typical of his circle. Nick never approached the Liberal Club and it never approached him. He was aware of Robin (later Sir Robert) Askin who led the Coalition to an election victory in May 1965 and ended 24 years of Labor rule. But Miklós Greiner was the family member who had the close interest in contemporary politics. A conservative, a devout Catholic and a refugee from the Eastern bloc, he rejected the line of the NSW church hierarchy that the Communists in Australia were not dangerous and that it was in the interest of Catholics to maintain their historic connections with the Labor Party. Miklós became a strong supporter of the breakaway, anti-communist Democratic Labor Party (DLP). His two sons handed out DLP how-to-vote cards at their father's behest.

Politics on the campus, conscription and the Vietnam War generally passed Nick by in the mid-1960s. With individual exceptions, Economics students were not major figures in the gathering protest movement, and were more moved when a lecturer hanged himself in the University Union's shower rooms in March 1965. The two "political" events Nick remembers clearly were the Freedom Ride and the shooting in June 1966 of Arthur Calwell, the Leader of the Federal Labor Opposition. In any case, the extent of protest should not be exaggerated. In September 1966 *Honi Soit* could report that a poll of over 5,500 students found that 68 per cent supported sending Australian troops to Vietnam, 59 per cent supported conscription and a third supported the presence of Australian conscripts in Vietnam.[6]

The timing was relevant. Demonstrations did not become seriously disruptive until the sit-ins of April 1967 prompted by the issue of library fines. By the end of what was Nick's final year, there was almost continual agitation on the campus over Vietnam and university governance. The more moderate students preferred reasoned dialogue, and Nick instinctively favoured such an approach. He was, in 1967, a member of the Sydney University team which failed to make a convincing case in the national universities debating championship that America's involvement in Vietnam was justified. But he was never seriously involved in current issues. He did not stand for election to the SRC nor did he participate in Union Night debates. Neither his membership of the University Regiment, nor his record of absenteeism, reflected political motivation. Nick had joined the Regiment to avoid the military call-up, and did not care for Army life. It took a letter from Les Bury, the Minister for Labour and National Service, reminding him of his obligations to persuade him to improve his attendance record. Perhaps, if he had arrived at university in 1967, he might have become more immersed in the issues of the day. He might have had more contact with Percy Allan, an activist from Cranbrook and of Austrian-Jewish and Danish parentage, who became a central figure in the spectacular militant protests of 1969-70. As Secretary of the NSW Treasury, Allan proved critical to the implementation of the Greiner reform program.

For Nick Greiner between 1964 and 1967 his university world remained largely bounded by the Faculty of Economics, the Economics Society and an increasingly pleasant personal life. Peter Collins, Greiner's Deputy Leader between 1986 and 1992, offered in the year 2000 a brief portrait of the future Premier whom he met outside the Fisher Library during Orientation Week in late February 1965. Nick himself has "no recollection of such a significant event".[7] Whereas the Collins memoir seems preoccupied with Greiner and Greiner's effect on the career of Peter Collins, the fixation is not shared.

For Collins, the initial meeting mattered because of what would follow. "Our backgrounds were worlds apart." Nick was the Riverview boy from Killara "who could choose any course he wanted at any university". Collins, the Waverley College boy from Coogee, "had struggled and clawed my way into my university of first preference". It was a case of "(r)ich man, poor man". But their common interests meant, for Collins, they got on well from the outset. They were very close in age. Nick was 19 days older. According to Collins, they both enrolled in Government in order to study political science (Nick was actually enrolled in Economics to take economics and never took a course in Government). They both joined the Newman Society and the University Regiment and, while Collins became President of the Arts Society, Nick became President of the Economics Society. Whatever Collins thought at the time, in 2000 he described his new friend as "a strange combination: shy but self-assured to the point of arrogance; obviously very bright but not what we would now call streetwise; warm when he wanted to be but capable of switching off." Others, including Greiner himself, have noted these characteristics.

Nick had three extra-curricula interests at Sydney University. One of them proved to be brief. He joined the Newman Society, which had a membership of 500-600 Catholics, and stood for President – unsuccessfully – against Peter Manning, later a prominent journalist and television executive. At issue was the Society's response to the Second Vatican Council of 1962-5. Australian Catholics were divided over the reforms initiated or promoted at Vatican II affecting, among other matters, the liturgy, approaches to other Christian churches, the relationship with the secular world, and the role of the laity and the hierarchy in Church governance.[8] Some Catholics saw the pace of change as too fast and destabilising, others as too slow and obstructed. Perhaps influenced by the way the Jesuits at Riverview had welcomed the Council, and probably by what became his characteristic and instinctive response to change, Nick represented what he called a "left-liberal" position in contesting the election as a supporter of the Vatican II reforms.

The Economics Society, of which Butlin was the Patron, was another and more enduring interest. Day students in the Faculty of Economics were automatic members of the Society by virtue of their payment of enrolment fees. In his second year Nick joined the Society's office-bearers at the time when Ian Hutchens, later Australia's Ambassador to Egypt, was President. Phillip Smiles, with whom Nick would have a "difficult" relationship after Smiles entered the Legislative Assembly in 1984, was a publicity officer. Two *ex officio* office-bearers in 1965 became friends: Tony Berg was then Treasurer of the SRC and Michael Kirby had by then become President of the Union Board and was the elected student member of the University Senate. In 1966 Nick was elected President of the Society and the office-bearers again included Berg, Kirby and Smiles. The Society commanded much of his attention. He was on hand for visits from Les Bury, Sir Roden Cutler, the Governor of NSW, and the Soviet Ambassador, and was a speaker in a public debate where H.D. Black was also a participant.

In addition to organising "educational, social and sporting activities", including the formal Balls of 1964 and 1966, and a "Miss Economics Quest", the Society produced the annual *Economic Review*, a non-profit publication which offered an outlet for the academic writings of students and for the views of leading economists. Nick published articles in the journal in each of the three years, 1965 to 1967, all reflecting an approach he later adopted in politics and government. He cut through issues of principle to those of practicality. Instead of joining the interminable arguments about rights and wrongs, the economics undergraduate argued the case for looking at practical alternatives, ones which would actually work and fitted into an Australian context.

The first article, "The Economic Case for State Aid",[9] was published after the Menzies Government and the recently-elected Askin Government in NSW began providing various forms of financial assistance to non-government schools. He steered clear of the sectarian and philosophical arguments which had characterised so much of the debate during the previous decades. Rather, given that State aid, "for better or worse, is here to say", it was appropriate to consider the economic advantages. Greiner began with the proposition that education "is an industry", and "ordinary industry concepts such as productivity and efficiency" could be applied. Subsidising private schools would create healthy competition and yield greater efficiency. Discriminating against them locked up resources which could have been reallocated to secure a higher level of education. The supply side was also affected. State education departments pursued standardisation, resisted change and restricted choice. But economics could not settle everything. Although investment in this "industry" was critical, economics could not reconcile differences grounded in value judgments. Nevertheless, it should be understood that State aid was "not without its economic advantages".

The Economics III student in 1966 examined burgeoning overseas capital investment in Australia. The Commonwealth-appointed Vernon Committee of Economic Inquiry (1963-5) had argued for limiting the inflow to the levels of recent years, given a possibly unacceptable degree of foreign ownership and balance of payments problems caused by servicing debt. Nick did not want to comment on either the pros or cons of investment or on the need for controls. He regarded a discussion of these issues as "essentially a futile one conducted in an academic and/or political vacuum", and "delusory" because "in practice" there was no real choice; Australia remained "capital-hungry". The alternative to reliance on capital inflow and to the pressure on the balance of payments was to increase domestic savings. Compulsory savings through tax increases was obviously one approach. Nick argued it was preferable to encourage voluntary savings. He examined several methods tried overseas, drawing extensively upon a paper presented to the Australian Institute of Management in November 1965 by Bede Callaghan, his future father-in-law. Nick found most of the methods wanting, partly because they would enhance what Syd Butlin had called Australia's "penchant for institutionalising interest groups". He had no magical solution of his own, except to urge economists to look at methods for increasing productivity without requiring considerable capital expenditure, and to examine practicable ways for augmenting savings and mobilising them effectively.

This article provided a foretaste of what became an article of faith, namely, that governments should not negotiate deals to resolve the claims of competing interest groups. There was also a preview of his approach to arguments he considered irrational or without foundation. In the mid-1960s he dismissed them as "futile" and "delusory". Twenty years later he preferred calling them "a nonsense".

Nick returned to the subject of domestic savings in his third article.[10] Prompted in part by a developing interest in housing finance, he noted how, while there had been a substantial increase in the volume of personal savings during the previous decade, the savings banks had not matched the building societies in gaining a share of that increase. The author explained that periodic rises in interest rates had done no more than enable the banks to maintain their competitive position. Total savings did not respond to changes in the rates; rather, a change merely shifted funds from one form of savings to another. The building societies were providing a higher rate and, as in the United States, concentrated on establishing a record for soundness; that is, Australians could achieve a higher return on a "no risk" investment. This success of the building societies put pressure on the structure of housing finance interest rates while weakening regulatory control over a vital sector of the economy. At the same time, the capacity of the savings banks to counter inroads by the building societies was limited because most of their investments were in the form of long-term, fixed interest securities. They did not have the rate flexibility. To help the savings banks compete on more equal terms the regulations could be liberalised to reduce the 65 per cent rule which required the preponderance of government securities in their asset portfolios. The rule itself reflected a time when the Commonwealth Government had problems in raising loan money. Meanwhile, there was a need "from a national economic viewpoint" to foster private savings and increase the size of the cake to be divided, while cushioning the impact on any one group of institutions. The "problem" was being addressed abroad but ignored by economists and policy-makers in Australia.

A striking feature of this article is how the Economics IV student had developed research-based and increasingly sophisticated arguments, in this instance to support his concern that government regulations were hampering one sector of the finance industry from competing with another. It is tempting to see here a foretaste of arguments which Greiner would use as Premier to support a level playing field, except that he applied them in reverse: government trading enterprises should not enjoy special privileges in competing with private companies.

Nick's other main outside interest was the University Union. In October 1966 he sought to join the board of directors of the Sydney University Union. Established by and for men in 1874 – it did not amalgamate with the Sydney University Women's Union (established in 1914) until 1972 – the Union provided eating facilities, a library, meeting rooms, shops, a theatre and club rooms. The Union itself was a substantial business. In 1966 it had a turnover of $3.7m and owned or managed property worth more than $1m.[11] Members, who included 15,000 graduates as well as teaching and administrative staff, paid $20 to join and an annual membership fee of $20. Controversially, fees were doubled in the year Kirby was President to meet costs for a new building. During 1966 a majority on the Board diverted $120,000 to refurbish some existing premises. Tony Berg led the opposition and formed a "ticket" to fight the Union Board elections. Nick Greiner was part of his ticket, and campaigned on what he called "bread and butter issues", a theme he adopted after winning the leadership of the State Liberal Party in 1983.

Although there were Faculty and factional tickets in the Union Board elections Nick argued that the Union was primarily about providing services for students. *Honi Soit* at first ridiculed candidates who promised better and cheaper food, and did not focus on the two key issues: secret Board meetings and whether to construct a new building or to renovate existing premises. On the eve of the election *Honi Soit* remembered why the Union existed: "It remains to be seen whether any candidate or team of candidates emerges with credible plans to convert the Union into a student service responsive to the needs and wishes of its day-to-day users".[12] Nick's "bread and butter" approach clearly addressed the challenge. Perhaps, however, the most notable feature of his campaign was the last-minute act of crossing the road from the University to canvass votes in a student pub. Campaigning in this manner never came naturally to him.

Tony Berg was elected President, defeating the outgoing President by 290 votes in a valid poll of 3,136. Twelve directors were elected to the Board, including Geoffrey Robertson, a Law student from Epping Boys' High School with whom Nick had established a rapport. "N.F. Griener [sic]" was placed 13th with 1,032 votes, 33 behind the last director to be elected. He had done well, especially given his virtual seclusion in the Economics Faculty. His tilt at the Union Board was not in vain. An elected director resigned early in 1967 and Greiner's name (this time, correctly spelt) was added to the Board. He served out 1967 as a member of the Finance Committee.[13]

**Academic Results**

In his second year Nick had taken the compulsory course of Economics II which focussed on the theory of price formation, the allocation of resources with a given level of aggregate employment, and the factors which determined the growth of, and fluctuations in, aggregate income and employment. He also took Economic History II, a study of the American economy from colonial times to the New Deal and of the British Empire since 1815. Law II, his third subject, encompassed property law, commercial law and bankruptcy, company law and practice, and tax law and practice. His results continued to be impressive: a Distinction in Economics II and a High Distinction in Economic History (he topped both classes) and a Pass with Credit in Law II. He also collected a second General Proficiency Prize and a prize in Law II, taking home a total of £12-10-0. Economics may not have been a favourite subject but he was more than holding his own.

Nick's third year was even more successful. He scored a Distinction in Economics III, a study of economic policy, the economics of development and under-development and advanced macro- and micro-theory. He was beaten for top place, however, by John Hewson, who would build a varied career upon his qualifications as an economist. Nick topped Economic History III with a High Distinction in a course which examined Australian economic and social development from 1788 to the post-1945 years. He also came first in Industrial Relations I, an inter-disciplinary course which explored the general factors affecting industrial relations and included a special study of developing countries. There were more cheques to collect: a third one for general proficiency, the Federated Ironworkers Association Prize in Industrial Relations (worth $21, after the introduction of decimal currency in 1966), and the Anthony Squires Prize for Economic History ($21). Nick also won a Commonwealth Bank scholarship valued at $200 awarded to meritorious undergraduates in the Faculty who were proceeding to a final honours year.

By this time Nick was acutely aware of three things: he enjoyed studying economic history and industrial relations; he was not interested in pursuing an academic career in economic history, for all the encouragement he received from the Faculty's economic historians, such as Boris Schedvin and Sybil Jack, and he was no more interested in economics, despite his very good results in the subject.

Completing his degree in 1967, Nick was awarded Second Class Honours (Division I). He might have achieved a First if he had written his thesis on an aspect of Economic History rather than writing about the housing industry. But Nick thought he had been judged fairly, as he had not mastered economics and felt isolated from its theoretical and mathematical tendencies (not unlike Butlin himself). In any case, he did well enough to collect the $10 prize for coming top of Economics IV, beating Hewson who was awarded a Second Class Honours (Division 2). He could now contemplate taking his studies a stage further and more in the direction of management. The University of Sydney had given the young man further reasons to feel confident about himself, and had proved to be more than "an extension of school".

## Endnotes

[1]  W. Connell, G.E. Sherington, B.H. Fletcher, C. Turney and U. Bygott, *Australia's First: A History of the University of Sydney Volume 2 1940-1990*, University of Sydney and Hale & Iremonger, Sydney, 1995, p.205.

[2]  Interview: Greiner, 7 September 2011.

[3]  The Pass with Credit (awarded for a "specially meritorious pass") was the maximum possible result in 1964 for first year and some later year subjects in the Faculty of Economics.

[4]  *Good Weekend*, *SMH*, 1 July 1989.

[5]  Interview: Kathryn Greiner, 14 September 2010.

[6]  Connell *et al.*, *Australia's First*, p. 353.

[7]  Peter Collins, *The Bear Pit*, Allen & Unwin, Crows Nest, 2000, pp.19-20; interview: Greiner, 7 September 2011.

[8]  Patrick O'Farrell, *The Catholic Church and Community: An Australian History*, rev. ed.,

NSW University Press, Kensington, 1985, p. 406ff; Edmund Campion, *Australian Catholics: the contribution of Catholics to Australian society,* Viking, Ringwood, 1977, p. 205ff.

[9]   *Economic Review,* vol. 11, 1965, pp. 12-13.

[10]   "Savings Banks and the Pattern of Personal Saving", *Economic Review,* vol. 13, 1967, pp. 16-19. Jim Spigelman, a future Chief Justice of the NSW Supreme Court, wrote an article in the same issue discussing "the mentality of paranoia" afflicting the DLP.

[11]   *Union Recorder,* 23 February 1967.

[12]   *Honi Soit,* 27 July, 28 September 5, and 12 October 1966.

[13]   *Union Recorder,* 20 Oct. 1966 and 9 March 1967.

# 4

# Harvard: "what would *you* do?"

After leaving Sydney University, Nick Greiner won a scholarship to attend the Graduate School of Business, Stanford University, California. His father was profoundly unimpressed. He had never heard of Stanford. But he did know of the Harvard Business School, and agreed to pay fees amounting to more than $US 9,000[1] and other living expenses for his elder son to undertake the two-year Master of Business Administration (MBA) course.

Nick's application to Harvard was successful. With a guaranteed place and, producing evidence of a capacity to meet his costs for two years, he was awarded a Fulbright scholarship to pay travelling expenses. He knew something of what to expect. In the issue of the *Economic Review* which published Nick's article on State aid, James Wolfensohn, BA, LLB (Sydney), MBA (Harvard), wrote about his time at the Business School in the late 1950s. Although Wolfensohn's stellar career was well ahead of him,[2] he clearly took more of lasting value from Harvard than he extracted from Sydney University. It was "no holiday" because students worked on average 70-80 hours a week. But Wolfensohn found the institution "dynamic, exciting, thought-provoking", the environment "alive with ideas and stimulants to the mind", the teachers "outstanding" in their fields and in touch with business and government, and the students "a cross-section of the best graduates in the United States and abroad".

An ambitious and talented young Australian could thrive in such an environment. Advanced study of management practices, with limited time spent on economic theory, constituted a further attraction. Fortuitously, too, Greiner applied for Harvard in a year when, as Anthony G. Athos, the admissions director in 1968, later explained, the Business School sought to diversify its intake.[3] There were minor changes in the gender and racial balance. Of the 742 students selected from about 3,000 applicants, 31 were women (one of them Black) and 25 were Black males.[4] Of greater significance, the School deliberately reduced the proportion of "elegant sheep", the sort who came from Williams, Yale or Harvard and wore wool fabrics and button-down shirts. Nick's class "was destined to bridge the era between the Organization Man and an era that glorifies individual initiative". It was also the last one to wear a jacket and tie to school. "We looked for people who stirred the pot rather than guarded it. The world was changing, and it was time for Harvard to change." Within the United States, the admissions director looked for gifted graduates of the military academies, the technical colleges and the state universities. And, in order to foster debate, recruits were divided into sections where they were likely to clash. Nick Greiner may have come from the outside and was probably the youngest member of his cohort yet, as someone who liked to pit himself against the best, he was a good fit.

### Before departure

After visiting Taipei to work with one of his father's suppliers, Nick spent six months in 1968 as a senior research officer in the Commonwealth Department of Housing, appointed on the strength of his housing industry study in the final honours year. There was one important rite of passage to undergo before leaving for Harvard. Nick turned twenty-one on 27 April. His mother, assisted by Gourmet Caterers of Lane Cove West, stage-managed the mandatory party. Eighty guests were served savouries, punch, champagne and beer for a total cost of $A260-11. John Flynn, one of Nick's early childhood friends, wrote to "Auntie Clare" on 4 May referring to the "usual . . . masterpiece". She should start "Clare's complete classes in classic catering, cooking and kindness". He felt "privileged" to be there and "proud" to have grown up with Nick:

> there aren't too many people who have achieved and done so much as Nick in twenty-one years; how many boys of his age can put after their name B.Ec. (Hons)? how many can boast a string of positions in so many clubs, societies, councils & committees? how many are as widely traveled, well read & well informed? and lastly, how many are true Christian gentlemen? There are very, very few.

Kathryn, who had attended at least one earlier birthday gathering, spoke of the "usual . . . Greiner touch" and thanked the family for "allowing me to be a part of this very happy evening".[5]

Nick's relationship with Kathryn was now firmly established although, at his suggestion, they had "cooled it" before coming back "on strong" prior to his departure in August. Kathryn "cried buckets" when he left but the two had not made commitments tying each other down. There was no bar placed against social or more intense dating, and she acknowledged that there was "one serious contender" during his absence.[6] As will be seen, Nick was no recluse in the United States.

Clare Greiner kept the letters Nick wrote home in his first year away. Unfortunately, the tapes he sent did not survive, nor did anything he wrote or recorded in his second year. The letters exchanged with Kathryn and with others (he briefly corresponded with Peter Collins) are not available. For obvious reasons, letters to parents need to be read with caution. There are limits to what a son might tell. Parents keep asking questions which become tiresome, and some of Nick's letters reflected a mild irritation. His answers, however, provide a picture of how he lived and, more importantly, in volunteering stories about his world, reveal much about his values, priorities and preoccupations. A literal reading would catch the unwary. Nick had a way then, and now, of sounding a bit too full of himself than is conventionally acceptable. Read closely, these letters reflect his other side: the self-mockery which balances the self-confidence, as well as an amusement about the way he is judged. He could pass off a blood donation in March 1969 as showing "I'm not completely uninterested in others". The letters also demonstrate how readily he adjusted to the demands of the Business School and how, though driven to succeed at the highest level, he managed to sample so much of life outside the School walls. The well-rounded Sydney boy became an even more well-rounded young man.

## August-December 1968

Unlike most Australians, who went abroad for the first time to take a postgraduate course, Nick's venture to Harvard was the fourth occasion he had left Australia since arriving in 1951. It was also his second visit to Harvard.

While it was no longer unusual for an Australian postgraduate to go to the United States rather than the United Kingdom, it was uncommon to enter America after journeying across Canada. His father's contacts decreed that Nick should spend a week in Vancouver with a Hungarian family. He visited two plywood mills and "pretended to know more about the Aust. timber industry than I do".[7] After collecting introductions to companies in Montreal, Toronto and New York, he drove to the township of Banff in the heart of the Rockies. By then he had enhanced his reputation with "the Hungarian aristocracy in Vancouver" and become "a major talking point – big deal"; by way of expressing thanks, he had sent roses. He wrote to Kathryn around this time pointing out they had just 95 weeks to go before seeing each other again. His next main stop was Toronto ("quite a swinging place") where he learnt about the Soviet invasion of 21 August which crushed the "Prague Spring" in Czechoslovakia. He wrote to his mother imagining how she would be upset though she could "thank her lucky stars – again". Nick spent just one day in Ottawa, and was happy to leave, and visited "Expo" in Montreal, which was "surprisingly good": there "are girls everywhere", the food was "just delicious" and he had been enjoying the company of two boys from New York. There was only one problem: the mail from home was slow. He had just received his first letter from Kathryn: "C'est la vie."

Leaving Canada, Nick flew to Boston and booked himself into the Sheraton Hotel before moving into his quarters in the Business School's Gallatin Hall. Gallatin, built in 1927, was named after a Swiss-born American diplomat, linguist and politician who holds the record as the longest-serving Secretary of the Treasury (1801-14). Nick opened both a cheque and a savings account, depositing $A350 in the latter, and set up a charge account at the store located in the basement in his building which "has almost everything one would need".

He liked his room-mate from Detroit. Dave Zimmer was "a nice guy" who had the added advantage of owning a car, liked eight hours of sleep, sport, politics and economics – "so that's OK". Nick's contacts included six Australians as well as "French, Colombians, Chileans, Brazilians, Filipinos, Japs, Pakistanis etc . . . It's really quite a fantastic atmosphere." The rooms were "OK" although the bedroom was small, and he and Dave had to spend "a fantastic amount of money" fitting themselves out and getting settled (which included taking a subscription to the *New York Times*). An amused Dave Zimmer recalled having reservations about his new companion. He had asked not to be roomed with a foreign student; the course was going to be tough enough without having to deal with a foreign language "though that would have been easy compared to what Nick spoke!" He added: "It took a while to adjust to Nick . . . he always wanted to be in charge but we had to do things equally a lot of the time, so we got that sorted out."[8]

The Harvard which Nick described to his family was really just the Business School, though it did cater for more than the MBAs.[9] The School offered a doctoral degree in business administration and courses for middle management and even for trade unionists. The second largest group after the MBAs consisted of older businessmen enrolled in the Advanced Management Program (AMP). They were being groomed for top management – Richard Todd reported they had "moved vertically and now face horizontal problems" – and usually lived off-campus whereas the unmarried first-year MBAs stayed in the halls of residence.

Yet wherever the students lived, and whatever their age and marital status, they inhabited a self-contained world.

Separated physically by the Charles River, the inmates of the School's Georgian-style buildings could eat, drink and work without having much contact with the rest of the University. One School student, interviewed after Nick had arrived at Harvard, offered an explanation for this absence of contact: "[M]ost of us are just not used to living around so many beards and 'unwashed masses'." Another thought that the undergraduates across the Charles think "we're a bunch of robber barons" and a young wife of a recent School graduate said that what the MBAs all had in common was "rank, gross greed". Yet, if the School stood apart at Harvard in the late 1960s, it was closely connected with another world. Each year it sent out 700 graduates who were mostly "destined for unusual influence and success". In 1968, nearly 2,000 School *alumni* were presidents of corporations or board chairmen.

The new MBA intake was divided into sections of 90 to 100 students. Each section met in a tiered amphitheatre shaped as a horseshoe to assist the discussion which was central to the School's case method. Students, with their name cards placed in front of them, attended three classes daily, each of 90 minutes duration, starting at 8.10am and concluding around 2.00pm. They had previously been given case notes, comprising about 100 pages which they studied overnight. Peter Cohen, one of Nick's contemporaries at Harvard, who became a playwright after obtaining his MBA, described what happened next in terms of a military metaphor. The cases, he wrote, were real business campaigns (with names changed), sometimes "giving a general's grand view", at others "a corporal's blurred vision", with reports on conditions "in the trenches and bunkers of the business front", and of "the progress of armies of salesmen marching against each other . . . [and] of supply convoys steaming down channels of distribution". At the end of the exercise there would be one question to haunt you in your sleep: "[W]hat would *you* do?"[10]

Sydney University had not prepared him for this kind of exercise. Instead of someone standing in front of a class and delivering a set piece, a professor would invite argument and ask questions which became especially searching in the compulsory first-year courses where the School had imported ideas from the social sciences and mathematics. Decision theory, for example, informed Managerial Economics, Reporting and Control I and II (MERC I and II) where students learnt to draw "decision trees" to represent the "options" available, to eliminate some because of a weak branch further down the tree, and to guide their actions by a rational assessment of risks and probabilities. Professors taking classes in MERC I and II would sometimes lead a student onto an unsound limb and then "saw" it off. "Sawing off", with its attendant public embarrassment, was considered acceptable teaching practice in the School. Across the Charles, undergraduates were more likely to be led by the hand.[11]

Nick's ability to think incisively and quickly through arguments and options enabled him to flourish in this unfamiliar environment. He was also highly competitive, and understood that, in the Business School, "if you were not interested in being competitive it was not possible to exist". It was "like a war", though not so much a war against each other as against the examiners. He was competing with "the system", and wanted to defeat it and not to be defeated by it.[12] His contemporaries agreed with Dave Zimmer that he "always wanted to be the best". One later described him as "smart as a whip. Sometimes he's too smart and he gets cocky, like all you Aussies. But we love him." Another, who thought him cynical, reasonably critical and yet constructive, noted how when he set a goal "he normally achieved it".[13]

Early on, Nick warned the family about his "very hard" workload, telling them he would not be "doing brilliantly", and how he would be pleased to come in the middle of the class while learning "a great deal". By 7 October he was "coping fairly well" and getting on with most of the people he met. Within a month he told the family he was the only student of the entire intake to obtain a Distinction in Written Analysis of Cases, a result which counted towards his final grades.[14] Expecting he would soon come back to the field, Nick nonetheless described the mark as "good for my morale". Yet, little more than a week later, he failed a maths subject (nearly everyone in his section did) while accountancy, his second worst one, was yet to come. Human Behaviour in Organisation would right matters. This subject, designed to accustom students to the psychological implications of management decisions, was "more in my line". A month later he was confident of finishing in the top third in his year.

In the midst of these reports Nick did not lose sight of other important matters. He was pleased to learn that South Sydney took the 1968 rugby league premiership by defeating Manly 13-9. Nick could also tell home about one of the School's attractions; on consecutive days, he attended a lecture by the President of the Radio Corporation of America and a lecture by Professor Samuelson, "one of the world's best known living economists". But there was a downside. One of his neighbours had succumbed to the pressure and quit the School, and another had suffered a nervous breakdown and was taken to the local mental institution.

Despite the pressure, Nick found time for a life outside of case preparation. Early in October he reported talking to Kathryn on the telephone. There was just one problem. "The wicked child was at some 'guy's' beach house (NB 'guy = bloke')". In the same letter he spoke of meeting two girls he thought were Jewish and were "fairly nice". Twelve days later he could tell his mother that he and Dave were about to take two girls out to dinner. Next month he was trying to decide whether to visit New York or take a trip to the Niagara Falls and Toronto with the Australian President of the Student Association and two girls. Around this time he also reported:

> I still haven't met any US girl I like but they are very persistent. I get cards & invitations to invite them out etc. but I've decided it is better to be firm & maybe get some sleep on Saturdays. This idea hasn't worked: I've been out every week so far.

Early in December he informed his brother that "things are pretty good – weather putrid, food moderate, girls moderate". He attended the School's formal in mid-December – "my girl was quite nice" – where they ate a "lovely Polynesian dinner ($24 per couple without wine!)" and his section went through eight dozen bottles of champagne in their suite between dances. At the end of December Nick was drinking tequilas in Acapulco and, after staying in Mexico with Aunt Camilla (Edward Redlinger's mother), visited Houston in Texas (which "has its delusions of grandeur") where he saw a Brecht play, attended a concert, a cocktail party and then a dinner party – and discovered that the "southern girls were more my cup of tea than the ones I've met in the North".

Two events – the Olympic Games in Mexico City in October and the American presidential election in November – received a passing mention. Nick admitted spending two hours a day watching the Games on television and thought Australia was "doing surprisingly well". He had arrived in the United States after the strife-torn Democratic Convention in Chicago but observed the increasing excitement of the latter stages of the presidential election campaign. Noting how Hubert Humphrey, the Democrat candidate, had improved his position in the polls and been endorsed by the *New York Times*, Nick still thought Humphrey had left his run against Richard Nixon too late. He considered both men to be "uninspiring speakers" while even an Australian politician would not say some of the things they did. There was a similarly enigmatic comment about the Australian political scene. He was "glad to see Mr H got the big Liberal job – makes it easier for me to become P.M." ("Mr H" was Bede Hartcher, the father of Nick's fellow Riverview debater, Chris Hartcher, who had been appointed Federal Director of the Liberal Party.[15]) Later Nick told his brother that Nixon's team was "a pretty lacklustre" group" and reported people were already wearing "Kennedy in '72" buttons. Meanwhile, his own "political" career had already been boosted with his election as a section representative on the Student Association. Whereas one Harvard contemporary thought that Nick had no interest in politics, Dave Zimmer remembered how for his room-mate "politics were there from the start".[16]

## January-June 1969

Three subjects dominated Nick's letters home in the first half of 1969: his academic progress; a seemingly crowded social life; and his quest for summer employment.

His letters were full of stories about the tests he had to face and about his continuing High Pass average which placed him near the top of the year, although there were "guys" in the other sections who were doing better. At one point he warned his parents, who may have been considering a visit, that his last exam was on 31 May, "so I trust I will not be seeing you in late May – *there are four exams in the last week!*" [emphasis in the original]. The pressure was not unremitting. On 8 May, in the course of wishing Clare well for Mother's Day, he talked about the courses he expected to take in his second year, about the plans he had made for "a week of culture" in New York after his exams, and the immediate prospect of seeing the film, *The Prime of Miss Jean Brodie*, and of attending a number of parties (but without a "date"). In a letter sent a week later he spoke of 18 classes and 4 exams to go, of a coming round of cocktail parties and conversations with professors, and of changes in the courses he would take next year.

He was still trying to find acceptable and relatively inexpensive accommodation off campus for his second year at the School. The good news was that he had been elected to the Century Club, an elite group chosen from the top 10 per cent of the class for leadership and intellectual ability. Typically, he described his election as "no big deal", merely involving meetings over dinner to hear, and holding discussions with, non-business speakers. Writing a week later, Nick spoke of having to sit only three more exams, of hoping to maintain his High Pass, and of looking forward to listening to a Nobel Prize winner at the Century

Club and of watching the "amazing", "direct" and live pictures from the Apollo mission to the moon.

For all his concerns about doing well, it is evident that Nick had learnt, in a few months, how to cope with the pressure. The tempo at the School also dropped off around March 1969. It helped that he was not inclined to procrastination, and could find time for skiing, squash and even rugby. He told his brother Chris in April how he was playing rugby "with unaccustomed success" and had run 50 yards after an intercept to score a try against Harvard College. Nick found he could remain free of trouble as a breakaway and had managed to stay in "reasonable shape". It was best, however, not to spend more than a weekend on Long Island with the "real NY Jewish family" of a close School friend: "altogether too much. It's lucky I left or I would look like a balloon in a week."

His social life also prospered. Dave Zimmer chuckled as he pointed out that his room-mate "was good with women" while Kathryn, being in Australia, meant "he had a lot of licence he might not normally have".[17] Nick told his parents in February of a date with a girl from Wellesley College which he explained was one of the "Seven Sisters", the prestigious women-only liberal arts colleges.[18] They dined at the better of the two Hungarian restaurants in Boston and went to see *Oliver!*. The exercise involved a borrowed Chevrolet Impala and a lot of driving through snow (his weather reports were frequent and thorough). Early in the following March he went to New York with "a very nice blonde from Virginia", the one he took out in Boston, who wanted to interview religious editors for a job when she graduated. On this trip he saw a play, stayed at the Yale Club, went to St Patrick's Cathedral and the Guggenheim Museum, and visited Scarsdale – "the rich Jewish suburb" – to see a friend who drove Nick, his date and her room-mate back to Boston.

In mid-March he had "a most enjoyable time" at Montego Bay, Jamaica: "very informal, beautiful weather, excellent French/Jamaican food & drink, 13 nice girls from a college near N.Y. (Briarcliff [sic]) & lots of money". On 21 May 1969 – the fifth anniversary of his first meeting Kathryn – he told his parents of an invitation to a "girlfriend's place" in New Jersey for a couple of days and of several plays he planned to see. Writing from the Yale Club in New York after his exams were over, Nick spoke of earlier and future outings which included a dinner party given by two Wellesley College girls for their families on the eve of their graduation followed by a concert and a "traditional singsong under the stars". Nick found it interesting to talk to "my girl's parents" from Virginia who had very different views from those he was accustomed to hear in the "East".

Nick's social life included looking after a visitor from Australia, and it was an encounter to have significant ramifications. Geoffrey Robertson, a friend from Sydney University, arrived in Boston in March 1969. Robertson described how he looked up "a friend from student politics" who, "once the most indolent of pupils", was in "a lather of frenetic preparation for his class the following day". Nick introduced Robertson to the School's case study method, to the role-playing, the decision tree, the consideration of options, and the critical question: "What would *you* do?". Robertson would later write: "My discovery of the new world of the 'hypothetical' happened in Boston one wintery afternoon in 1969." After observing the impact of the technique on "the young Greiner", Robertson developed it as the host of "Geoffrey Robertson's Hypotheticals".[19]

There was pressure on each School intake to secure employment during the northern hemisphere summer break. Nick originally had three preferences: management consulting work in New York, Chicago or London; something in international trade; the paper manufacturing company Crown Zellerbach of San Francisco. He asked, in the case of the latter, "doesn't Father have some good contacts there?": "some push" was needed because the company normally did not take foreign students. His preference by February 1969 was McKinsey and Co., the global management consultancy firm, even if, as he felt, his age and lack of experience would count against him. The publishing company Harper

& Row had promised to make contact and other companies had been in touch.

McKinseys turned him down in late March but Harper & Row appointed him to investigate expansion opportunities for book stores and correspondence schools in Asia. He was also expected to report on general educational trends and publishing needs in the region. Nick was to be in Australia from about 23 June to 20 July and based in Crows Nest. He would then spend a week each in Singapore, Malaysia, Thailand, Hong Kong, and the Philippines followed by a few days in Tokyo before returning to New York to write a report. It sounded, he wrote, "pretty interesting". Nick started work in June soon after finishing his exams. Unfortunately, the air conditioning in New York had failed, and the company was in "a state of turmoil" because the new boss had fired almost everyone and no one knew much about anything. But Nick liked the boss who was "sharp", and the two got on well together. He finished the same letter by warning his parents that there was so much to do in Australia they might have trouble seeing him.

## Other preoccupations

Throughout his first year Nick was careful to remember birthdays and other significant dates, and was sensitive to family concerns. He noted how Camilla, his aunt in Mexico, was working for up to ten-and-a-half hours a day, six days a week, and that she was "like Mum in many ways but much harder – she doesn't cry anymore". He expressed his concern a few times about Edward, concluding that "it really seems he's beyond hope".

The older brother would occasionally admonish and advise his sibling. Chris might well have felt patronised. His brother urged him to stick with maths despite a score of 101/195, to take as many courses as he could in the HSC, and to use rowing to build him up for the football season ("you never know you might be lucky & crack a GPS crew"). Pleased because Chris had received a rave review in the *Alma Mater* for his drama and debating activities, Nick advised him to seek a decent role in the school play, while enjoining him to remember that the purpose of theatre was to entertain. Chris should not become "too arty about culture generally", given that he was "somewhat left and above his brother's down to earth pragmatism". There was also encouragement and instructions: Nick congratulated Chris on his "inevitable" appointment as a school prefect and told him to arrange an international driving licence for his elder brother and "*send it forthwith*" [emphasis in the original].

Nick provided regular reports to his father on the state of the timber industry in the United States. Lumber and plywood prices had risen sharply in late 1968 and the new Nixon Administration had set up a committee to investigate, while requiring government departments to reduce their orders. Relying on the *New York Times* and the *Australian Financial Review*, Nick was ever-ready with stock market advice. He told his parents near the end of 1968 to buy Broken Hill South mining shares at $A4-00 because they would double in value by June 1970 (they did once reach $6-00 but hovered around $3-60 in mid-1970). Nick read in the *Wall Street Journal* of the planned mergers of the Bank of New South Wales and the Commercial Bank of Australia, and of the ANZ Bank and ES&A Bank: "I'm not at all sure that this is good for the 'small man' [but] at least it'll give Mr Callaghan [Kathryn's father] something to do – he won't be the biggest anymore".

The rare references to Kathryn in his letters home were brief and not especially warm. In mid-November he reported having dinner with a married classmate and his German wife in a "pretty grim" unfurnished apartment consisting of a room, a bathroom and a kitchen costing $100 a month. The price of such an establishment helped him get over the "occasional feelings that it would be nice to have K. over here next year". In April of the following year he told his parents he had received a present "and a somewhat desultory card from K" to mark his 22nd birthday. Evidently, he did not think it necessary to tell them how he and Kathryn were writing to each other about once a week.[20]

Money, or the lack of it, was a minor irritation, though the subject was often mentioned in letters. Towards the end of 1968 he raised the subject of a credit card with his father who was clearly not keen on the idea even though it would be, as Nick saw it, "convenient". Just the same, "there will be no need for foreign aid supplements in the immediate future". He resented some of the prices he encountered, including a Customs charge of $6 to collect a tape recorder. At least he had overcome the temptation of buying a car. While he thought a play he saw in New York in June 1969 was "most enjoyable", he was shocked to find that a scotch and water cost $1-75. He had previously sought a grant of $1,000 from Harvard, but was not confident of getting one despite his grades, and there was no further mention of the application. Money was not the only factor, however, in causing him to revise plans for living off campus in his second year: Nick admitted, "I'm just too lazy to do my own housekeeping, cooking, etc.".

Nick kept up an interest in Australian politics. Noting the major write-up for Sir Paul Hasluck in the *New York Times* after his appointment as Governor-General early in 1969, he described Gordon Freeth, Hasluck's replacement as Minister for External Affairs, as "the epitome of (the) useless Australian Cabinet Minister". Nick's own political career received a slight setback. Standing in February for re-election as section representative on the Student Association – "presumably I will get elected but politics is a funny game!" – he lost by three votes in the fourth ballot, beaten by his "good friend" Gerry Dwyer "who has all the Air Force medals the President can give & 3 kids". Bob Ryan, "our black boy", had been a "cert" because everyone liked him. "It's the first election I've lost in a while" but the defeated candidate could console himself knowing that half the incumbents were defeated, he would now have more time to himself, and he had "got all the personal benefits I can from the position".

Nick's Harvard years coincided with the acceleration of protest in the United States over the Vietnam War and, within the universities, a preoccupation with university governance.[21] On 8 April 1969 the

Harvard chapter of the Students for a Democratic Society issued a list of demands to the University which included a call to abolish the Reserve Officers Training Corps. At lunchtime on the following day some 30 students occupied the University Hall, an administrative building located in the historic Harvard Yard, which they re-named "Che Guevara Hall". Joined by another 300, they ejected staff and rifled through confidential papers.

Nathan Pusey, the President of Harvard since 1953, decided on a quick "bust". He called in some 400 city police and state troopers who "liberated" the building in 20 minutes, roughly evicting the occupiers and arresting 196 of them. The large majority of students, hitherto either repelled by, or indifferent towards, the radicals, were immediately aroused. Fearful of an attack on the Business School, the authorities locked the gates, posted guards and announced that students could leave the campus "due to the possibility of violence". On Monday 14 April, between 10,000 and 12,000 students assembled at the Harvard football stadium, located within a decent punt kick of the Business School. The meeting eventually voted for a strike which lasted for several days. Nick was one of more than 300 MBAs who attended the rally, along with two "platoons" of AMPs, faculty members, office staff and the Dean of the Business School. Meeting separately, the Business School voted not to participate in strike action.

Throughout the occupation, eviction and strike Nick's entire first-year class was engrossed in a management simulation game via computer. The class had been divided into 24 "corporations" in an exercise which extended the "what would *you* do?" routine by requiring "decisions" within a three-hour period. The results were graded to assess the performance of the "managers" and the "boards of directors". Nick was the Marketing Vice-President of his corporation. He sat with a computer ("which never works") or wandered around his corporation's three divisions advising and co-ordinating. On the night of the football stadium meeting he had "a gruelling Board meeting" where three staff members – two of them AMPs and the other a second year student – "grilled us, mainly me, on our strategy". He learnt the next day that his corporation was adjudged top of the 24.

The letters home in mid-April referred both to the management game and to the events on the campus. He told his brother on 15 April how he attended the stadium meeting. It was the "usual uni political rally" though "very well organized". He continued:

> There is a move for the B School to join the strike but it has no chance of success. There really are no grounds for striking – that's why the use of police the other night was a dubious move although it seems there really were vital personal files etc which may otherwise have been destroyed. If I had time I'd do a write up for *Honi Soit*.

Nick spent the rest of the letter reporting on the management simulation game, which he found "pretty interesting but very tiring", and on his plans to visit New York and the Soviet Union. He told his parents on 18 April that his corporation continued to do well although no longer coming first. The game remained "pretty gruelling": he started at 8.00am on the day before and went through to 3.00am that morning. He also told them about the market research project he wrote before visiting Jamaica. It was one of the best two in the class; as a result, he had to give a presentation. He referred briefly to the strike. It had been suspended and the Business School had refused to join, but there was "tremendous turmoil" in the universities throughout the United States which could reach Australia "if an issue can be found". For Nick, as for the School as a whole, however, it was a case of business as usual. As one contemporary, later a director of McKinsey & Co, put it: "We really were an island of conservatism in a sea of discontent."[22]

The "Harvard Strike" changed many aspects of the university's governance, recruitment and curriculum policies, and community relations were never the same again. The Business School was not entirely insensitive to the "turmoil". It decreed a day off classes on 24

April to allow attendance at a symposium on "Student initiated change and administrative response". Pusey addressed it, and so did Professor Archibald Cox of the Harvard Law School. Cox had been Solicitor-General in the Kennedy Administration, had led the commission of inquiry into the Columbia University riots of 1968, and subsequently became the first Watergate Special Prosecutor. Nick's one comment to his parents on the proceedings was that he found them "fairly interesting".

He did not write about the Harvard strike for *Honi Soit*, though he did publish an article in the *Economic Review* recounting his first-year experience of the Business School.[23] Explaining that "the case method is virtually the sole method of instruction", he reckoned to have read 500 cases – three a day – and worked up to 70 hours a week, though most students tapered down to about 55 as the year unfolded. The first-year course was "completely practical in orientation". Lectures were almost non-existent with the instructors merely guiding discussions. Staff-student relations "are extremely close and forthright", unlike Nick's experience in Sydney. There were regular lunch meetings and drinks in the pub. Because the majority of students were single and lived on campus in their first year, each section became "very closely knit through social, sporting and academic activities".

Significantly, Nick advised future applicants not to follow the route he took to the MBA. The better strategy for securing admission and for personal development was to take a part-time Master's degree in the field while undertaking two years of employment. Harvard placed weight on business experience in its admissions policy and Nick, in effect, admitted he was inadequately prepared by entering the Business School only nine months after graduating with an Honours degree. He warned about costs. Harvard involved a considerable investment of around $US 6,000 a year for fees and living expenses, there were few Australian scholarships for study in the United States, and the School did not provide financial help to foreign students in their first year. Harvard was clearly ahead of Stanford in reputation and starting salary on completion of the degree, while Stanford was marginally ahead of about ten other business schools in the United States. Stanford had the better climate, smaller classes and a Pacific orientation, but Harvard had the "name", the better balanced and broader curriculum, "and access to the corporate nerve-centres of New York and surrounding areas".

## Second Year

Nick returned to Australia in mid-June 1969. His reunion with Kathryn led to an important decision: they decided to get engaged. She almost certainly precipitated the event. Kathryn saw no point continuing the relationship if it did not have a destination.[24] Nick's own memory of the moment is closely tied to the captain of his flight announcing that Neil Armstrong had landed on the Moon.

After visiting the selected Asian capitals he returned to Harvard for a second year. Vince Colarco, the CEO of the chemical company, Crompton & Knowles, described the difference between the first and second years at the Harvard Business School as follows: "In the first year the objective was to grind you down. You could do no good. And in the second year, they built you up. You could do no wrong." Nick agreed with this assessment.[25] He found 1969-70 so much more "relaxed". There was only one compulsory subject – Business Policy – and for the rest, "you could do what you liked". He chose to take Marketing Management, Urban Land Development, Interpersonal Behaviour and Management of New Enterprises, as well as write a research paper on Marketing in Foreign Environments. He went to the main Harvard campus and took Economics of the Arts with J. K. Galbraith. The famed economist, author of *The Affluent Society* and a former Ambassador to India, had served in every Democratic Party administration from F.D. Roosevelt to Lyndon Johnson. Galbraith offered this cutting assessment of the Business School: "We should be grateful to it for training people who will shoulder the dull, tedious administrative jobs in organisations."[26] From Nick's standpoint, eager to hear the great man lecture, it was a pity that Galbraith "distinguished himself by mostly being drunk and not turning up".[27]

Nick's social and cultural life, if anything, increased in tempo, although his male friends made sure the women he met understood he was engaged. He shared accommodation in his second year with Andy Jitkoff. Born of Russian parents in Houston, Texas, and a graduate of Rice University and the University of Texas Law School, Jitkoff was four years older than Nick. Of the two, Nick was the brighter and Andy was the more worldly-wise and socially adept. As Kathryn pointed out, Andy knew which lecturers with whom to play tennis.[28] The two men remained close friends after leaving Harvard, despite going very different ways. Jitkoff became an investment adviser before founding a financial planning company of which he was president. He also involved himself in good works. At 46 years of age, Jitkoff died of a heart attack in 1989 while on a flight to Tulsa. Nick, the godfather of his two children, has maintained contact with Andy's widow (now remarried) and the family.

Nick graduated in 1970 as a Baker Scholar. George F. Baker, the financier and philanthropist, funded construction of the School with a gift of $5m. The School's library also bears his name. Baker Scholars were the outstanding achievers. Selection was based on first-year grades and limited to the top 2.5 per cent of students in the year. Greiner was placed in the top half of the best. He graduated with a High Distinction; some Baker Scholars did so with a High Pass. Nick also belonged to another select group. Of the 19 (all male) Baker Scholars in 1970, four were from England, one was French and four were Australians and, of the Australians, three – Greiner, Bill Ferris and Tony Berg – were economics graduates of Sydney University who have remained close friends.

Importantly, the Baker Scholar had a job. In deference to his father's wishes, Nick turned down higher-paid offers in other fields and accepted a position as Assistant Vice-President of the Boise Cascade Corporation based in the north-western State of Idaho. Boise Cascade was formed in 1957 following a merger of two longstanding lumber companies. After three dozen mergers and acquisitions the company had grown into what the *Wall Street Journal* described as "a sprawling international giant", operating from Hawaii to New Hampshire. It had diversified and expanded into building materials, packaging, office supplies, factory-built houses, resort and hotel complexes, urban and recreational land development and, briefly, cruise ships. Boise Cascade's annual sales which, in 1957, amounted to $35m, topped $1.7bn in 1969. In the previous four years it had risen from the 154th largest industrial company in the United States to 55th. Nick Greiner had every reason to believe he was joining a growing conglomerate, "the darling of Wall Street".

There was another reason for taking the job. Robert V. Hansberger, a graduate of the Harvard Business School, the company's first president and the driving force behind its expansion and success, was committed to "decentralizing . . . a high degree of authority and responsibility". Hansberger attracted scores of the brightest "young tigers" (as he called them) from the top American business schools and put them in charge of individual areas. The newly-anointed Baker Scholar, a middle-level executive aged 23, would be able to make and implement important decisions. As Premier of NSW, Greiner adopted the Hansberger philosophy. He, too, believed in letting the managers manage.[29]

## The Harvard legacy

In 1973 the *National Times* interviewed a number of Australians who had graduated from the School, including Rod Carnegie of Conzinc Riotinto Australia and Tony Berg and David Clarke of Hill Samuel Australia. Many acknowledged they had made a financial sacrifice in returning to Australia. Nick Greiner thought he was about 30-35 per cent worse off in real terms than when he was a middle-level executive in Idaho. But money "isn't all that important". He then pointed to a characteristic of Harvard MBAs:

they all tend to think and talk in a very ordered way. I remember
last weekend, when I was thinking about going to see the football,
I thought of all the alternatives that were open to me at the time. I
must say that is very much the Harvard MBA way of doing things.

The young man who left Harvard in 1970 recognised he had
been through a "mind forming" rather than "knowledge forming"
experience.[30] Forty years later Greiner recalled how the Business School
had "inculcated a strong, rational approach to everything" and "taught
us not to show emotion".[31] The case method had trained him to look at
options and make evidence-based decisions, to place outcomes above
following prescribed or historical processes, and to seek what was feasible
above what was ideologically consistent or desirable. Harvard, in effect,
confirmed and developed patterns of thought which would determine
his approach in politics and government and in business.

# Endnotes

1   Except where otherwise stated, all references in this chapter are to US dollars. The
    exchange rate in 1968 was, approximately, $US 1-00 = $A 0-90.

2   The self-styled "late developer" – a cellist, financier, philanthropist – was a two-term
    President of the World Bank . For an extended account of his Harvard years, see *A
    Global Life: My Journey among Rich and Poor, from Sydney to Wall Street to the World Bank*,
    Public Affairs, New York, 2010, ch. 4.

3   *International Business Week*, 18 June 1990.

4   Nick provided a different set of numbers: he thought there were 720 students in
    his intake, of whom 80 came from outside North America, 30 were female and 35
    were Black Americans. Around 40 per cent were married; the age range of the total
    was 21 to near 40; a third had an engineering background, another third came from
    economics or business, and the remainder had degrees in physics, law or arts. Nick
    Greiner, "The Harvard M.B.A.: An Antipodean View", *Economic Review*, vol. 15, 1969,
    p. 61. In 1990, women made up 27 per cent of the total, and minorities accounted for
    13 per cent. *International Business Week*, 18 June 1990.

5   Family Letters, Greiner Papers.

6   Interview: Kathryn Greiner, 14 September 2010.

7  Unless otherwise stated or self-evident, the quotations in this chapter are taken from Nick's letters contained in a folder entitled "Letters from Nick", Greiner Papers.

8  *DT,* 4 June 1990.

9  The following five paragraphs and quotations draw upon Richard Todd, "Where Money Grows on Decision Trees", *New York Times Magazine,* 10 November 1968. Nick sent a copy to his parents, describing the article as "really quite a good description".

10  Peter Cohen, *The Gospel According to the Harvard Business School,* Doubleday & Company, Inc., New York, 1973, pp. 16-17. Cohen's book upset many members of Nick's class.

11  Robert McNamara, the former President of the Ford Motor Company, the Defense Secretary in the Kennedy and Johnson Administrations and one of the School's best known *alumni,* famously popularised the notion of "options" in the 1960s while escalating the American commitment in the Vietnam war. The story in the School was that he did not draw the trees out far enough.

12  Interview: Greiner, 7 September 2011.

13  *DT* and *SMH,* 4 June 1990.

14  The available grades for his first-year courses were Distinction, High Pass, Pass, Low Pass, and Unsatisfactory.

15  Hartcher did not last long enough to be of any assistance. He was dumped in 1974 following the intervention of the so-called "McKinsey set", armed with their MBAs, who considered Hartcher to be a dinosaur. Tim Pascoe, who replaced Hartcher as Federal Director, once interviewed Greiner in 1969 for a summer job with McKinsey and Co. Nick did not get the job, and neither man recalls the occasion.

16  *SMH,* 4 June 1990.

17  *Sunday Telegraph,* 4 June 1990.

18  Hillary Rodham (later Clinton) was in the same year as Nick's "girl".

19  *Geoffrey Robertson's Hypotheticals: Dramatisations of the moral dilemmas of the 1980s,* North Ryde, 1986, Introduction.

20  Interview: Kathryn Greiner, 14 May 2012.

21  For three accounts of these events at Harvard, see Cohen, *Gospel According,* chs 11-12; Lawrence E. Eichel *et al, The Harvard Strike,* Houghton Mifflin Company, Boston, 1970; and Archie E. Epps III, "The Harvard Student Rebellion of 1969: Through Change and Through Storm", *Proceedings of the Massachusetts Historical Society,* Third Series, vol. 107, 1995, pp. 1-15.

22  *International Business Week,* 18 June 1990.

23  Greiner, "Harvard M.B.A", pp. 61-2.

24  Interview: Kathryn Greiner, 14 September 2010.

[25]  *International Business Week,* 18 June 1990; interview: Greiner, 25 March 2012.

[26]  *Wall Street Journal,* 1 April 1969.

[27]  Interview: Greiner, 25 March 2012.

[28]  Interview: Kathryn Greiner, 14 May 2012.

[29]  The above two paragraphs, and the quotations, draw upon, *Time,* 12 Apr.; *Business Week,* 15 May; *Wall Street Journal,* 29 December 1971; and Herman L. Boschken, *Corporate Power and the Mismarketing of Urban Development: Boise Cascade Recreation Communities,* Praeger Publishers, New York, 1974, pp. 8-9.

[30]  *National Times,* 9-14 July 1973.

[31]  Interview: Greiner 29 March 2011.

# 5

# Into Politics

Nick and Kathryn were married on Saturday 1 August 1970 at the Chapel of St Ignatius College, Riverview, in a ceremony beginning at 6.00pm and followed by a reception at the Menzies Hotel in the City. It was a formal affair with the three males of the bridal party dressed in white tie and tails. Chris Greiner was a groomsman and Geoffrey Robertson the best man. For someone who would be criticised for making bad political judgments, or for lacking political nous, Nick's choice of Robertson was a shrewd one, and not because his best man became a celebrity. By appointing a later arrival in his life, the bridegroom did not have to choose between friends he had known since his early school days.

After spending one night in Sydney the young couple had a week in Tahiti, and then flew to San Francisco and hired a car to drive to Boise, the State Capitol of Idaho. Nick took up his position with the Boise Cascade Corporation while Kathryn secured a job with the Human Resources Center. They spent the next 18 months in what was a small conservative State, firmly in the hands of the Republicans at both the State and the Federal levels. Idaho had a strong tradition of opposing "big government" and standing up for individual rights. Nevertheless, personalities mattered more than ideology in Idaho, which explains why Frank Church kept being returned to the Senate as a Democrat after 1956, despite his criticism of America's involvement in the Vietnam War in a strongly pro-war State.[1]

Nick did not have the inclination or the time for Idaho politics and, fortunately, the successful timber division of Boise Cascade was not affected by the problems elsewhere in the Corporation. Boise Cascade plunged into the red in the fourth quarter of 1970, hit by a recession and by law suits arising out of consumer and environmental anger over its recreational land developments in California. It was forced to write off $250m worth of assets in 1971-2 while its share price tumbled from $80 in 1969 to $8 in 1972 and, for a brief period, it appeared that Boise Cascade might go under.[2]

Returning to Australia in January 1972, the Greiners bought a house in Castlecrag, later moving to Wahroonga. Their son, Justin, was born on 19 August of that year; Kara followed on 5 December 1974. Nick became the Executive Director of the White River Corporation which issued its first prospectus in 1973 after acquiring the three Greiner timber companies. He was also managing director of two private building companies, and a director of Harper & Row, responsible for revision of publishing, printing and distribution policies in Australia, south-east Asia and Japan. It was not, however, a full or absorbing workload, principally because of the frustrations he experienced at the White River Corporation.

Having met his father's wishes at every turn – taken economics at Sydney University, gone to Harvard rather than Stanford, joined what was originally a specialist timber company – Nick came home to work in, and expected to take over, the family business. But neither his father nor the employees of the White River Corporation welcomed his ideas, his father did not allow his manager to manage, and Nick had trouble coming to terms with the "European way" of doing business through deals and bartering. He needed to be in control, and he was not.

> Part of the problem was that my father hung on very grimly. We were discordant, we had very different attitudes on lots of things . . . I actually spent most of my time doing other things. I went to work every day, but I spent a lot of time playing squash, being in the Harvard Club, and being in the Liberal Party.[3]

Acknowledging that the son of a European father could not walk out of the family business to join another company – for example, Hill Samuel Australia where friends like Tony Berg were employed – Nick had to find an escape route his father could accept.[4] Forty years after leaving Harvard Greiner described his political career as an "accident": "I would never have gone into politics if my father had let me run the family business."[5]

### "I quite like this"

Nick joined the Turramurra branch of the Liberal Party where he entered the orbit of Dorothy Peters. A gregarious and well-meaning senior Liberal of distinctly "progressive" views, Peters was one of several influential women who were the Party stalwarts on the North Shore. Encouraged by Peters, Nick served as secretary and president of the Turramurra branch, became a delegate to State Council from 1974, a vice-president of his State Electorate Conference, and a member of the Party's State Economic and Urban Committees. He also worked for the Liberals' Electorate Assistance Committee which raised and distributed funds and organised manpower for campaigns in marginal seats and frequently acted as an adjudicator for Young Liberal debates.

The contrast with the Liberal hopefuls of his age group could not have been starker. They were apprenticed to politics. Chris Puplick, like John Howard and Philip Ruddock before him, had come through the Young Liberals. When both Greiner and Puplick sought pre-selection in 1977 (Puplick nominated for the Federal seat of Mackellar), Puplick's record in the Party was far more significant and substantial. It would take paragraphs to list all the offices he held at the Federal, State and branch level, as well as his positions in the Young Liberals. Puplick could fairly describe himself as "a child of the Liberal Party". He knew its history, had imbibed its culture, and was a true believer. Nick, by contrast, was an outsider, mainly by inclination. As will be seen, there were advantages and drawbacks in following his separate path.

On the eve of the December 1972 Federal election, which brought

Labor to power, the *National Times* invited "two young professional men" to air their views on the two political leaders: Bill McMahon and Gough Whitlam.[6] Greg Woods, in 1972 a Senior Lecturer in Criminology at Sydney University and later a QC and Judge of the District Court of NSW, regarded support for McMahon as like "voting for a Ford Edsel".[7] Nick Greiner was more charitable in writing about Whitlam. He admired "a man of considerable charm with a sharp intellect and a quick wit" who had shown "great determination" in presenting Labor as "an acceptable alternative Government". But Nick raised questions about Whitlam's temperament and about his lack of prudence, patience and self-control. He saw Whitlam's panacea for every problem – a national commission to undertake detailed planning in Canberra – as "simplistic and superficial". It failed the test of "good organisational design": the top-down approach, whether applied to business or government, "will only increase resistance to change, stifle initiative and destroy morale at the levels where the ultimate activity takes place". He also saw the practical difficulties confronting Whitlam's attempts to translate "Utopia" into reality. Above all, he concluded, a Whitlam Government would be "an intellectual luxury which my commonsense says I cannot afford".

The Coalition's Federal defeat in 1972 prompted the Liberal Party's "younger brigade" to challenge long-serving backbenchers or former ministers, or to nominate for seats where sitting members were preparing to retire.[8] Nick Greiner nominated for two Federal seats. Bradfield was the first, one of the safest Liberal seats in Australia, held since 1952 by Harry Turner, no friend in the Party Room of Sir Robert Menzies. Greiner once met Turner, an occasion he remembered for being asked whether his tie was a regimental one. Greiner did not figure prominently in the pre-selection ballot won by David Connolly.[9] Typically, Nick later made light of the moment: "I had the choice of going to the timber company picnic or Liberal pre-selection for Bradfield, so I went to the pre-selection, and I didn't get in, but I thought, 'I quite like this'."[10]

He did much better in the contest for North Sydney held two weeks later. This seat, also considered safe, had been held since 1966 by a former RAAF pilot, Bruce Graham, who had previously represented the marginal seat of St George (1949-54, 1955-8). Graham was a convivial backbencher who was apt on drawn-out evenings to detach his artificial leg, the result of a war wound, for the sake of amusement or to make a point. Like Harry Turner, he held a seat which might usefully have been occupied by someone with a realistic prospect of entering Cabinet.

Greiner was aged 26 at the time of the North Sydney pre-selection on 15 December 1973. The selection panel consisted of 30 members of branches within the North Sydney Federal Electorate Conference and ten representatives each from the Liberal Party's State Council and State Executive. Several members of the panel would cross paths with Greiner in later years. They included Senator John Carrick, formerly the long-serving General Secretary of the NSW Division of the Liberal Party; Kevin Rozzoli, the Speaker of the Legislative Assembly when Greiner was Premier; Neil Pickard, a Greiner Government minister whom Greiner controversially appointed NSW Agent-General in London; and Lyenko Urbanchich, a leading right-winger, whose alleged Nazi and anti-Semitic associations during the Second World War periodically embarrassed Greiner in the 1980s.

Candidates had to make a short speech – two, if they survived the first cull – and to answer questions. Greiner's probably disarmed, antagonised or seduced the panelists with his frank, seemingly offhand comments. An elderly North Shore gentleman asked whether he would be happy to run for a "hard luck" seat, a term Liberals then applied to safe Labor electorates. Many in the Party thought that fresh-faced Liberals should first prove themselves in Labor's heartland. Nick explained that, in terms of horses for courses, he would not be effective working in a Labor stronghold. Invited to explain why he had not followed the normal practice of submitting references with his nomination, Greiner said he did not have any to present but, if he did produce any, they would all be "first class". Otherwise, he would not have submitted them. Given these responses, and the fact that he was largely unknown, Greiner came "perilously close" to victory. He tied second with John Lockhart, a future Federal Court judge, after 14 ballots.[11] The sitting member survived only because he had a loyal following in North Sydney. A Greiner victory would have seen him accompany John Howard to Canberra after the 1974 election.

Greiner might have tried again for North Sydney if the sudden double dissolution in 1975 had not protected Graham from a further internal contest. Instead, in 1977, Greiner switched his attention to the State seat of Willoughby on the North Shore, an electorate which included Chatswood, Artarmon, and Castlecrag, as well as Willoughby itself. Lawrence McGinty had held this safe Liberal seat since 1968. In 1976, when Neville Wran wrested government from Eric Willis, McGinty won 63.1 per cent of the primary vote, easily defeating the Labor candidate, Eddie Britt. A Catholic, a war veteran, and a solicitor by profession, McGinty had risen to prominence through his role in local government for which he was appointed MBE in 1967 after serving seven years as Mayor of Willoughby. A minister in the Askin Government from December 1973, and retained by Askin's successor, Tom Lewis, he was sacked when Willis replaced Lewis in January 1976. McGinty, a wheeler dealer and an old campaigner, was aged 56 in 1977. The Party wanted to replace him and two other long-standing MPs, all of them habitués of the parliamentary bar, at a time when it was touting Nick Greiner as "the future", and even "future Premier material".

Greiner was McGinty's sole rival for pre-selection. It was probably necessary, when competing with a much older man who could claim years of political activity, to include anything and everything on the nomination form. Nick set out his academic record, business experience and Party activities, and listed all the organisations with which he had been associated. Many Willoughby selectors would have approved of his membership of the University Regiment for three years, and there was no need to tell them anything more. Nick cited his six-month job with the Department of Housing in 1968 as evidence of experience in government. He claimed to have been a student member of the Senate, the supreme governing body of the University of Sydney when he was actually a student member of the Union Board. The entry reads like a slip rather than an intention to deceive. By declaring he spoke German and Hungarian as well as English, Nick no doubt created the impression of being equally fluent in all three languages. Perhaps, like most candidates of all ages, he occasionally stretched a point. The fact remains that, at age 30, Nick Greiner could demonstrate he was an inveterate joiner of, and active participant in, professional, cultural, welfare and sporting organisations. He could rightly present himself as someone with wide-ranging interests who had already packed a great deal into his life.

Liberals liked to know about wives, their candidates in the 1970s being overwhelmingly male. "A good wife" was an asset and Kathryn had the right kind of record: she was the Preschool adviser for the Department of Youth and Community Services and responsible for supervision of all early childhood programs in the electorate and surrounding areas. The two children also had a role in demonstrating the Greiners' commitment to Willoughby: they attended local playgroups and kindergarten and would attend school in the electorate.

On this occasion, Nick did provide references. Mervyn Watson of Harper & Row described him as "an exceptional citizen" destined to be at the forefront in any enterprise he undertook. He referred to Greiner's outstanding academic record and proven record as a manager who was noted for his self-discipline and for being a successful businessman. Watson added that Nick was "the true family man happily married with two children" and could handle difficult interpersonal conflicts. Clive Powell, a member of the Sydney Stock Exchange, emphasised his loyalty, balanced approach to life and work, his humanity, intellectual and speaking qualities, and capacity for hard work and for taking matters to a conclusion. Powell reinforced the notion of "a good wife": Kathryn possessed "a vivacious personality" and had "considerable social and professional qualities in her own right".

Assuming his re-endorsement was automatic, McGinty relied on the selectors knowing his record. He did not supply references or a full list of activities and achievements. Clearly, he expected almost the full support of the 30 branch delegates which included many well-known conservatives in the Party, even if he could not expect too many votes from the 20 State Council and State Executive selectors. The latter, after all, included Dorothy Peters, two other women who had mentored younger Liberals, and members of the ruling "Liberal establishment" who were looking for younger talent.

The pre-selection was conducted on 29 September 1977. Greiner knew for the first time just what he was doing.[12] His approach was not the laid-back one of 1973. He had already written to district progress associations, churches and other bodies seeking meetings, and had spoken to the Mayor of Willoughby and to Council staff. In his speech Nick emphasised his management experience and accentuated the differences between McGinty and himself. As the two men sat together in an ante-room the older man, anticipating an easy victory, patronised his younger rival, telling him the pre-selection should give him good experience. Nick noticed an unusual mannerism. McGinty would dip his fingers into his whisky to extract ice cubes which he would then suck. After the numbers were counted Greg Bartels, the General Secretary, came into the room to break the news: Greiner had won by 32 votes to 18. McGinty was initially stunned though he appeared to take defeat as a gentleman. He was "very disappointed" but "not bitter"; "I'll always support the party"; and he understood the desire for "a new image".[13]

The successful candidate told the local press he had abandoned ambitions to go to Canberra; he liked to have breakfast with his family.[14] Nick delivered a characteristic throwaway line about his 1973 challenge for Bruce Graham's seat: "I was only 26 then, and it was more or less something to do on a Saturday afternoon". On the basis of doing "fairly well" in that "dry-run" he felt encouraged to seek State pre-selection. Nick called his "fairly convincing" victory a decision for the "future". The Party needed new blood. Wran was "doing it well", and the Opposition was "doing it hard". Importantly, Greiner emphasised he had received support from every section of the Party. The State Liberal Organisation was becoming progressively factionalised between liberals and conservatives, the so-called "Trendies" and the "Uglies". Greiner wanted good relations with the conservatives in the Party, and it helped to have Judith Barton, a leading conservative, as his campaign director for Willoughby.

Following the pre-selection, Greiner told the local Chatswood paper, *The Star*, of his concern about the two areas of local government which needed attention, namely, housing and urban development.[15] He deplored the entry of politics into local government as Labor had done, though he wanted to see State and local government working more closely together. *The Star* obliged with good publicity, enhanced by an appealing photo on the front page featuring Nick, Kathryn and the two children.

Feeling assured of victory, and not expecting a poll for some 18 months, Nick saw no need for intensive electioneering. Besides, McGinty kept saying he remained totally committed to the Liberal Party and had no plans to run as an Independent. The timetable changed, however, when Eric Willis abruptly retired from politics in 1978 after his removal as Party Leader. Labor took his Earlwood seat with an absolute majority in the subsequent by-election, and Wran grasped the opportunity to call an early poll for 7 October. The Liberal Party was swamped by what became known as the first "Wranslide". The Liberals shed 9.3 per cent of their primary vote and were reduced to 18 of the 99 seats in the Legislative Assembly, only one more than the National Country Party (NCP).[16] Peter Coleman, the new State Liberal Leader, lost his seat, while the swing against the Liberals in five "safe" North Shore seats averaged 12.7 per cent.

Despite the electoral carnage, Nick Greiner should have won

Willoughby. Eddie Britt, once again the nondescript Labor candidate, was certainly not the "future". He won the seat principally because McGinty reneged on his promise, stood as an Independent and directed his preferences to Britt. Although the Liberal vote fell by 24.4 per cent on the 1976 figures, Greiner led Britt on the primary count by 10,438 votes to 10,014. McGinty, however, had garnered 4,076 votes and, after his preferences and those of the Australian Democrat were distributed, Labor took the seat with a 424-vote majority. There were few, if any, recriminations directed at Nick Greiner. The President of the Castlecrag Branch described him as "an excellent candidate" who had worked "exceptionally hard and . . . thoroughly deserved to win". The Chairman hoped Greiner would offer himself again for pre-selection.[17]

## Ku-ring-gai

Bruce McDonald, the Deputy Leader of the State Parliamentary Party, wrote to Greiner on 23 August 1979 to report on Britt's dismal record in parliament and to discuss the possibility of Greiner standing again in Willoughby. McDonald, who had been a selector when Greiner defeated McGinty in 1977, also raised the prospect of Greiner nominating for North Sydney. Bruce Graham had sensibly decided to retire and a number of high profile candidates eventually offered themselves for selection. It was as well Greiner was not tempted because the pre-selection contest proved to be one of the dirtiest in Liberal Party history.

His next attempt to gain Liberal pre-selection followed the retirement in 1980 of John Maddison from the very safe North Shore State seat of Ku-ring-gai. Maddison had been a reforming Minister of Justice in the Askin, Lewis and Willis Coalition governments, and Deputy Leader of the Liberal Party after 1975. Thirteen other candidates applied, including the Mayor of Ku-ring-gai and two future Liberal MPs – John Booth and Phillip Smiles – as well as Andrew Caro, a former manager of World Series Cricket and considered by some Liberals to be the favourite.

Judging by his preparations, Greiner's approach to this pre-selection was even more thorough than in 1977. He asked Clive Powell to use his earlier reference while adding that Powell himself was a lifetime resident in the area and felt it did not want a "trendie" (sic) but "an intelligent business oriented person with clear leadership potential (Ra Ra)". Nick reckoned he could secure 15-20 votes in the first ballot, and sought to make contact with each of the selectors. He assembled notes on more than a dozen topics in anticipation of questions. His planned speech, to be delivered before the first ballot, began by quoting Malcolm Fraser's stress on "freedom of choice, of decision and of responsibility" and concluded with Alfred Deakin's injunction to Liberals "to tread as ever the paths of progress". The important message lay in between. Nick referred to "management" or "managerial" on four separate occasions. Observing that there was not one member of the State Parliamentary Party who was an economist or had top level experience in manufacturing, he defined the problems of NSW in such a way that the selectors would see the need for someone of his training and experience to address them.

In his second speech to be delivered after the initial cull – he did not contemplate failing to survive it – Nick focussed on leadership, correctly sensing that the selectors would want to reserve this blue ribbon seat for someone capable of reaching the very top. He pointed out how a range of different styles had proved successful in State politics, citing the contrasting examples of Don Dunstan in South Australia and Askin in NSW. At the same time, he identified some general principles: the person chosen to join the team must command respect for competence, integrity and sincerity at the local and broader level; must have the ability to relate to all segments of the community – big and small businessmen, trade unionists, the elderly and the young, academics, ethnic groups and the normal families; must be aware of personal appearance and style and relate effectively to the media and the public; and must have the capacity to attract the right people and get the best results from them. Whereas in the 1970s the emphasis was on consensus and pragmatism and *ad hoc* responses, voters in the 1980s wanted principled and honest politicians.

"The era of politicking is the past." The NSW Parliament of the future:

> should be like a vibrant board of directors in which we are all
> shareholders, while acknowledging the additional human element
> in politics. At present, it is generally ill-informed and largely
> powerless at the hands of the Executive, Public Service and
> statutory authorities.

Greiner's nomination was supported by three referees: in addition to
Clive Powell, who wrote the reference he was asked to provide, Nick was
supported by John Walton, the Chairman of Waltons Limited, and Justice
Michael Kirby of the Law Reform Commission, Greiner's friend from
university days. Kirby had the most to say, partly because he felt obliged
to explain at length why his judicial office precluded him from expressing
views about party politics. He had to limit himself to character and
personality. Kirby spoke glowingly about Greiner's "very considerable
intellect, sharp mind . . . good practical instinct and . . . keen business
sense". This "generous host", "good family man" and "forward-looking
Australian" with "a friendly disposition", would work towards improving
society "in an orderly and systematic way" and promote change, not for
its own sake, but in order to better society. All three referees stressed how
Kathryn added value to Nick's candidature, and all mentioned she was the
daughter of Sir Bede Callaghan. Walton thought "Katherine" [sic] would
be "a real asset"; Powell described her as "an excellent organizer, with [a]
sound understanding of many current social and human problems"; and
Kirby found her "charming and highly intelligent", while noting how he,
as deputy to Sir Bede as Chancellor of the University of Newcastle, had
a further link to the Greiner family.

The pre-selection was conducted at Liberal Party headquarters in
George Street on Saturday 5 July 1980. Greiner faced an imposing panel
which included David Patten, the State President, and John Mason, the
new State Parliamentary Leader, as well as Bruce McDonald and a number
of leading women from the State Executive and the local branches
(including Dorothy Peters). Greiner probably counted on the vote of one

young man who would figure prominently in his political life, ultimately to his detriment. In 1980 Terry Metherell would himself be selected for the safe seat of Davidson by a panel which included Nick Greiner.

It took several ballots to narrow the candidates to two, before Greiner emerged with a 30-20 vote majority over Caro. The Liberal Party commissioned a survey of voter attitudes soon after the pre-selection.[18] The 109-page report observed how there had recently been an erosion of the Party vote. It was important, therefore, to make a good showing in the coming by-election to serve notice that the Liberal Party "was far from a spent force" and would be pushing hard to return to the government benches. Ku-ring-gai was important in its own right and as a possible morale booster for the Liberal Party. In addition to unexceptional findings relating to policy and Wran's total dominance, the survey noted Mason had "an extremely low profile", McDonald was considered "brash" – although at least he was noticed – and Greiner had achieved "some awareness". What was known of him was "positive": he was young, energetic, a brilliant speaker who grew up locally, and was well-educated. The report suggested projecting him as a dynamic young politician possessing a lot of practical experience and the kind of vitality the Liberal Party lacked.

The by-election was held on 13 September. Labor stayed out of the contest to concentrate on the by-elections for its safe Sydney seat of Bankstown and the safe Coalition electorate of Murray. Brian Buckley was Greiner's only opponent. A former Liberal and an avowed republican who had previously tried to win Liberal endorsement, Buckley's candidature did not excite general interest. Tim Moore managed Greiner's campaign. Son of the then President of the Australian Conciliation and Arbitration Commission, Sir John Moore, and first elected to the Legislative Assembly in 1976, Tim Moore was the most "liberal" of the Liberals in the State Parliamentary Party. Within a dozen years his friendship with Metherell would be the catalyst for Greiner's fall from the premiership.

Nick's campaign opening was a low-key affair. Ordinary supporters

were almost outnumbered by Liberal Party politicians headed by Mason
and McDonald and including Peter Collins, the newly-endorsed candidate
for Willoughby. There was a well-composed flyer with photographs of
Nick posing with a businessman (he "knows the problems of industry"),
standing outside the Sydney Adventist Hospital ("health care is very
important to Nick"), sitting on a bench at Turramurra railway station
("Nick Greiner will monitor transport facilities in this electorate"), and
standing with Kathryn next to their children sitting on swings ("a family
man"). Kara was still at primary school, did not understand why she
had to appear in public, and felt very confused about what it all meant.[19]
The flyer also listed Greiner's academic qualifications, noted that he was
the Executive Director of a company which supplied components for
3,500 homes a year, was a Liberal Party member for 13 years, a branch
president for five and a State Council delegate for seven, and was an
accomplished debater and public speaker and a keen sportsman. John
Maddison endorsed his friend of "over ten years" and recommended
him for his hard work, and his ability to wrestle with problems and argue
a case.[20]

The turnout on by-election day was low, about 68 per cent compared
with 89 per cent in the 1978 general election. Greiner won with 66 per
cent of the vote, achieving a slight improvement on Maddison's margin
over Labor in 1978. Acquaintances and friends were quick to congratulate
him. John Hewson, by now the Professor of Economics at the University
of New South Wales, pointed out that he had first learnt of Greiner's
political ambitions some 16 years earlier and was "tempted to say its [sic]
about time!". He further remarked that "timing is the essence of success
in politics". Greiner had got it right given the state of NSW politics
and of the Liberal Party. Greiner replied, saying it was more a matter
of good luck than good management on his part; the timing of his
entry into politics had been "fortuitous". But he hoped their "somewhat
intermittent" personal and professional contact would continue.[21] Leon
Punch, the Leader of the State NCP, saw it as an "excellent result" and

Nick said he was looking forward "to establishing a mutually beneficial working relationship".

## The new MP

Starting a new career required relocation. The Greiners bought a house in Koora Avenue, Wahroonga, within the Ku-ring-gai electorate. Moving proved to be a drawn-out process. The family had to shift in and out of rental properties and parental homes because unavoidable building delays added months to what normally took a few weeks to install a Cape Cod extension. The goldfish, which survived every disruption, expired on the day they took occupation.[22]

Nick Greiner was sworn in on 25 September 1980. Two other newly-elected MPs – Tim Fischer, the NCP member for Murray and a future leader of the Federal National Party, and Richard Mochalski, the Labor MP for Bankstown – took the oath of allegiance on the same day. Six years later and after an investigation found evidence of improper conduct, Greiner, as Leader of the Opposition, sought to have Mochalski expelled from the Legislative Assembly. Mochalski was a founder and director of the $110m Balanced Property Trust which collapsed in 1983 and cost thousands of pensioners their life savings. The Labor Government pre-empted Greiner by forcing Mochalski to resign his seat on 1 December 1986, and the former MP subsequently faced fraud charges, was convicted and struck off as a solicitor.[23]

On 15 October, late in the afternoon, Greiner made a 30-minute maiden speech in the Legislative Assembly.[24] The circumstances were partly responsible for what was an unusual event. Entering parliament after a by-election rather than a general election, Greiner did not have the option of speaking in a debate on the Address-in-Reply. In normal circumstances, the new arrivals generally roamed far and wide. They would combine effusive expressions of gratitude to family, mentors, friends, supporters and the electorate at large with insights into personal philosophies and world views, along with aspirations or promises to leave this world a better place. Greiner chose to speak in a budget debate, and his contribution was almost entirely devoted to an analysis and critique of the Wran Government's Budget. He did not regard the occasion as "any big deal", and could not recall, nearly 28 years later, whether any members of his family were in attendance.

Greiner did pay homage to his predecessor in Ku-ring-gai: "a fine parliamentarian", "an outstanding liberal in every sense of the word", "an outstanding human being." He promised to do all he could to advance the interests of the people of his electorate, and alluded to some of the problems in Ku-ring-gai. There was also a brief "policy statement" which consisted of agreeing with Lord Hailsham's Sir Robert Menzies Oration delivered in the Great Hall at the University of Sydney in May 1978.[25] Hailsham had contrasted two alternative views of democracy: one he characterised as a centralised democracy or an elective dictatorship, and the other as the theory of limited government or a belief in freedom under the law. He argued that the latter offered justice in place of rigid equality. Greiner concurred.

The rest of his speech addressed the 1980-1 Budget. He began by pointing out how the Premier, who was also the Treasurer, had claimed that his economic strategy since 1976 had been to protect the State from the worst effects of the Fraser Government's policies. Quoting the Under-Secretary of Treasury, he contrasted Wran's position with the Treasury standpoint that State economic policies were of marginal significance only. The Premier's "Mr Fix-it fantasy", of keeping the NSW economy safely on the straight and narrow, did not stand up to reality. While State governments should not abdicate responsibility in favour of the Federal Government, they should not make "absurd and fatuous claims . . . for economic miracles". The Premier had done so in his Budget Speech by talking about creating 150,000 new jobs and leaving NSW with the lowest unemployment rate in Australia. Patiently and effectively, providing figures where necessary, he questioned or undermined many of the Premier's self-congratulatory assertions. Citing the figures for public sector spending between 1975 and 1979, Greiner showed how the public sector deficit in NSW had increased at a faster rate than it did for the whole of Australia. He showed how the NSW Government was the highest taxing State in Australia, was following tax policies which lacked "imagination and innovation" and was, through inflation, "accentuating the repressive and counter-productive effects" of the taxes it imposed.

Greiner's concluding remarks amounted to his real "policy statement", and he re-stated it at every opportunity in the following decade. He believed that Parliament and the general public should be able to evaluate how well the Government was spending money and how efficiently its programs were performing. Pleased that government departments were drawing up corporate plans, he could not understand why they did not also consider the financial implications of these plans. The two should be presented together and the information should be available to the Parliament and to the people working within the departments. Departments could then question where they were going and could question government priorities. "I am in favour", Greiner said, "of allowing management to manage." To that end, departments and authorities should have greater flexibility and the discretion to apply the funds made available to them. If all these steps were taken, the public would become more aware of how government programs were working and might take greater interest in their evaluation. Parliament could then perform what Greiner saw as one of its first duties, namely, to analyse the effectiveness of public spending and the quality of government programs, and to enable all members to know whether ministers' proud objectives were being achieved.

Greiner summed up his own speech. The Government's claims of economic management were "spurious": it had failed to present its programs in a manner which allowed them to be evaluated; the Budget lacked imagination and innovation on both the expenditure and revenue side; it was a "cosmetic, do-nothing" Budget which failed to offer a "fair-go" and did not face the major structural problems of the public and private sectors in the 1980s.

As Greiner resumed his seat, "Lin" Gordon, the minister at the table, called out to Mason: "Make him the Leader now, John."[26] No doubt it was in Labor's interest to praise Greiner's speech as a means of highlighting the inadequacies of the Opposition front bench. But a number of Labor members went beyond point-scoring in commenting on his remarks. One Government backbencher called it a "strong speech" and expected Greiner to make his mark in Parliament; another referred to the research Greiner had undertaken in preparing his speech and predicted that the member for Ku-ring-gai would be a "great asset" to the House. Laurie Brereton, one of Labor's rising stars, thought that Greiner's commitment to financial answerability "will go a long way towards improving the stand of accountability in the Parliament". Rosemary Foot, the MP for Vaucluse, who spoke first for the Opposition after Greiner, failed to mention him at all. Other Liberals did take notice. The conservative Jim Cameron thought he showed "magnificent promise" and described his contribution as "one of the most learned and, indeed, instructive speeches heard in this House for many years."[27]

Greiner's first months were normal fare for a new Liberal Party MP. He attended branch and electorate conference meetings and functions, board meetings of Harper & Row and White River, the opera, the opening of the Annual Art Show by the actor Jackie Weaver of the Elizabethan Trust Sydney Committee, the annual general meeting of the Hornsby/Ku-ring-gai Hospital, and Remembrance Day at the Cenotaph. He met a delegation from Odyssey House who wanted to discuss alcohol addiction and drug dependence, voted at two pre-selections, and hosted visits to Parliament House and small lunches in the Strangers' Dining Room. His diary was full of engagements for Christmas drinks within the electorate and for school speech days or nights. Nonetheless, he managed to fit in several games of squash and to watch some tennis at White City.

One of Greiner's first tasks was to appoint an electorate secretary. He did not have to look far. After inheriting Janet Mahon from Maddison, the two gave each other six months to test their relationship. Mahon remained with Greiner for 16 years.[28] A single woman in her forties when she joined him, Mahon had previously worked in private enterprise as a secretary to a solicitor in Wagga Wagga, a naval attaché in London, a world-renowned scientist in Canberra, and a Hereford breeder in Sydney. She initially found Parliament House "daunting" but soon fitted in with "a very interesting man to work for. He's very hardworking, and he likes people to be hardworking." Greiner later described the woman known as "The Organiser" as "perfect" – dependable, honest, diligent, with common sense – "you name it". Janet occasionally mothered him, gently eased him into accepting unwanted invitations, and protected him from invasions without alienating potential intruders as some in her position were wont to do.

He was already making his mark, and the press was pleased to provide space for his views. Greiner told an interviewer he believed Parliament could not continue to be almost exclusively made up of lawyers, public servants, school teachers, trade union officials and farmers. Politics needed people with experience in business. Areas such as health and education required "a large dose of management", and that meant bringing into Parliament people qualified to test the efficacy of government programs being run by bureaucrats. He believed that the traditional philosophical differences were breaking down. Younger voters were more likely to swing, not on the basis of prejudice but in their estimate of which party was more likely to be more competent in government. He wanted a rationalisation of government services between Federal, State and local spheres to reduce the duplication, and hoped that the Federal Government would take the lead. For example, the States should have unfettered control over health and education and specific purpose grants should be abolished. He hammered these points as Premier when negotiating with Hawke and Keating between 1988 and 1992.

As for his own ambitions, Greiner would like to sit on the front bench and make a significant contribution towards getting back into government. In government, he "would like to be a minister of something interesting and significant". Reporters, in the meantime, noted how Greiner had impressed both sides of the Assembly with his well-researched and well-delivered speeches. They also detected annoyance among some colleagues who thought the new boy was too inclined to tell the Party how to go about its business.[29] If he appeared brash it was because he was impatient to get on with the job.

## Liberal woes

Nick Greiner was a delegate and Kathryn an observer in February 1980 when State Council debated a motion to expel Lyenko Urbanchich from the Liberal Party. He was accused of publishing "virulently anti-Semitic propaganda" during the Nazi occupation of his native Slovenia, a sub-committee having decided it was too difficult to prove he had collabo-rated with the occupation forces and had committed war crimes. Greiner supported the expulsion motion which was carried by 270 votes to 203 but fell 15 votes short of the required 60 per cent majority.[30] The mo-tion itself marked the culmination of five years of increasing tension between the left and the right in the Liberal Party Organisation. It also heralded a new phase where organised factions dominated contests for Party positions and pre-selections. For the most part Nick Greiner was able to remain aloof.

The Parliamentary Party, which had remained largely unaffected by the factional brawls, had its own problems. The Leader, John Mason, had neither the intellectual capacity nor the stomach to match Neville Wran. Dismal polls kept registering his inadequacies. Greiner had little respect for him, remembering him mainly for his inane giggling.[31] A survey conducted in February 1981 found that Mason had "a very low profile . . . even among Liberal supporters", while a "very high level of respondents" had "no view about what the Liberal Party stands for". Liberal policies were "not well understood in the community, and particularly amongst Liberal supporters".[32] Sensibly, at the end of May, Mason decided to resign. Persistent rumours about a leadership challenge and his own manifest failings had rendered his position untenable.

The Party Room elected Bruce McDonald, the member for Kirribilli since 1976 and the Deputy Leader since 1978, to replace him. McDonald brought aggression and self-promotion to the task, as well as a reputation scarred for some in the Party by questions raised about his business dealings and whether he was the "right type". Jim Cameron, one of the five members of the so-called "Prayer Group" – the one organised faction within the State Parliamentary Party – won the deputy leadership. Cameron believed in lower taxes and small government and considered the permissive society an abomination. The Rev. Fred Nile, the National President of the Call to Australia, and newly-elected to the Legislative Council, had hoped Cameron would become the Liberal Leader.[33]

McDonald was an energetic talker whose commitment to economic development through private enterprise, and to small government over big government, was spelt out in charts and accompanied by references to "Strategic Task Force Groups", "the discipline of a proper strategy", "market place perception", "positive attitudes", and "attitudinal awareness and instant issue research". For all his self-belief, vigour and aggression, McDonald failed to impress the NSW electorate. On 19 September the Liberal Party endured a second "Wranslide". Although its primary vote improved by 0.6 per cent on the 1978 result, and Peter Collins regained Willoughby, the Liberals lost two more seats to Labor and Mason's seat of Dubbo to the National Country Party. At least the arrival of Collins and Metherell boosted the available talent in the 14–member Liberal rump in the Assembly.

Greiner had no difficulty in retaining Ku-ring-gai, securing 66 per cent of the primary vote. McDonald, whose seat of Kirribilli was abolished in the redistribution, failed to win the new seat of North Shore. Labor "ran dead" and its preferences assisted the North Sydney Mayor and Independent candidate, Ted Mack, across the line. Even if

McDonald had retained his seat, his days as Liberal Leader were surely numbered; he was so discredited by the election result and appeared more obviously not the "right type" as further information emerged about his business activities.[34] McDonald's defeat in North Shore averted one form of leadership contest. When the Liberal rump assembled to choose McDonald's successor, Leon Punch threw out a different kind of challenge. Accusing the Liberal Party of dragging the Opposition down "like a sea anchor", and pointing out that the Coalition parties each held 14 seats, he proposed becoming Leader of the Opposition until the Liberals recovered their sense of direction. The Liberals flatly rejected what they unanimously regarded as impertinence. Instead, they elected John Dowd to replace McDonald.

Dowd was a lawyer who had held the seat of Lane Cove since 1976 and held strongly civil libertarian views on issues such as homosexual law reform. His election ended coalition arrangements with the National Party (NP). Oddly enough, Dowd won the leadership on the votes of the five-member, Protestant-Catholic "Prayer Group". It decided that the other candidate was too young and inexperienced and probably a little too "liberal". Nick Greiner had nominated with the encouragement of Lloyd Lange, a lawyer and the leader of the Liberals in the Legislative Council. He lost by a handful of votes but, at the age of 34, Greiner knew he could afford to wait. Besides, he had polled remarkably for someone who had been in Parliament for just 13 months.

# Endnotes

1. F. Ross Peterson, *Idaho: A Bicentennial History*, Norton and Company, New York, 1976, chs 8-9; Robert H. Blank, *Individualism in Idaho: the Territorial Foundations*, Washington State University Press, Washington, 1988, pp. 76-81.

2. *Wall Street Journal*, 29 December 1972; *Los Angeles Times*, 8 July 1973; Boschken, *Corporate Power, passim*.

3. *International Business Week*, 18 June 1990.

4. Interview: Greiner, 10 September 2012.

5. Quoted by Paul Barry, 21 Oct. 2011, in http://www.thepowerindex.com.au/Sydney/nick-greiner.

6. *National Times*, 27 November-2 December 1972.

7. The Ford Company's Edsel, manufactured in the late 1950s, was a marketing fiasco and its name became synonymous with failure.

8. *Sun-Herald*, 16 December 1973.

9. Connolly, a former diplomat, held the seat until 1996, having lost a pre-selection battle in the previous year to Dr Brendan Nelson, a future Liberal Party leader.

10. http://www.thepowerindex.com.au/Sydney/nick-greiner.

11. *SMH*, 16 March 1983; Interview: Greiner, 24 September 2009.

12. Interview: 24 June 2009.

13. *North Shore Times*, 12 October 1977.

14. *Ibid.*

15. *Star*, 18 October 1977.

16. The Country Party in NSW had changed its name to "National Country Party" in 1977 and the change to "National Party" was made in 1982.

17. President, Castlecrag Branch to Members, 17 November 1978, Greiner Papers.

18. Max Stollznow Research Pty Ltd, Market Research Report, 8 August 1980, Liberal Party of Australia (LPA), ML (Mitchell Library), MSS 3340, Add-On 1454, H 1121.

19. Interview: Kara Greiner, 19 April 2011.

20. Ku-ring-gai file, Greiner Papers.

21. Hewson to Greiner, nd; Greiner to Hewson, 14 October 1980, Ku-ring-gai file, Greiner Papers.

22. Interview: Kathryn Greiner, 14 May 2012.

23. David Clune and Gareth Griffith, *Decision and Deliberation: The Parliament of New South Wales 1856-2003*, Federation Press, Leichhardt, 2006, p. 561.

24. *NSWPD*, Third Series, vol. 156, pp. 1684-92.

[25] Lord Hailsham of St Marylebone, *How Free Should We Be?*, The Speakers Forum Limited, Sydney, 1978. Hailsham, formerly a Tory MP in the HFouse of Commons, was Lord Chancellor in the Heath Government (1970-4) and later served as Lord Chancellor (1979-87) in the Thatcher Government. He disclaimed his inherited title in 1963, but received a life peerage in 1970.

[26] Interview: Greiner 24 December 2012.

[27] For comments see *NSWPD*, Third Series, vol. 157 for 21 October 1980.

[28] Following her death on 16 October 2001 the Legislative Assembly passed a condolence motion on 23 October moved by Barry O'Farrell, then Deputy Leader of the Opposition. *NSWPD*, Third Series, vol. 288, pp. 17775-80.

[29] *SMH*, 3 January 1981.

[30] For an account of the Urbanchich episode, see Ian Hancock, *The Liberals: A History of the NSW Division of the Liberal Party of Australia 1945-2000*, Federation Press, Leichhardt, 2007, ch. 6.

[31] Interview: Greiner, 24 September 2005.

[32] NSW Marginal Seat Survey, Summary and Initial Conclusions, February 1981, Electorate Profile 1980-1981 - 1, Collins Papers, ML, MSS 7442/52.

[33] *SMH*, 2 June 1981.

[34] I am grateful to David Clune, the former Manager of the NSW Parliament's Research Service and the Parliament's Historian, for his advice on this point.

# 6

# "We will focus on
bread-and-butter issues"

At the end of 1981 the Liberal Party in NSW was in dire straits at both the organisational and parliamentary levels. Phillip King, the Chairman of the Organisation's Political Strategy Committee, described the Liberal Party in NSW as "a demoralised and spiritless association of people".[1] Many branches were moribund or operated as closed shops. Seemingly immovable conventions and structures and factional warfare inhibited change at all levels of the NSW Division. The 14 seats held by the Parliamentary Party in the Legislative Assembly (Neville Wran had 69 in a House of 99 members) were, with the exception of two outposts – Vaucluse in the Eastern Suburbs and Wagga in the country – located in the North Shore bunker. In March 1982 the NSW Liberals lost Bill McMahon's Sydney seat of Lowe in a by-election, and lost four more Federal seats when the Fraser Government was defeated on 5 March 1983. They now held only 11 seats in the House of Representatives compared to 19 in 1975; their primary vote in NSW for the same period had fallen from 39.7 to 31.6 per cent. At least the NSW Liberal Party was not alone in its embarrassment. The State Liberal Governments of Victoria and South Australia and the Coalition Government in Western Australia were all out of office by February 1983, while the break-up of the Coalition in Queensland in August 1983 left the National Party governing alone.

The one consolation in NSW was that the Wran Government suffered a 10.4 per cent fall in its primary vote in Drummoyne, the State seat vacated by the popular Labor member who had won Lowe in 1982. Under attack for his seeming insouciance, John Dowd's "meet-and-greet" campaign had certainly contributed to the biggest-ever swing against the Wran Government. But Dowd's poll ratings throughout 1982 stayed marooned in the low 20s, despite his relentless attack on police corruption. John Valder, a former Chairman of the Sydney Stock Exchange and the State President of the NSW Division of the Liberal Party, concluded at the end of 1982 that Dowd was not the man to lead the Liberals to victory. Valder commanded respect because he had orchestrated the dramatic rescue of the Division's finances. Conservatives in the Party were wary of him because he wanted State Council to drop its traditional opening prayer and the singing of "God Save the Queen" and because he "looked after the (left-wing) Establishment" of the Party.[2] In fact, like Nick Greiner, the State President came from outside the ruling clique and was not "a Liberal Party animal".[3] Again, like Greiner, he had a limited grasp of the Party's culture and of the histories of those with whom he had to deal.

Valder regarded Greiner as "the only hope" for the Party in NSW, despite claiming to know little about him.[4] The State President knew more than he was letting on. It is unlikely that the conversation was restricted to Greiner's shadow portfolio of Treasury when the two men lunched together at the Union Club on 17 February 1983. By then the mutterings about Dowd had extended into manoeuvres. On 14 and 21 February Greiner met Lloyd Lange, his principal numbers man, and the two men discussed a possible leadership challenge. Greiner was also in touch with Rosemary Foot. Eleven years older than Greiner, a grazier's daughter, educated at Frensham School and the University of Sydney, divorced with two daughters, Foot had an impeccable political pedigree. Her paternal grandfather, James Ashton, had been a minister in the Carruthers and Wade Liberal governments in the first decade of the 20th century and her maternal great grandfather, Sir John See, had been Progressive Party Premier of NSW from 1901 to 1904. Given their very different backgrounds, it is not surprising that a journalist dubbed

Greiner and Foot "The Odd Couple".[5]

Labor's decisive victory in the Federal election on 5 March 1983 became the catalyst for change. Valder did not feel constrained by the Liberal Party convention whereby leaders of the Organisation did not comment publicly – unless with enthusiasm – about the parliamentary leadership. "All of us in the Liberal Party", he said, "have got to lift our game." He referred to a Morgan Gallup Poll in the previous December which put Liberal support in the State at 29 per cent, the National Party at 8 per cent, and Labor at 54 per cent. Dowd's approval rating stood at 22 per cent whereas Wran registered 47 per cent. "When", Valder pointed out, "we are opposing a Government that has made just about every mistake in the book, our public opinion poll ratings ought to be a lot higher." While denying his comments amounted to serving notice on Dowd, Valder added that the Leader had to "address himself more to the major issues", one of which was the financial management of NSW. He noted how Greiner was commanding the limelight on this issue, and suggested the State Leader and the Deputy Leader might also be pitching in on the subject.[6]

Lange and others, acting with Greiner's approval, began canvassing. The numbers rapidly slid away from Dowd who took few steps to protect his leadership. It was not his "style" to be what he later called "a good pocket pisser".[7] Two of his lieutenants – Kevin Rozzoli, who had replaced Cameron as Deputy Leader in 1981, and Tim Moore – started a rescue mission and Dowd heaved into action on the weekend before the Party Room vote. Dowd's supporters pushed several lines: Greiner lacked the experience to fight the election against Wran due in 1984; Leon Punch might dominate him; another leadership change would destabilise the Party and further hold it to ridicule. But the Greiner camp remained confident of securing 18 of the available 26 votes to support a spill motion.[8] Promises of preferment helped. So did Dowd's reputation as a "trendy". At least three members of the Prayer Group had decided that Dowd was much too liberal. Either they were unaware of, or prepared to overlook, Greiner's own predilections which included support for homosexual law reform. Overall, however, Dowd's miserable poll rating was probably the decisive factor in shifting votes to Greiner who looked and sounded a better prospect for leading the Party out of despair.

The conflict was not, as some have claimed,[9] between the Party's "conservatives" and "progressives". Apart from the Prayer Group, there were still no real factions within the Parliamentary Party. The Prayer Group itself lost a member when Jim Cameron resigned from the Liberal Party on the day before the leadership vote, saying he had "no appetite for this comic farce of annual decapitations of leaders". Andrew Peacock's election as Federal Leader compounded his unhappiness because Cameron disapproved of his small "l" liberalism. Nor did he agree with the Party's decision to reverse what he saw as a principled stand not to accept public funding for elections.

Greiner had several duties to perform in the week preceding the Party Room vote. Peter Collins was due to marry Dominque Fisher on Saturday 12 March. A bucks party for Collins was organised for the Monday after the Federal election, and the Greiners hosted a dinner for the bride and groom at their home on the following Thursday. Moore may have been lobbying for John Dowd but the Moores, as well as the Metherells, were guests at the dinner. Greiner did some scrutineering on the Friday for Don Dobie who just held on to his marginal Federal seat of Cook. On the Saturday afternoon Nick and Kathryn attended the Collins-Fisher wedding at the Royal Motor Yacht Club, Point Piper. He had had a busy week outside of the politicking Greiner preferred to leave to others, and was quite relaxed about the outcome.

The Liberal MPs assembled on Tuesday morning 15 March, the Ides of March, ten days after the Federal election, and 105 years after the Greiners in Hungary had observed the uprising against the Hapsburgs. The *Sydney Morning Herald* editorial told them that their Party "continues to give the appearance of a body in free fall". Against this background, Fred Caterson, the Liberal whip and a member of the Prayer Group, moved a spill motion, which Metherell seconded. After it was carried by 16 votes to 8 Dowd announced he would not be nominating, and Greiner was elected to the leadership unopposed. Foot defeated Rozzoli by 8 votes to 5 in an election for the deputy leadership (Liberal members of the Legislative Council were not entitled to vote for this position). Anticipating rejection, Dowd had prepared a press statement where he graciously conceded defeat and promised his loyal support.

Greiner met Punch twice on the day he was elected Leader. Punch had already talked privately to him and to Foot about reviving earlier coalition co-operation.[10] He had laid the groundwork for co-operation by rejecting Cameron's offer to join the Nationals, and by announcing he would not seek to lead the Opposition despite the parity of numbers. Punch promised that the Nationals would give Greiner their full support should he be elected and so welcomed the Party Room result; almost anyone would have been better than Dowd. He expected the Nationals and Liberals to form a more cohesive and united front, to establish a joint shadow cabinet and revive regular joint party meetings.[11] Greiner was more cautious but did promise much closer collaboration.

Notwithstanding the pessimistic expectations of one senior National, the two men worked well together.[12] Speaking on a condolence motion for Punch in 1992, Greiner acknowledged that "Leon Punch and I were about as different as chalk and cheese".[13] Punch was 20 years his senior and the two differed "in a whole variety of personal attributes and in our attitudes towards intellectual pursuits". Yet they had "nary a disagreement", basically because Punch "always called a spade a spade". Greiner then appeared to contradict himself by saying there were some "jolly good fights", although he also stressed how Punch was always straight in his dealings and had the view, like Wal Murray, his successor as Leader of the Nationals, that, if a deal was made, "it was to be honoured".

The new Leader declared that the Liberal Party "will be different in both substance and style". He also offered an early glimpse of the Greiner frankness which would disarm and charm the media. The Liberal Party, he said, would try hard to play a positive role. The notion of an Opposition which automatically criticised every government action "is an insult to the intelligence of the electorate and destructive of its own credibility". Instead, the Opposition should assume the initiative in setting the agenda of debate and not simply respond to the Government's measures. On matters of substance, he told a news conference:

> We will focus on bread-and-butter issues: jobs and economic
>
> development, industrial relations, State taxes and charges and the quality of services provided in major areas such as education, health, transport and housing.

Greiner did not consider that organised crime, a favourite Dowd subject, should constitute a basic concern of the alternative government in NSW.

In a separate interview on the day of his elevation, he foreshadowed some of the themes which became the touchstone of his approach in government. He explained his entry into politics not in terms of wanting to change the world, or to conserve it; he just thought he could do a better job of running the State Government, the biggest corporation in NSW.[14] But Greiner did not want to be considered a faceless technocrat. Rather, if labels were unavoidable, he was an economic rationalist with a social conscience (the harbinger of the slogan, "Warm and Dry", used to describe his Government in 1988). Politics was "ultimately . . . about people": good management and economic rationality had to be tempered with a concern for people, especially the disadvantaged. He was a critic of middle class welfare. Resources were scarce and should be directed to those most in need. He wanted to introduce "the cold breeze of public accountability" to government. If the Electricity Commission was subsidising some sections of the community at the expense of others, then the people should know about it. The people should know how much government cost, and decide whether those costs should be borne by users or by the community as a whole.

Greiner acknowledged that winning the 1984 election would not be easy because of the Opposition's poor performance over the years. Yet it could be won. Three factors would help: the dwindling popularity of Neville Wran and his Government, the volatility of the electorate and, paradoxically, the defeat of the Fraser Government. The Premier, he said, was "no political Messiah"; he could be beaten. And Wran's standard excuse for everything which went wrong – Canberra – would be harder to justify because of the election of the Hawke Labor Government.[15]

Greiner officially informed the Assembly of his election when it met at 2.15 pm. Soon afterwards, he asked the Premier his first question as Leader of the Opposition. He was neither combative nor probing. Bob Hawke had called an economic summit and had spoken of the desirability of extending the current wages pause. Greiner asked whether the NSW Government would support a pause for twelve months, seek to persuade the other States to follow suit, and extend the scope and duration of the NSW freeze on government charges. Wran's response to a fair and measured question was to ignore it. He attacked the record of the previous Fraser Government, accused Greiner of not understanding that the summit would examine the national economy and industrial relations, said he had not expected Dowd to go down without a fight, took a sideswipe at Rosemary Foot, and announced that his Government would go to the summit in an endeavour to reach a consensus between all the interested parties.[16] The Premier clearly intended to treat his young opponent to the familiar Wran tactic: abuse, diversion, and more abuse. It had, as yet, never failed.

The media generally welcomed Greiner's elevation. One journalist remarked that on the day of his victory he wore the grin "of a man who clearly sees himself as a born leader, a man who rejoices in his intellect, a man who feels he has the backing of the captains of industry". The same writer said Greiner "is ambitious and it shows", and claimed that, having in the morning "cut down the dispirited John Dowd with not a pang of conscience", he took the Leader's seat in the Assembly in the afternoon "with some authority".[17]

Another journalist saw some grounds for thinking Greiner might become the first long-term Liberal Leader since Askin. Writing in the *Bulletin,* Bob Carr noted how Greiner could address the issues of finance and management "which are the heart of State politics" and, having marketplace experience, might win back some business support for the Liberal Party. Even so, he thought that the Liberals "had taken a big punt", not least because of Greiner's limited experience in Macquarie Street. Carr noted, with approval, that Greiner would be starting out by pressing ahead with "bread and butter" issues instead of the "scattergun" and "cheap populism" approach of his predecessors. Nevertheless, the two "Wranslides" meant it was unlikely Greiner could win in 1984. Failing Wran's own departure from State politics and some Labor Party disasters, he would have to wait until 1988. In the meantime, should Michael Baume, having lost the seat of Macarthur in the recent Federal election, enter State politics, he might become a focus for any internal opposition to Greiner.[18] Neville Wran, however, constituted Greiner's immediate problem. The Premier's mastery of the 30-second media "grab" and of Question Time meant he controlled journalists' perceptions of previous Liberal Leaders. Carr warned the new Leader of the Opposition he needed "a potent parliamentary and media performance" to win a greater approval rating.[19]

## The inheritance

Nick Greiner became Leader just one month before his 36th birthday. In case he had any illusions about his new job, the *Sydney Morning Herald* reminded him of the past. He was the eighth Liberal Leader in eight years. Greiner had to convince his colleagues that "eight is enough".

Greiner was well-placed in one respect. Dowd as Leader could afford four staff, including one press secretary. The Wran Government was not disposed to be generous to the Opposition (the Premier alone had a personal staff of 16). But the generosity of the "Hungarian connection" (Frank Lowy of Westfield and Joseph Brender of Katies were major donors), the Liberal Party and other business donors enabled Greiner to employ nine staff, three of whom were press secretaries, one was an office manager and others worked in a research unit.[20]

Two of his early appointments proved to be inspired choices. Ken Hooper had started his working life as a lad with a country newspaper in Horsham, Victoria. He joined the *Age* when it was edited by the legendary Graham Perkin. Starting as a police roundsman, he managed the paper's Sydney bureau, travelled abroad, and had himself deported from South Africa for interviewing Chief Buthelezi. Returning to Sydney, he joined the *Daily Telegraph* as the State political reporter (he claims to have asked the chief of staff over a beer in Castlereagh Street the name of the Premier and for directions to Parliament House). He later worked in the Canberra Press Gallery and as an editor in Sydney with the *Australian* and the *Sunday Telegraph*. Hooper tried – and hated – public relations before becoming John Dowd's press secretary. Greiner approached him on the eve of the leadership challenge but Hooper remained loyal, though he did think of strangling Dowd if he used the term, *non sequitur*, one more time. Hooper did not hesitate when Greiner approached him after winning the leadership.

Hooper's role was to deliver messages to an electorate more attuned to a tabloid than a broadsheet. Stories were fed to the *Daily Telegraph* and the Sunday papers to take Greiner into unfamiliar territory and to promote an "image". Hooper also sought exposure on television and radio, in the case of the latter to win the attention of Alan Jones, who was clearly onside, and John Laws, who was something of a loose cannon. Hooper had Greiner wearing make-up because his five o'clock shadow could arrive by late morning making him look "shady". Hooper also worked the State Parliamentary Press Gallery which for years had been in Wran's thrall. He could drink and mix with the best of them and, in doing so, had an ally in his close friend, Bryce Osmond, a journalist who worked for Punch. Hooper understood how the system worked but he also had a very good base from which to launch a media campaign.

The private Greiner he knew to be shy and with his own insecurities; in public, he was a "natural", and did not need glib lines written for him. Hooper gave up writing speeches because Greiner would simply turn his offerings into dot points. The trained debater was someone who could think on his feet and preferred to do so.[21]

The second key appointment, Gary Sturgess, arrived in mid-1983. A Mormon and a university graduate from Queensland, Sturgess had come to Sydney to write for the *Bulletin*. Malcolm Turnbull's return from Oxford "made things a bit crowded". After meeting Jim Carlton, the Federal Minister for Health, through the Centre for Independent Studies, he joined him as his private secretary for the remaining ten months of the Fraser Government. Sturgess planned to return to the *Bulletin* and complete a Master of Laws. He had already met Greiner through the Crossroads Group[22] and saw him as "one of us". He thought of working for Rosemary Foot, decided against it and, after a phone call from Greiner, agreed to head the Leader's research unit.

Sturgess was the intellectual, the thinker, ideas man and ideologue. He and Greiner were in familiar and comfortable territory together, though Sturgess was the more deeply read. They differed in approach in one key area. Sturgess saw himself as a libertarian and Greiner as a "consequentialist". Sturgess explained the difference between the two positions in a letter to *Quadrant* in November 1983: libertarianism was a rights-based philosophy which regarded individual liberty as the ultimate virtue; the so-called "new economics" or economic rationalism was utilitarian or "consequentialist" in being concerned with efficiency and where the enthusiasm for economic freedom stemmed from a belief that it would minimise social costs. In working for Greiner, Sturgess had to adjust his own thinking to the fact that his employer was primarily a manager. But their association remained "very much a collaborative effort".[23]

Greiner's speech delivered to local government bodies in Sydney on

17 August 1983 was an early example of this collaboration and of the strong Sturgess imprint:

> It is a fundamental tenet of liberalism that governmental power should be minimised and that, where it is necessary, should be decentralised as much as is practical . . . [Liberals] would prefer local to State authority, State to Federal authority, and private individual decision-making to them all.

Local government must be allowed to decide what services it would provide and be permitted to levy rates accordingly. Whereas, for the sake of fiscal conservatism, Margaret Thatcher imposed greater restrictions on local councils, the State Liberals had faith in ratepayers being vigilant, would encourage them to determine remuneration, and support local councils having greater flexibility in environmental planning, subject to broad State government guidelines.[24] The consequentialist could adopt the approach of the libertarian because, as the former had written about Whitlam in 1972, the "top-down" approach increased resistance to change, stifled initiative and destroyed morale where the ultimate activity took place.

## Corruption

John Hewson was right in his comment to Greiner after the Ku-ring-gai by-election: timing is, indeed, "the essence of success in politics". Luck is also important. Napoleon, who had wanted to know if one of his generals was lucky, would have approved of Nick Greiner's early brush with good fortune.

On Saturday 30 April 1983 the ABC program, *Four Corners*, aired "The Big League", an investigation into the administration of rugby league. One allegation was that in 1977 Neville Wran had influenced the then Chief Stipendiary Magistrate, Murray Farquhar, to drop a case against Kevin Humphreys, the secretary-manager of the Balmain Leagues Club, who had been charged with misappropriating $52,519 from the Club. In August 1977, Kevin Jones, SM, cleared Humphreys of all alleged offences. A number of other magistrates had told *Four Corners* of their concern about a high-level intervention in the case. Citing ill-health, Humphreys stepped down as Chairman of the Australian Rugby League the day before the program was screened. Neville Wran responded to the program by declaring the allegations involving him to be "absolutely false" and said he would sue the ABC for defamation.

Greiner seized a great opportunity handed to him just six weeks after he took the leadership. He called for a royal commission because "a reputable organisation and a reputable program have made the gravest charges about the integrity of the system of justice". At the very least, aspects of the court hearing should be the subject of a judicial inquiry, preferably – to ensure its independence – conducted by a judge from interstate. Wran, he said, should welcome an inquiry because the Premier felt he had nothing to hide. But the Premier said a royal commission was unnecessary; his defamation case would get to the truth of the matter. Meanwhile, Paul Landa, the Attorney-General, asked the Crown law officers to obtain documents from the ABC and sought reports from Kevin Jones and from "Clarrie" Briese, the current Chief Stipendiary Magistrate. Greiner kept up the pressure: it was inappropriate for Landa and the Crown law officers to be conducting an investigation; that was the job of the police or "better still, of a judicial inquiry". He was now making progress. At his request, the Acting Police Commissioner agreed to ask the new police Internal Security Squad to investigate another of the *Four Corners'* claims, namely, that Fred Hanson, a former Police Commissioner, had intervened in the original police investigation of Kevin Humphreys.

The allegations were hurting the Premier personally and damaging the Government. On 10 May Landa, with Wran's agreement, sprang the appointment of a royal commission on an unsuspecting Cabinet. Wran agreed to step aside for the duration of the inquiry in favour of "Jack" Ferguson, the Deputy Premier and leader of the Left faction. Ministers from the dominant Right wanted one of their own to be Acting Premier, and blamed the already-unpopular Landa for what they saw as a looming disaster. The Premier's actions had prevented an implosion, but Greiner could still maintain his attack because the Crown Solicitor had drawn up very limited terms of reference. The Commissioner – Sir Laurence Street, the Chief Justice of NSW – was asked to report on whether Farquhar had influenced, or sought to influence, the outcome of the committal proceedings and, if so, whether he was acting at the direction or request of Neville Wran. Greiner pointed out how these terms ignored Hanson's alleged interference and did not include the consideration of whether the Premier influenced or sought to influence Farquhar. Anybody, he said, "can see you can influence without directing or requesting".

Six days after Landa announced the appointment of the Street Royal Commission, Mick Young, the Special Minister of State in the Hawke Government, visited Ferguson in Sydney. Young informed the Acting Premier about information gleaned from phone taps pointing to the possible involvement of a NSW minister in criminal activities relating to the early release of prisoners. Separately, and earlier, the Federal Police Commissioner had requested Cec Abbott, the NSW Police Commissioner, to take no action lest an ongoing drug smuggling operation be compromised. Abbott let the matter rest for a month.

While unaware of the contacts made with Ferguson and Abbott, Greiner did know of disquiet about the early release system. Under the scheme introduced in April 1982, prisoners with a non-parole period of up to three years and a good record inside prison could be released on licence after serving at least a quarter of their non-parole period. Some 640 had been released on these terms by mid-1983 and Rex Jackson, the Minister for Corrective Services, declared the scheme to have a 95 per cent success rate. Several judges, however, pronounced it to be a "farce". The scheme had usurped the proper role of the courts to fix non-parole periods. Greiner shifted the focus of criticism when, on 11 June, he called for a judicial inquiry into allegations about prisoners buying their way out of prison by paying sums ranging from $2,500 to $15,000. The head of the Prison Officers Union said it was common knowledge at Long Bay that inmates could buy their freedom. Questioned by the press, Jackson said the allegations were "news to me" and pronounced the whole idea to be "not possible" because "it's something you would guard against at the very start".[25] Ferguson then announced that the Police Commissioner would appoint a special task force to investigate Greiner's claims.

The Street Royal Commission concluded that every investigation of Wran's alleged involvement in the Humphreys case ended "specifically in his favour". Street did, however, recommend laying charges against Farquhar. Returning to office on 28 July, Wran said he was neither relieved nor gratified because he "should not have been involved in the first place". Although improved polling indicated that he had more than survived a difficult period, the Premier now faced further problems. Punch revived claims that one of his ministers, Laurie Brereton, had earlier conspired to corrupt four aldermen of Botany Council. Greiner kept up the pressure over the early release system. He could now cite the extraordinary case of Stephen Cooley. Cooley had already served a prison term for three armed robberies in Victoria and had since pleaded guilty in Sydney to four charges of armed robbery and committed further offences while on bail. Not only was he given a "soft sentence"; Jackson had approved his early release, against the advice of two parole officers, on the ground that Cooley wanted to get married.

In mid-October Abbott finally reported to Gerry Gleeson, the head of the Premier's Department, on the charges Greiner had made in June.[26] After a "most thorough investigation", a task force had found no evidence to justify criminal proceedings. Abbott admitted he had not released sensitive and classified information to the task force but insisted that his "integrity and sincerity of purpose" could not be questioned in recommending that neither a royal commission nor a judicial inquiry was warranted. Wran told the Legislative Assembly on 11 October how his Government's approach had been "proper", how the Police

Commissioner's investigation was "thorough", and how it would be "irresponsible" to release the task force report. Greiner was unimpressed, especially with the Premier's line that the relationship between corrective services and drug trafficking was so close that inquiries about the former would prejudice investigations of the latter. When Greiner asked Wran about Jackson's covert association with drug traffickers, the Premier fired up his backbench by accusing unnamed Opposition members of having covert relations with tax dodgers, pimps and crooks. Jackson assured the Assembly he had never knowingly had contact with drug traffickers. He denounced Greiner for doing an interview about corruption with *Penthouse*, a magazine which, Jackson said, pedalled "filth and obscenity".[27]

It was, apparently, all a matter of "integrity": Wran had it, so did Ferguson and Peter Anderson, the Police Minister, and Cec Abbott. Greiner, of course, had none at all. On 20 October Ferguson said the Leader of the Opposition was "beyond contempt". He "skulks around the corridors, whispering corruption" and "did not have the guts to stand up in this House and make a direct accusation".[28] But neither the confected nor the genuine outrage diverted or intimidated Greiner, Punch, their Federal colleagues in Canberra nor the broadsheet press. Questions continued to be asked about police corruption, drug trafficking and the activities of a NSW minister. Ferguson might speak warmly of Jackson as "my friend and comrade" but his continued presence in the Government was an embarrassment. Fortunately, the Minister for Corrective Services had publicly contradicted information he had earlier given Parliament relating to the prison release system.[29] The Premier could demand and obtain Jackson's resignation without having to acknowledge the minister's practice of taking bribes to finance his gambling habit.

Belatedly, the Government took action on other fronts by improving the machinery for investigating complaints about the police and instituting a three-member Police Board (two of them were civilians) to administer the force. It also established a special commission of inquiry into corruption. Greiner pointed out that it had limited powers though Justice Cross, the Commissioner, did investigate three cases, dismissing allegations of malfeasance or misadministration in all of them. Not everyone survived: Jackson, Humphreys and Farquhar were later convicted and jailed. Senator Chris Puplick, a Dowd supporter, once mischievously asked Greiner whether corruption had become "a bread-and-butter issue".[30] The fact remains that Greiner, assisted by the research efforts of Sturgess, had seized the moment and benefited from the exercise. Neville Wran, meantime, had lost some of his reputation for being cool and in control.[31]

## "I have always had a healthy opinion of myself"[32]

Throughout 1983, or at least until late November, the media regarded Greiner as a welcome break and very good copy. Greiner obliged with interviews, candid comments and self-analysis. He was quickly seen to be different from earlier Liberal Leaders: a Catholic with a Hungarian background was now leading a Party which had been overwhelmingly Protestant and Anglo-Scottish. The Harvard graduate could talk authoritatively about budgetary and broader economic issues, understood what had to be done to win government, and knew what he wanted to do when he succeeded. The commentators also noticed he was not fussed about getting on well with the Liberal Organisation. He performed the necessary tasks of attending and addressing State Council and State Executive but Greiner and his personal staff aggressively and separately pursued their own agendas.

Two-and-a-half months after the leadership election he told a journalist that the key to his approach was "honesty".[33] For two reasons he was not prepared to change. "It sits easier, I don't have to act it. Secondly, I think it is a better political position . . . If you're honest and have nothing to hide, it defuses criticism." The electorate was ready for politicians to acknowledge their blunders, "as long as they don't do it every day of the week". While some viewed his candour as a weakness, he saw it "as one of my greatest strengths and if I succeed in NSW politics that will be one of the reasons". It was also an advantage in being a practising Catholic and a European by birth because one-third of the electorate had a similar background. "It shows we are open to all people." Greiner described himself as "very ordinary" (which plainly he was not), the product of a migrant family "who made good". He had a broad range of interests and was equally at home watching Rugby League or attending the opera, but liked to use sporting analogies because a large part of the population thought in sporting terms.

Finally, asked how he saw himself, he replied:

> I think I'm charismatic, positive. I think I come over positively both in person and on television which is really the ultimately important thing. I'm intelligent, honest, open, not lacking in self-confidence and I accept the criticism from my colleagues that humility is not my greatest virtue.

In August he said he expected to win in 1984. There was no other "sensible objective". "You don't go into a fight with the object of losing." Ever since he could remember he wanted to be the leader in whatever he was involved. Whereas his father thought him too honest and straightforward, and lacking the killer instinct necessary for political life, the son pointed out how he generally achieved what he set out to do. In any case, European and Australian parents had different outlooks. The European world of Miklós Greiner was one where you crashed or crashed through whereas Nick Greiner believed you could succeed with an objective approach and without relying on a killer instinct.

He referred once more to bread and butter issues, to jobs, economic and industrial development and quality in education, transport, housing and energy (he did not mention health). These matters, he said, affected people in their daily lives, much more so than investigations into organised crime. He also wanted to raise the level of parliamentary debate above the "bear pit". "The standards of parliamentary behavior [sic] in New South Wales are deplorably low but high in personal abuse." To rectify this situation, and as a disciplinary measure, he wanted proceedings in the Assembly to be televised. Wran set the tone, and he was the problem. The moderate and reasonable Premier appearing on the TV news was not the man in Parliament. "The one thing I admire about Mr Wran is his acting ability." But the voters were tired of performance and sick of all the mud-slinging.

At the conclusion of this post-breakfast interview the journalist told Greiner he had "the unmistakable gloss of middle Europe". Taken by surprise, he was all the more shocked when Kathryn agreed. After all, he felt "totally Australian".[34]

In November, after Andrew Peacock praised Greiner as the key to a Federal Liberal resurgence, Greiner said he was "not yet leaping tall buildings in a single bound". Rather, he was trying to sell himself as a different kind of politician: to be straight with the public, not to promise the world, not to oppose automatically everything the Government did. He could also be candid when acting against the character he was trying to project. After Geoffrey Ferrow, the cleverest member of the Right faction in the Party Organisation, had worked for two weeks on a speech, Greiner told him he would deliver his own off-the-cuff version. So, he promised more roads, hospitals and water and sewerage facilities for the marginal seat of Gosford. Greiner acknowledged he was engaging in "straight-out, traditional pork-barrelling . . . I think the difference perhaps is that I am prepared to admit it".[35] No doubt it helped to own a healthy self-respect.

## Four "very public political blunders"

The year appeared to be ending well. The results of four by-elections held in October 1983 for Labor-held seats looked highly encouraging. The Government retained all four, and delivered Bob Carr to Macquarie Street as the MP for Maroubra, but the anti-Labor swing averaged around ten per cent. Greiner declared the result to be "fantastic". If the trend continued, he predicted, the Government would be out of office at the next election. He attributed this "resounding kick in the pants" to the "overall stench" and to simple bread-and-butter issues such as increased electricity charges. Neville Wran blamed a poor turnout by Labor voters, the "mud-slinging" and the state of the economy, although he acknowledged that the Opposition had received a "morale boost". The *SMH* declared that Greiner "has played a big part in fostering . . . dissatisfaction among many voters who supported Labor in 1981". His task now was to convince the electorate that he was leading "a credible alternative Government".[36] The State Director of the Liberal Party was sceptical. He thought the actual Liberal improvement, amounting to 5-6 per cent, would deliver just 6-7 seats in Sydney. A Liberal Party scrutineer added her view that the Western Suburbs constituted a "no man's land" for the Liberal Party.[37]

The polls remained encouraging. A Morgan Gallup Poll in April recorded an approval rating for Greiner of 32 per cent; by mid-year his rating was more than double John Dowd's figure for most of his last twelve months in the leadership; in November the Morgan Poll placed him equal with Wran on 46 per cent, with the Coalition standing just two points behind Labor. But in the second half of November Greiner's rating nose-dived. Peter Collins wrote a diary note for 6 December 1983 referring to what he called Greiner's four "very public political blunders" committed during the closing two weeks of parliamentary sittings. Greiner had named two police informants in the Legislative Assembly, opposed establishment of the Police Board, proposed a merger with the National Party, and said the Coalition did not deserve to win government. Collins noted how Greiner had consulted no one except Punch before taking these positions. There were also minor "tactical" errors. The fundamental problem, according to Collins, was that Greiner was "a lone wolf" and had been for as long as Collins had known him. He was not accustomed "to working with a team".[38]

Greiner freely acknowledged he had blundered in naming his informants: "I was badly wrong."[39] Handed evidence of high-level interference with a secret police unit based in Penrith, Greiner said several times during an urgency debate that his information came from "impeccable" sources inside the unit. Goaded by Labor's frontbench he made a spur-of-the-moment decision to name the two policemen – Detective Sergeant Lionel Hanrahan and Detective Bob Clark – who had provided oral and documentary information to his office about an alleged conspiracy involving the poker machine industry, including the delayed arrest of one of the principals.[40] Wran applied the blow torch to the belly, as he had once threatened. Both prior to Greiner's speech and in its aftermath he had his backbench baying at every insult and unsupported accusation he hurled at members of the Opposition. Greiner, he said, could never be trusted because, "at the first bit of pressure, he weakened and revealed his sources. That is unforgivable. That is a laughable situation. Even the Leader of the National Party, we could hear him over here, was becoming hysterical and saying: 'do not do it: do not do it'." [41] Frank Walker, emerging as the principal head-kicker even before Wran retired, chimed in: Greiner had made a "pathetic, snivelling and grovelling apology", he was a "failed businessman", "the boy who now wants to be Premier . . . lacks the ability for mature reflection". The *Daily Telegraph* on 25 November lectured him on the necessity for Oppositions to authenticate information they received and to guard the identity of their informants. Otherwise, Greiner's "current successful assault" on the Wran Government might "lose its impetus due to a shortage of ammunition reaching the frontline".

The second "blunder" was less serious. The Police Association and the Commissioned Police Officers branch of the Association both criticised the proposal to establish a Police Board. They feared political appointments and manipulation and protested about the lack of prior consultation. Even Abbott initially expressed opposition. Nick Greiner was quick to join the critics. He described the proposal as a vote of no confidence in the Police Commissioner and undertook to disband the Board once he took office. When Wran condemned the Association's plan to implement bans and limitations Greiner spoke out against industrial blackmail yet observed how the Government did not apply such strict standards to other unions. He also raised the question of prior consultation.[42] But he had to back down in relation to the composition of the Board because the two civilian appointments were manifestly not "political". The Government had chosen Sir Maurice Byers, the former Commonwealth Solicitor-General, to be the Chairman; the other civilian was Sir Gordon Jackson, the highly-regarded, former head of CSR Ltd.

It was not immediately obvious that Greiner had committed a "blunder" on 25 November in raising the subject of amalgamation in a public statement. The issue had re-surfaced in part because of disputes between the Liberals and the Nationals over contests for two seats, and in part because optional preferential voting had rendered three-cornered contests – once an electoral plus – as dangerous territory for the Coalition. Greiner said that Australia was a country of "umbrella parties" and he was intent on "providing the maximum sensible umbrella for the non-Labor parties" in NSW. In any case, the Liberals and Nationals had identical principles on "the gut issues". He had talked to Punch about amalgamation and they had agreed a merger was a serious option within two or three years. Two days after Greiner made these comments Leon Punch said he could see no moves towards an amalgamation in the near future because "certain groups in both parties" opposed the idea. The Premier, inevitably, seized the moment: the merger idea was just "a smokescreen of unity" to hide the fact that the two parties "are at each other's throats".[43]

Collins evidently thought that Punch's very public rejection was embarrassing. But Collins would have been aware that Greiner had merely given voice to long-standing Liberal policy. From its inception, the modern Liberal Party in NSW had consistently advocated a merger with the Country Party and its re-branded successors. Rebuffed every time, the Liberals were left with two choices: either pursue co-operation or adopt the approach of a former Victorian and Federal President, W. H. Anderson, that the rural party "must be destroyed – like Carthage".

Greiner would certainly have blundered if he had advocated the Anderson approach. In fact, he had always been a committed coalitionist. Perhaps, therefore, Collins was concerned either about the timing or about Greiner's failure to make sure Punch was onside. Or perhaps Collins just wanted to find fault.

Greiner's final "blunder" was to be utterly candid in saying that the Coalition did not deserve to be in government because it had not been positive enough: "We've managed only to convince people that this Labor Government is not good enough, without presenting ourselves [as] a credible team." Oppositions should not rely on governments performing badly; they should "project themselves as an alternative government". The Coalition "has to begin packaging its policies to make them more meaningful and so they can be understood". Wran and Collins were agreed: the former described Greiner's comment as "another major blunder".[44] Yet there is no evidence that Greiner's refreshing honesty, which so amused or appalled the professionals in Macquarie Street, actually cost his party any votes in the 1984 election.

For all the real or imagined stumbles at the end of 1983, Nick Greiner finished the year in good fettle. There was no clearer indication he had unsettled the Government than the savagery of its response. Importantly, whereas some of his predecessors had been inwardly as well as outwardly bruised by Neville Wran, Greiner looked upon him as a skilled thespian and was, therefore, largely untroubled.

# Endnotes

[1]   P. J. L. King, Memorandum, 29 Sep. 1982, State Executive Committees, LPA, ML, MSS 7205/25.

[2]   Interview: Gary O'Gorman, 30 May 2005.

[3]   Interview: Valder, 1 December 2005.

[4]   *Ibid.*

[5]   Richard Ackland, *National Times*, 18-24 March 1983.

[6]   *SMH*, 8 and 10 March 1983.

[7]   *SMH*, 10 March 1983; Interview: Dowd, 20 January 2006.

[8]   *SMH*, 14 March 1983.

[9]   Mike Steketee, *SMH*, 15 March 1983.

[10]  *Australian* and *SMH*, 15 March 1983.

[11]  *SMH*, 16 March 1983.

[12]  Ian Armstrong in Paul Davey, *The Nationals: The Progressive, Country and National Party in New South Wales 1919 to 2006*, Federation Press, Leichhardt, 2006, p. 278.

[13]  *NSWPD, Third Series*, vol. 228, pp.46-8, 25 February 1992. Punch died on 30 December 1991.

[14]  *SMH*, 16 March 1983.

[15]  *Australian, DT*, and *SMH*, 16 March 1983.

[16]  *NSWPD*, Third Series, vol. 174, p. 4561.

[17]  John Campbell, *SMH*, 16 March 1983.

[18]  Interviewed in Greiner's office and before the leadership vote, Baume said, "Nick is an able and intelligent person and . . . would do well as leader". But he was prepared to stand for the soon-to-be vacated seat of Mosman if the Party wanted him. *SMH*, 12 March 1983. Baume entered the Senate in 1985.

[19]  *Bulletin*, 29 March 1983.

[20]  Interview: Greiner, 24 September 2005; *SMH*, 9 May 1983.

[21]  The above two paragraphs draw upon an interview with Hooper on 20 April 2011.

[22]  The Crossroads Group, consisting of "economic dries", first met in February 1981, ostensibly to discuss Wolfgang Kasper's *Australia at the Cross Roads*. For the meeting, see John Hyde, *Dry: In Defence of Economic Freedom*, IPA, Melbourne, 2002, pp. 108-9.

[23]  The above two paragraphs draw upon an interview with Sturgess on 21 June 2011.

24  Warm and Dry: the Evolution of Greinerism, Speeches and Papers written by Gary Sturgess, 1982-1992, pp. 23-5.

25  *Sun-Herald*, 12 June 1983.

26  An edited version of Abbott's report is available in *SMH*, 12 October 1983.

27  Presumably, Jackson observed in passing some full frontal female nudity and stories of schoolgirl crushes in the article headed, "To Sir With Lust", in the October 1983 issue while searching for serious articles such as the one on El Salvador as the Spanish version of "Vietnam" and Greiner's views on corruption.

28  *NSWPD*, Third Series, vol. 176, pp. 2115-17.

29  *Ibid.*, p. 1998; *Sunday Telegraph*, 23 October 1983.

30  Interview: Greiner 17 February 2010.

31  See, Ken Turner, "Back to a contest, 1981-4" in Ernie Chaples, Helen Nelson and Ken Turner (eds), *The Wran Model: Electoral Politics in New South Wales, 1981 and 1984*, OUP, Melbourne, 1985, pp. 196-201.

32  Jane Cadzow, *Australian*, 17-18 September 1983.

33  Alison Stewart, *Sun-Herald*, 22 May 1983.

34  Nan Musgrove, *DT*, 21 August 1983.

35  Mike Steketee, *Australian*, 24 November 1983.

36  *Sun-Herald*, 23 October, *SMH*, 24 October 1983.

37  S. Litchfield, Winning Government in New South Wales, 20 October 1984, Strategy, LPA, ML, MS 7205/80, and Sandra Simpson in *ibid.*

38  Diary Note, Liberal Party (Valder), Collins Papers, MSS 7442/68.

39  *Sun-Herald*, 27 November 1983.

40  The debate and divisions on the urgency motion can be found in *NSWPD*, Third Series, vol. 177, pp. 3220-72.

41  This comment was made on 24 November in reply to a question about the development of the first Government House site. *NSWPD*, Third Series, vol. 177, p. 3433. For Wran in full flight see esp. *ibid.*, pp. 3264-9 and pp. 3433-6.

42  *Ibid.*, pp. 4008-10.

43  *SMH* and *DT*, 25-6 and 28 November 1983.

44  *Daily Mirror*, 29 November 1983.

# 7

# The 1984 Election – the First Test

Nick Greiner thought he would face an election in May or September of 1984. It was, therefore, a relaxed family which sat down for an interview in February with Liz Hickson of *Woman's Day*.[1] There were several references to the Greiners having "a happy marriage", which Kara playfully explained in terms of them never actually seeing each other. Kathryn said she tried be awake when her husband arrived home, often at midnight. Her own job was time consuming but fulfilling. She had continued to work for the NSW Government Department of Youth and Community Services as a psychologist dealing with children's services, and had found "a perfect fit between the results and the expectations so we do indeed have a happy marriage". Some five-and-a-half years later Kathryn acknowledged that, soon after Greiner was first elected for Ku-ring-gai, she wondered whether to stay in the marriage. She issued her husband with an ultimatum: "unless you make some changes, help more about the house . . .".[2]

Kathryn expected to have a job if Greiner became Premier. "Keeping on at a job of your own is important because I think the political world can be a bit of a fairyland. I've seen a lot of other political wives destroyed because they're out of touch with reality." She had told her husband he should not spend 25 years in politics: that "would make him a very boring politician and a very boring man." She would tell him when to go and, if he disagreed, they would have a good row. Not that Greiner would need persuading. He had no intention of spending the rest of his working life in politics, nor would he retire on leaving politics. He expected to have at least one more career.

Next to the happy marriage was the happy family. The father said he tried to be there for his children's sporting activities on Saturdays. ". . . I'm sure the children would agree that we're a very happy family. The family comes first and I expect the electorate to understand that." Coming "first" did not mean the family spent much time together. *Woman's Day* did not report how Justin and Kara saw a lot of their nanny and ate countless microwave meals. Years later Justin recalled how his father was not physically affectionate or demonstrative, as he was with his grandchildren, and Kara remembered him as "absent".[3] Sunday nights were, however, family nights, and there were memorable family occasions such as the ten year-old Justin's trip to Melbourne with his father to see the Boxing Day Test in 1982 – memorable in part because driving home to Sydney they encountered a man meditating in the middle of the road and the son heard his father swear for the first time. Importantly, both children were encouraged to speak their minds, just as their parents did to each other. Kathryn told the magazine that her first impression was of his honesty. "I found him very refreshing. He was perhaps too frank at times. If he didn't like your hairstyle or a dress you were wearing you certainly got to know it."

On Sunday 4 March 1984, five days after the *Woman's Day* article was published, Neville Wran called an election for 25 March.[4]

Wran had said at the end of January there would be no poll in the first half of the year. But a new scandal had emerged. Unnamed NSW police had released illegally-recorded tapes to the Melbourne *Age* (the tapes would in time involve Wran's friend, Justice Lionel Murphy of the High Court, in a Senate investigation). Greiner asked five parliamentary questions between 21 February and 1 March based on the recordings. Wran responded by talking about holding an election to clear the air of corruption allegations so that the ordinary business of government could proceed. Although the Government remained in firm control of both the Assembly and the Council, an early election would force the Opposition "to put up or shut up" while closing down its best avenue for attack. Deprived of parliamentary privilege, the Opposition would have to rely on its colleagues in Canberra to pursue what Wran called its "sustained muckraking". One of the shortest campaigns in the State's history would also restrict the Opposition's exposure and, providing the Government won, it would have four years rather than four or more months to deal with any further charges or revelations. Another benefit was that the next election would fall close to the bicentennial celebrations allowing Wran or his successor to exploit the likely euphoria.[5]

On the day Wran called the poll Greiner and Ken Hooper were travelling in a car together to attend an engagement. On hearing the news, the Leader of the Opposition asked his press secretary, "So what do we do now?" Hooper replied: 'Just wing it; it'll be alright on the night". As Greiner put it, "we were totally unready".[6] The Liberal Party also felt it was caught on the hop by the early election.[7] Yet, in its post-election review, the Party acknowledged beginning its campaign when Greiner was elected Leader. Some policies had been publicised before Wran made his announcement; one of which promised to allow small business to negotiate voluntary agreements with employees outside of award conditions. The Liberal Party had already launched television commercials and a catchy slogan, "Together, we can clean up NSW". A direct mail campaign, a method borrowed from the Republicans in the United States and including a personally-addressed letter from Greiner, was expected to reach 670,000 families by 5 March. A strategy was formulated on paper in October 1983 to launch "Greiner and the Liberals", with careful financing, developed policies, candidate training and a focus on 27 seats. Phase One was to project Greiner as the alternative Premier and to make him known to the electorate (43 per cent of those questioned in Sydney during September had never heard of him). Phase Two involved selling the team with thoroughly-prepared policies built around a new management style of government. This latter stage never eventuated.

The Coalition lagged well behind at the start of the contest. A Morgan Poll taken two weeks before the Premier called the election placed the Government on 52 per cent and the Coalition on 40 per cent. Wran's approval rating headed Greiner's by five percentage points. Another poll taken immediately before Wran's announcement had the Government leading the Coalition 54-39. Nevertheless, the Opposition Leader was telling everyone he was "relaxed", which was palpably true. He was never anxious about what he could not control. It was certainly in his interest for the election to be held later in the year. The Government was on the back foot over the corruption allegations and was bound to become more vulnerable over unemployment, education, taxes and charges. Yet Wran controlled the timing, and Greiner had to work within the timetable set for him. The important thing was to be calm and appear confident. Greiner claimed the Coalition had an excellent chance of winning although it would be "ridiculous" to delude himself or the electorate about the task ahead. The odds on victory, he said, were about evens when Wran announced the poll.[8] He introduced a golfing analogy to explain his intentions: he was trying to get onto the green in one, not pitching short to be there in two in 1988.

Having deprived Greiner of his parliamentary forum to pursue the *Age* tapes issue, the Premier sought to pre-empt the Opposition by revealing his anti-corruption strategy on the day he called the election. His Government would appoint a Judicial Commissioner for Public Complaints who would be a Supreme Court or Federal Court judge, to hold the office for five years. The Commissioner would examine complaints made against elected and appointed public officials and determine how they should be handled. There were to be statutory guarantees of full independence and reference could be made to Parliament if action on the complaint was unsatisfactory. All complaints would be heard in strict secrecy and, although the Commissioner would not have powers of investigation, support would be provided by the police, the Ombudsman and the Corporate Affairs Commission. The Opposition's alternative, devised by Sturgess, differed in several key aspects. Greiner promised to establish a *permanent* anti-corruption commission which could initiate inquiries in the absence of a formal complaint; the commission would report directly to Parliament instead of the Government; and it would be allowed to conduct inquiries in public and have the powers of a royal commission, including those of investigation.

Greiner accepted that corruption had been around for a long time in NSW and did not expect to eliminate it altogether. Besides, it was a matter of degree: how close was corruption to government and to the administration of justice? Corruption involving prostitution, the licensing police and black market alcohol did not go to the heart of the State's main institutions.[9] Greiner was concerned about the integrity of ministers, of government, and of the public service and of the administration of justice, rather than "who's running the girls this week". Simultaneously, he wanted to establish the statutory independence of his proposed creations – the special anti-corruption commission, the Director of Public Prosecutions, and the Ombudsman – to ensure "the integrity of our basic institutions" which should function "without reference to the political process".

The *SMH* thought that the idea of a permanent commission was probably "best left as a last resort". It might be necessary in the future, "but not yet".[10] Wran adopted a different approach. He departed the corruption battleground and headed for the safer territory of conventional politics. After declaring he would not be making a "grab bag of promises" which could not be fulfilled, the Premier proposed to deliver six more high speed XPT trains and 450 new carriages costing a total of $470m (the Armidale area was still waiting for the XPT promised at the 1981 election). Leon Punch, on the other hand, kept to the script when he delivered his policy speech in Grafton on 7 March. He spoke at length about corruption. Greiner, who sat on the platform for the launch, also urged Wran to act. He suggested replacing the ill Justice Cross to enable the Jackson inquiry to proceed so that the public might learn the truth of the matter. Neville Wran was very happy for nothing to be revealed, let alone concluded, before 24 March.[11]

Greiner launched the Coalition's education policy on 11 March.[12] It was a well organised media event, and widely reported in the press and on radio and television. The policy bore a striking resemblance to the program later identified with Terry Metherell although, in 1984, Neil Pickard was the (barely noticeable) shadow minister and Lloyd Lange authored many of the proposals. The aim, Greiner said, was to give parents and children more choice, the children a better education and the parents more say in what was taught. To promote choice, the existing zoning regulations in the State system would be abolished, and selective schools and specialist schools (with a focus, for example, on sport or music) would be encouraged. Quality would be improved by introducing a three-year probationary period before teachers would become eligible for tenure. Those "below standard" could be dismissed, and good teachers would be rewarded with higher salaries. School councils, composed of parents, teachers and community representatives, would have a major involvement in school governance and course selection and a degree of financial independence. In addition, Greiner produced a raft of proposals relating to staffing formulas, TAFE colleges, access to library facilities for infant and primary school children, an external literary and numeracy test for students completing Year 10, the streamlining of the State education bureaucracy, and the development of computer networks.

The NSW Teachers' Federation was predictably scathing, especially in relation to the three-year review and the proposals to sack incompetent teachers and scrap school zoning. The Federation's State President found aspects of the policy "so silly" he assumed they emanated from people who did not know how the education system worked (arguably, the policies were devised by those who knew precisely how it operated). Another official said that the existing 12-month probation system for teachers already involved strict supervision. The Federation announced it would have to reconsider its bi-partisan stance on the election (the existence of such a stance would have surprised most Liberals, and even some in the Labor Party).[13] In a paid advertisement in the *Daily Telegraph* of 17 March the Federation accused "Mr Greiner" of attacking "our professionalism". This attack was "naturally" rejected. The Federation had studied the two sets of policies "with the welfare of one group in mind – the children". While not endorsing Labor's education policies, it considered them "clearly superior" to the Coalition's proposals which revealed "a grave lack of concern for public education" and would lead to all manner of travesties, including "the running down of many public schools". The NSW Teachers' Federation gave the Greiner reform agenda in 1984 a foretaste of what to expect in 1988.

Nick Greiner, alone on the stage, delivered his policy speech to a half-full Concert Hall at the Opera House on 12 March. Andrew Peacock and John Howard and the State shadow ministers sat in the front row, not far from Kathryn and the children and Clare Greiner, in a wheel chair following a recent leg amputation caused by cancer. Leon Punch delivered a warm-up speech mainly on the theme of corruption and "the network of slimy inter-connections that entwines itself around this Government" which he promised would disappear after the Coalition won the election. Greiner also dwelt on the corruption issue, and made some telling points: Wran had accused the Opposition of muck-raking but it was merely wielding the rake; and the muck would not disappear just because the Premier had called an election. In fact, the election was held in haste, "not to let the people decide but to deny them an effective vote". His administration would restore faith and trust in government, principally by creating a special and permanent commission and increasing the powers of the Ombudsman.

The main focus of the policy speech, however, was on improved management and the attendant consequences for people's lives. Greater efficiency in running departments and authorities would help pay for a housing interest subsidy and for cuts in financial, land, liquor and payroll taxes. Greiner said he had no intention of matching Wran with a spending spree, although half of his 42 promises did involve increased expenditure or decreased revenue. There would be a two-year freeze on all taxes while the new government reviewed the State's mechanisms for raising taxes and charges. At the same time, the Coalition would abolish the Harbour toll, boost police strength by 1,600 over four years and increase spending on pre-schools and day-care centres. The *SMH* detected a note of cynicism underlying one of the promises: any cut in payroll tax would be offset by allowing inflation to reduce the value of the concession. It further described the home buyers' assistance scheme as belonging to "the worst tradition of cynical vote-buying". Yet the editorial allowed that Greiner "has managed to give us the best Opposition policy speech in NSW since 1976", thus placing him on a par with the Wran assault on the Willis Government.

Inevitably, with Wran making promises of his own, one of them being not to enter a "Dutch auction", exchanges about costings dominated the ensuing days. Wran had some good lines: "Mr Greiner hasn't just promised the world but the moon and half the milky way as well", and was "trying to emulate his namesake, St Nick." Greiner described Wran's costings as "a real Alice-in-Wonderland assessment", and "a tissue of lies, misconceptions and mistakes". He dubbed his opponent "the Billion Dollar Man" after Wran announced that $5bn would be spent on roads by 1988. The Premier countered with "the $600 Million Man", after producing what he claimed was a Treasury analysis of the Greiner promises which would account for $245m in the first year rising to $272m in year two. Ross Gittins argued in the *SMH* on 15 March that both sides played fast and loose with the facts and figures. He pointed out how Treasury would have taken a week to measure the Opposition's costings, not the 24 hours it took for Wran to produce them. The Government, he wrote, had clearly over-stated the expenditure required to meet Greiner's programs. On the other hand, Greiner had not costed a number of long-term objectives and necessarily vague promises. As the *Herald* headlined the Gittins article, it was "all good, clean fun".

Some things were not so "clean". One of the most effective ways of corrupting the democratic process is to use the public's money to promote a government's policy and image. This practice has now become endemic and expensive, though underpinned by the saintly avowal of keeping the public informed. Midway through the election campaign the Electricity Supply Industry, comprising the County Councils and two statutory bodies (the Electricity Commission and the Energy Authority), went on an advertising bender in the press and on television. The objective was to broadcast its record for reducing domestic electricity charges to the lowest in Australia and its decision to freeze charges until 1 January 1985.[14] There was no reference to Wran, the Government or the Labor Party. Instead, the Electricity Supply Industry took the credit. Greiner produced correspondence revealing that the campaign followed discussions between the Industry and the Minister for Energy. He also drew attention to a Department of Main Roads publication recording its achievements with a blatantly "political" intent, and he claimed to have evidence of public servants being employed to prepare "political" material to assist Labor Party candidates.[15] But the Liberal Party failed in its bid to have all officially-funded advertising withdrawn during the election period. Gerry Gleeson explained that statutory bodies were not funded from consolidated revenue.

While newspaper and television channels continued to advertise and extol the State's cheap domestic electricity and cuts in third party insurance, Greiner promised that a Coalition Government would review all senior positions in the Public Service in order to restore its impartiality. Labor, he said, had "turned jobs for the boys into an art form", and had politicised the top levels of the Public Service and the statutory authorities. Greiner clearly had John Ducker in mind when referring to "quite clearly blatant political appointments" to the Public Service Board. Wran had appointed the English-born Ducker, a Catholic convert who became the most powerful union official in NSW, a Labor member of the Legislative Council, and the major right-wing powerbroker in the NSW Labor Party, to the Public Service Board in 1979. Yet Greiner also stressed that a review of appointments would be on the basis of

merit. Two of Labor's appointments – Nicholas Whitlam, the son of
the former Prime Minister, and David Hill – had "overwhelmingly good
credentials" to remain as heads, respectively, of the State Bank and the
State Rail Authority. Nor would the Coalition sack any public servants;
rather, it would make the Public Service revert to its traditional role of
acting in the public interest instead of serving the interests of a particular
political party. On the other hand, appointments to the personal staff of
ministers could be, and would be, "political".[16]

## The thinking man's campaigner

On 19 March, five days before NSW went to the polls, Greiner delivered
the 1984 Edmund Barton lecture.[17] The lecture had been timetabled
well in advance of the early poll announcement but it was decided to
proceed anyway. Prepared by Sturgess, the Barton lecture foreshadowed
a key element of "Greinerism".

The starting-point was a question: "how can modern Governments
govern for all the people instead of merely making deals with powerful
interest groups?" Greiner rejected the proposition that the interests of
the people were well served when a sufficient number of private interest
groups competed for governmental favours. For one thing, ordinary
citizens did not have the same access to governments as the articulate
and influential lobbyists representing pressure groups. For another, it was
more difficult organising a diversified mass of consumers than managing
a concentrated and narrow body of producers. Greiner highlighted
the latter point by contrasting the problems faced in identifying and
assembling the diffuse body of potential beneficiaries of a tariff cut on
imported cars when the three local car manufacturers could command
government attention with full-time lobbyists and public relations
specialists. Even the consumerist elites, which claimed to act for the silent
mainstream, were not representative of the large majority of Australians
who did not identify with the anti-business ideologues and zealots who
ran these bodies. The political parties were no better. They cultivated

vested interests and actually created new interests – for example, "ethnic affairs" – in their quest for votes, and they became isolated from the ordinary taxpayers and consumers while relying on pressure groups to interpret the supposed middle ground of politics. As a result, Australian politics had become an undignified brawl among powerful private interests, and governments did not govern but simply made "deals".

The task of the Liberal Party was to make "a genuine attempt to govern in the long-term interests of all the people". Greiner, in effect, was remodelling a longstanding and recurrent theme of non-Labor politics since Federation, namely, that, in contrast to Labor's class-based politics, liberal-conservatives saw themselves as governing for all Australians. Part of Greiner's thesis was that the old consensus had broken down. Traditionally, political power in Australia was divided between three powerful interests: business, labour and the land. This arrangement no longer applied in the 1980s. The Liberal Party, more so than Labor and the Nationals, was ideally placed "to formulate a new politics of the public interest". It had successfully liberated itself from an association with a specific interest group. Moreover, it was the party for both taxpayers and consumers, freeing the one to spend more of their own incomes, and emphasising the sovereignty of the other as production existed only for the sake of consumption which was best served by a healthy and competitive market.

Greiner conceded that governing in the public interest was not easy. There were risks in refusing to make deals with private vested interests. But there was no future for the Liberal Party in "private interest politics". Instead, the Party should "take a leadership role in producing government of the people, by the people and for the people".

Greiner was not a hostage to dogma. On the day he delivered the Barton lecture, Peter Bowers and Ross Gittins of the *SMH* tried to pin him down as a supporter of "small government".[18] He agreed he stood for the appropriate use of government which, in NSW at present, probably meant smaller government. But he was not in favour of small government or deregulation for their own sake; to oppose government doing things was "absurd, non-rational". If governments could do useful things they should do them. He would not, therefore, want to "flog off" the State Bank or the GIO (later, when in government, he sought to privatise both). He would sell the State Building Society which did nothing for the people of NSW. What mattered was the best result for the people, and who or what could provide it best. "I am not an absolutist, nor an ideologue. I'm trying to duck being tagged. I don't think tags are useful." Incidentally, Greiner also disavowed a doctrinaire commitment to States' rights. The journalists did not pursue the point. Yet he had told them, in effect, that he had rejected Liberal Party Holy Writ.

Throughout the campaign both Neville Wran and the print media (and especially the *Daily Telegraph*) kept hammering Greiner's lack of experience. On election-day Wran said the poll revolved around "trust and experience". His article, published in the *Telegraph*, referred to experience, or the lack of it, on five separate occasions.

Greiner's response was complex and sensible.[19] He noted how the Premier wanted NSW to vote for an experienced team: that is, "experienced in covering up corruption, experienced in breaking election promises, experienced in giving you the highest unemployment rate in Australia". He identified Brian Burke as an example of someone seemingly lacking in experience who had starred as Premier of Western Australia (Greiner was less sure about John Bannon in South Australia and was less than impressed with John Cain in Victoria). The argument about experience was the "classic" one used by a man heading towards 60 being confronted by a much younger opponent. The argument for experienced government was really one for more of the same, for opposing change. Greiner acknowledged that the electorate had to take alternative governments on trust. He cited the case of Bob Hawke. No one knows what someone will be like until they get there, and Hawke "has been a surprising Prime Minister". Greiner also said he did not have "a concrete vision" of what he would be like as Premier or of how he would respond to the "stresses of government". But it was possible to get a view of him personally and of his style from what had been achieved in the previous twelve months. Moreover, as evident in his policy speech, he had given a different meaning to the notion of Liberalism. And, unlike the typical Liberal approaches of the past, he had spent time in Labor strongholds and areas of disadvantage because he believed "a government should be about the people and ought to be about their problems".

## The highs and lows

Kathryn quickly proved to be an asset in the Greiner campaign. While Jill Hickson, the Premier's wife, continued her work as a literary agent, Kathryn took leave from her job in the Department of Youth and Community Services. Frequently sallying forth on her own, she worked the Labor seats of Maitland and Newcastle.[20] Wran once referred to his wife as "one of my secret weapons", and journalists decided she remained very secret in the 1984 campaign. Kathryn Greiner, in the words of one commentator, was more of a "guided missile". She was out there and upfront, making speeches, knocking on doors, and giving radio and television interviews. "Being flippant", Kathryn told a journalist that, while she and Jill were both good looking and intelligent, she was the more relaxed with people from all walks of life. Kathryn had the advantage – occasionally it was a disadvantage – of being quick-witted, sharp-tongued and independent. When a car parts salesman in Campbelltown told her she was "prettier" than her husband she shot back, "I've got the better legs as well". On the other hand, her comment on the John Laws program on 8 March that Bob Hawke, who had such a high approval rating, was "a creep" caused Greiner some embarrassment. He countered by saying the Prime Minister had to be a good bloke because he liked sport so much.[21]

Throughout the campaign the *SMH* virtually ignored the shadow ministers, and most of Wran's ministers as well. The *Daily Telegraph* did run a series where the relevant Labor minister and Liberal shadow minister outlined their respective policies on education, transport, law and order, employment, the environment, health, charges and taxes (Greiner, as the shadow treasurer, was responsible for the last-named category). In most cases, the shadow ministers simply repeated what Greiner had announced in his policy speech or in separate policy statements. Despite this exposure, a *Telegraph* editorial on 24 March described "most" members of shadow cabinet as "unknown outside their electorates" and accused the Coalition of having "done nothing to convince the electorate it has an alternative team capable of doing a better job". Greiner, it said, "has proved beyond doubt he is a worthy political leader and a skilled campaigner" but had "been working as a man alone".

On the eve of the election Greiner complained about the contest becoming too "gladiatorial". Too much emphasis was placed on the contest between Wran and himself.[22] He would have preferred promoting his whole team of shadow ministers. It is unlikely he was wholly serious. Although he thought the *Telegraph* comment on the shadow cabinet was unfair, most of the shadow ministers were demonstrably undistinguished and were best kept out of sight. An academic commentator supported this view: Greiner had effectively presented himself as the alternative Premier but his frontbench was "largely an unimpressive, faceless lot who did little to support the Opposition's claims for government".[23] There were exceptions. Peter Collins had considerable media experience. He made himself known, and his separate announcement of the Coalition's environment policy received good coverage. Nevertheless, in general, Greiner took the limelight and, unlike Wran, who could call on Hawke as a useful support act, Greiner found that Peacock had little to offer.

Not everyone in the Coalition camp was happy about the emphasis on projecting Greiner. Bruce Baird, a senior executive with Esso Australia who won Northcott in 1984, was concerned because shadow ministers were appearing in "sports clothes or 60's suits". He was even more worried because the focus on Greiner had lifted his rating without having any impact on the Coalition's standing. Baird wanted more emphasis on the team.[24] A member of a post-election review committee echoed Baird's views.[25] Twelve days before the poll a prominent businessman, Alderman W.B. Northam, took a different approach to the focus on Greiner. He told Valder of his intention to remain a member of the Party and to give a small donation though he would not "invest" in "a hasty ill-prepared scramble for a most unlikely result". The Opposition should be getting its house in order before assuming the stance of a potential winner. He urged the formation of a "team" rather than relying on "the desperate attempt to sell a personality". Greiner had a long way to go before he could convince anybody he had sufficient maturity. Valder should save his money for the next election.[26]

Every modern election campaign is marked by well-reported gaffes and Greiner's cause in 1984 had its share. On the day of his policy speech, Rosemary Foot refused at a press conference in Albury to rule out a challenge to Greiner's leadership should there be a poor result for the Liberal Party. Wran jumped at the opportunity. He accused Foot of planning to challenge Greiner, and called it almost unprecedented for a deputy leader to raise questions about the leadership during an election campaign. Foot subsequently and emphatically denied having any intention of issuing a challenge; "Nick and I complement each other" and have made "a strong impact as a team". But the damage was done, and the media kept finding evidence of strain between the two of them.[27]

John Valder committed a glaring blunder when speaking at a breakfast meeting of businessmen two days before the poll. The Liberal State President said it would take "one of those rare miracles" for the Coalition to succeed on Saturday. Greiner tried to retrieve the situation. Valder's remark merely highlighted the "very difficult task" of trying to achieve the biggest-ever swing in a NSW State election. So, his use of the word "rare" was reasonable, even if "miracle" was not "quite appropriate". Greiner said he would prefer to put his trust in the people of NSW than the Almighty. Leon Punch was less charitable; perhaps Valder was "not experienced much politically and maybe he would be wise to stay out of the political arena".[28] Not that Punch himself was always astute. It was not clever to suggest that motorists with good records should be permitted to register a blood alcohol reading of 0.08; nor was it wise for a Liberal shadow minister to raise the prospect of a second runway for Sydney airport.

Greiner himself made two mistakes. Defending local government's financial autonomy was itself sound enough, especially given his 1983 speech to the Local Government Association. But it was imprudent to tell councils they could lift rates by 100 per cent because they were answerable to their electors. At the same time he had been attacking the Government for raising taxes and charges.[29] The Liberals had to use advertising funds to counter Labor claims that a Coalition government would increase local rates.

More seriously, six days before the election Greiner sent the Police Commissioner a number of documents relating to the Sydney Entertainment Centre where the Government held a 20 per cent share. Copies were also forwarded to the Auditor-General and to Gerry Gleeson, the Government's representative on the Centre's board. They contained allegations that some employees of the company managing the Centre had defrauded it by making wage payments to "ghost" workers, fiddled ticket sales, pilfered liquor stocks, and sold goods privately. These practices, Greiner claimed, had cost the Centre upwards of $1m. He acknowledged later that he probably "overreached" in trying "to get something out of the box". People who were already worried about corruption did not need more evidence but here was a chance to widen the net.[30]

Wran reacted so vehemently that Justin Greiner, then aged eleven, was for the first time upset by criticism of his father.[31] The Premier said Greiner must be in a "desperate situation" and have "sick advisers" to think allegations of this kind could curry favour with the general public just before an election. He was "shocked at the immaturity and inexperience" of those who kept "bringing up muck-raking allegations". The Centre's board rejected any claims of fraud; there had been problems in 1983 and three forced resignations had solved them. The Police Commissioner weighed in two days before the election, describing Greiner's allegations as "completely without basis". In response, the Leader of the Opposition noted this "premature" finding; Abbott had issued his statement within 24 hours of interviewing Greiner and before he had spoken to the senior Liberals identified as witnesses. Greiner had a fair point but his case required a more thorough preparation; the charge fell flat.[32]

## The results

The Liberals gained nine seats on 24 March: winning eight from Labor and regaining Northcott which had been previously held by Jim Cameron as an Independent. The Nationals took two seats from Labor which also lost Wollongong to an Independent. Labor's share of the primary vote had fallen from 55.8 in 1981 to 49.1 per cent in 1984 and its majority, while remaining larger than any Askin had ever achieved, had been reduced from 39 to 17. The Liberal Party's primary vote had risen from 27.6 to 32.2 per cent while Greiner retained his own seat with 77.8 per cent of the vote, an increase of almost 13 per cent on the 1981 figure. Notably, all the Liberal Party's gains occurred in, or close by, the Sydney area. They failed to make any advances in non-metropolitan NSW. In the Legislative Council the Coalition and the Labor Party each won seven seats, the fifteenth being taken by Jim Cameron who headed the ticket of Fred Nile's Call to Australia group. Labor maintained its Council majority with 24 seats over 11 Liberals, seven Nationals, two Call to Australia and one Australian Democrat.

The day after the poll was a good time to confess. Greiner told the media he never expected to win: "If I hadn't lied to you about our chances of winning you would have pilloried me the way you pilloried John Valder." He was doing no more than the obvious: that is, keeping up the Party's morale.[33]

Whereas Wran called it "the sweetest victory of all", Greiner described the result as "a kick in the pants" for the Government, and was "genuinely happy" because the chances of coming first rather than second "were always small". Besides, the swing was the second-largest in NSW election history and the largest ever achieved by an Opposition. Nor was it just a case of disgruntled Liberal voters returning to the fold. He was prepared, therefore, to accept the accolade for being the most successful Liberal Leader since Askin. More importantly, Greiner reckoned the Coalition was in a winning position for 1988, and "very few people have the opportunity of being Premier at 40 after seven or eight years in Parliament". In the meantime, by almost doubling the numbers in the Assembly, the task of Opposition had become "a lot easier".[34] Nor was it simply a matter of numbers. The 1984 Liberal intake included one future Premier (John Fahey) and five future ministers (Bruce Baird, David Hay, Ron Phillips, Michael Yabsley and John Hannaford, MLC). Two Nationals from the "class of '84" – Ian Causley and Robert Webster – would also become ministers in the Greiner Government. The one real downside was that Neville Wran immediately foreshadowed a redistribution which every commentator concluded would mean creating more Labor seats in outer western Sydney.[35]

Valder told the State Executive on 2 April that Greiner had helped to restore public esteem for the Liberal Party and given the Party a boost. Writing to Sir Charles Court, the former Liberal Premier of Western Australia, he said the election result was "a great boost to the Party's morale" and the Party was "now poised to move ahead strongly in New South Wales with a new sense of purpose and new direction". He admitted that "some fool (me) was quoted as saying that it would have required a miracle to win!"[36] Being criticised internally for this "gaffe" did not bother him. Leon Punch was another matter. Valder told Punch there was "a limit to our patience and tolerance in the face of unnecessary and provacative [sic] remarks made publicly from time to time from your side".[37] Nick Greiner stayed well clear of this exchange. The important achievement was that, by holding 23 seats in the Assembly compared with the National Party's 14, the Liberal Party was the unassailable senior partner in the Coalition. Neither Punch nor any of his successors would ever again suggest that the rural hindquarters should assume Coalition leadership.

Some commentators and a mischievous Neville Wran argued that Greiner had botched a winning hand. The Liberals, who seemed to leap ahead in the first week, lost momentum when they focussed on the "bread-and-butter" issues in the second.[38] Greiner stressed how the Party had decided to spend the first week hammering the Government over corruption and their excuses for holding an early election to avoid a time bomb; to spend the second week "being essentially positive" by announcing policies it would have preferred to reveal before the campaign; and to go hard on the "integrity issues" in the final week. He did not know then that claims of a "million dollar swindle" at the Entertainment Centre would fall flat. Greiner later argued that 80 per cent of the Party's advertising attacked the Government over corruption. The Party's slogan – "Together, we can clean up NSW" – "could not have been more explicit". He argued further that the Party's market research justified an emphasis on taxes and charges in the metropolitan area and that Punch's attacks on graft and corruption did not resonate in rural NSW. Greiner might also have said the Government's action in calling an early election had ensured that accusations of graft, especially those relating to Rex Jackson, had not yet been proven.

Greiner's own post-election observations signalled his determination to make key appointments and to take charge of State election campaigns. He had not wanted to use the Masius advertising company in the election campaign but the Organisation had insisted on renewing its contract. Acknowledging that the company had performed better than he expected, Greiner told Valder its record was "certainly not brilliant", worth at most 7 out of 10. He succeeded in appointing his preferred agency – Campaign Palace – for the 1988 election.

Greiner felt just as strongly about another area strictly outside the province of the Parliamentary Leader, namely, the role of field officers. When John Carrick was General Secretary approximately half his annual budget was spent on employing them. Their tasks ranged from forming branches, enrolling members and advising office-bearers to mixing with local communities and looking out for potential candidates. They were, above all, his eyes and ears throughout NSW, his trouble shooters and early warning system. Carrick regarded them as more reliable than opinion polls in assessing public opinion. If money were no object he would have employed field officers in every State and Federal electorate in NSW. Greiner did not accept what he called the "Carrick view" of placing field officers "all over the place" – and he did not then know that Carrick's successor as General Secretary thought over half of the 17 he inherited ought to be dismissed on grounds of incompetence.[39] Greiner believed four field officers would be sufficient: two operating in the marginal seats of the inner west, south west and south east of Sydney, and two looking after an area stretching from Albury, through the Blue Mountains and Bathurst to the Hunter and the North Coast. Resident field officers were not needed north of Newcastle. Members of the Legislative Council and a senior official in the Party's Secretariat could do what was required. "The practice of simply lobbing a $25,000 per annum person into, say, Coffs Harbour and expecting them to produce results is ridiculous."[40]

On the Sunday after the election Greiner said the Party leadership should and would remain unchanged: "stability was a virtue". On the Monday he said the leadership team of himself, Foot and Lange had achieved "an excellent result" and it would be in the Party's interest for the team to be retained. Yet all Liberal MPs were entitled to stand for any leadership position, and he would not intervene to prevent any contest and would not be involved in any internal lobbying. His comment was interpreted to mean that Foot's position was in jeopardy, although Greiner clearly intended to back her in any ballot. Once again, he was forced to deny he had a difficult working relationship with her, though he did admit, "like any relationship of that sort, there are tensions". Valder was emphatic. He told any Liberal who sought his opinion that Foot should be re-elected deputy leader. A number of senior Liberals remained unconvinced. Names of potential challengers were mentioned – Collins and Rozzoli being the most prominent – but it was clear by the end of March that Foot would be re-elected, largely on the votes of the nine new members who had never seen her perform.

The Parliamentary Party met on Tuesday 3 April and re-elected Greiner unopposed. Foot defeated Rozzoli by 16 votes to five with one informal, and repeatedly told a press conference she would never seek the leadership. Rozzoli qualified his support for the leadership team by saying it did not extend to Foot. Greiner could live with Rozzoli's ambitions. But he was initially unnerved by the election of Ted Pickering to lead the Liberals in the Legislative Council.[41] Supported by the 1984 intake, Pickering defeated Lange by six votes to five. Greiner did not at the time appreciate his own good fortune. Pickering became the critical figure in delivering votes in the Party Room and the backing of the Organisation either to shore up support for a potentially stranded Leader or, more often, to help him get his way. Hence, the 1984 election and its immediate aftermath marked an important stage in Greiner's progress towards the premiership.

# Endnotes

1   *Woman's Day*, 27 February 1984.

2   See the interview with Craig McGregor *SMH*, the *Good Weekend*, 1 July 1989.

3   Interviews: Justin and Kara Greiner 19 April 2011.

4   For an account of the election, see Ken Turner, "The 1984 campaign: twenty hectic days", in Chaples, *et al.*, *The Wran Model*, ch. 17.

5   See the editorial, and comments by Malcolm Mackerras, in *SMH*, 3 March 1984.

6   Interviews: Hooper, 20 April 2011; Greiner 24 December 2012.

7   C.J. Middleton, 1984 Election: A Review of the History of the Campaign, Mar. 1984, State Campaign Committee, LPA, ML, MSS 7205/43 and Pre-Election, *ibid.*, 80.

8   *SMH*, 3 March; *Sun-Herald*, 4 March 1984.

9   *SMH*, 20 March 1984.

10  *SMH*, 6 March 1984.

11  The hearings were due to commence on 12 March but were indefinitely delayed after Cross resigned on health grounds. The Premier refused to appoint a replacement, invoking the convention about not taking fresh action once an election had been called.

12  *SMH*, 12 March 1984.

13  *DT*, 13 March 1984.

14  For one of the two-page advertisements, see *DT*, 16 March 1984.

15  *SMH*, 15 March 1984.

16  *SMH*, 16 March 1984.

17  Nick Greiner, "Restoring the Public Interest", *Quadrant*, vol. 25, no 5, 1984, p. 59-63.

18  *SMH*, 20 March 1984.

19  *SMH*, 20 March and *DT*, 25 March 1984.

20  *SMH*, 5, 19 March; *Sun-Herald*, 11 March 1984.

21  For comment on the wives, see *SMH*, 5 and 19 March; *Sun-Herald*, 11 March 1984. Asked later about her description of Hawke, Kathryn replied, "prescient, wasn't I!". Interview: 29 March 2011.

22  *DT*, 22 March 1984.

23  Chaples, "24 March 1984", in Chaples *et al.*, *Wran Model*, pp. 223-4.

24  Baird to Foot, 23 January 1984, Pre-Election, LPA, ML, MSS 7205/80.

25  Liberal Party 1984 State Election Review, Liberal Party – 1984 Election, Collins Papers, ML MSS 7442/69.

26   Northam to Valder, 16 March 1984, Strategy 1984, April, LPA, ML, MSS 7205/80.

27   *SMH*, 13 March, *DT,* 14 March 1984.

28   *SMH* and *DT,* 23 March 1984.

29   See *DT,* 22 March 1984.

30   Interview: Greiner, 15 Sepember 2010.

31   Interview: Justin Greiner, 19 April 2011.

32   *SMH,* 19 Mar., *DT,* 23 March 1984.

33   *SMH,* 22 and 26 March 1984. He reiterated the point in an interview on 14 September 2010.

34   For post-election comments, see *Sun-Herald,* 25 March, *SMH* and *DT,* 26 March 1984. For an upbeat Liberal Party election review, see Middleton, 1984 Election.

35   *DT,* 26 March 1984.

36   Minutes of State Executive, 2 April 1984, LPA, ML, MSS 7205/10; Valder to Sir Charles Court, 9 April 1984, LPA, ML, MSS 7205/76.

37   Valder to Punch, 9 April 1984, *ibid.*

38   For a review of the arguments about the Liberal strategy and about the role of corruption in the campaigns, see Turner, "The 1984 Campaign", pp. 212-14 and Ernie Chaples, "24 March 1984: what happened and why", in Chaples *et al., Wran Model,* p. 223.

39   Field Organisation, 1 September 1972, Field Organisation, LPA, ML, MSS 3340, Add-On, 1454/H1156.

40   Greiner to Valder, 30 March 1984, Strategy 1984, April, LPA, ML, MSS 7205/80. For the Carrick approach to managing the NSW Division, see Graeme Starr, *Carrick: Principles, Politics and Policy,* Connor Court, Ballan, 2012, chs 5-7.

41   Born in 1939, Pickering graduated in Science, worked in the coal industry in Wollongong, entered the Legislative Council under the old system in 1976, supported Dowd against Greiner in 1983 and, later in that year, earned his reputation as a "numbers man" when, working with Dowd, he produced a winning slate in pre-selections for the Legislative Council. In the process, he thwarted Bronwyn Bishop's parliamentary ambitions, partly because she represented "the unacceptable face of the Liberal Party". David Leser, *Bronwyn Bishop: A Woman in Pursuit of Power,* Text Publishing, Melbourne, 1994, p. 63.

# 8

# Four More Years

It was never easy holding the worst job in NSW politics. Wran kept up his attack and the backbench jeered "Greiner the Whiner" and mocked his physical likeness to "Kermit the Frog".[1] Labor repeatedly sought to undermine Greiner's managerial credentials and embarrass him over the existence of "right-wing extremists" in the Liberal Party. Greiner's assaults on the Government sometimes misfired. Gary Sturgess, who liked to explore Labor's dark side, occasionally attracted unhelpful publicity. Greiner was powerless to deal with factional warfare inside the Liberal Party Organisation, and struggled to restrain the Organisation from fighting the Nationals. Even Wran's retirement in July 1986 had a negative aspect. After early staggers his successor, Barrie Unsworth, presided over a revival of Labor's fortunes in the first half of 1987 with his "Back to Basics" approach. Personal issues also intruded. Kathryn pleaded guilty after registering a middle-range reading on a random breath test in January 1987, and received bad publicity after the magistrate discharged her without conviction on account of a long and good driving record.

For all the difficulties he faced, Greiner never seemed bothered by self-doubt. He rode the punches, held his ground, and worked long hours. He kept fit by skiing and playing squash and tennis. In part conscious of the need to expand the Liberals' electoral base, and in part more aware of his own family's history and of the migrant experience, he accepted as many invitations as he could to attend ethnic community functions. He spoke on one day in 1987 at the Lakemba mosque and two days later attended a Mass in Lidcombe celebrated by the Patriarch of Antioch. There were many pleasant diversions: family holidays; nights at the Opera House with Kathryn; travel overseas (twice in 1985); lunches or meetings at Parliament House with the editor of cricket's *Wisden* or with Paul Eddington and Derek Fowlds of *Yes, Prime Minister*; attending games in all four football codes; regular contact with the Harvard Business School Association. There were important meetings with Rupert Murdoch, Sir Peter Abeles, Lindsay Fox and the Jewish and Budapest-born Larry Adler of Fire and All Risks Insurance (FAI). He met John Howard several times. The two men had little personal rapport but contact was necessary because Howard had replaced Peacock as Federal Leader in August 1985. Greiner was often in contact with Sir Charles Court, the former Premier of Western Australia, and Jeff Kennett, the Liberal Leader in Victoria. On one day he would be talking to the "Uglies", and next day meeting trade unionists such as Jennie George of the NSW Teachers Federation, John Halfpenny of the ACTU and Jack Mundey, unionist and conservationist.

For all the difficulties and occasional setbacks, Greiner emerged from four more years in Opposition well prepared for winning and managing government. He had established the priorities and methods of operation, developed his own election strategy, and formed a strong partnership with a new National Party leader, Wal Murray. Two close and shrewd observers admired what they saw. Ted Pickering believed his Leader did a "fabulous" job managing shadow cabinet, having surprised them by holding regular meetings, imposing discipline and requiring policy documents. It helped that his "enormous intellect" gave him a "phenomenal" capacity to get "to the guts of any issue".[2] Bob Carr, watching Greiner in the Legislative Assembly, spoke later of his "textbook Opposition". The seemingly "cold-blooded", "always competent" and "highly articulate" Greiner worked hard to maintain morale and convince his side that victory was possible. He made it increasingly difficult for the Government at a time when "things started going seriously wrong". Importantly, he cultivated the ethnic communities and kept the Opposition in the public domain with a stream of stories for the print media and with regular spots on radio and television. When Carr became Opposition Leader after the 1988 election, he set about applying the Greiner model.[3]

## Greinerism

Anyone who had taken notice of Greiner's words and actions in this period would have known in broad terms what to expect of the Managing Director of NSW Inc.

Many fellow Liberals feared he was no social conservative. On homosexual law reform Greiner had adopted John Stuart Mill's "classic liberal position": "The only purpose for which power can be rightfully exercised over any member of a civilised community, against his will, is to prevent harm to others." Sturgess provided him with the words but Greiner spoke his own mind when responding in May 1984 to Wran's Private Member's Bill to decriminalise homosexual acts between males 18 years and over. Unlike the Premier, he did not want to bring the law closer to contemporary standards. Instead, he saw the existing law as wrong in principle, irrespective of time and context. As for claims that changes to the law would undermine social cohesiveness, he argued that what was needed "to hold society together is not some common morality enforced by the State, but the mutual tolerance of different moralities". Wran's Bill eventually passed the second reading by 62 votes to 35.[4]

In September 1984 Sturgess provided Greiner with more words to set out what would become the Greiner Government's approach to business. Entitled "Government by Wink and Nod – the Future of Business under Labor" – this speech, delivered to Liberal Party donors in Melbourne, criticised the entrepreneurial interventions of the Labor governments of Victoria and Western Australian. It specifically queried the Hawke Government's commitment to competition and to the regulating mechanism of the market. Federal Labor was now just more sophisticated and less confrontationist as economic and social planners. Subtle interventionism had replaced explicit nationalisation, and the wink and the nod caused business to turn somersaults and comply over matters such as affirmative action. By contrast, a Greiner government would apply rules known in advance and applicable to all, thus ensuring a fair and level playing field and giving favours to no one. A sporting metaphor seemed apt: whereas Liberals sought to make rules applying to each player on the field, Labor wanted the referee (the government) to make them up as he goes along, and even to participate in the game.

Greiner and Sturgess were very conscious of the need to counter crude Labor and media images of "Greinerism". In several speeches delivered during 1985 Greiner denied he believed in small government for its own sake, or was beholden to a "New Right" market-driven philosophy which ignored the interests and needs of "ordinary Australians". He was uncomfortable with the notion of "deregulation"; the aim was for less and better regulation. He did want the public service to be more like the private sector and to resemble the market as closely as possible. Private sector managers, Greiner argued, were more efficient because they faced the discipline of competition. Governments tolerated inefficiencies because they could not allow their enterprises to go broke. Selling these enterprises, however, was not the only option; it may be sufficient to create competition between them and private companies.

Following an internal office discussion, Greiner introduced a slogan to the Liberal Party's State Convention in August 1985 designed to soften the image of economic rationalism. Sturgess wanted "a clear and distinctive image which conveyed the fundamental concern in our policies for people". He pressed the case for presenting policies as "Dry and Warm" (later represented as "Warm and Dry").[5] Greiner spoke of a dry wind blowing through all parties but the Liberal Party must emerge as "dry and warm" rather than "dry and cold". To be "warm and wet" meant throwing money at people, and most taxpayers had given up believing that worked. To be "dry and warm" meant politicians had "a warm heart and a hard head", creating a situation where consumers, workers and taxpayers would all be better off.

Greiner's speeches were also designed to counter Labor's success in painting the Liberal Party as the party of, and for, big business. Despite its successful raid on seats outside the North Shore in 1984, the Liberal Party in NSW was too easily dismissed in public discourse as a middle-class – and Anglo-Celt and Protestant – enclave. Greiner wanted the Liberal Party to be one for all Australians. Anyone familiar with its history would have known that the first Federal President, Tom Ritchie, expressed this aspiration in formally launching the Party in 1945. Greiner could rightly insist there had been changes. The Liberal Party now had more contacts with "ordinary Australians", was more representative of the community in ethnic and religious terms, and had thrown aside much of its born-to-rule mentality. It was "led by the son of a service station owner (Howard) and the son of a Hungarian immigrant". Yet the Liberal Party was one of the few liberal-conservative parties in the world unable to claim a significant proportion of the blue collar vote. The Liberals were not seen as the Party for those struggling to obtain a reasonable standard of living, as the natural choice for those who left their homelands for freedom and opportunity, or for the young who placed a high value on personal freedom and choice. Greiner enjoined his side of politics to show the "so-called working class" that it would be better-off under Liberal policies because there would be more jobs and a higher standard of living.[6]

On 4 January 1988 Greiner addressed the Young Liberals National Convention in Sydney in a speech which mapped out what would become "a complete revolution in the management culture of the State Government".[7] It was a speech which brought together the "dry" elements of the Greiner-Sturgess thinking of the previous years, expressed in the language of management rather than ideology and focussed on outcomes and not on processes.

Greiner argued that Australian liberalism was essentially "practical" and "anti-ideological". The test of any idea was not its "ideological integrity" but "Does it work?". The Managing Director of New South Wales Inc. ("the biggest business in the nation") would be concerned with results, securing better services for the company's customers (the consumers), better returns for the shareholders (the taxpayers), and better results for its employees through improved management practices, working conditions and productivity. Most of the speech focussed on the methods for achieving these objectives: a moratorium on expenditure growth; a separation of the commercial and social objectives of government programs; an expansion of user-pays; a comprehensive audit of the State's assets and liabilities; a good rate of return for commercially-oriented authorities and programs; the awarding of contracts on purely commercial grounds; competition by each government agency in the market place on a competitively-neutral basis; and increased departmental autonomy to allow the managers to manage.

## Liberal Party matters

While Wran ridiculed, patronised and mimicked Rosemary Foot, the support from her own side of politics was ambivalent, notwithstanding the improvement in her relationship with Greiner. Peter Collins kept files recording Foot's gaffes and outspokenness, and was occasionally obliged to deny any intention of challenging for the deputy leadership.[8] He scraped through an exhaustive ballot to succeed her when the legal costs of a lost defamation case forced Foot to leave Parliament in February 1986. As part of the leadership team he could no longer complain about its failure to consult the Parliamentary Party. The Greiner camp was never quite sure, however, whether he ever belonged in the same tent, although Greiner and Collins met frequently during 1986-7 and did mark their 40th birthdays by holding a joint dinner party at the Buon Ricordo Ristorante in Paddington on 2 May 1987.

The emergence of the Group after February 1984 was a critical development for the Liberal Party, and for Greiner himself. It was formed to thwart the Right in contests for pre-selections and party positions. The inner circle included four State MPs (Pickering, Dowd, Moore and John Booth) and two Federal senators (Peter Baume and Puplick).[9] An outer circle, drawn from the Women's Council and the Young Liberals, spread the Group's influence throughout the Party Organisation. The inner sanctum developed a number of "understandings", one of which was to support the decisions and preferences of the parliamentary leaders.[10] Pickering evolved as the overall "leader", partly because the 1983 pre-selection ballot for the Legislative Council had confirmed his standing as a "numbers man", and partly because his membership of the Legislative Council gave him the time and resources to establish networks throughout the State. He was also fairly conservative and could never be labelled a "trendy".[11]

John Howard was not sure about the Group's loyalty when he was Federal Leader between 1985 and 1989. Greiner, on the other hand, knew he could usually rely on support for his agenda and preferred candidates.[12] First, however, he needed a sharp reminder of the Group's independence and of its complex make-up, and to learn he could not automatically have his way.

Greiner hoped to secure a spot for a staff member when the Liberal Party conducted a pre-selection during a weekend in November 1986 to choose the Legislative Council ticket for the 1988 election. The Group was not interested. Greiner also wanted to avoid a "winner-take-all" ticket by including a conservative. He held talks with two members of the Urbanchich sub-faction of the Right, and Gary O'Gorman, a lawyer and a Catholic from the North Shore, emerged as the preferred candidate. Although Dowd opposed any accommodation with the conservatives, Pickering agreed to back Greiner. Protracted negotiations during the latter part of 1986 over many Chinese meals failed to secure agreement. Michael Photios, the President of the Young Liberals in 1984-5 and normally Pickering's close ally, was a principal obstacle. The Young Liberals had delivered the numbers when the Group needed them. Now they insisted on the selection of one their own instead of O'Gorman. Greiner mistakenly chose two "nonentities" as his floor managers for the vote in November 1986 and did not endear himself to the Young Liberals by appearing to threaten them. After a tight and tense contest the Young Liberal candidate – Stephen Mutch – defeated O'Gorman for a winnable place on the ticket.[13] This result had many ramifications for the internal politics of the Liberal Party, including the Right's increased determination to organise the numbers.

Nick Greiner realised that he was better placed to influence decisions when not trying to obtain concessions for the Right. He was successful, for example, in securing Group acceptance of his preferred candidates for the Blue Mountains and Georges River for the 1988 election. His achievement was all the more remarkable in Georges River, held by Frank Walker of the Labor Left and one of Greiner's principal adversaries in the Assembly. The Group had already selected a candidate and a Party elder of known good judgment had advised Pickering not to touch Greiner's choice – Terry Griffiths – "with a forty foot barge pole".[14]

Supported by conservatives, and opposed by the Group, Bronwyn Bishop was elected State President in September 1985. Anticipating dismissal, the State Director immediately resigned. Bishop secured the appointment of Graeme Starr as his replacement. An academic and a Carrick protégé, Starr had worked in the Federal Secretariat and more recently had been employed in John Howard's office. Bishop regarded the Starr appointment as one of the significant achievements of her presidency.[15] Nick Greiner, who was involved in the selection process, sat with Bishop and Starr at the press conference announcing the appointment. Greiner maintained a fixed smile while Starr said his job was to make sure everything ran smoothly and that a chief executive of a voluntary organisation "can't go around directing people". In quick time, Greiner decided that Starr, "a personally reasonable, intelligent guy" cast in the Carrick-Howard mould of a State Director, was "a weak flunky", unable to "execute and implement", "a bit of a naysayer", "very narrow", "rule-bound" and with "a limited strategic perspective". Whereas Greiner saw Starr as someone fixated on processes, the new State Director saw cutting corners and bending rules as breaching tradition and forsaking good practice. Greiner the outsider who judged tradition, convention and rules on the basis of what they achieved or inhibited, decided to spend as little time as possible in the Party's new headquarters in Riley Street. And, to circumvent the State Director, Greiner and his office mounted a separately-funded election campaign.[16]

## A new opponent

Neville Wran stunned State Labor's Annual Conference on 7 June 1986 by announcing he would be resigning as Premier on 4 July. Of the obvious succession candidates, Laurie Brereton was Greiner's preferred successor because Brereton would be seen as a continuation of the Wran style which he felt was losing its edge.[17] The kingmakers of the Labor Right chose instead to install Barrie Unsworth, a former electrician and Secretary of the Labor Council. Unsworth had been in the Legislative Council since 1978 and a minister and Leader of the Government since 1984. The brutish and successful lobbying on Unsworth's behalf "crippled him from the outset".[18]

The long-serving Labor MP for Rockdale obligingly stepped aside for Unsworth to enter the Legislative Assembly. The by-election for this supposedly safe seat was set for 2 August, coinciding with the contest for Wran's seat of Bass Hill. The Liberal Party's Strategy Committee, headed by Starr, decided not to take a high profile in the fight for Rockdale. The State Director considered the seat a lost cause, and wanted to conserve resources for the 1987 Federal campaign.

The arrival of Ian Kortlang on 16 June 1986 was central to what followed. A former Whitlam supporter who still belonged to what he called the "small 'l' inner city liberal tradition", Kortlang had risen to officer rank in the Australian Army and worked in the Joint Intelligence Organisation and the Department of Foreign Affairs. He took over preparations in Lusaka for Malcolm Fraser's visit to Zambia for the 1979 Commonwealth Heads of Government Meeting, and was then employed privately to help companies get into Africa. Kortlang joined the Liberal Party on the eve of the 1983 Federal election, principally to expand his business contacts. He sought, and won, Liberal pre-selection for the seat of Ryde which he contested unsuccessfully in the 1984 State election, and never attended another branch meeting.[19] Kortlang left his job selecting staff for aid projects in Africa and joined Greiner's office as Principal Private Secretary. Priding himself as a planner and organiser, he quickly decided that the office "couldn't run a bar". But he fitted in easily with Sturgess and Hooper as Greiner's closest advisers. They constituted a triumvirate, each had a distinct role and there were "no territorial pissing matches". Inside the office, Greiner was no more than *primus inter pares* and discussions were often "robust"; outside, "he could walk on water".[20]

Kortlang, Sturgess and Hooper convinced Greiner to go hard, and mount "a very strong suburban" campaign in Rockdale. They exhumed the career of an experienced local candidate and secured Greg Daniel of Campaign Palace to undertake the advertising. They acted "without any Party involvement at all".[21] Yet Greiner held several meetings with Starr over the campaign for Bass Hill and Rockdale, and the Liberal Party mounted an extensive grass-roots campaign, including a full door knock.[22] Greiner himself visited Rockdale on five occasions, although by polling day he was coming down with a severe dose of 'flu.

A Young Liberal captured Bass Hill on 2 August. After several tense days of counting and preference distribution Unsworth survived the indignity of defeat by 54 votes. Greiner saw it as a perfect result: Unsworth had been seriously embarrassed by a swing of 14.5 per cent but would remain Labor Leader. Greiner left it to Federal and State Labor to decide whether the swing was mainly anti-Hawke or anti-Unsworth. He had grasped the principal message. The Labor voters who turned against Labor objected to Labor's performance. They were not converts to the Liberal Party.[23]

Describing Wran as "the New Labor model" – "stylish, professional, pragmatic", Greiner depicted Unsworth as "the Old Labor model" run by the Labor machine – "narrow, ideological and sectional". It would be "easier to fight Old Labor" because Unsworth would not be such a formidable opponent inside or outside Parliament. In a rare admission, which his office found difficult to accept, Greiner later said it was "perfectly apparent that I was unnerved both by Neville Wran and the machine". Although "we got Wran's measure to a significant extent" he could turn even the best-prepared attack. Unsworth could not do that even if the attack was "mediocre". He described dealing with Unsworth's "non-policies and non-decisions" as "like wrestling with a wet blanket". The upside was that whereas Greiner had found it hard to make an impression when he and Wran were attending the same social function, "I now actively seek opportunities to be side by side with Mr Unsworth". Better still, there was not a day in Parliament since Wran's retirement where the Government "has managed to walk all over us".[24]

## Preparing for 1988

Greiner and the triumvirate interpreted the by-election results as arguments for conducting campaigns with minimal reference to Riley Street. Starting with David Dale's account of how Labor in 1976 created the perception of Wran's inevitable accession to government and, after studying other successful Federal and State Labor campaigns, they applied Labor's strategies to their overriding goal: to make Nick Greiner Premier of NSW. Harnessing the Liberal Party to the cause was essential, but the success of the Liberal Party would be a by-product, not the prime objective.

On 1 June 1987 – Greiner called it "Brainstorm day" in his appointment diary – the core of what became the key campaign team met in Janet Mahon's house in Bowral over bowls of pumpkin soup. Greiner, Pickering, Collins, Kortlang, Sturgess, Hooper and Daniel engaged in some hard-headed talk. Some "brutal" comments were directed at Greiner, and Pickering marvelled at the way he took them. Everyone was assigned tasks, and the Leader's included contacting the media proprietors, looking into ways and means of setting up and financially supporting independents in Labor-held seats and of dealing with the environmentalists and the NSW Teachers' Federation.[25]

Hawke called an early Federal election for 11 July and Greiner took time off to make the requisite public appearances for Howard. Hooper joined the proceedings and reported on the folly of the machine and the Leader's office running separate campaigns. The important thing was to establish who, overall, was in charge. Greiner observed how the Federal Opposition was ill-prepared with its policies and had banked heavily on buying the votes of a cynical electorate. Howard's cause was further blighted when Joh Bjelke-Petersen, the Premier of Queensland, decided he was a suitable tenant for the Lodge. Fortunately, for Greiner, the "Joh for Canberra" campaign, which clearly hurt the Federal Coalition, did not turn the NSW Nationals into allies of the Queenslander's preposterous ambitions.

The Greiner family went to Charlotte's Pass for a week of skiing on the day after Hawke was returned with an increased majority in the House of Representatives. Plans were already under way to hold a State election dress rehearsal.[26] Kortlang drew upon his military experience: the Army rarely did anything without first practising it. Greg Daniel's slogan, "We're Ready", provided a clever cover for a situation where "we couldn't have run a campaign in a fit". The Liberal Party machine "was non-existent", the local organisation was poor, and selected candidates were taking Greiner around pubs but never to meet Parents' and Citizens' Associations. The rehearsal was meant to convince the media that "we were a professional unit" and not "a bit of a joke", to get attention, create momentum, and make Greiner "look like a Premier". A simultaneous television commercial portrayed him as a long-time leader who had survived "the toughest political forum in the country", had built a strong team, and was ready to deliver "a Change for the Better". The rehearsal itself focussed on a campaign launch and the second last week of a projected campaign, timed to coincide with the Liberal Party State Convention in August. Adjudged a success, it allowed the "classic mistakes" to be made while securing a 30 per cent increase in suburban media coverage.

Money was a problem. The Federal campaign had left the NSW Liberals with a deficit of $597,000 at the end of 1987.[27] Greiner knew he had to look beyond the Party for funds. He also believed that the Secretariat, manifestly more interested in winning power in Canberra, would divert any funds raised to Federal campaigns. Graeme Starr considered it wasteful to spend heavily fighting a State election when victory was assured, and made no secret of his approach. As he said later, "I don't think it matters terribly much who governs in New South Wales".[28] The Greiner team turned, therefore, to a new organisation – Community Polling – to meet its needs.

Community Polling was established in 1985 by Metherell and his electoral assistant to conduct opinion polls in marginal seats. The assistant left by 1987 to be replaced by a recent Sydney University graduate, John Stirton, who organised volunteers to conduct telephone polling for what had become a central polling organisation. Kortlang, Stirton and Metherell were later registered as proprietors of Community Polling which had no formal connection with the Liberal Party. Once registered, it opened investment and cheque accounts to accommodate donors who wanted to fund the State campaign. Kortlang's dress rehearsal was an early recipient of Community Polling handouts. Greiner, Bob Frost, a property developer and the Finance Vice-President of the NSW Liberal Party, and James Yonge, a merchant banker and the Deputy Chairman and Managing Director of Wardley Australia Ltd, actively and successfully sought donations from the business community. Some of the money found its way into Community Polling.

Like Community Polling, the Kaldor Committee had no ties with the Liberal Party. Hungarian-born Andrew Kaldor, whom Greiner had known since his Sydney University days, was the Managing Director of

Columbia Products Pty Ltd of Milperra. He chaired a group of Greiner's friends and associates, most of whom, like Greiner, were members of the Young Presidents Organisation. The Kaldor Committee delivered funds to Sturgess' Policy and Research Unit, and paid for polling and research assistance for shadow ministers, met Telecom, helicopter and charter charges, and made at least one payment to Kortlang as a salary supplement. In round figures it paid out $45,000 in cheques in the 1987 calendar year and another $16,000 in January-March 1988. Donors arrived when needed. The Melbourne-based "Dick" Pratt, with whom Greiner had some meetings, provided $25,000 on Christmas Eve 1986. The Lewis Land Corporation donated $10,000 to be used in the Gosford and Blue Mountains seats (both were won in 1988) or at Greiner's discretion, and an additional $10,000 for advertising and $15,000 to assist – again at Greiner's discretion – five or ten Liberal candidates.

Starr and the Strategy Committee accepted funds from Community Polling even though its very existence, and that of the Kaldor Committee, defied Liberal Party Holy Writ. Since 1945 the Organisation alone was supposed to raise and disburse funds.[29] But Greiner had no qualms about by-passing the "dysfunctional" Liberal Party. He had an election to win. Pickering recalled how Greiner had inherited nothing from the Liberal Party's "gene pool" in relation to finance, and had resisted when Pickering, on one occasion supported by Valder, tried to dissuade him from collecting money. Judging by a letter he wrote to the Organisation's office-bearers in December 1987, Starr was aware of an even more serious problem; Greiner was handing over receipts and assuring potential donors they were immune from disclosure when, under the *Electoral Funding Act*, they were not. Frost thought Nick was "naïve", and he had to intervene when Bill Roche of the skin-care company, Nutrimetics International (Australia), donated the largest single sum – $100,000 – on behalf of his company. Roche was horrified to learn that the money would have to be declared; his company did not authorise political donations. The Roche money appears on the official register in two tranches as a personal donation.[30]

## Nick Greiner and Wal Murray

Their improved showing in the 1984 election had emboldened some Liberals to challenge the Nationals for rural seats not currently held by the NP and in defiance of an agreement reached with the Nationals in 1982. At the same time, there were divisions between and within the two party organisations about amalgamation. Leon Punch spoke in favour of a merger at the NP's State Conference in June 1985 when announcing his resignation as Leader.[31] He believed circumstances had changed because of optional preferential voting, the continuing contraction of the rural population, and the financial disclosure laws. Greiner again floated the idea of amalgamation. David Brownhill, State President of the Nationals, was greeted with acclamation after saying a strong and independent NP was needed more than ever "to protect the interests of non-metropolitan people".[32] Despite clear NP opposition, a joint party committee was formed to consider mechanisms for working more closely together, including the possibility of a merger.

Wal Murray was subsequently elected to succeed Punch. At first sight, Murray and Greiner seemed an unlikely couple. Indeed, Greiner hoped that Ian Armstrong, the more liberal-minded, would win the leadership. Murray admired Winston Churchill and Henry VIII, partly because of their common "cylindrical shape". He did not share Greiner's taste for opera and theatre: he liked a good comedy, enjoyed films like *Crocodile Dundee*, *South Pacific* and *Bridge on the River Kwai*, while spurning murders and mysteries because he wanted to know the result from the start.[33] But a man who was more likely to call a spade "a bloody shovel", and whose word – once given – was unbreakable, proved to be a perfect match, after a few matters were sorted.

Murray declared there was no point discussing a merger because his State Conference had rejected it.[34] His worry was that Greiner, "a very strong character", was not "overly enamoured of the National Party" and inclined to issue instructions.[35] Opening the NP campaign for Punch's former seat of Gloucester in September 1985, the two men engaged in what a *Herald* journalist described as "a bloodletting ritual". Murray said that the NP, unlike the Liberals, was not answerable to big business and the corporate bureaucrats. Greiner branded the comment "stupid". Yet, because the ritual demanded that both leaders insist there was no split, Greiner described Murray's swipe as "understandable". It was "fair enough" for Murray to demonstrate that the National Party was independent of the Liberals.[36]

Unbeknownst to Greiner, the Liberal Party had supported an independent candidate in Gloucester against the NP's Wendy Machin. The Party had also decided to nominate for Labor's second most marginal seat of Northern Tablelands centred on the city of Armidale, and formerly a Country Party stronghold.[37] Greiner and Murray agreed to meet representatives of the two organisations on 18 December 1985. According to Liberal records, the meeting agreed to hold regular consultations and to conduct an analysis of three-cornered contests. When Greiner twice declared he was sceptical of such contests another Liberal sharply reminded him that the Coalition never won rural seats from Labor except in triangular contests. Bronwyn Bishop did not help by saying that Greiner and Brownhill had agreed that a Liberal candidate in Northern Tablelands would assist the Coalition. Brownhill objected to the airing of "an informal and private conversation". Murray was forthright. He unequivocally rejected any suggestion of the Liberals having communicated their intention to run.

Murray sent a one-line note to Greiner on 20 December, asking him to confirm in writing his repudiation of the January 1982 agreement. Greiner replied that the agreement was a matter for the two Organisations. He forwarded Murray's letter to Bishop and offered, though on leave until 6 January, to have a personal chat at Murray's convenience. Murray fired back a long letter accusing Greiner of condoning or committing several slights directed at himself or at the National Party. In view of Greiner's "dogmatic statements" at the meeting on 18 December, Murray thought Greiner needed only to confirm the views he had expressed; a written agreement should not be repudiated in conversation. Murray was also angry because Greiner was not immediately available and had not taken other opportunities to meet. He concluded by quoting Greiner's alleged comment, "it's finished", made when Murray said the NP was not beholden to big city interests. Assuming the comment referred to the Coalition, Murray said he had more reason than Greiner to say that.

Soon after Murray sent this letter the two men met and worked through the issues. "That blue", Murray said later, "was the only one we had in our time working together."[38] From this point Greiner, like Howard at the Federal level, argued in Liberal circles against taking on the National Party in its backyard. The critical moment came when the State Executive had to decide whether to endorse the locally-selected Liberal candidate to contest the by-election for Northern Tablelands on 23 May 1987. The seat had become vacant following the death of the sitting member. Greiner pre-empted the State Executive decision by announcing that the Liberals would not be contesting Northern Tablelands. He warned the Party it would be looking for a new State Parliamentary Leader if it endorsed the selected Liberal. The Executive voted 21-17 not to do so.[39]

Labor, meanwhile, selected the widow of the sitting member and Unsworth engaged in all-out pork-barrelling and appealed to local Liberals who had been "left in the lurch by the Sydney apparatus". Greiner attended Murray's campaign launch and accused Unsworth of undertaking "the most cynical political exercise" he could remember. He noted how at "the very first sign of pressure" Unsworth had abandoned his "back to basics" approach. In the event, all sides salvaged something from the result. The NP eventually won the seat with a small four per cent swing. Murray called it "a bloody good win" and Greiner thought the result vindicated the Liberals' decision not to stand. He promised to sit down with Murray and work out where it would be beneficial for both parties to stand candidates in a general election. Greiner did not mention that he was talking outside his formal responsibility. The important point was that, heading into 1988, the Coalition was secure.[40]

## Labor attacks

On 23 November 1983 Wran accused the White River Corporation of stripping assets, issuing loans when it was virtually bankrupt, and milking public funds. Supported by an audit report from a firm of chartered accountants, Greiner declared Wran's claims "a complete fabrication". His father said the Premier's stocks were so low he was now accusing without any basis "honest and reputable people" – himself and past and present co-directors – "to score doubtful political points".[41] One week after Wran's attack Richard Face, the future Minister for Gaming in the Carr Government, raised 61 questions on notice about the Greiner operations which expanded upon the Premier's allegations. He admitted receiving "expert assistance" in framing them.

The Corporate Affairs Commission (CAC) conducted an investigation over 18 months. It found that Nick Greiner and his father had committed a number of indiscretions and had failed "to act honestly and use reasonable diligence". But it did not recommend prosecution. Terry Sheahan, the Attorney-General, tabled the CAC report on 21 March 1985, declaring it evidence that the Leader of the Opposition, "who portrays himself as a paragon of virtue, is shifty". He was a tax avoider who wanted to be seen as a professional manager of a State with a $12bn budget. Sheahan failed to tell the Legislative Assembly of the Government's advice from Brian Toomey, QC, recommending against legal action. Sickened by Labor's attempts to fabricate a case against Greiner, a well-placed trade union official had passed on the details of Toomey's recommendations in secret meetings with Sturgess.[42] In the Assembly Greiner defended himself and his father against Labor's "political witch hunt". There was nothing in the CAC report – in the general or the particular, or in terms of the spirit or the letter of the law – to substantiate claims of dishonesty. Greiner also asked why the Toomey report had not been tabled. He knew the reason: "the advising does not suit the Government."[43]

Despite occasionally revisiting the subject, the Government's attempts to "expose" fraudulence or business incompetence simply petered out for want of a case. The point of attack switched in late 1985 to Greiner's "toleration" of a Nazi, anti-Semitic presence in the Liberal Party. On 30 October Frank Walker, the Minister for Housing, claimed that "Mr Urbanchich has taken over the Liberal Party and his forces now control the New South Wales branch [sic]". Given his background, Greiner "should be most concerned about the Nazis controlling the Liberal Party".[44] Greiner replied that the Right faction constituted just 20-25 per cent of the membership and that Urbanchich did not control all of it. Urbanchich hardly helped Greiner's cause by claiming his people could "make" some Liberal MPs and "break" those who were "bad" for the Party.[45]

Walker returned to his theme on 16 April 1986, drawing this time on evidence released by the US State Department, the British Foreign Office and ASIO. A long-worded motion referred to the actions of the Menzies Government in allowing war criminals to enter Australia, and censured the Liberal Party for allowing Nazis to reach positions of influence in their organisation and Greiner for his willingness to appear in public with Nazis and not publicly to condemn them. While identifying six of the alleged war criminals, Walker focussed on Urbanchich whom he described as "a leading member" of Rupnik's Government in Slovenia[46] and of the Domobranci or White Guard and who, as part of its "poisonous propaganda machine", was responsible for an "endless stream of rabid anti-Semitic speeches and writings". Excitedly brandishing documents which he said had been leaked to him by senior Liberals (they had been on the public record for some seven years), he seized on Greiner's earlier comment that the Right controlled between 20 and 25 per cent of the Liberal Party. Noting Bishop's recent victory in the elections for State President (he called her the "pro-Nazi candidate"), Walker said that 40 per cent was the more appropriate figure, and rounded on Greiner for his "role and culpability . . . in this sordid affair". Greiner should have used his "immense power" to expel Urbanchich, and should have

been "very angry" about having Nazis in the Liberal Party. His family
had direct knowledge of what happened to Jews in Hungary. Perhaps
Greiner, like John Howard, depended on the votes of the "Uglies"
to remain leader.[47]

Nick Greiner spoke immediately in reply.[48] Like Walker, he had
partisan points to make, especially about the role of the Chifley
Government, the tardiness of the Hawke Government in acting on
recent revelations and the difference in outlook between Walker and
some Federal ministers. Greiner then turned from the political to the
personal. Walker either did not know the truth or sought not to tell it:

> The truth is not simply that my family lived through the sort
> of crimes that the Minister was talking about. My family was
> subject to some of those crimes. My mother suffered directly and
> personally at the hands of the Nazis . . . This is real life for me.
> This is suffering and ignominy for members of my family. I do not
> stand behind anyone, and certainly not behind this Minister, in my
> hatred for what happened, and I expect the Minister not only to
> acknowledge that but to say so publicly.

As he spoke, Greiner had tears in his eyes and his voice faltered. The
"Bear Pit" was almost silent.

No one was better placed to say he was "sick to the stomach" at the
thought that either he or the Liberal Party gave succour to any Nazis or
to anyone with anti-Semitic views. He promised that his government
would act against racial hatred and sectarian bias. Every effort had been
made within the Liberal Party to find the truth about Urbanchich. Should
"adequate evidence" be found, action would be taken immediately. Proven
Nazis should be deported, despite concerns about what the Yugoslav
Government might do to them. He wanted to dismiss a "ridiculous
furphy". Urbanchich was no more representative of the conservative
wing of the Liberal Party than Bill Hartley of Victoria – "Baghdad Bill"
had been a persistent source of embarrassment to the Labor Party –
was representative of Labor's Left. Finally, Greiner accused Walker

of trivialising an issue important to the whole human race by drawing attention to a photograph of Greiner standing next to Urbanchich. It was "ridiculous" to suggest that a joint photograph implicated one individual with the views of another. In doing so, the minister had revealed his lack of care for Jewish sensibilities in order to score a political point.

Walker's efforts now looked very shabby. Hammering home his advantage, Greiner said he did not apologise for wanting to hunt Nazis to the grave. Justice had to be done. But it would not be done while Walker tried "to drag down the debate . . . from the levels of real human emotion and suffering . . . into the political gutter".[49]

## The final months of the 48th Parliament

After staging an impressive revival in the polls in the first half of 1987, Labor slipped badly in the second half of the year. Greiner and his front bench hurt the Government over populist issues ranging from hospital waiting lists, the unsightly and misplaced monorail and the (temporary) demise of the Darling Harbour project, to some worrying crime statistics and serious problems inside the State's jails. Stephen Loosley, Labor's General Secretary, acknowledged that the Government had taken a "mauling" in the last two or three months of 1987. It decided, therefore, against holding another parliamentary session, thus locking itself into a February/March election in 1988.[50]

On 25 November, the last sitting day of 1987, Frank Walker decided to tip another bucket over Nick Greiner. He had primed the media of his intentions to link him to the "extreme right wing faction of the Liberal Party". Walker moved a motion condemning the Leader of the Opposition for selecting Fontana Films to produce the Liberal Party's television campaign for the coming election. Walker referred to three individuals associated with Fontana Films who belonged to "a very disreputable group of extremists": Urbanchich; the "very sinister and dangerous" Ray Lord who owned Fontana Films; and Bedrich Kabriel who drove around in a huge Mercedes with tinted windows, wore dark glasses and was accompanied by a bodyguard. In the course of a 26-minute rant Walker threw in a new charge – the Leader of the Opposition had failed to pay for a pizza in Turramurra – and made the requisite reference to White River. But the main object was to challenge Greiner to dissociate himself from the "Uglies" or resign.

At the mention of Fontana Films, Collins spoke briefly to Greiner, left the Chamber to phone Greg Daniel, and returned bearing information he handed to his Leader. Greiner began his reply as if following a pre-planned course of disassociating himself from the Far Right. Then he delivered the mortal punch:

> on this very day . . . Fontana Films, this terrible company controlled by these terrible international gangsters with which no self-respecting person should have any connection at all, are shooting a random breath testing commercial . . . for the Government of New South Wales.

Greiner, his voice heavy with irony, listed other clients of Fontana Films which, like the Opposition, must be linked with Nazism and terrorism: the Bicentennial Authority, American Express, Leed Lemonade, Honda, Union Carbide and McDonalds. Reading out the names of advertising companies which used Fontana Films, he noted that Phillip Adams was the director of one of them. He must be "a terrible person" and "a strong Liberal supporter way to the right of the spectrum".

A number of ministers threw their heads back and stared at the ceiling and the Labor backbench "took on the appearance of stunned mullet". Rodney Cavalier, the Minister for Education, referred in his diary to the episode as an "unmitigated disaster"; the Coalition benches, previously apprehensive, were "baying in the way we did behind Neville, cheering and jeering at our monumental stupidity". The Government had contrived "to send our backbench out into the boondocks utterly depressed", and had "saved our very worst performance – our *very worst performance* – for the last day of Parliament before an election" [emphasis in the original].[51] Unsworth tried to save the day by announcing that the

Government had decided to sever all links with Fontana Films. Walker later acknowledged his research might have been defective, and withdrew his allegation about the pizza bill. Collins concluded that Greiner had achieved his "single best tactical victory" in Parliament and demonstrated to him "just what he and I could do when we worked closely together".[52]

The tactical victory was followed in the evening by what amounted to a free kick: Brereton resigned from Cabinet after Unsworth sought to demote him out of public sight. At the end of 1987 an election victory in the New Year, which Greiner and Sturgess had always believed they would achieve, looked even more certain.

## Endnotes

1   After Kara gave her father his first Kermit, Greiner quickly acquired several plastic frogs, drawings and mugs to play up the joke and deflect any belittling connotations. He removed them from his office early in 1986 to "de-Kermify myself": "the jovial days are over." *Bulletin,* 25 February 1986.

2   Interview: Pickering, 13 July 2011. Similar views of him in shadow cabinet were expressed by Yabsley, 29 November 2011, and Baird, 3 January 2012.

3   Interview: Carr, 30 January 2012.

4   For Greiner's speech, see *NSWPD,* Third Series, vol. 179, 10 May 1984, pp. 699-701. A number of Liberal frontbenchers also supported the second reading. Greiner did, however, side with a conservative majority to make it a crime to counsel a male under 18 years of age to engage in homosexual activity.

5   Sturgess thought that the metaphor did more harm than good, because it made the difficult task of communicating the benefits of good government seem easier than it was. Interview: Sturgess, 21 June 2011.

6   For Greiner's Liberal Party speeches in 1985, see his address to State Council in February, to the Australian Liberal Students Federation in May, and to the State Convention in August, in Sturgess, Greinerism.

7   "A Management Strategy for New South Wales", in Sturgess, Greinerism, pp. 97-103.

8   Liberal Party (Valder), Collins Papers, ML, MSS 7442/68.

[9]　Collins, *Bear Pit*, pp. 145-7. Booth, who won Wakehurst in 1984, had been a member of Senator Carrick's staff.

[10]　Interviews: Dowd, 20 January and Puplick, 30 March 2006.

[11]　Interview: Pickering 13 April 2004.

[12]　Interview: Greiner, 23 September 2005.

[13]　Interviews: Pickering, 13 April 2004 and 13 July 2011; O'Gorman, 3 May 2005; Greiner 2 November 2005; Photos, 21 April 2006. Personal communication: Mutch, 24 January 2012. If the final ticket lacked factional balance it did, with the inclusion of Helen Sham-Ho, broaden the ethnic composition.

[14]　Interviews: Pickering, 13 April 2004 and Greiner, 2 November 2005. Griffiths was later forced out of John Fahey's ministry and of the Liberal Party over claims of sexual harassment.

[15]　Minutes of State Council, 17 October 1987, LPA, ML, MSS 7205/5. Starr became very critical of Bishop as too interventionist and thought "the distinguishing feature of her presidency was the endemic factionalism which brought the party to its lowest point in history". Leser, *Bronwyn Bishop*, p. 78.

[16]　Interviews: Starr, 28 July 2004; Greiner, 23 September 2005 and 22 November 2011.

[17]　Stephen Loosley and Gary Sturgess in Public Policy Forum, *The Campaign Managers: The 1988 New South Wales State Election – by the people who ran it*, Australian Graduate School of Management, Sydney 1989, pp. 8-11.

[18]　Rodney Cavalier, "Barrie John Unsworth" in David Clune and Ken Turner (eds), *The Premiers of New South Wales*, vol. 2, 1901-2005, Federation Press, Leichhardt, 2006, p. 441.

[19]　Peter Collins, *Bear Pit*, p. 148 wrote of "the urbane and well-travelled" Kortlang that his "single best career move" was probably not to win Ryde.

[20]　Interview: Kortlang, 12 July 2011.

[21]　Public Policy Forum, *Campaign Managers*, p. 12.

[22]　John Carrick regarded the subsequent vote in Bass Hill and Rockdale as a triumph for a "grass-roots campaign" which he associated with the Party Organisation. Women's Council, LPA, ML, MSS 7205/40.

[23]　*Sun-Herald*, 3 August; *SMH*, 4-6 August 1986.

[24]　*DT*, 14 March 1987; *Australian*, 11 February 1988.

[25]　Interviews: Kortlang, 12 July and Pickering, 13 July 2011; Campaign '88, Collins Papers, ML, MSS 7244/8.

[26]　For an account of the rehearsal, see Public Policy Forum, *Campaign Managers*, pp. 18-21.

[27] Treasurer's Report, 5 February 1988, Finance Committee January 1988-June 1989, LPA, ML, MSS 7205/106.

[28] Interviews: Starr, 28 July 2004 and 26 March 2006.

[29] For a copy of the code, see LPA, ML, MSS 7205/59.

[30] The above three paragraphs draw on interviews: Pickering, 13 July; Frost, 14 July and Greiner 22 November 2011; Starr to Ron James, 16 December 1987, Office Bearers Committee, LPA, ML, MSS 7205/40; Research Material, Various Matters; Election Funding; 500 Club; Kaldor Committee; Liberal Party – including Finance; K. McCann file, Greiner Papers.

[31] *SMH*, 15 June 1985.

[32] *SMH*, 16 June 1985.

[33] *The Leader*, Vol. 7, no. 3, 1988.

[34] *SMH*, 18 June 1985.

[35] Davey, *Nationals*, p. 281.

[36] *SMH*, 18 Sep. 1985.

[37] For exchanges over Northern Tablelands, see Coalition Relations Agreement, 1983-1989, LPA, ML, MSS 7205/186.

[38] Davey, *Nationals*, p. 281.

[39] Information provided by Joe Hockey, 29 October 2012.

[40] For material on the by-election and comments on the result, see *Australian*, 5 and 25 May and *SMH*, 4, 11, 12, 25 May 1987.

[41] For the audited statement clearing Greiner and the Corporation of any wrongdoing, see *SMH*, 25 November 1983.

[42] Interview: Sturgess, 11 July 2011.

[43] *NSWPD*, Third Series vol. 184, pp. 4897-9; 4902; 4909-12. Although the Government refused to reveal the total cost, it later admitted that two CAC investigators devoted 60 man days to the operation between December 1983 and July 1984 and that the Government had also sought, and paid for, advice from Senior Counsel. See also Sheahan's reply to Dowd's question on notice 1 Oct. 1985, *ibid.*, vol. 186, pp. 7443-4.

[44] *Ibid.*, vol. 187, pp. 8952-6.

[45] *SMH*, 12 November 1985.

[46] The British Government delivered General Rupnik to the Yugoslav authorities after the War. They executed him as a Nazi collaborator.

[47] *NSWPD*, Third Series, vol. 190, pp. 1963-81.

48  *Ibid.*, pp. 1982-9.

49  For a favourable assessment of Greiner's speech, see Dennis Shanahan in *SMH*, 17 April 1986.

50  Public Policy Forum, *Campaign Managers*, p. 25.

51  Quoted in Clune and Griffith, *Decision and Deliberation*, pp. 493-4.

52  Collins, *Bear Pit*, p. 152.

# 9

# "A Real Change for the Better"

Some members of Nick Greiner's staff were concerned about Barrie Unsworth occupying the centre stage during the Bicentennial celebrations. Assuming they were a success, the Premier was bound to benefit politically. At best, the Leader of the Opposition would be an official guest for the formal occasions but placed at stage right. Kortlang became nervous when Greiner was unnoticed by the public on Australia Day.[1] On another important occasion he was not even meant to be there. A British official discovered that the State Government had not included the Greiners on its list of proposed invitees to see Prince Charles hand over Britain's Bicentennial gift on 25 January. By that time Greiner probably had had enough of the festivities. He wrote "Whatever" in his appointment diary next to the message referring to his apparent exclusion. It appears, however, that British officials contacted some counterparts in the Federal Government, and the Greiners were duly added to the list. After all the "fuss", Janet Mahon asked if he would accept. He wrote "OK" next to her message.[2]

January was a hectic month. In between attending Bicentennial openings, receptions, lunches and dinners, the Greiners went to the opening performance of *Carmen* at the Opera House, and Greiner attended – as previously discussed – the Young Liberals National Convention, as well as the World Jamboree luncheon and the official opening of the Sydney Football Stadium and of the National Convention. His first direct "political" acts involved some door knocking on 5 and 7 January in Labor seats in the inner Western Suburbs, followed a few days later by

169

more door knocking in Queanbeyan and Georges River. On 18 January Greiner had a quick breakfast meeting with John Elliott, the Liberal Party's Federal President, and Tony Eggleton, the Federal Director, before campaigning in the Blue Mountains and the seat of Kogarah. Next day he was in Wollongong for a shadow cabinet meeting where he also met members of five local councils in the region. Within a few days he was back in Wollongong to meet Prince Charles and Princess Diana, returning to Sydney to watch the mostly dreary and drawn Bicentennial Test against a depleted English team at the Sydney Cricket Ground. By now there were daily campaign meetings at Riley Street, starting at 8.30 in the morning.

## Towards an election

Once again, Greiner appeared to be a lucky general. At the end of January Bob Carr, the Minister for the Environment, alleged that the wood-chipping company, Harris-Daishowa, had made a $20,000 donation to the Coalition, thereby raising questions about the Coalition's environmental credentials. One day later it emerged that the same company had made a $10,000 donation to the Labor Party for the 1987 Federal election campaign. Carr's gaffe, similar in character to Frank Walker's over Fontana Films, was the first of several self-inflicted wounds which hurt the Labor Party before the election date was even announced. It transpired that Stephen Loosley had placed the Harris-Daishowa donation in the Party's administrative fund without disclosing it publicly. Loosley, Labor's overall campaign manager, had to remove his name from the Party's advertising. The Hawke Government did not help by advertising the prospect of timed telephone calls – which would have hurt Labor's own constituency – on the eve of a by-election for the "safe" Federal Labor seat of Adelaide. On 6 February the Coalition won Adelaide on the back of an 8.5 per cent swing. Then Mick Young, a Hawke Government minister and Labor's Federal President, suddenly resigned two days after the by-election, and accepted a well-paid consultancy with

Qantas. Almost overnight it had become even easier for Nick Greiner to claim that Labor was "out of touch" with its own "heartland" and was simply looking after its mates, while the misplacement of the Harris-Daishowa funds kept the corruption issue in the headlines.

Greiner had to make quick decisions, of which the most important related to guns. Following the "Father's Day Massacre" at Milperra in September 1984 the Wran Government had amended the *Firearms and Dangerous Weapons Act* to require all shooters to have a licence. The amendment did not come into force because the police computer system was not fully operative. In December 1987 Unsworth joined the Prime Minister and the other Premiers at a gun summit to discuss ownership and use. He subsequently gazetted new regulations under the existing legislation to come into force on 1 January 1988. These regulations banned possession of self-loading rifles and introduced a two-month amnesty to allow shooters to hand in these weapons and receive compensation. In addition, licences for other firearms – which were to be stored in a locked cupboard – would be granted only if the owners belonged to a sporting club approved by the Police Commissioner, or needed weapons to earn a living or to shoot vermin. Further regulations, gazetted on 19 February, applied to the purchase and registration of firearms.

Greiner supported the restrictions. So did Kortlang. Hooper and Sturgess, on the other hand, had both grown up in the country and understood the deep resentment about Unsworth's gun laws, and knew they would be "a big winner". Pickering agreed with them. He had been attending gun lobby meetings and, finding himself in front of audiences of 2-3,000 protestors, visualised up to a dozen seats being affected. When Unsworth made his move on 1 January Pickering told Greiner, "we've just won the bloody election". As Pickering recalled their conversation, Greiner said the Coalition could not oppose Unsworth on this issue. Hooper intervened, and Greiner eventually agreed to a change of policy on the possession of semi-automatic rifles on condition that the word "gun" was not mentioned in the city. Greiner agreed to meet the Firearms Advisory Council and the Sporting Shooters' Association on 20 January in the expectation that these two bodies would provide valuable assistance during the campaign.

Pickering and Wal Murray shouldered responsibility for presenting the case in the country against Unsworth's gun laws. Voters in the city, who invoked horror stories about mass shootings, were told that users and not weapons were the problem. The Coalition, Greiner promised, would apply the strictest standards in granting licences to use firearms. Its policy could also be justified on the principle of preserving private ownership and the rights of individuals. One man, who felt strongly about his rights, was so important that a busy schedule was amended to accommodate him. Kerry Packer bluntly told Greiner on 11 February he must have the right to defend himself. So, for the first and only time during the election period, Greiner found himself committed to a position he did not want to take. It was not, however, exclusively or even primarily a matter of winning rural seats. After all, he knew of city seats which could be threatened if he supported a less restrictive policy. Greiner accepted that the National Party would not budge on the question of shooters retaining semi-automatic weapons. His overriding consideration was to keep the Coalition together. Unsworth must not be allowed to use the gun laws as a "wedge" issue to divide the Coalition.[3]

Other decisions were easier to make. Greiner turned up when Bronwyn Bishop insisted he attend a reception for businessmen in her office. Other politically sensitive meetings were best avoided. Greiner put off meeting the new Managing Director of Phillip Morris on 1 February – "Sorry – after election". But he found time on that day to meet the more acceptable Brian Loton, the Managing Director of BHP. Greiner also made time available to establish a presence in traditionally non-Liberal areas. Greiner liked the idea of the Liberal Party being "relevant" in Labor strongholds and placing Labor under pressure in its safest seats. So it was "sensible" and "legitimate" to support centre or right-of-centre Independents in Labor-held seats where their preferences could boost the Liberal vote or where an Independent might take a Labor seat as happened in the case of Swansea. In response to a request from John Hannaford, MLC, Greiner agreed to back the Independent in Wentworthville who was supported by the Right-to-Life movement and who, with the Liberal candidate, an Australian Democrat and another Independent forced Labor's candidate to preferences.[4] The decision to back Independents was easy to take and cost a mere few thousand dollars.

On Sunday 21 February, just as Labor's standing in the polls had plummeted, Unsworth called the election for 19 March. The most recent Morgan Poll placed the Government eight points behind the Coalition on a two-party preferred basis. A Newspoll published on 23 February had Labor trailing the Coalition by 15 percentage points in primary support.[5] The Bicentennial had not delivered. Instead, recent events – the wood chip donation embarrassment, Young's resignation, the new gun laws – had evidently registered. When these setbacks were added to the Government's 12-year term in office, Laurie Brereton's decisions as Minister for Public Works in inner urban Sydney, and the scandals of the past, it is not surprising that Labor had slipped well behind the Coalition. On 21 February the Coalition looked to be well placed to win a majority in the enlarged Legislative Assembly of 109 members.

Claiming underdog status, Unsworth referred in his election announcement to Labor's central theme for the campaign: "a fair go for all". He said the shift from Neville Wran's "lifestyle politics" to "back to basics" would ensure social justice and equity in NSW. Greiner was quick to respond: Labor's slogans represented "the most clear-cut admission of failure that there has ever been by any Government, particularly one that has been in power for 12 years". He had a point: if there was now to be a "fair go" for the poor, the aged, the sick, the homeless, the migrants and ordinary families, where had NSW been for more than a decade? Greiner said the people of NSW now had the opportunity to vote for "a change for the better in the performance and priorities of the Government", for the removal of an "arrogant, sleazy and corrupt government", and for a program "dedicated to open government, integrity and giving power back to the people". Unsworth tried to shift the attention. The Opposition, he said, was "offering a change for the worse", being committed to the philosophy of user-pays rather than to one based on community needs. But, as the *Sydney Morning Herald* observed, the problem for a 12-year old government was that voters "will be inclined to give the Opposition the benefit of the doubt".[6]

## The first two weeks

The Coalition's approach to the campaign looked highly professional, even though it was hardly a unified effort. The Greiners moved into the Regent Hotel in the city which became the Leader's campaign headquarters. The inner circle, consisting of Greiner, his office advisers and the polling and advertising representatives met each day at 6.00 am. The Secretariat was relegated to the "B-Team" which attended the campaign meetings at 6.20 am after the "A-Team" had already made the tactical decisions for the day. According to Kortlang, "it was important that we kept the same level of advice, and the same type of people giving him advice". Significantly, only two of the 18 closest advisers and support staff were members of the Liberal Party. Greiner, Kortlang said, had "chosen poker rather than canasta players – hard heads" who would leave if Greiner lost: "We're all Greiner people".[7]

The contempt for Graeme Starr and the Secretariat was never disguised. When the State Director had said he was writing a history of the campaign, Kortlang shot back: "We're down here making it".[8] Effectively, the Regent Hotel campaign was a replay, albeit on a more advanced level, of Askin's 1973 election strategy. The then Premier – admittedly with the assistance of the Party's General Secretary (Jim Carlton) – ran his own, separate campaign and left it to the Organisation to look after the nuts and bolts. In 1988 the State Director could not even be trusted with the practicalities. Andrew Kaldor sat in an office in Parliament House driving a marginal seats campaign on behalf of the "A-Team". In common with Greiner and his personal staff, Kaldor thought Riley Street was "hopeless".[9]

The Regent Hotel campaign proceeded with military precision. Every day was planned well in advance, including which meals to eat. Kortlang's influence was everywhere; 8 March, for example, was designated "D-Day minus 11". Graeme Starr might have found the walkie-talkie messages and conversations during car rides at once amusing and over-the-top,[10] and there may have been many slip-ups along the way. Nevertheless, the media received the impression of a well-oiled machine capable of outsmarting Sussex Street. Robert Haupt of the *SMH* noted how Unsworth once spent a tiring day in the air flying to Albury in a Fokker Friendship for which he achieved a 30-second slot on local television. Sussex Street had rejected an invitation to speak to Derryn Hinch because time was too short to spend some of it talking to Victorian television. Greiner and his team jumped at the opportunity, having grasped the point that, in the Riverina, the border with Victoria was really the Murrumbidgee rather than the Murray. As a result, the Leader of the Opposition was seen on television in Albury for four minutes and did not have to leave Sydney.[11]

According to Kortlang, "we made a conscious decision to run Greiner's campaign on a Presidential basis". Nick Greiner was to look like a Premier. They knew they had someone who was intrinsically more publicly attractive than Unsworth. Yet something had to be done about his dress sense; to get rid of the shiny suits, introduce him to wool and ban him from casual clothes and especially his choice of shirts.[12] He was to travel in style, and the "A-Team" was delighted when the cardigan-wearing Unsworth chose to be "a Man of the People" by using a minibus. Their research revealed a perception that Unsworth "wasn't statesmanlike" or would be straight back into his limousine should he be re-elected.[13] Either way, Unsworth, from Greiner's perspective, looked desperate and even less like the Premier of the Premier State.

Unsworth sensibly rejected Greiner's call for a televised debate. He described the challenge as "a red herring" and a "gimmick" to elevate

Greiner "above his station". The Premier may have recalled how Peacock outshone Hawke in a televised debate in 1984, and decided that a haughty dismissal would cover his retreat from a verbal stoush he would probably lose. Greiner was not at all concerned by Unsworth's response. He expected it, and would do the same to Bob Carr in 1991. Greiner's principal means of capturing the early attention was to announce policies on virtually every day for the first two weeks. He began on 22 February with a package of tougher law-and-order policies. They included longer prison sentences for serious crimes and automatic life imprisonment (effectively, 20 years) for murder; a review of maximum sentences to ensure they reflected community views of particular crimes; and truth in sentencing to be achieved in part by requiring the non-parole period to be 75 per cent of the original sentence. Although Greiner ruled out reintroduction of the death penalty, even if the community wanted it, he described Labor's stand on crime as "soft, soft, soft".[14] In the following days, and accompanied by the relevant shadow ministers, Greiner announced policies relating to health, education, corrective services, the formation of the Independent Commission Against Corruption (ICAC), organised crime, and compensation for victims of crime.

Labor's strategy was to lie low in this period. Sussex Street reasoned on the basis of its research that the more Greiner became visible, the further his personal rating would fall.[15] Having ceded the campaign initiative, the Government limited itself to criticising Coalition policies. Unsworth described the ICAC proposal as "another Mickey Mouse idea from Mr Greiner", a proposition which lost impact when the Police Commissioner appeared to endorse the notion of a permanent anti-corruption commission. Reduced to playing catch-up on the issue, Labor promised in its first policy announcement of the campaign, made as late as 2 March, to establish a State Crime Commission modelled on the Commonwealth's National Crime Authority to deal specifically with organised crime. Unsworth had now decided that Greiner's "Mickey Mouse idea" would become "the greatest travesty of civil rights perpetrated anywhere in the western world".[16]

Labor's strategy required Greiner and his inexperienced colleagues to make serious gaffes in the first fortnight. Greiner appeared to oblige at the start of the campaign. Although he made much of allowing students to enrol at government schools outside their area, he did not propose extending the free bus pass system to them, yet retained it for private school students. Attacked on talkback radio and in press interviews, Greiner conceded the arrangement might be unfair.[17] But the issue simply disappeared. Ted Pickering, the Shadow Minister for Police, appeared to be more accident-prone. Within the space of a few days early in the campaign, he managed to embarrass himself, Greiner and the Liberal Party on four separate occasions, most dramatically by contradicting Wal Murray and creating confusion over the Coalition's policies on the gun laws. Touchingly, Pickering asked the *SMH* on 3 March to make allowances for his inexperience. The fourth estate duly reported and repeated this story, found Pickering to be out of his depth in the "hurly-burly" of politics, and decided that his career was almost finished. Either the Group had been wholly successful in staying out of the limelight or journalists had failed to recognise Pickering's indispensable role in the Greiner team. Describing himself as "a sensible, understanding man", and one "who looked at results over time", Greiner declared Pickering's performance to be "absolutely all right" and confirmed he would be Minister for Police in his government. Pickering himself thought Greiner backed him "1,000 per cent".[18] In any case, as Shane Easson, Unsworth's Executive Officer, said later, the mistakes made "didn't really matter because the person (Greiner) we needed to make a mistake never made one during the entire election campaign".[19]

Greiner acted quickly to dispose of one potential embarrassment. Arthur Incekara was a prominent figure in the Sydney Turkish community and the founding vice-chairman of the Ethnic Communities Council. Selected by the Liberal Party to contest the safe Labor seat of Auburn, he was described in the Party's official biography as a highly qualified economist who held a master's degree in economics and political science from the London School of Economics. Auburn's local newspaper published a photograph of him standing alongside Greiner and headed, "Economist as Candidate". Incekara was forced to withdraw in the week after Unsworth announced the election date. He admitted never having attended the LSE, and never having graduated from any tertiary institution. Incekara's highest formal qualification was the equivalent of the leaving certificate from a Turkish high school. Describing himself as a "battler" and "one of the people", Incekara said he was "man" enough to admit what he called an "error". Greiner was not at all sympathetic. He quickly defused the issue by disowning Incekara for lacking the integrity expected of a parliamentary candidate and said Incekara had been dealt with "appropriately" for misleading the Party.[20]

The Government's strategy for the first two weeks allowed the Coalition to take charge of the campaign. An early Labor commercial, aired on the weekend after the election announcement, actually forced its own side on the defensive. In 1987 Labor had run advertisements for the Banks and Heathcote by-elections depicting Greiner as Kermit the Frog. John Singleton, Labor's advertising agent and for whom refinement was not a professional necessity, now depicted Greiner as an octopus, a monster from the deep extending its tentacles to gobble up the people of NSW, the victims of the user-pays system. First shown on prime time television on 28 February, accompanied by scary noises and a chilling voice over, the advertisement provoked widespread adverse comment. The creative director of Saatchi & Saatchi thought it "(c)rude, cheap and nasty". Unsworth, who had apparently expressed reservations about the commercial, said Singleton had done no more than equal what the Liberals were in the habit of doing. Frank Walker pretended to discover "gentle symbolism" in an advertisement meant to shock and terrify. Nick Greiner likened the octopus image to "the sort of thing that a Rugby League team does when it is 20 points down with five minutes to go".[21] Labor, he said, must be absolutely desperate. Cavalier later confirmed this view. Describing the television commercial as "unprecedented bile", he thought the act of screening it "meant that the inner group reckoned there was nothing more to be lost".[22] The advertisement lasted only a few days. Sussex Street denied it had been "withdrawn" and said it was time to move on to other Singleton creations. The Greiners ordered a meal of octopus at a restaurant, confident that the advertisement had been counter-productive.

They were soon given another cause for celebration although, initially, they were angry. On 9 March, the day set down for Unsworth's policy speech, the Canberra-based journalist, Alan Ramsey, had a story on the front page of the *Sydney Morning Herald*. He quoted Rod Cameron, the Labor Party pollster, who claimed his research showed how married women with children in marginal Sydney seats did not like Kathryn Greiner. She was "too pushy", "too outspoken" and "above us", and should not have left her children to join her husband in the Regent Hotel. According to Cameron, "Mrs Greiner" was "a plus for the Government among women voters". Margaret Gibbs, a director of Cameron's company, ANOP, said Kathryn Greiner was seen as "overstepping the mark as a politician's wife". Gibbs compared her unfavourably with Tammy Fraser, Hazel Hawke and Jill Wran who all played the perfect supportive roles. Gibbs brought up the drink-driving incident, reporting how "They" remembered it, and how "They" thought she was not treated as "an ordinary person". As for Barrie Unsworth's wife, Pauline, ANOP found that "They" did not know much about her but thought she was "nice", "the backbone of the family".[23]

The Greiners were at a motel in Young when they learnt of the *Herald* story. The husband was incandescent. He called it "mongrel politics", the equivalent of "wife-beating", and paced about using what Kathryn called "colourful language". Outraged because of the attack – as he saw it – on Kathryn, and frustrated because he could not retaliate, he allowed himself one savage (and insensitive) comment: "I don't think Mr Unsworth would want us to move into a debate on parenting skills."[24] As his rage subsided, he commented that the polling would backfire on a Labor Party trailing the Opposition by 11 points in the most recent Morgan Gallup Poll. It was Kathryn, however, who went onto the front foot. John Stirton said later she "handled it brilliantly". Greiner told Sturgess he wished he could be half as confident in the capacity of the shadow cabinet to handle an issue. Kathryn did a number of interviews, wrote a column for the *Daily Telegraph*, and captivated a Liberal Party women's lunch at the Regent Hotel on 10 March. She pointed out how the reported research was unfair as well as hurtful because the parents had talked over the Regent Hotel arrangement with the children in January and they had accepted the decision. Besides, Justin and Kara spent at least one night a week in the hotel while the family stayed together at the weekends.

Senator Janine Haines, the Federal Leader of the Australian Democrats, said she was "appalled" by the survey and believed Labor had panicked because of Mrs Greiner's success as a campaigner. Haines also implied that, by "asking the right questions", ANOP may have secured the results it wanted. The Liberal Party pollster, Ron Klein of Brian Sweeney and Associates, confirmed Haines' suspicion about answer-driven findings. He found no adverse reaction to Kathryn Greiner – "not a cracker" – in the qualitative research conducted in several marginal Sydney seats. Pauline Unsworth absolved her husband who, she said, knew nothing about the poll. She was sorry for the attack and declared she would never make personal remarks about Mrs Greiner. Rod Cameron told the ABC's radio program, *AM*, he was merely doing his job, and the polling was "undoubtedly a plus" for Labor. Neville Wran disagreed. He thought one of Unsworth's handlers needed "a kick up the arse". John Della Bosca, the Assistant Secretary of Labor's NSW Branch, said later that the incident cost Labor "buckets full of votes" while giving "the final impression of panic on our side of the fence". Ironically, Sussex Street had not officially commissioned the research or approved its publication. The Liberal Party capped a good week with a full-page advertisement in the *Sun-Herald* showing the four Greiners as one close and happy family.

## Policies

Nick Greiner delivered his policy speech on Sunday 6 March at the Rockdale Town Hall in the heart of Barrie Unsworth's electorate. The choice of venue was not a planned intrusion into enemy territory. The original bookings were for Hurstville or Parramatta. Both fell through because the Liberal Party, unsure of the election date, could not give firm commitments. The Opera House and Centrepoint had been considered and rejected; Sturgess and others wanted "a more Western Suburbs image". It transpired that Rockdale was the only suitable venue available.[25]

Kara, Justin, Kathryn and the Greiner parents sat prominently in the front row in the Rockdale Town Hall. It was in most respects a well-staged and tightly-managed affair: in the words of one observer, "a presidential spectacular, at once thrilling and tacky, arousing and awful".[26] The live rock music might have contrasted sharply with the Chopin on offer when Hawke launched Federal Labor's campaign at the Opera House in 1987 but there was something of the modern Labor Party about the theatricals. Yet Labor would never have made the mistake of allowing its political opponents to infiltrate such an occasion. Greiner's speech was occasionally drowned out by Labor supporters inside the Hall. Attempts to eject them by men wearing T-shirts bearing the words "Nick Greiner's Young Liberals Hit Squad" led to Catherine Easson attending Casualty at St George Hospital. She was shaken though not otherwise injured. Unsworth raised the spectre of Hitler's Brown Shirts and spoke of neo-Nazis in the Liberal ranks. Greiner preferred to call the Young Liberal activists "over-enthusiastic". He might well have asked why the wife of Unsworth's Executive Officer was there in the first place.

Written largely by Gary Sturgess, Greiner's speech stands out for something the State Liberal Party had lacked for more than a decade: a real sense of purpose. There was a "mix of economic reform, anti-corruption and populism"[27] which gave Liberals a cause to believe in and not just something to oppose. And if the objectives were a call to arms and for reform, there was no better way to begin than by adapting Gough Whitlam of 1972 (and his borrowing from John Curtin of 1943): "Men and Women of New South Wales, We Stand at a Cross Roads. We Stand Facing a Signpost. One Road Leads to the Future. One to the Past." There was even a reference to "It's Time for a Change", although the Party's slogan for the election – "A Real Change for the Better" – more accurately reflected the intention. And Greiner could point out how one of Labor's slogans – "Back to Basics" – amounted to an admission of failure. After twelve years in government, Labor was "offering to deliver us out of the hands of the Labor Party!".

The speech listed Labor's alleged failures: the rise in crime, the soft penalties, the traffic jams, the crowded hospital waiting lists, the decline in education standards, the corruption. Greiner promised to restore the authority of the family, the police and the courts, to attack corruption through the Independent Commission, and to establish a comprehensive code of ethics for ministers. The Coalition would ensure excellence in the education system through basic tests in reading and writing, the restoration of the Year 10 School Certificate, the inclusion of a scaled aggregate mark on the Higher School Certificate, and the establishment of new selective high schools. It would take power from Labor's machine and return it to the people through freedom of information, an administrative appeals tribunal, strengthened powers for the Ombudsman, greater public scrutiny, and better and more efficient management of the State. While Labor talked about compassion, Greiner promised to ensure that government services reached those who were in need: "There is no inconsistency between better management of the State's services and a better deal for the disadvantaged." One of his critical themes was to offer "better" not "bigger" government, and "quality" rather than "quantity" government, with a stress on improving hospitals, education and housing, on uplifting the conditions of the homeless and of Aboriginals, and on dealing with crime. In sum, there were four planks: the restoration of the basic institutions; greater access by the people to their government; better management of the public sector; and a better deal for the disadvantaged.

Unsworth called Greiner's speech "one of the most pathetic documents I have ever read". Greiner had just "regurgitated" his speeches of the previous two or three years and rehashed old policies. It is not clear whether he was merely being mischievous, or had simply missed the point. Greiner would enter government with a planned reform program and a clear agenda. There were no half-prepared ideas. Greiner's policy speech brought together four years of preparation and planning. Even so, the stress was on themes rather than details. The basic requirement was to win a mandate for reform, not to invite a discussion about its cost.

Unsworth delivered Labor's policy speech in the Bankstown Town Hall on 9 March, ten days before the election. His advisers, including two on loan from the Hawke camp, had pressed the case for a new start and for handouts. So, in response to the Greiner strategy of highlighting "twelve years of Labor rule", the Premier asked voters to elect a "new Unsworth Government" and to give it a "mandate for change". In effect, the Premier dumped a campaign based on providing sound financial management in favour of the "fair go" approach. His election promises, costing at least $260m, were designed to appeal to Labor's traditional heartland. Principally, Unsworth promised a cut in weekly travel fares, a reduction in motor registration fees, the abolition of stamp duty for first-home buyers on houses costing up to $105,000, and educational supplements for school-age children. Greiner described the proposed handouts as a bribe, and said the Government was "simply seeking to throw money at social problems". Just as the voters had not warmed to Howard's proposed tax cuts in 1987, the NSW electorate would reject Unsworth's "far more irresponsible promises". The Premier called it a well thought-out and thoroughly-costed social justice package. Greiner said that a re-elected Labor Government would have to pay for the handouts by tax increases, or heavier borrowings, or reduced capital works. Alternatively, facing reduced funding from the Commonwealth, Unsworth would have to break his promises.

Greiner was in an unusual position for a Leader of the Opposition. Not only had the Government declared itself to be the "underdog"; by promising so much it left itself open to the question usually directed at Oppositions – "where is the money coming from?". Greiner could legitimately portray the Government as a collection of desperate men and himself, by contrast, as measured and responsible. He could also invoke an old favourite of politicians trying to appeal to "ordinary" men and women: the limits of the household budget. Australians knew "if you go to the larder and the larder is bare, you don't prepare a feast".[28]

## The campaign continued

A striking feature of the campaign was that Greiner and Murray rarely had contact with each other. The two leadership groups had marked their territory before the election was called, sorted out their joint approaches to the seven three-cornered contests,[29] worked out itineraries to avoid clashes, and ensured that the "minders" restrained any agitated supporters with different ideas about who constituted the real enemy. As an extension of Greiner's pact with Murray over Northern Tablelands, the Liberal Party remained locked out of the entire North Coast and the North-West, allowing the National Party Leader to concentrate on the southern half of the State. The Nationals adopted more conservative positions on gun laws, logging and land rights, but never threatened the united front. Sturgess noted how, on land rights policy, Greiner was "selling it from a warm perspective and Wal was delivering it with more of the traditional country flair" (that is, the Nationals wanted to scrap Indigenous title). Greiner never regretted the differences in delivery style because he could see no substantial point of difference. Greiner's concession over Northern Tablelands had secured its reward; the Nationals had, in Kortlang's words, "sacrificed a lot" for the unity theme.[30]

Throughout the campaign the Coalition used a number of issues – notably, health, law and order, logging and guns – to detach groups from Labor's support base.[31] Greiner occupied the centre stage in pursuing the law and order issue. Collins led a sustained and clever attack on the "crisis" in the health system. Pickering and the National Party assaulted Labor over guns and logging. Inevitably, the deliberate "presidential" approach to campaigning meant most shadow ministers were rarely sighted. Inevitably, too, there were serious journalistic pieces discovering that the shadows were invisible, or using their absence to ponder what kind of government would take office should Greiner succeed (and concluding it would probably be lacking in talent). The "presidential" approach had one other implication. Greiner stayed out of the "ruck". There was a deliberate attempt to keep him one step removed from becoming "negative", let alone getting dirty. Not that this campaign entered too many depths. The "octopus" advertisement was as low as it got.

Speaking at the National Press Club three days before the poll, Neville Wran predicted that Unsworth would defeat "that other little bastard" (presumably John Howard was "the other"; as for "little", Greiner stood 5"10" tall in the old measurements).[32] Wran was evidently influenced by polling during the previous fortnight which showed Labor clawing back votes lost before and after Unsworth called the election. As the campaign wore on, some in the media thought Greiner appeared tired and red-eyed, and was more inclined to become snappier at public appearances and in handling journalists.[33] But he showed no signs of fatigue on the Friday before the poll as he walked through the crowd at a lunch-time rally in Australia Square. He knew he was going to win.[34]

## Victory

On election night the Greiners watched the early results at their Wahroonga home. Greiner was reluctant to express too much of the internal elation, but he did allow one break-out. He was almost ecstatic about the early results for Georges River: "If there was one seat I dearly wanted the Liberal Party to win it was Frank Walker's – my opinion of him is abysmally low." When a bored Kara turned the television channel to the *Golden Girls,* her father quietly insisted on returning to the election results. While supporters in the room ate ham and pineapple pizza, and Kathryn snatched a can of Mr Sheen away from a roaming television camera, Greiner mused about the future: "We're going to play it slow, calm and sensible." There would be no rush to change things overnight in the manner of the two-man ministry of Gough Whitlam and Lance Barnard in December 1972. When Fred Nile came on television to announce that his Call to Australia would fight to ban the Gay Mardi Gras, Greiner remarked that outlawing it "will be very low on my list of priorities". He claimed victory when he arrived at the Tally Room where he briefly encountered an incoherent John Singleton of the Octopus advertisement who struggled to make himself understood. From there he went to the Inter-Continental Hotel where the Liberals held their celebration party.[35]

What the *Sydney Morning Herald* had dubbed "The Tightrope Election" turned out to be a landslide. Labor suffered a swing of 8.4 per cent on a two-party preferred basis and endured a greater disaster than its defeat in 1932.[36] Twenty-one notionally Labor seats were lost (three of them to Independents); seven ministers (including Cavalier and Walker) were defeated. From a Liberal perspective, there were some important breakthroughs: the Party had gained seats in Sydney's west and south, established a foothold in the Hunter Valley by winning Cessnock, took Labor's remaining two seats in Sydney north of the Parramatta River, and now held six seats in the country and two on the Central Coast. With the count complete, the Liberals had 39 seats, the National Party 20, Labor 43 and the Independents seven.

Yet not everything went the Liberal Party's way. Its primary vote, which had lifted from 32.2 per cent in 1984 to 35.8 per cent in 1988, was lower than the vote received in 1976 when Wran ousted Sir Eric Willis. Returning Bass Hill to Labor was hardly a serious blow but it did matter that Michael Yabsley lost Bligh to an Independent, Clover Moore, and that the Independent Ted Mack retained North Shore. The Liberals also failed to take several winnable seats. Finally, despite having a majority of nine over Labor and the Independents in the Assembly, the Coalition held just 19 of the 45 seats in the Council. Even with the support of Fred Nile's three-member Call to Australia, Greiner required the vote of one of the two Australian Democrats to pass any controversial legislation.

Nick Greiner did not need to give the downside his attention on election night. Interviewed when he remained uncertain of the extent of the victory, he thanked the people of New South Wales for showing confidence in himself and his colleagues. "That is a confidence that we will most certainly repay over the next four, eight or more years." He was well aware of what had been necessary to achieve such a result. "I would like to thank all the people who have worked so hard to rebuild the Liberal Party, indeed the National Party, into a dominant force in NSW politics."[37] He promised to be "tough" with his Cabinet, requiring ministers to perform or be removed. He also promised there would be no "bloodbath" in the senior levels of the public service. The new Government would not proceed with Labor's policy of gun registration or the confiscation of semi-automatic guns. Instead, there would be tougher requirements for obtaining licences and tougher penalties for carrying guns while committing offences.

The *Sun-Herald* greeted his victory with the observation that it was all the more "creditable" because he achieved it "almost singlehandedly". With few exceptions, "his support team has been a rather lacklustre bunch". Justin Greiner called the result "brilliant", adding that both children expected to see less of their father. John Howard said he was "over the moon" and thought the real message was to be found in the Western Suburbs of Sydney where Labor had been "de-throned". Inevitably, Federal Liberals saw unmistakable signs of a general conservative renaissance but, though Howard wanted to include Hawke among the causes of Unsworth's defeat, he did not want "to take anything away from Nick Greiner. Tonight belongs to him."

It did so, perhaps even more than Howard imagined. Ordinarily, a Federal Liberal Parliamentary Leader, who happened to come from NSW, would have the authority and status which placed him ahead of the NSW State Parliamentary Leader. Howard, however, was in the weaker position in 1988; he had just lost a Federal election and his own leadership was perpetually under a cloud. Greiner's triumph assured him of complete authority within Cabinet and over the State Parliamentary Party. With the help of Pickering and Dowd, he could even "best" Howard at the State Executive of the Organisation, normally not his "territory" and whose conventions the Federal Leader better understood.

Greiner spoke further about his plans on the day after the election. He said the Government would be "sensible, moderate but progressive", and promised quick action to establish a standing corruption commission and to provide for greater accountability of the Government and public servants. Kathryn announced her own plans. She would give one month's notice for her job with the Department of Youth and Community Services. Knowing liberationists would criticise her, Kathryn said she was doing what the liberation movement was all about; that is, being able to do what you wanted to do. She also intended to be herself: a "people person", an extrovert who enjoyed the social side of life more than a lot of other politicians' wives, who liked to bounce off other people's ideas and to hear what they were doing. She would spend more time with her teenage children and develop an interest outside the home, so long as it was not "political".[38]

In the days following the election the Labor Council warned of industrial chaos if the new Government tried to abolish compulsory unionism and supported workplace agreements which by-passed the Industrial Relations Commission. Jennie George of the NSW Teachers' Federation promised a troublesome time if Greiner and Metherell sought to implement some of their "outlandish" policies. The Labor Party engaged in the customary "blame game" and fingers were pointed in many directions, and often at Bob Hawke.[39] A consensus emerged that the Party had become detached from its heartland and paid the price for longevity in government. In some despair, the Party pulled what turned out to be a master stroke. It by-passed Brereton and prevailed upon Carr to forgo his Federal ambitions to take on the leadership of what in 1988 threatened to be at least eight years in Opposition.

Victors, as much as the losers, need to look hard at election results. Whereas John Carrick was too shrewd to allow success to induce complacency, there is little evidence that the Liberal Party in NSW investigated the disturbing elements in the 1988 election, most obviously, the divided local branches and the encroachment of Independents into both Liberal and National Party territory.[40] It was well to recognise that many of the votes cast for Liberal candidates were votes against a 12-year government, an asset which disappeared overnight. Nick Greiner probably needed to think about the trap which had befallen generations of military generals. Fighting the last war rarely worked; mounting a second "presidential campaign" might not, therefore, be a winner. Understandably, in getting down to the business of managing NSW Inc., and with another election four years away, Nick Greiner had different considerations in mind.

## Endnotes

[1]   Interview: Kortlang, 12 July 2011.

[2]   Appointment Diary: January 1988, Greiner Papers.

[3]   The above two paragraphs draw heavily on interviews with Greiner, 22 November 1910; Sturgess, 21 June and Pickering, 13 July 2011; on Diaries and Appointments, Greiner Papers, and on Public Policy Forum, *Campaign Managers*, p. 50.

[4]   Diary, 9 February 1988, Greiner papers; Interview: Greiner, 22 November 2010.

[5]   *Australian*, 23 February 1988.

[6]   *SMH*, 20 February 1988.

[7]   *Australian*, 12-13 March 1988.

8   Interviews: Sturgess, 21 June; Kortlang, 12 July 2011.

9   The above paragraph draws upon Public Policy Forum, *Campaign Managers*, p. 19ff. Interviews: Kaldor, 13 Oct. 2010; Kortlang, 12 July 2011.

10   Interview: Starr, 28 July 2004.

11   *SMH*, 7 Mar. 1988.

12   Public Policy Forum, *Campaign Managers*, p. 34; Interview: Kortlang, 12 July 2011.

13   John Stirton and Ron Klein in Public Policy Forum, *Campaign Managers*, pp. 33-4.

14   *SMH*, 23 February 1988.

15   *SMH*, 9 March 1988.

16   *SMH*, 3 March 1988.

17   *SMH*, 25 February 1988.

18   *SMH*, 4-5 March 1988; Interview: Pickering, 13 July 2011.

19   Public Policy Forum, *Campaign Managers*, p. 57.

20   *SMH*, 27 February 1988. The Liberals subsequently endorsed Virginia Schrader, a 25 year-old executive trainee, who achieved a swing of more than 6 per cent.

21   *SMH*, 29 February 1988.

22   Cavalier, "Unsworth" in Clune and Turner, *Premiers*, p. 440.

23   For this, and the next two paragraphs, see *SMH*, 9-11 March; *DT*, 10-11 March; and *Australian*, 11 March 1988. See also Jim Hagan and Craig Clothier, "1988", in Michael Hogan and David Clune, *The People's Choice: Electoral Politics in New South Wales*, vol. 3, 1968 to 1999, Parliament of NSW and University of Sydney, Sydney, 2001, p. 367 and Public Policy Forum, *Campaign Managers*, pp. 55-7.

24   In 1978 Unsworth's eldest son, aged 20, died of a heroin overdose in Penang. For its effect on the family, see Richard Glover's article in the *SMH*, 10 June 1986. Unsworth had, injudiciously, said of Greiner on 6 March that he "should go back where he came from", but the remark slipped out of sight. *SMH*, 7 March 1988.

25   Public Policy Forum, *Campaign Managers*, pp. 51-2.

26   Robert Haupt, *SMH*, 7 March 1988.

27   Greg Melleuish, "Nicholas Frank Greiner" in Clune, and Turner, *Premiers*, p. 448.

28   For the Unsworth speech and Greiner's reactions, see, *SMH*, 10-11 March 1988.

29   The Liberals won five of them on 19 March (four – Albury, Bathurst, Burrinjuck and Cessnock – were previously Labor-held seats and the other – Bega – was a new one), the Nationals won one (Monaro, previously Labor), and Labor retained Broken Hill.

30   For this account of Coalition relations before and during the campaign, see Public Policy Forum, *Campaign Managers*, pp. 36-8 and p 51.

[31] Hagan and Clothier, "1988" in Hogan and Clune, *People's Choice*, pp. 268-72.

[32] *DT*, 17 March 1988.

[33] See, for example, Dennis Shanahan, *SMH*, 12 March 1988.

[34] So did those who drank long and expensively on election eve at the Party headquarters in Riley Street, leaving it to the State Director's wife to clean up the vomit the next morning. One of Starr's severest critics remarked that this single act amounted to a more useful contribution than anything her husband managed to achieve for the entire campaign. Private information. See also *SMH*, 29 August 1989.

[35] *Sun-Herald*, 20 March 1988.

[36] For this assessment and a survey of the results, see Hagan and Clothier, "1988" in Hogan and Clune, *People's Choice*, pp. 272-9.

[37] *Sun-Herald*, 20 March 1988.

[38] *SMH*, 21 March 1988.

[39] For a summary of the various accusations, see Tony Stephens' article in *SMH*, 22 March 1988.

[40] For the problems in the seat of Waverley in the Eastern Suburbs, see Electorate Campaign Assessment, LPA, ML, MSS 7025/95.

# 10

# Managing NSW Inc.:
# the First Twelve Months

Nick Greiner was sworn in as the 47th Premier of NSW on 25 March 1988. Not yet 41 years of age, he supplanted William Foster, who became Premier in 1859, as the youngest to enter the office. Greiner did not wait for a formal swearing-in ceremony to start implementing his reform agenda. Despite the promise to hasten slowly, he set a frenetic pace. After one month he could list 25 "achievements" embracing anti-corruption initiatives, open government and law and order, as well as a number of miscellaneous actions.[1] Within three months the Government had introduced or had passed 49 bills. By the end of his first year Greiner had made substantial progress in identifying and reducing debt, improving general financial management, placing government trading enterprises on a surer commercial footing, restructuring the Public Service and changing its culture, increasing the levels of accountability and openness, and laying down principles and procedures to promote efficient and good governance.

Greiner rejected what he called the "soft option" whereby governments avoided doing anything significant in the first six months after winning office. He also implicitly rejected Wran's judgment of 2000 about making a difference, namely, that "[y]ou can't really have any cataclysmic changes. The system doesn't allow it. Indeed, the mindset of the Australian public doesn't allow it."[2] Greiner sought office because he believed he could change the way NSW was governed. And he saw himself entering office "well prepared" and with "a clear idea of what we wanted to do in the priority areas".[3]

Everything Greiner undertook in his first year was in some way related to everything else, although more on a higher plane for the cerebral Gary Sturgess, the intellectual, than for Nick Greiner, the pragmatist. Sturgess, the Premier's closest adviser on policy, looked at issues and expounded arguments within a broad philosophical and theoretical framework, and kept pushing boundaries.[4] Greiner was more inclined to think and talk about reducing debt, bringing private sector methods and values into the public sector, being more open and accountable, restoring respect for institutions, and delivering good government. Labor tried to depict the Premier as a dangerous ideologue, hell-bent on destroying the social fabric in order to protect the "bottom line". Some commentators claimed that his "king hit" approach was "dressed up in the apparently non-ideological language of management and markets". They saw a strategy of replacing deliberation and consensus-building with one of conviction, and of substituting market mechanisms for traditional forms of political control. Greiner regarded his approach to financial management as "pretty much applied common sense". It was not necessary to spend time at Harvard to understand where NSW was going if the railways continued to lose half a billion dollars.[5] What others saw as an ideological commitment to market liberal reform he saw as the obvious and necessary course for the better management of NSW.

### The reformers

While Greiner drove the reform process it helped to have an amenable Cabinet. No minister had ever served in a cabinet or worked near the top of government but the very able – such as Baird in Transport, Metherell in Education and Dowd as Attorney-General – were committed reformers who set their own fast pace in implementing change. Regrettably, for Greiner, one of the brightest, Peter Collins, was a major disappointment. Greiner thought that Collins' idea for the Health portfolio was to build a hospital in each marginal seat.[6] Importantly, however, the Premier was not a lone reformer in the ministry although, until the return of Robert Webster to the front bench (he initially lost his place because the proportion of Liberals in the Coalition had increased at the election), Greiner was short of true believers among the National Party contingent.

In Greiner's direct field of interest – the integrity of public institutions, financial management and public sector reform – the key figures were the senior bureaucrats. Gerry Gleeson, Secretary of the Premier's Department since 1976, was not among them; he had already signalled his intention to retire. John Ducker wanted to remain, and cried when Greiner told him that the Public Service Board was to be abolished.[7] The heads of Health, Housing and Industrial Relations were smartly removed and the head of the State Rail Authority (SRA) sensibly resigned after the election. Greiner wanted chief executive officers appointed on merit, committed to the reform program and capable of implementing it. He insisted, in the face of reasonable Labor claims about Kortlang and Sturgess being "political" appointments, that they were exceptionally well qualified to head departments.

Kortlang spent the first few weeks recruiting staff for the Premier before taking State Development with a brief "to stop the National Party from concreting the North Coast".[8] He left the post within a year to join Andrew Peacock, recently re-elected as Leader of the Federal Liberal Party. The Sturgess appointment was more contentious. As Director-General of the newly-created Cabinet Office, his principal jobs were to co-ordinate development of government policy through the cabinet process, and to act as the Premier's primary source of policy and strategic advice.[9] The Cabinet Office managed the agenda, analysed the issues and, where possible, resolved conflicts before they reached Cabinet. Sturgess described the advice he provided as "politically sensitive" rather than "political". The Labor Opposition and some traditionally-minded public servants felt the distinction became blurred. They considered he was too close to the Government. Several ministers resented his sitting next to the Premier in the Cabinet Room and disliked his influence behind the scenes. When Tim Moore, the Minister for the Environment, dubbed him the "twenty-first Cabinet Minister", many colleagues nodded their agreement.[10]

Greiner had planned to replace Percy Allan, Secretary of the Treasury, with a former Deputy Secretary. It will be recalled that Greiner had overlapped briefly with Allan at Sydney University. Allan was a President of the SRC and stood for Labor against Les Bury in Wentworth in the 1972 Federal election. With Wran as his campaign director – Wran's principal contribution was the slogan, "Point Percy at the Parliament" – he almost took Bury to preferences.[11] After a stint with the Bank of New South Wales, the rising star became the senior economist at the NSW Treasury (1976-82) and adviser to the Treasurer (Ken Booth) and to Wran (1982-6). Appointed Secretary of the Treasury in 1986, Allan was the driving force behind a program of financial management reform. Greiner recognised in Allan a kindred spirit. The two men formed a creative partnership broken only by Greiner's resignation in June 1992.[12]

Richard ("Dick") Humphry was the third member of what became the Sturgess-Allan-Humphry triumvirate at the head of the NSW Public Service. Born and raised in Perth, Humphry left school aged 15 and was employed by the Bank of New South Wales before joining the Commonwealth Treasury as a trainee computer programmer. He later worked in Defence, Finance and Aboriginal Affairs. Appointed Auditor-General for Victoria in 1986, he came under notice for criticising practices of the Cain Labor Government. He had previously met Greiner and in 1988 received a call for "a bit of a chat". Interviewed in Greiner's dining room, with Sturgess and Kortlang present, Humphry was selected at the age of 49 to run the Premier's Department with a brief to implement a management reform program designed to create "a truly professional public service".[13]

Greiner's relationship with the triumvirate and with most other heads of department and statutory authorities went beyond one of mutual respect. Allan expressed two of the elements which impressed the bureaucrats. First, Greiner was "a terrific boss to work for. You got certainty." Secondly, he "didn't put politics before evidence-based policy. With him it was always a case of what's the problem, how do we solve it, and then how do we sell it." Greiner was sometimes so "blasé" about the political consequences he alarmed Treasury officers. Humphry highlighted another aspect of Greiner's appeal: he directly involved senior officers in the reform program, meeting them alongside their respective ministers in annual departmental reviews and encouraging them to participate and put forward ideas. This approach cut through the "dictatorial service" over which Gleeson had presided. For Greiner, the dividend was the enthusiasm of the upper levels of the NSW Public Service for reforms designed "to break the mould".[14]

## The Independent Commission Against Corruption (ICAC)

Nick Greiner regarded the restoration of respect for public institutions as central to his reform agenda. On 26 May, in one of his first legislative actions as the new Premier, he introduced the bill to establish the Independent Commission Against Corruption. Sturgess, assisted at one stage by John Dowd, was the real architect.[15] He devised the anti-corruption package – Greiner acknowledges that without him the policy would have been more timid[16] – and chaired the committee which determined the finer details of the legislation in the weeks following the 1988 election. Nevertheless, if the second reading speech bore the Sturgess stamp, Greiner was fully committed to its substance.

He began by pointing out that the Government had "a clear and unequivocal mandate" to establish ICAC.[17] It was prepared to accept constructive amendments, and wanted to reassure civil libertarians and to dispel notions of a witch-hunt directed at the Wran-Unsworth era.[18] But the Opposition and the Legislative Council should understand he had the authority to confront and defeat corruption by means of a permanent anti-corruption body. Liberal democracy could not flourish in NSW unless and until the credibility, integrity and accountability of its institutions were restored and safeguarded. Because "the people of this State are fed up with half-hearted and cosmetic approaches to preventing public sector corruption", it was essential to establish what in effect was a standing royal commission with wide-ranging powers and not restricted to a particular issue nor restrained by narrow terms of reference.

There were limitations and safeguards. ICAC could not punish for contempt, nor conduct prosecutions for criminal or disciplinary offences, nor dismiss public servants. No individual would have his or her reputation publicly "impugned" without the Commission making definite findings. ICAC would not be a general crime commission nor intrude upon the territory occupied by the National Crime Authority, though it would co-operate with existing law enforcement agencies in addressing public corruption. ICAC would not, however, be a purely investigatory body. Greiner stressed its constructive roles: to educate public officials about what it meant to hold an office of public trust and to highlight the damaging, long-term effects of corrupt practices.

ICAC was to be independent and accountable. The Government might refer matters to the Commission but would not have privileged access. The Commission could decide what to investigate, except where ordered by a resolution of both Houses of Parliament. It could also determine that some allegations were too remote in time to justify investigation. Sturgess ruefully pointed out later that ICAC's independence proved to be of two kinds: one (desirable), where the institution was free of external control or influence; and the other (dangerous), where "a self-confident, strong-willed and free thinking commissioner" could act as he saw fit.[19] As for accountability, an Operations Review Committee consisting, eventually, of the Commissioner, an Assistant Commissioner, the Police Commissioner, a nominee of the Attorney-General's Department and four lay persons, would advise the Commissioner about action to be taken on complaints. A Joint Committee of the Parliament would monitor and review ICAC's activities in the exercise of its functions.

The Commission was also required to provide the Parliament with an annual report.

Greiner made four separate statements in the course of his speech which seemed more poignant after he was found in 1992 to have engaged in "corrupt conduct".

First, he said that ICAC was not intended to be "a tribunal of morals". It was "to enforce only those standards established or recognised by law". Secondly, he insisted that the Commission's jurisdiction extended to all public officials, including the Governor, ministers, MPs, judges, all holders of public office, and all employees of departments and statutory authorities. "There are no exceptions and there are no exemptions." Thirdly, Greiner said that "corrupt conduct" had been "carefully defined". The definition in section 8 of the Act included conduct which adversely affected the impartial or honest exercise of official functions, or itself constituted a dishonest or partial exercise of functions, or constituted or involved a breach of trust or the misuse of official information. Yet under section 9 of the Act, conduct could not be deemed corrupt if it did not constitute or involve a criminal or a disciplinary offence or reasonable grounds for dismissal. The "carefully defined" definition generated intense argument for years after the Greiner finding.

Fourthly, Greiner promised that "from this time forward the people of this State will be confident in the integrity of their Government". In his 20-minute speech Greiner used the word "integrity" seven times, once in relation to the qualifications of the Commissioner and six times in referring to public administration and institutions. Although the word itself is "imprecise . . . and not amenable to legal definition or objective determination",[20] a Premier who rightly prided himself on possessing "integrity" would be slammed four years later for falling short of what others thought it entailed.

The ICAC legislation placed Carr in a difficult position. To be obstructive would lead to accusations of covering up Labor's past, but here was a threat to legal rights "accumulated over centuries".[21] Resisting internal pressure from Labor's Right, Carr agreed to support the Bill's passage through the Legislative Council, while promoting amendments approved by the NSW Bar Association. He tried to shift attention: the legislation was hastily assembled; it was designed to root out "rotten apples" rather than institutionalised corruption; the provisions for oversight were inadequate; Parliament rather than the Government should appoint the Commissioner; ICAC should not become "a statutory base" for a witch-hunt directed at the Labor Party.

The original Bill encountered problems in the Legislative Council, partly because of concerns about ICAC having access to communications between lawyers and clients and between doctors and patients, and about the protection of the religious confessional. Further delays held up a replacement Bill and, knowing he could count on public support, Greiner threatened to call a referendum if they continued. Eventually, after changes restoring professional legal privilege and receiving guarantees about the religious confessional, the Australian Democrats and the Niles helped the second Bill pass into law in August 1988.[22]

Greiner's next step was to select the Commissioner. He told the Legislative Assembly on 13 September that after "extensive consultation" – Greiner himself held just one informal discussion with the successful candidate – the Government intended to appoint Ian Temby, QC. Born in 1942, Ian Temby was educated at Perth Modern School and graduated in law from the University of Western Australia. Early in his career he worked with Fred Chaney, a future Liberal Party senator, and Peter Dowding, a future Labor Premier, to form a shop front legal advice bureau. He polled well in March 1982 as the Labor candidate in a by-election for the State seat of Nedlands vacated by Sir Charles Court and won on preferences by Court's son. Appointed the first Commonwealth Director of Public Prosecutions (DPP) by the Hawke Government in 1984, Temby antagonised many in the Labor Party for prosecuting Lionel Murphy, then a justice of the High Court and an icon of the Labor Left.

He compounded this "offence" by prosecuting Wran for comments he made on the Murphy case, and Loosley for his involvement in the Harris-Daishowa affair. Lionel Bowen, the Federal Attorney-General, refused Temby's request for an extension of his term of office. Offered a seat on the ACT Supreme Court, Temby chose to resign in October 1988 and contemplated re-entering private practice.[23]

Bob Bottom, an investigative journalist and anti-corruption fighter, and two former DPP colleagues sounded out Temby for the ICAC position. Sturgess visited him in Canberra, and Greiner and Sturgess met him together at the Premier's Wahroonga home. Sturgess was well aware of Temby's history, but liked his energy and reputation for taking people on. Greiner liked what he saw. Temby would be tough and not too liberal, and had two of the essential qualifications: he was "available and interested". The Government had not been overwhelmed by expressions of interest.

Greiner and Sturgess were bothered by just one thing. Both have a clear recollection of Temby asking for an appointment to the bench after his five-year term of office expired. Temby does not have a similar recollection, though when he saw Dowd after the Wahroonga meeting he raised with the Attorney-General the very real problem he would face at the end of his term in 1994. He would then be aged 52 and have been out of private practice for the ten years when a barrister could expect to make serious money. Dowd told him there would have to be a waiting period for the sake of "appearances". Temby wanted the matter dealt with up front, to avoid any notion of "a secret deal". When Greiner announced the appointment he used a form of words worked out between Temby and the Attorney-General:

> The commissioner from time to time not only will be a person who is eligible for appointment to the Supreme Court, but will be highly suitable for such an appointment. It follows that the appointment of a person to the position of commissioner will not detract from eligibility for appointment to the Supreme Court,

and ordinarily, a person having served as commissioner would be considered suitable for an appointment to the Supreme Court.[24]

It was not a promise but, in 1988, it looked close enough.

The Premier told the Assembly that Temby possessed that "strength and independence, that experience and judgment, impartiality and integrity" of which he had spoken when introducing the ICAC legislation in May. There was, indeed, no reason to doubt Temby's qualities – or his self-belief – although Greiner felt afterwards he should have undertaken careful vetting and looked more closely at someone disposed to taking high profile positions. The DPP had told a seminar at the Australian Institute of Criminology in November 1984 that it might be better to prosecute holders of high public office faced with allegations of impropriety, even if the evidence did not appear strong enough to secure a conviction; an acquittal would serve to "clear the air". This so-called "Temby doctrine" was interpreted to mean that public figures, when faced with such allegations, should be prosecuted to give them a chance to clear their name. Temby's rider, that no prosecution should proceed unless there was a *prima facie* case, was conveniently overlooked, and so was his comment that consideration should be given to the possibility that, far from clearing the air, a prosecution might "muddy the waters".[25]

Bob Carr spoke briefly. Temby saw him before agreeing to the appointment and had assured Carr he would be balanced and act without fear or favour.[26] The Opposition Leader had two reservations: some matters which had received publicity when Temby was DPP amounted to "[t]rial by media"; and the "Temby doctrine" raised the possibility of public figures being prosecuted to "clear the air".[27] A *Sydney Morning Herald* editorial accused Carr of misrepresenting the "Temby doctrine" and suggested he was doing the bidding of elements in his own Party or expressing Labor's "unreasoned hatred" of Temby.[28] Bruce Hawker, Carr's legal adviser, had reassured him: "Temby's performance re Murphy suggests he is his own boss. Would investigate allegations against the government."[29]

Nick Greiner had no worries on this score at the end of 1988. He could believe his Government had taken major steps towards restoring integrity and improving accountability with a program which also included a ministerial code of conduct and freedom of information legislation. He could look forward to a well-armed ICAC and its crusading staff causing trouble for the corrupt and the corruptible.

## Financial management

Greiner and Sturgess knew there was no momentum for some of the financial reforms they wished to undertake. They had to invent a sense of crisis "to create a popular demand".[30] The Commission of Audit became what Greiner called the Government's "agent of reform". Established ten days after Greiner became Premier, the Commission was asked to determine the State's total indebtedness, to consider ways of introducing a user-pays system for public services, identify public asset sales for up to $1bn, leave the way open to increase taxes and charges, open the books of public sector bodies, and establish a framework for effective and efficient program delivery.[31]

Charles Curran, the Deputy Chairman of the merchant bank Kleinwort Benson Australia Ltd, was appointed chairman. Curran was a longstanding friend who played a significant role in Greiner's campaign for the 1988 election.[32] He was "immortalised" by a contrived tax avoidance scheme bearing his name. John Howard as Treasurer moved against the "Curran Scheme" as the first stage of an attack on "bottom-of-the-harbour" arrangements. The other two members of the Commission of Audit also came from the private sector. Jim Dominquez, the Chairman of Dominquez Barry Samuel Montagu Ltd, was a one-time member of the Liberal Party's 500 Club. James Yonge, it will be recalled, worked with Frost and Greiner to collect funds for the 1988 election, and he led a team manning polling booths in a marginal seat. Don Nicholls, the Deputy Secretary of the NSW Treasury, was appointed Executive Director of the Commission. Supported by staff from Treasury and the Auditor-General's Department, he prepared most of the two-volume report. The Commission canvassed the opinions of some 60 senior representatives of business, industry and the professions while Sturgess presented the case for corporatisation which became a major Commission recommendation.[33]

Awaiting the Commission's report, Nick Greiner delivered a mini-budget on 2 June. The objectives were to eliminate the $245m overdraft, to retire $350m of debt in the current financial year and reduce borrowings by $314m in the following one; conduct asset sales (principally, the NSW Investment Corporation, the State Brickworks and the site of the Homebush Abattoir); and cut recurrent departmental budgets by 1.5 per cent in real terms. At the same time, Greiner increased charges for education, electricity, hospitals, motoring, and public transport, almost all of them above the rise in the Consumer Price Index, despite the promise in Opposition to keep increases below the rate of inflation.

The *Daily Telegraph*, Hooper's preferred outlet for Greiner Government news, announced "GREINER KING-HITS FAMILIES FOR $450". Greiner had "fired a . . . mini-Budget torpedo packed with savage price rises", launched "a hard-hitting assault on wage earners"; and applied "draconian measures". A cartoon depicted him as the "Grim Reaper" and the editorial said his budget risked an all-out war with the unions, had hit "battling families" and broken election promises. Susan Adler of the *Telegraph* staff wrote the requisite hardship story. She described how "we" voted Liberal to get a better deal and instead got these "unfair price rises". Adler invoked images of her children wearing poorer quality shoes to meet food costs and possibly growing up with damaged feet, and of them going to an inferior school because of higher bus fares. The comforting news for the Government was buried down the editorial page. Greiner had "little choice" except to act firmly; the State's finances were in a "dreadful mess".[34]

Others viewed the mini-budget very differently. Ross Gittins described

Greiner "as a smart political operator – and also as a promising managing director of New South Wales Inc". He was "smart" because he acted early in his term knowing that the electorate would calm down and forget the pain by the next election. He had targeted the unions least likely to gain sympathy – public servants, teachers and railway workers – and looked after the doctors, nurses and police who enjoyed public support. Greiner was a "quick learner": deliver all the bad news in one hit and preferably just after a Premiers' Conference and a tough Commonwealth mini-budget; blame the preceding government; and hold back on tax cuts until just before the next election.[35]

One week before he released the Curran Report, the Premier announced that the Government would reduce debt by $1bn in the coming year, principally by utilising asset sales and repaying part of the Treasury Corporation's loans. Greiner also said the Government would pay off the 56-year loan used to finance the Sydney Harbour Bridge. The debt, he acknowledged, was not large but was "symbolic of the fact that we're in hock up to our eyeballs". The *SMH* obligingly produced a front page photograph of Greiner standing alongside the debt-free Bridge. The Premier had engaged in repayments with which the public could identify.

Greiner released the Curran findings on 1 August. The report, of more than 400 pages, began with a simple proposition stated in capital letters and bold type: **NEW SOUTH WALES HAS BEEN LIVING BEYOND ITS MEANS!**[36] This situation had occurred because of "excessive spending, the heavy drain of losses from government business undertakings, poor management of the State's assets, a failure to recognise and pay for operating costs as they are incurred and an increasing reliance on debt". Curran found the State had liabilities of $46bn, the equivalent of $25,000 per household. Servicing the debt cost 12 cents in every dollar the government spent and, at the present rate, would take 315 years to clear. The remedy lay in "fundamental reform". Appendix 2 set out possible courses of action to achieve "a significant down-sizing of Government". They included: immediate corporatisation of some statutory authorities to make them subject to commercial principles; eventual privatisation of other business operations; elimination of borrowings to fund non-income producing capital works; asset sales to pay off debt; and better management of the State's property holdings.

Specifically, Curran recommended that the Government withdraw from 24 activities (including the State Bank and the Government Insurance Office), cut departmental spending by $500m, reduce taxes by $300m by 1993-4, and sell government properties to raise $1.5bn. The report was particularly critical of several statutory authorities for their inefficiency and management practices, notably, the SRA, the Electricity Commission (Elcom), the Grain Handling Authority, the Maritime Services Board, the Sydney Opera House Trust, and the Sydney Cricket Ground and Sports Trust. Of lesser importance, though not to Greiner, it savaged the management of the Legal Aid Commission. Its Director, John Cooke, had previously been in charge of the CAC investigation into the White River Corporation and had, in Greiner's opinion, been dilatory in investigating the role of the Labor MP, Richard Mochalski, over the collapse of the Balanced Property Trust.[37]

Greiner complimented the Commission of Audit for its "outstanding contribution" which illustrated the capacity and readiness of private sector managers to contribute to the public interest. He committed the Government to implementing the recommendations, with two riders: the changes would be gradual, and some of the proposals were probably too dangerous politically for his Government to execute. Although the Premier highlighted the "cowardly and incompetent leadership" of his immediate Labor predecessors, he acknowledged that Curran had delivered a "scathing indictment" of governments of both persuasions. They had "spent too much, taxed too much and above all borrowed too much". But it was not all "unadulterated gloom and doom". Taxpayers and the users of government services would benefit from the envisaged changes.[38]

Margaret Thatcher arrived in Sydney on Thursday 4 August for a brief stopover on her visit to Australia for the Bicentennial celebrations. Journalists related stories about Greiner giggling nervously, repeatedly adjusting his shirt cuffs before meeting her, and having difficulty unwrapping Thatcher's gift of a silver platter commemorating the 400th anniversary of the Spanish Armada. One observed that Thatcher referred to him as "Prime Minister" on four occasions instead of "Premier", saying she was "not used to these French words". Matthew Moore reported how Carr overshadowed Greiner with his speech at the black tie dinner at the Regent Hotel, while acknowledging how Greiner had forsaken Wran's practice of shutting out the Opposition from such occasions. The British Prime Minister pointedly praised Carr's performance. Typically, Nick Greiner remained unfazed by the attention given to Carr. Some in the media did notice that Thatcher's arrival in Sydney coincided with the publication of the Curran Report and referred to its "whiff of Thatcherism".[39] But Greiner was also reported saying that, unlike Howard, he did not regard Thatcher as one of his heroes. Although the two found much in common in talking about debt and the teaching unions, Greiner maintains he "wasn't an ideologue in the Thatcher sense".[40]

The commentators had generally endorsed the Curran findings and recommendations. The *Daily Telegraph* was very supportive. "NSW is first, all right. First for debt; first for waste; first for mismanagement; first for over-staffing." Nevertheless, the editorial warned Greiner to move cautiously: the balance sheet was important and "so are the people". Bob Carr could say or do little. He defended the record of the previous Labor Government, and insisted that much of the information provided by the Commission was already available in reports from Treasury, the Public Accounts Committee and the Auditor-General. Yet his prognosis was much the same as Greiner's.[41] Criticism of the Curran Report usually focussed on its political role of justifying pre-existing Greiner approaches and allowing the Premier to modify pre-election promises with tougher financial measures. It was often pointed out – either to put the report down or simply to place it in context – that the adoption of a "corporate management framework" for government trading enterprises and support for privatisation were predated by developments in the UK and, especially, in New Zealand.[42]

Sturgess neatly pinpointed Curran's significance for the Greiner Government: "If the electorate in May 1988 gave Nick Greiner the mandate to govern, it was the Curran Commission which gave him the mandate to govern the way he did."[43] In a key step the Sturgess-led Steering Committee on Government Trading Enterprises subsequently formalised the five principles upon which the Government's financial management reforms and corporatisation program were based. The first four also applied to public service reform:

- public sector organisations must set out clear objectives;
- managers at all levels must be allowed to get on with their job;
- performance should be carefully monitored and appropriate rewards and penalties should be applied;
- incentives should apply to senior management in the form of remuneration packages on the basis of comparable commercial worth;
- a level playing field should apply between government trading enterprises and private sector firms.

These words and the intent of these principles are normally associated with Sturgess who, in turn, was influenced by the ideas and practice of Roger Douglas, the radical Minister of Finance in the New Zealand Labour Government of the 1980s. The five principles became the Greiner Government's mantra, expounded with conviction by senior public servants as well as by Greiner himself.[44] He probably first aired them as a single message when addressing the Young Liberals Convention in January 1988. But, for Greiner, they had a long gestation period, beginning with business courses at Harvard and the experience gained at Boise Cascade and with the White River Corporation, and developed through contacts with the Crossroads group in the early 1980s. He had long been committed to micro-economic reform and improved management practice.

Seven weeks after publication of the Curran Report, Greiner delivered his first annual Budget, designed to promote financial rehabilitation and better management. The Budget embodied a five-year strategy to eliminate all non-income producing inner budget borrowings, to reduce debt as a proportion of Gross State Product, introduce accrual accounting, deliver major tax cuts, achieve a more effective and efficient public sector, and improve services for the disadvantaged.[45] Notable features of the recurrent strategy for 1988-9 included one-line budget allocations; further productivity savings in departmental expenditure; priority spending on education, health, housing and law and order; financing non-revenue capital works in the Inner Budget Sector by asset sales and taxes rather than borrowings; and extension of user-pays principles to services between government departments.[46] The capital works strategy involved shifting resources from leisure and cultural facilities to roads, courts and prisons, hospitals and other health facilities, schools and technical colleges; encouragement of private investment in toll roads and private hospitals; and reduction of borrowing in the non-revenue producing social and economic infrastructure areas.

Greiner could claim to have produced the "first fair dinkum balanced Budget" in the State's history because the Government had abandoned the traditional practice of treating borrowings as revenue and not as liabilities. The projected surplus of $8m was a real one, unlike the fictional surpluses declared by the Labor States of Victoria, Western Australia and South Australia. The next step, which Percy Allan did not regard as so important, was that, by replacing cash budgeting with accrual accounting, the accumulated liabilities such as asset depreciation and future superannuation and long service leave obligations, would also be included in the calculations.[47]

Debt reduction was a central objective. As Greiner put it, the NSW public sector was "heavily addicted to the debilitating drug of debt" and it was time to "start weaning the patient". The Premier planned to reduce debt from 28 per cent of Gross State Product to 20 per cent within five years. He anticipated Carr's populist response: the withdrawal symptoms would be accompanied by "accusations of cruelty", and the patient's "enemies" would be prescribing more "fixes". Greiner praised the Unsworth Government for making a start towards a "leaner public sector", claiming no more for his own efforts than the intention to extend and implement earlier moves to sell surplus assets, develop user-pays, promote commercialisation and involve private enterprise in infrastructure development.

Although the *Australian Financial Review* on 22 September called the Premier's first Budget "a worthy one", many commentators said he missed an opportunity and was clearly affected by the reaction to the mini-budget.[48] Greiner admits he had been so "spooked" by the outcry following the June mini-budget, he baulked at further spending cuts in September.[49] Having promised zero real growth in recurrent spending in his first term, Greiner's handouts amounted to a three per cent real growth for the 1988-9 financial year. Business leaders nonetheless applauded the Budget; the executive director of the NSW Chamber of Commerce said the Premier had kept his promise of running the State like a business.[50] Yet the reputed hell-bent reformer showed in September 1988 that he was not immune to electoral considerations.

## Public Service Reform

During the 1980s, facing new and ever more complex tasks and "beset by a crisis of confidence", the public sector in many countries, including the United Kingdom, looked to the private sector for ideas. What emerged was a developing movement in administration variously labelled "new public administration", "new public management", "new managerialism", or just "managerialism". The core of managerialism was the focus on achieving desired objectives rather than on traditional public service concern for process. Managerialism was about "managing for results". It involved applying business techniques and insisting on cost-effectiveness by means – among others – of corporate planning, program budgeting, program evaluation, allowing and requiring the managers to manage, a system of user-pays, performance indicators and performance-based pay.[51] By the time Greiner came into government the various elements of managerialism were well known in public services in many countries, including Australia. It was in 1988 a controversial subject but not a new one. The important point here is that Greiner did not have to invent a managerial approach to administration. It was more a case of his Harvard and business experience rendering him receptive to such an approach.

Greiner, with Sturgess at his elbow, had several plans for improving the governance of NSW.[52] Many of their reforms – formation of the Cabinet Office, abolition of the Public Service Board and devolution of its functions to departmental heads for day-to-day management, introduction of well-ordered cabinet processes, and the annual departmental reviews over which Greiner and his Public Service triumvirate presided – contributed significantly to the workings of government without being much noticed outside official circles.

When Greiner set out to change the culture and jettison some of the traditions of the Public Service, the impact was more obvious. His starting-point was that public sector organisations, like successful private companies, should be responsive to their customers. They should have forward-looking policies and strategies, be sensitive to the "bottom line", encourage entrepreneurial characteristics, and be innovative and risk-taking. Greiner saw an underlying similarity between managing in the public and private sectors, and believed that the management skills required by the private sector could improve the performance of the NSW Public Service:

> the days are gone when the public and private sectors were
> separated by a chasm, with totally different cultures and value

systems. . . . The ultimate aim would be to have much the same
values, culture, risks and rewards in the public and private sectors.[53]

Greiner highlighted the logical corollary: "public sector managers, if
given the right resources (a productive, rewarding climate in which to
work, and clear goals to work towards) will have the same motivations
and pressures to perform and excel as their private sector counterparts".
In fact, they were in a position to out-perform them. After all, "they
were likely to be substantially better educated, better trained, smarter and
harder working than the average senior or middle manager earning the
same amount of money".[54]

Greiner's plan for a senior executive service (SES) was founded on
these assumptions. The idea, however, of establishing an elite body within
an Australian Public Service was hardly a new one. The Boyer Report
in 1958 had effectively proposed one for the Commonwealth Public
Service.[55] Victoria established an SES in 1982 and the Commonwealth
did so in 1983-4. Peter Wilenski in 1982 had proposed the formation
of a similar body in his second report on government in NSW. Gerry
Gleeson, supported by Wran, stomped on the idea. Greiner, on the
other hand, was attracted to it. He committed himself to some of the
implications when delivering a speech in Sydney on 30 August 1983.
Entitled "A New Management Strategy for New South Wales Limited",
he spoke of introducing contracts for senior public servants and heads
of statutory authorities, a review of tenure, and relating pay scales to
ability as well as seniority.[56]

Soon after taking office Greiner announced plans to form a Management
Council to advise the Premier and ministers on the administration
and machinery of government. Chaired by Humphry, and assisted by
the new Office of Public Sector Management within the Premier's
Department, one of its first tasks was to recommend the creation of a
senior executive service. Cabinet approved a proposal in December 1988
for implementation the following year. A scheme was in place within ten
months. Under it, 1,400 positions were to be filled on renewable contracts

for up to five years. Flexible salary packages were based on market-related remuneration. Performance was to be reviewed annually, performance-based incentives were available, and rewards and sanctions would be applied depending on performance. Officers had a "right of return" to positions below the SES, and a special tribunal – not the Government nor the Industrial Commission – determined remuneration.

At a stroke, Greiner abolished security of tenure for the upper levels of the NSW Public Service. Of all his public sector reforms this was the most radical.[57] He removed a central pillar of a "traditional" public service, namely, that non-partisan senior officials offered frank and fearless advice in the knowledge that their own jobs were secure. Greiner was unrepentant on this issue: he wanted flexibility, accountability and performance management. He was not criticising the Public Service. But he did want to change "the job for life" culture and conditions of employment. To this end, Greiner chose a method which he thought would actually reduce political patronage, promote smaller and more focussed government, greater accountability, better staff morale, higher productivity, "and, most importantly, better service delivery to the public".[58]

## A report card

After twelve months in office Nick Greiner published his own report card.[59] He pointed out how he came into office "with the clear philosophy of running New South Wales like an efficient and effective business in the interests of its shareholders, the people of the State". His Government believed that this approach alone would contain State debt, and ensure that the community received full value for each dollar the Government spent, that welfare services were directed to the truly disadvantaged, that future generations did not have to pay for services enjoyed but not financed by present users, and that taxes were lowered. Greiner's account of his first year carried a warning. Although there had been "an exceptional level of achievement" the benefits "will be felt gradually rather than instantly". The gain beyond the pain would take time to materialise. Time did not look to be a problem in March 1989.

The Government did not have to face the electorate for another three years. Whether the Premier was yet communicating with his constituency is another matter. He described the managerial approach of "downstream autonomy", "performance monitoring", "management incentives" and "competitive neutrality" as "social objectives". Clearly, report cards of this kind were meant for those who understood report cards of this kind.

The commentators argued about whether "Greinerism" in its first year went too far or not far enough. They also debated the question of how far "Greinerism" was new to NSW or whether it was original in itself. Dr Barry Moore, who had a long-term involvement with public administration, pointed out how three of the hallowed five principles of financial management predated the arrival of the Greiner Government. According to the Book of Exodus, Moses restructured Israelite administration in order to let the managers manage, while the idea of performance monitoring had been around for 15 years and the formulation of clear objectives for 14. The terminology had changed, but not the substance. Moore concluded that management incentives and competitive neutrality were the sole innovations.[60]

The critical point in the case of Greiner himself is how so many elements of his own past, how many long-held assumptions, along with his disposition always to choose change over maintaining the *status quo*, influenced his approach to managing NSW Inc. He may not have been familiar with the history of the Liberal Party but he was acutely aware of developments in recent decades in Australia and in the world beyond. Greiner described his outlook as "post-ideological". He was part of a global movement which saw governments, irrespective of their proclaimed political positions, adopt similar policies in pursuit of economic efficiency, managing the "retreat" of the public sector from "non-strategic areas", and getting debt under control. He, rightly, made no claim to originality. What he could fairly say was that the Askin and Wran-Unsworth Labor governments were part of the same conservative "continuum", whereas the Coalition constituted "the parties of change in NSW."[61]

# Endnotes

1   For Greiner's annotated copy of the list, see Peta Seaton, "Decision-making in Greiner's NSW Inc [sic]: An insider's perspective", in Ken Turner and Michael Hogan (eds), *The Worldly Art of Politics,* Federation Press, Leichhardt, 2006. Seaton was a member of Greiner's office.

2   Interview (Diana Giese), 25 Aug. 2000): NLA, ORAL, TRC 4628, p. 94.

3   *Age,* 23 June 1988.

4   See, for example, his approach to corporatisation in his address to the ACT Division of the Royal Australian Institute of Public Administration in July 1990, *Canberra Bulletin of Public Administration,* no. 65, 1991, pp. 84-8.

5   For the above comments and Greiner's own assessment, see Martin Laffin and Martin Painter (eds), *Reform and Reversal: Lessons from the Coalition Government in New South Wales 1988-1995,* Macmillan, South Melbourne, 1995, pp. 8-9.

6   Interview: Greiner, 24 September 2005.

7   Interview: Greiner, 29 March 2011.

8   Interview: Kortlang, 12 July 2011.

9   Cabinet Office, *Annual Report 1989-1990.*

10  Interviews: Sturgess, 21 June; Richard Humphry, 26 September 2011. According to Greiner's appointment diary, Sturgess attended a political strategy meeting at Bowral on 15 October 1990 along with senior Liberal ministers involved in election planning, members of Greiner's office, the Liberal Party State Director, a Liberal Party pollster and the head of its advertising agency. Kortlang was also present but was not then a public servant.

11  Interview: Allan, 8 December 2010; Mike Steketee and Milton Cockburn, *Wran: An Unauthorised Biography,* Allen & Unwin, Sydney, 1986, pp. 59-60.

12  Interview: Allan, 14 September 2011; Percy Allan, "The Financial Management Improvement Program of the New South Wales Treasury", *Australian Journal of Public Administration,* vol. 50. no. 2, 1991, p. 107; Martin Painter, "Microeconomic Reform and the Public Sector", in Laffin and Painter, *Reform and Reversal,* p. 92.

13  Interview: Humphry, 26 September 2011.

14  Interviews: Allan, 14 September; Humphry, 26 September 2011.

15  Sturgess wrote in a conference paper that ICAC "did not spring fully grown" from his, or Dowd's, mind; rather, like Topsy, it just "grow'd". Gary L. Sturgess, "Guarding

the Polity: The NSW Independent Commission Against Corruption". For a copy, see Parliament of New South Wales, Committee on the ICAC, *Collation of Evidence of the Commissioner of the ICAC,* 4 March 1994.

[16]   Interview: Greiner 10 September 2012.

[17]   *NSWPD,* Third Series, vol. 201, pp. 672-85.

[18]   Dowd had, in the previous week, said that ICAC "will spend much time examining the workings of the Labor Party". *Ibid.,* pp. 296-7.

[19]   Sturgess, "Guarding the Polity", p. 14.

[20]   Peter D. McClellan, "Administrative law and the Independent Commission Against Corruption", *Australian Institute of Administrative Law Forum,* No. 4, 1995, p. 21.

[21]   For Carr's speech, see *NSWPD,* Third Series, vol. 201, pp. 822-32.

[22]   For a summary of the legislation and its subsequent history, see Marie Swain, "The Independent Commission Against Corruption: An Overview", NSW Parliamentary Library, Briefing Note, 018/94, 1994.

[23]   Interview: Temby, 23 November 2011.

[24]   *NSWPD,* Third Series, vol. 203, p. 1173. The above two paragraphs draw upon interviews with Sturgess, 22 June 2011; Temby, 23 November 2011; Greiner, 26 March 2012.

[25]   *SMH,* 14 September 1988.

[26]   Interview (Chris Cunneen): Ian Temby, May-June 1995, NLA, TRC, 3258/209-10.

[27]   *NSWPD,* Third Series, vol. 203, pp. 1172-4.

[28]   *SMH,* 14 September 1988.

[29]   Undated briefing note, quoted in Andrew West and Rachel Morris, *Bob Carr: A Self-Made Man,* HarperCollins, Pymble, 2003, p. 166.

[30]   Laffin and Painter, *Reform and Reversal,* p. 9; and Gary Sturgess interview, 1994, quoted in *ibid.*

[31]   *SMH,* 5 April 1988.

[32]   Interview: Ken Hooper, 20 April 2011. Following a social occasion with the Greiners and the Currans in January 1988, Colin Reynolds of the Chase Corporation (Australia) sent Greiner a cheque for $15,000 to assist the election campaign. Liberal Party – including Finance, Greiner Papers.

[33]   Interview, Sturgess, 21 June 2011. For Nicholls' account of the Commission's work, see Don Nicholls, "The New South Wales Commission of Audit", in Chris Pirie

and John Power (eds), *Economic Management Pressures on Australian Pubic Administration*, CCAE, Canberra, 1989, pp. 97-109.

[34]  *DT*, 3 June 1988.

[35]  *SMH*, 3 June 1988.

[36]  New South Wales, Commission of Audit, *Focus on Reform*, Sydney, 1988.

[37]  Cooke, a member of Frank Walker's branch of the Labor Party, resigned within a week of the Curran Report being made public. For material relating to Cooke, see *Australian*, 5 and 6-7 August; and *SMH*, 9 and 11 August 1988. A Labor-appointed inquiry exonerated Cooke over the Balanced Property Trust in February 1989 and implicitly rebuked the Premier. Refusing to apologise, Greiner did not resile "one iota" from his claim that the CAC management had behaved in "a totally incompetent and irresponsible manner", adding that some 5,000 pensioners had lost their life savings. *SMH*, 25 February 1989.

[38]  *NSWPD*, Third Series, vol. 202, pp. 2212-13 and *SMH*, 2 August 1988.

[39]  *Australian Financial Review* (*AFR*), *DT*, 5 Aug.; *SMH*, 5 and 6 Aug.; *Australian*, 6-7 Aug. 1988. See also, Nick Greiner, "How to Treat an Opposition", *IPA Review*, vol. 42, no. 3, 1988/89.

[40]  Interview: Greiner, 29 March 2011.

[41]  *NSWPD*, Third Series, vol. 202, pp. 2213-14.

[42]  For commentaries and critiques, see Eric Groom, "The Curran Report and the Role of the State", *Australian Journal of Public Administration*, vol. 49, no. 2, 1990 (including Martin Painter's comment), pp. 144-56; and Evatt Research Centre, *State of Siege: Renewal or Privatisation of the Australian State Public Services?*, Pluto Press, Leichhardt, 1999, pp. 179-82, 213.

[43]  Interview: Gary Sturgess, 27 September 2004.

[44]  Painter, "Microeconomic Reform", pp. 91-2. See, for example, Humphry, "Comment" on Patrick Weller, "Financial Management Reforms in Government: A Comparative Analysis", Australian Society of Certified Practising Accountants, 1990; Allan, "Financial Management Improvement Program", pp. 107-116; Greiner, *NSWPD*, Third Series, vol. 204, 18 Oct. 1988, pp. 2407-9.

[45]  For the full Budget speech, see *NSWPD*, Third Series, vol. 203, pp. 1469-79.

[46]  NSW Government, *A New Direction: 1988-89 NSW Budget Strategy*, nd.

[47]  Interview: Allan, 20 September 2011.

[48]  See Alex Mitchell in the *SMH*, 22 September 1988.

[49] Interview: Greiner, 30 March 2011.

[50] *SMH,* 21 September 1988.

[51] There is a brief description of managerialism and a summary of different viewpoints in David Corbett, *Australian Public Sector Management,* 2nd ed., Allen & Unwin, St Leonards, 1996, pp. 246-50.

[52] A very good overview of the changes undertaken in the NSW Public Service can be found in Martin Laffin, "The Public Service" in Laffin and Painter, *Reform and Reversal,* ch. 5.

[53] NSW Premier's Department, *Executive Bulletin,* vol. 1. no. 5, 1989. See also, David A. Lamond, "Establishing a Senior Executive Service: The New South Wales Experience", *Australian Journal of Public Administration,* vol. 50, no. 4, 1991, p. 506.

[54] NSW Premier's Department, *Executive Bulletin,* vol. 1, no. 8, 1989.

[55] R.S. Parker, "Senior Executive Services: Variations on a Theme", *Canberra Bulletin of Public Administration,* no. 61, 1990, p. 54.

[56] Sturgess, Greinerism, pp. 27-32.

[57] For an analysis of how the scheme went further than those operating at the time in the Commonwealth, Victoria and Western Australia, see Ken Baxter, "Senior Executive Service in New South Wales", *Canberra Bulletin of Public Administration,* no. 61, 1990, pp. 129-31.

[58] *Reforming the State's Finances: the First Year,* March 1989. For commentary on the reforms, see especially Barry Moore, "Developments in New South Wales Public Administration", *Australian Journal of Public Administration,* vol. 48, no. 2, 1989, pp. 109-22; David A. Lamond, "Establishing a Senior Executive Service", pp. 501-14; Martin Laffin, "The Public Service", in Laffin and Painter, *Reform and Reversal, ch. 5.*

[59] *Reforming the State's Finances: the First Year,* March 1989.

[60] Moore, "Developments", see esp. pp. 109-115.

[61] *DT,* 8 August 1988.

# 11

# Managing Politics and Change: 1988-90

Nick Greiner liked to say he was not a political animal, nor a career politician. He could never take the political game itself too seriously, be thrilled by a good performance in the Bear Pit, or enjoy giving Bob Carr a serve. He did what he had to do in Parliament; at best, he did it "tolerably well". Greiner considered himself "knowingly indifferent" to the politics of any given situation.[1] His own side sometimes despaired of him. Ted Pickering, who admired so much about Greiner, felt he had "unbelievably bad political instincts".[2] In pre-selections he sometimes backed the loser in what was effectively a two-horse race. He made wrong judgments about people – Terry Griffiths comes to mind – and took on causes which were bound to lose.[3] The common view around Macquarie Street and the State Office Block, and within the Liberal Party, was that Kathryn would have made the better politician. She had the social skills he notably lacked, and her presence was often essential when warmth and captivation were required.

Yet some of the conventional wisdoms about Greiner the politician, including his own, can be taken too far. He might have cared little for number crunching, courting popularity or massaging egos but he had to be, and was, sufficiently "political" to stay ahead of the field in his first term as Premier. Admittedly, he did have the political equivalent of a following wind. The 1988 election result had given Greiner total authority within Cabinet and the Party Room. Wal Murray, with whom Greiner had developed a "mutually respectful relationship", and who had made the transition from a traditional NP "tactical politician",[4] kept the Nationals in line. For all his thespian and oratorical skills, Bob Carr was hampered by self-doubt, a fractious Caucus and rival leadership ambitions. These advantages would have meant little, however, if Greiner had failed to deal with the threatening situations which confront any Premier. Carr, as Leader of the Opposition, saw how Greiner was especially effective in dealing with "brush fires" both in the Legislative Assembly and where it really mattered – in the media. Carr may have exaggerated in claiming that "no one said Nick was a poor politician until the night of the 1991 election" when he almost lost government. But Greiner's ability to "hose down" embarrassing issues was one reason why media proprietors kept telling the Leader of the Opposition that the Premier was a "master politician".[5]

Like Paul Keating, Greiner believed that good policy would have its rewards in good political outcomes; hence, the favourable response of the senior bureaucrats noted in the previous chapter. The problem with this approach in Greiner's case was that he often focussed exclusively on the overall strategy and assumed that the details would look after themselves, or be looked after by others. Fortunately, this approach rarely caused problems in his first term as Premier. Nor did his tendency to ignore, or fail to see, the political implications of what he regarded as sensible decisions.

Some of Greiner's failings as a politician – and as a manager – emanated from character traits many would find admirable. He was, on his own admission, probably too loyal. Influenced by his father's habit of forever sacking employees, Greiner was rarely comfortable confronting individuals or giving them marching orders. Kathryn would have had less of a problem.[6] Greiner, not surprisingly, had a Business School argument to justify inaction. Whereas his father's approach was "tactical", his was "strategic". Moreover, to dismiss an employee could reflect badly on the employer who appointed the person in the first place.[7] The important point is that despite the media and Opposition image of him as hard and uncompromising, Greiner knew that, at a personal level, he was not "tough". Percy Allan thought he was actually "quite a softie". Whereas Wran and Fahey could be bad tempered and volatile, and Keating and Kennett had the "mongrel", Greiner was "one of the politest of men". He was more in the Hawke mould of a consensus politician, a mediator who preferred persuasion. He was good in talking it out with ministers, but resolute in wearing down those who had to be persuaded. It just took time to do so. A Kennett would have pushed through a reform program much faster, and privatised the State Bank as soon as he came into office. The bureaucrats sometimes took the initiative where they could. They passed the word around that Greiner mandated certain actions and "bashed heads" in his name.[8]

Greiner's attitudes, strengths and weaknesses in managing politics were evident in his relationship with Terry Metherell, the controversial Minister for Education, in the way he handled the inevitable "brush fires", and in his approach to John Howard, Liberal Party conventions, the Eastern Creek "fiasco", Aboriginal affairs and Kathryn Greiner's possible career in the Senate.

## The Minister for Education

Terry Metherell was born in England in 1947, the same year as Greiner. His family migrated to Australia in the mid-1950s and, after attending Caringbah High School, he graduated from Sydney University as BA (Hons), DipEd, PhD (history) and Master of Town and Country Planning. He lectured at Sydney University and worked for two Fraser Government ministers – Robert Ellicott and John Carrick – before entering the Legislative Assembly in 1981 as the most academically-decorated of his contemporaries. An intensely private man, Metherell appeared to his colleagues as driven and obsessed and who, in government, seemed to relish unpopularity.

As Minister for Education, Metherell quickly implemented approved government policy. By the end of 1988 he had cut the numbers of teaching and support staff, increased teaching hours in return for higher salaries, and introduced promotion by merit and tests for basic skills for Year 3 and Year 7 students. He had established ten more selective schools, de-zoned schools, and increased funding for independent schools. He required TAFE institutions to focus on industry needs and on long-term vocational courses and established 24 new technology high schools. Metherell also decentralised the Department of Education and established regional administrations and budgeting at the local school level. The values underlying these changes included a diversity of educational offerings, freedom of choice, a core curriculum, increased community involvement and self-management of schools. They were the values embodied in much of what Greiner had taken to the electorate in 1984 and which he continued to advocate during Metherell's time as minister.

Metherell's reforms came at a high price. Within three months of taking the portfolio he had put almost every education lobby group offside. He even managed to make the NSW Teachers' Federation popular. Teachers, parents and students came together in strikes and demonstrations, with more than 50,000 protesting in Sydney on 17 August. The criticisms were as much about style as substance. "Dr Non-Negotiable Metherell" (a Teachers' Federation description) appeared to regard consultation as a device for telling people what he had decided. The principal of a leading Catholic School described Metherell as "astonishingly rude, arrogant and ill-mannered". A Liberal backbencher was appalled when Metherell told an HSC student who asked a question at a public meeting that she should be at home studying.[9] When John Stirton delivered his survey figures to Greiner in March 1989 he said "the superficial perception of what the Government is doing in education is still quite negative" notwithstanding strong support below the surface on specific issues. Nevertheless, 75 per cent of respondents thought Metherell had not been adequately consultative, and they also ticked arrogance, rudeness, inflexibility, ignorance and poor communication. His overall approval rating stood at just 19 per cent.[10] As Carr observed, Metherell provided a case study in how not to introduce change.[11]

Greiner loyally backed Metherell for the two years he was in charge of Education. Most of the Cabinet wanted him removed but stayed silent in view of the Premier's stand.[12] Early in July 1988 the Premier did acknowledge there was confusion about the reform process. He said the pace of change may have been too rapid, and student strike leaders did have legitimate concerns. Yet when a Cabinet committee looked at the most controversial issue – publication of HSC aggregate results – it supported Metherell, amending his program only by delaying changes to the HSC curriculum and requiring more extensive consultation. In January 1990, when Greiner said he wanted to build bridges with the teachers, he insisted this could be done with Metherell remaining at his post. Given this backing for his minister, and the public criticisms he endured for doing so, Greiner was understandably shocked when Metherell told ICAC in May 1992 that the Premier had not been sufficiently supportive during the education controversy.

Metherell believed that Greiner had betrayed him.[13] He had told a different story in July 1990. Speculation had mounted about a reshuffle, with Metherell being moved to a safer harbour, possibly State Development. At one point Greiner invoked a sporting analogy to quash any suggestion of censure, likening Metherell's role to that of the rugby league front-rower who did all the hard work early in the game and was then replaced. Metherell pre-empted Greiner's reshuffle by handing in his resignation immediately after hearing on 20 July that the Tax Office would charge him for failing to declare interest on assessable income of $38,054-25. Pickering recalled how ministers were "full of glee" upon hearing that "the smartest bastard in Cabinet" had gone.[14] In an exchange of letters Greiner praised Metherell for "the courageous and loyal way" he had implemented the Government's education reform agenda. The Premier also spoke of Metherell's "quite extraordinary courage and vision" in introducing reforms which would take State education in NSW into the 21st century. Metherell, in turn, referred to Greiner's "remarkable courage and vision, both personally and politically". He was "sure" the Premier "will not waiver or weaken", and looked forward "to continuing to make a constructive contribution to your Government both now and in the future".[15]

Early in September a magistrate ordered Metherell to pay $11,847 in fines, as well as pay back tax and costs. Greiner had provided a warm character reference and, after the case concluded, said Metherell had "a continuing place in public life in NSW" and would not rule out his return to the ministry "at some appropriate time in future".[16] It would never have occurred to Greiner in September 1990 that he would not have a free choice in the matter. For his part, Terry Metherell believed he was on a promise of redemption.

Greiner persuaded Virginia Chadwick to take Education and there followed an improvement in the Government's relationship with school principals and lobby groups; mass action became a story of the past. At some cost Greiner had stood by two of his principles; he had let a manager manage and supported unpopular reforms ahead of populist politics. If it was not smart politics to stick with Metherell for as long as he did it was sensible to support fundamental reform when his authority in the Government was absolute and an election was not due for two years. It was not, however, so smart to come into power to implement such reform without having a policy for managing change, and for carrying the interested parties. The Teachers' Federation was probably a lost cause but Greiner's own good manners and a commitment to real consultation might have eased the passage of reform.

## Handling "brush fires"

Greiner had made it difficult for himself by introducing a Ministerial Code of Conduct. Gary Sturgess felt on reflection that a written version was probably not a good idea.[17] Under the Code, ministers were required to perform their duties impartially, disinterestedly and in the best interests of the people of NSW, to be frank and honest with their colleagues and to maintain confidentiality. The Code set out desired practices ranging from registration of interests and the proper use of public property and services to dealing with gifts and hospitality and with post-retirement employment. Ministers were to report to the Premier every six months about their activities in relation to desired practice. If they had any doubts they were to talk to the Premier or the Director-General of the Cabinet Office. The overall aim was to maintain public confidence in the executive arm of government and to ensure its "proper working".[18] Greiner amplified the point in the Assembly on 1 September 1988:

> My Government will be squeaky clean; it is squeaky clean, and it will stay that way. I am personally committed to external accountability – I emphasize both those words with respect to both effectiveness and integrity.[19]

Within a few months Carr was reminding him of this declaration in the wake of several ministerial indiscretions, one of which led to a resignation.

The most serious case involved the NP's Matt Singleton, the Minister for Administrative Services. Greiner learnt in November 1988 that Singleton had failed to declare a directorship in the previous year and since then had lobbied the Planning Minister, David Hay, to lift a zoning restriction to enable some land owned by a company in which he had a 49 per cent share to be developed commercially. Greiner chose not to sack Singleton – Hay had not approved the development – but to embarrass him in Cabinet in the course of issuing a general order to comply with the Code of Conduct. By January 1989 Greiner had received more information about Singleton's activities, including his failure to disclose interests in at least three more companies. Yet the Premier was "persuaded only reluctantly" to act because he did not believe Singleton should be removed for what amounted to a "victimless crime". Appreciating that Sturgess would, all along, have taken a tougher moral stand, Greiner regarded Singleton's forced removal from Cabinet as "close to a sacrificial offering" for the sake of warning others and keeping the Government "squeaky clean". Wal Murray did not believe his "bloody good mate" should resign, and even thought of dissolving the Coalition over the issue. Singleton apparently dissuaded him. The good news, for Greiner, was the return of the National Party's Robert Webster to the front bench. The like-minded Webster pursued the reform program with vigour and intelligence.[20]

The other "bush fires" were comparatively minor. Murray had not declared the 4,000 shares he held in Singleton's finance and investment company. Pressed hard by Carr, Greiner invoked the maxim *de minimis non curat lex* (the law does not concern itself with trifles). Neil Pickard, the Minister for Minerals and Energy, had failed to disclose $1,400 worth of mining shares in the parliamentary public register. Greiner dismissed the Pickard shares as mere "penny dreadfuls", the sort which lay in bottom drawers after the last mining boom. On another level altogether, Paul Zammit, MP, the chairman of the parliamentary road safety committee, was fined for driving at 96km per hour in a 60km zone. Greiner rejected his proffered resignation. After saying he would "cop it sweet", Zammit blamed poor signposting, speculated that the police might be operating a quota system, and claimed that the speeding fine was his first traffic infringement in 20 years.[21] It was actually his seventh since 1978. The Premier accepted Zammit's resignation, if anything pleased to have his judgment confirmed about Zammit's lack of suitability for ministerial office.

Greiner felt confident he could counter Opposition attempts to expose transgressions of the Code of Conduct. Carr found a good line which he kept repeating: "Why castigate Dopey, Sneezy and Grumpy when it's Snow White who should be called to account?" He also sought to exploit the "squeaky clean" avowal. Greiner responded with references to Labor's long record of serious and uncorrected malfeasance, and highlighted his Government's initiatives with ICAC, the Code of Conduct and the *Freedom of Information Act*. He could point out that, unlike his predecessors, he acted as soon as matters came to his attention.[22] Greiner could also ask one devastating question: which government had one of its ministers end up in gaol?[23]

It was more difficult to dismiss a formal ICAC report. Adrian Roden, QC, an ICAC Assistant Commissioner and former judge of the NSW Supreme Court, conducted a long investigation into North Coast land development following a referral by the President of the Tweed Shire Council.[24] Roden found considerable and disturbing evidence of political donations being used to "purchase favourable treatment" for land development decisions. He also expressed particular concern about donations to political parties and politicians for administrative purposes being exempt from disclosure requirements. Both sides of politics were involved but the public hearings and Roden's findings were especially embarrassing for the Government. The ICAC report, released on 11 July 1990, cleared Wal Murray and the NP's Ian Causley, the Minister for Natural Resources, of acting dishonestly over North Coast land development. Both, however, had taken actions over disposing of Crown land which "put the public interest at risk and created a climate conducive to corrupt conduct". Roden found evidence warranting a consideration of prosecution against two National Party MPs – Beck and Don Page[25] – and against Jenny Gardiner, the Secretary of the National Party. Page and Beck were never charged. Gardiner was found to have breached the *Electoral Funding Act* but the court did not record a conviction.

The Roden findings presented Greiner with three problems. First, the indispensable Murray had been damaged, and Robert Webster briefly considered a leadership challenge.[26] Murray never fully recovered his reputation but survived, helped by Greiner's steadfastness and by a revival in the Government's standing in the polls in the latter part of 1990. Secondly, Labor threatened to use Greiner's own words in calling for the expulsion of Beck and Page from Parliament. Greiner had said in 1986 that the Labor MP, Richard Mochalski, had to be expelled to protect the reputation of the Parliament and Parliament did not need to wait for a conviction to protect its honour. Greiner immediately threatened retaliation. Should Labor proceed, he would move for the expulsion of the Labor MLC who was also cited unfavourably in the Roden report. The matter was dropped.

Thirdly, the Nationals were becoming even more critical of ICAC. They specifically objected to the public hearings which were mandated by the legislation because reputations were being trashed even where Roden had not found evidence of criminality. Sturgess came to ICAC's defence. Well aware of the personal and family suffering experienced by the National Party ministers, he argued that only an open and rigorous inquiry of the kind ICAC conducted could have cleared Murray.[27] Greiner agreed, and said the Government would not review the Commission's procedures. In fact, he was delighted with Roden's findings. They confirmed his confidence in Murray and Causley. The Premier claimed that the Assistant Commissioner had "categorically" found the two ministers to be of "great honesty and integrity".[28] That such a thorough investigation had occurred at all was, he argued, further evidence of the Government's commitment to cleaning up NSW. ICAC remained, for Greiner, one of his outstanding achievements.

During 1990 and early in 1991 the Opposition sought to undermine another of his success stories: the formation of the Senior Executive Service. It launched a series of attacks on individual appointments and on the cost of the system.

Labor had originally set its sights on Sturgess and Kortlang as "political" appointments but then seized on Ross Sayers, the CEO of the State Rail Authority (SRA). Formerly of New Zealand Rail, Sayers had antagonised the unions by tackling over-manning and dubious work practices.[29] In March 1990 Brian Langton, the shadow minister for Transport, accused Sayers of collecting $105,000 for personal expenses in little more than a year, and said senior management used petty cash to pay for lunches of devon and tomato sandwiches, fruit and juice. The State Secretary of the Australian Railways Union detected "rorting of Ceausescu proportions". Even though Sayers' personal expenses were included in his remuneration package, and the sandwich lunches hardly rated alongside the wining and dining at the SRA in the Wran-Unsworth era, Greiner called in the Auditor-General to inquire into Langton's allegations. Sayers was in intensive care after a heart attack when he was cleared of any impropriety. On 27 March Greiner turned on Carr and Langton, and was not challenged when he claimed that, while Sayers was in intensive care, Carr and his "cronies" used words similar to the following: "You don't take a hostage unless you are prepared to shoot him. It's easy because he's a public servant and we don't know him." Greiner's vigorous defence of the rail chief probably contributed to the high regard in which he was held by senior public servants.[30]

When Parliament met on 26 February 1991 Carr launched an attack on "the lurks and perks" received by the Senior Executive Service whose members were often better paid than officials of an equivalent status in the Australian Public Service. He conjured up images of ordinary workers struggling to meet their basic costs while paying $70 a year to sustain these packages, and of average taxpayers "footing the bill . . . for the nanny, the Darling Point apartment, the fees at Kings School [sic] and the soft top Mercedes for the New South Wales public sector elite". Individuals were not spared. Carr described Sturgess as "a political hack", and said Percy Allan – "the former left-wing firebrand" from NSW Young Labor – had more than doubled his income since 1988 and had previously worked better for less. He referred twice to "fat cats", once to "the corporate takeover mentality of the Premier" and once to "a bureaucratic master race". His substantive points were that the Greiner Government was wasting resources which would be better directed elsewhere, that it was paying public servants extra money to do what they were already doing, and that one of the arguments for an SES – to incorporate the values of the private sector – was being undermined by the lack of interest among private sector employees in becoming public servants.

Greiner insisted that NSW had "the best managed public service in Australia". Pointing out how Labor had voted for the establishment of the SES, he said that the shadow cabinet had been fully briefed on the implications of the scheme more than 18 months ago. It especially annoyed him that the Leader of the Opposition frequently and deliberately misrepresented reality. Carr had made allegations about secret arrangements in settling packages which were simply untrue; these determinations were published in the *Government Gazette*. Convinced that Carr would lie or exaggerate to make a point, Greiner treated his repeated "slurs" on the SES as third-rate theatre.

There was one matter on which Nick Greiner was potentially exposed. He had stressed, before taking office, that he would not be following Labor's practice of providing jobs for mates, and especially for mates who had no qualifications for appointment. In an article headed, "A parade of the party faithful", the *SMH* on 15 September 1990 drew attention to more than 30 men and women with Liberal Party connections, or a personal association with the Premier or other ministers, who had been appointed to statutory authorities. Lloyd Lange, for example, Greiner's former mentor, was appointed Deputy Chairman of GIO in 1988. Yet Greiner could reasonably argue that each elevation was justified on grounds of merit. He could certainly do so in the case of his friend, James Yonge, who was appointed Chairman of the Maritime Services Board in 1989. It was embarrassing, however, when Yonge was sacked in June 1990 as CEO of the Hong Kong Bank of Australia which had suffered huge losses on loans, and questions were raised in the *SMH* and by a QC's report about his associations with the discredited Laurie Connell, Alan Bond and Christopher Skase. Greiner and Baird were forced to raise the various accusations with Yonge who swore he had done nothing improper or dishonest. Greiner gave a spirited defence of Yonge and refused to sack him. Carr fulminated about how NSW Inc. "does its business" and how it appointed "walking disasters" to manage authorities, but the issue soon fizzled.[31]

## Greiner and Howard

One of the striking features of Greiner's later political career was that he so often found himself in opposition to John Howard. During 1988, for example, the two clashed over Asian immigration, multiculturalism and Liberal Party values and traditions.

A report for the Commonwealth Government on immigration policy, released at the beginning of June, referred to declining public support for immigration linked to disquiet about the emphasis on multiculturalism. It urged Canberra to affirm the pre-eminence of an Australian identity. When Greiner spoke as both Premier and Minister for Ethnic Affairs at a news conference at the end of July, he acknowledged there were concerns in the community about multiculturalism. But he saw no point arguing about whether Australia should be a multicultural society: in "reality" it was one. Any debate should focus on how the problems could be overcome.[32] On 1 August Greiner and Howard both spoke at the State Conference of the West Australian Liberals in Esperance. Howard used the occasion, as well as radio and television interviews, to criticise multiculturalism as divisive. He pressed the case for a "One Australia" policy, and called for a slowdown in Asian immigration in the interests of social cohesion. Returning to Sydney for the publication of the Curran Report, Greiner reiterated his commonsense views about what constituted reality and the need for better policies, declaring he was comfortable with the present level of Asian immigration.[33]

Greiner delivered a stronger message to Howard on 10 August. He saw no problem with the present level of Asian immigration, even if surveys were showing a majority of Australians wanted a cut. The realist pointed out how public opinion polls always recorded complaints about too many migrants, the most fervent complainants being migrants of the previous generation. Besides, "multiculturalism has really got the runs on the board" and should not be scrapped because politicians had failed to explain it properly. Australia had virtually no ethnic tensions and had done better than any other comparable country in managing large-scale immigration, and it was a fact that one-third of Australians had a non-English-speaking background. While Howard refused to comment on Greiner's sharp rejection of his views on Asian immigration, the Premier continued to distance himself from the Leader of the Federal Opposition. At the end of August, speaking at the annual general meeting of the NSW Ethnic Communities' Council, he described multiculturalism as "the greatest Australian success story", and repeated his call for better policies. Yet, in one respect, the assimilated son of migrants was not far removed from Howard's notion of "One Australia". He warned in December that migrants risked a backlash from other parts of the community if they refused to learn English; "putting Australia first" involved making an effort to learn the "national language".[34]

By the end of 1988 Greiner and Howard had clearly drifted apart in their attitudes towards Liberal Party rules and conventions, partly as a result of their vastly different experience of the Party Organisation.

Whereas Howard, mentored by Carrick since his time as a Young Liberal, sat for many years on the NSW State Executive and served as a senior office-bearer, Greiner was never part of the ruling establishment. Howard understood how the Liberal Party worked, he was careful to observe its rules and conventions, accepted the separate roles of the parliamentary and non-parliamentary wings, and always sought to carry the Party Organisation with him. In a masterly understatement, Howard said Greiner was "a little bit dismissive" of the Party Organisation.[35] As Leader of the Opposition, Greiner attended most of the monthly meetings of the State Executive; as Premier, he went to about a quarter of them. He sometimes addressed State Council but avoided further involvement, relying on Pickering, Dowd and the Group to keep everything under control. In October 1988, however, he became more involved because of criticisms of Community Polling and because he supported Starr's removal as State Director.

Starr had tried in the aftermath of the 1988 election to establish regular meetings with the Premier.[36] Greiner was content just to keep his

distance; Starr's preoccupations were irrelevant to the management of
NSW Inc. The Premier's office staff, along with Sturgess and Kortlang,
felt more strongly. Sturgess recalled telling Greiner that the State Director
was "totally disloyal" and "cannot be trusted on anything".[37] Sturgess had
a specific complaint, namely, Starr's "deliberately mischievous" decision
not to include the Community Polling details as Party donations in the
Liberal Party's return under the *Election Funding Act*. Instead of being
folded in "like an omelette", the Community Polling details were stapled
on the back of the official return. Starr, in fact, was not the official
responsible for filing the returns; the one who was probably saved
Greiner from investigation by the Election Funding Authority.[38] The
State Director became involved, however, when Hooper asked him to
use a particular form of words when dealing with the media. Community
Polling should be presented as acting "for and on behalf of the Liberal
Party" to enable it "to conduct public opinion research" to prepare for
a professional election campaign. Starr left a message for Greiner and
Hooper telling them the media would recognise the words as "a lie", and
he would not endorse them.[39]

The second, more serious, objection arose out of the Liberal Party's
practice of providing cars for members of Greiner's staff. Starr learnt in
April 1988 that new cars were to be leased by the Party and registered in
the names of Hooper, Kortlang and Sturgess (the latter two were waiting
the arrival of their official limousines). Bob Frost was involved in the
arrangement which Starr described as "contrary to the Party's finance
principles, ethically dubious and politically stupid".[40] On 29 April the
State Executive retrospectively authorised the lease arrangements "for
use by people not on the payroll", the funds being "provided by specially
committed donations not available for other purposes". The story about
the cars became public on Wednesday 19 October with a front page
piece in the *Sydney Morning Herald* quoting the State Executive minutes of
29 April and other "Liberal sources". Suspicion inevitably fell on Starr
because the material had clearly been leaked from within the Secretariat.

The State Director said he did not plant the story "but could not deny" having opposed the arrangement.[41] Greiner confirmed the *SMH* account in Parliament, pointing out that no law had been broken, tax dollars had been saved, there was no actual or potential conflict of interest, and Frost had acted in his official capacity as Finance Vice-President and had not personally provided cars or donated funds to pay for their lease.[42]

Starr's denials about the leak did not convince anybody in the Premier's office. At the very least, he was "guilty" because the Secretariat was the source. Greiner was now convinced Starr had to go, and the senior office-bearers of the Organisation agreed to act. They summoned the State Director to Riley Street on the evening of 19 October. Unlike the Labor Party, which dismissed a State Secretary in 1976 within a matter of minutes, the Liberal Party's office-bearers took four hours of emotive exchanges and tortured argument to extract a resignation from their State Director.[43] If he had been privy to the proceedings, Greiner might have concluded that the inability to "execute and implement" was not confined to Starr.

When the story broke on the following Friday, the *SMH* presented Starr's resignation as "Greiner 1, Howard 0 as top Lib quits". Starr was seen as Howard's man in the Organisation, and the Federal Leader spoke out on radio about his former staffer's "very high integrity" and "considerable competence". Howard refused to answer "Yes" or "No" when asked if he was engaged in a power struggle with the NSW Premier. He preferred to quote Greiner's comment of the previous day that the two men had "a very congenial relationship" (which would have surprised one of them).[44] Howard sought Starr's reinstatement when he and Greiner attended a meeting of office-bearers where it was agreed that the State Executive should settle the question at its meeting on 4 November. Howard and Carrick attempted in the intervening period to rally support for Starr although they realised two days before the Executive meeting the numbers were not there. Pickering and Dowd had worked on the numerically stronger though divided Group faction on the

Executive to ensure that Greiner would not be embarrassed. Greiner's telephone message book indicates he was in contact with others active on his behalf.[45] He met Howard again, two hours before the State Executive meeting. It appears they agreed to disagree in a way which would not be too divisive.

Greiner moved that the State Executive note Starr's resignation and resolve not to reinstate him. Acknowledging there was fault on both sides, Greiner said it was "not tenable" to retain a State Director who did not have the full confidence of the office-bearers and of the State Parliamentary Leader. After Howard spoke warmly in favour of Starr's work with the Federal Parliamentary Party, the Executive noted the resignation and, in the interests of sweetness and light, dropped any reference to a reinstatement which was not going to happen.[46] The Executive also noted how Community Polling's activities from mid-1987 had resulted from a breakdown in communications between the State Director and the State Parliamentary Party. Greiner assured the Executive that a similar organisation would not be formed again. The Premier could afford to be charitable. He joined Howard in a press statement which described the former State Director as "a man of complete honesty and integrity" who had "conducted himself in a highly professional manner", and implicitly cleared him of leaking.

Next day, 5 November, six former State Presidents publicly called for a return to the system of funding the Liberal Party which had applied since its formation.[47] On the same day, the Liberal Party chose Bronwyn Bishop to head the Senate team for the next election. She defeated Chris Puplick, Howard's Shadow Minister for the Environment, who, left in the vulnerable third place on the Coalition ticket, lost his seat in 1990. Puplick believes that Greiner turned vital votes against him in order to make sure that Bishop stayed out of State politics. Greiner simply regarded her as the stronger candidate and the better performer, and was also grateful for her assistance in delivering western Sydney seats in 1988.[48]

State Council at the end of November re-affirmed the principles which the NSW Division had regarded since its inception "as essential to its proper function, character and integrity". That is, the Organisation was solely responsible for raising and spending campaign funds, campaigns should be managed solely by the State Executive-appointed campaign committee through the State Director – "after full consultation with the parliamentary leaders", and Liberal MPs and candidates "should not have private election funds or handle donations".[49]  The Council had effectively condemned Community Polling, vindicated Starr's stand over Community Polling and the leasing of the cars, and implicitly rebuked Greiner for ignoring Party rules and conventions. Greiner was hardly bothered. The Party had provided him with a Leader's fund of $30,000. Community Polling, and the other financial activities which had passed unnoticed, had served their purpose in circumstances unlikely to be repeated. Secure in the Party Room and in the Cabinet, he could pursue his agenda without having to deal extensively with the Liberal Party outside Macquarie Street or the State Office Block.

Howard agreed that the Starr issue "caused friction" between Greiner and himself.[50] Crucially, Greiner had outfaced him because of a shift in the balance of power between the Federal and State parliamentary parties. Howard's defeat in the 1987 Federal election, Greiner's election victory in 1988, and the continuing Howard-Peacock conflict had effectively weakened the Federal Leader's position. The office-bearers of the Right faction who had moved against Starr did lose out in bitterly contested internal elections in September 1989. The new State President, Peter King, had moved the resolution at State Council condemning Community Polling. Nonetheless, the winning Group "ticket" claimed it was campaigning to "help Nick", and Greiner knew that the State Executive would not stand in his way.

His relationship with Howard, however, was further strained by the coup which brought Peacock back to the Federal leadership on Tuesday 9 May 1989. Caught unawares – he learnt of a spill motion the night before – Howard was defeated by 44 votes to 27. Greiner knew nothing of the moves against Howard and learnt of the spill motion only when watching television on the Monday evening. On the following morning Greiner threatened to sack anyone working for him who had been involved in the plot. Kortlang was in Canberra at the time lobbying on behalf of the NSW Government for a navy contract. Greiner did not know that his former aide had been brought into the secret planning by John Moore, a former Queensland State President and one of Howard's frontbenchers. After initial denials and confusion about his role, Kortlang acknowledged his involvement "over a number of weeks" because of his known ability for strategic planning.[51] Returning to Sydney, Kortlang told Greiner he could not forewarn him because the Premier was "such a blabbermouth" and might leak the story. The two men had a blazing row but they quickly made up.[52] Kortlang resigned from State Development soon afterwards and became Peacock's chief of staff, a position he left after two months.

Kortlang had done Greiner a service by keeping him out of the picture. Howard's staff believed Greiner was involved in the plot; Howard now accepts he was not.[53] Some commentators tried to link Greiner to the affair by referring to the immigration debate and the "Starr wars", and some – rightly – asked whether it was appropriate for the head of a State government department to be politicking in the Federal arena.[54] Greiner said that public servants "are entitled to have political involvement as long as they're doing their job". He could not resist a gentle dig by suggesting that Kortlang – "an important part of my Government's election" – had "taken on another, and some might say greater, challenge". Was it unreasonable for commentators to conclude that Greiner "will not be shedding any tears" over Howard's demise? After Puplick, a key plotter, was jeered at a subsequent meeting of State Council, he recorded in his diary how Greiner had been "friendly and positive".[55] But the Premier was always at pains to deny that his relationship with Howard was anything other than "perfectly amicable and appropriate". The customary code word – "professional"

– had been replaced by a new one – "appropriate" – to describe their contacts and meetings.[56]

## Eastern Creek

On 5 October 1989 Greiner announced at the Sydney Motor Show that a new race track would be built at Eastern Creek near Blacktown in the Western Suburbs. Bob Barnard, an English-born engineer with a gift for pitching a sale, was to construct the track with the objective of bidding for the 1990 Motorcycle Grand Prix. Greiner was none too pleased when Melbourne beat Sydney for the right to bid for the 1996 Olympic Games and Victoria won a lucrative frigate contract. NSW could now take over an event which Barnard had previously managed at Phillip Island in Victoria. The package offered to Barnard included an agreement to underwrite the venture to the value of $2m for six months and to fast-track the planning processes.

Everything started to come unstuck publicly from 17 January 1990 when the *Fédération de Internationale Motorcyclisme* (FIM) announced that the Grand Prix would not be held at Eastern Creek in 1990 because the circuit had not been completed, as required, by the previous 31 December. Barnard was already involved in two separate matters before the Victorian Supreme Court, having fallen out with the Auto Cycle Council of Australia which managed the Grand Prix on behalf of FIM. On Australia Day, Barnard told a magazine that, weather permitting, the track would be finished by mid-February, weeks ahead of schedule. He also said the Government "has been fantastically supportive" and that, while the Premier had yet to visit Eastern Creek, he had flown over it several times and said, "keep going, it looks great".[57] The *Sydney Morning Herald* was now running daily stories headed, "The Grand Prix Fiasco", as very public and sometimes heated arguments proceeded over who promised what in relation to dates of completion. Greiner intervened directly – and unsuccessfully – in an attempt to rescue the event in 1990. Under pressure, he revealed that the Government had provided the consortium building the raceway with a $20m loan at a concessional interest rate of 13.75 per cent, and had guaranteed repayment of a State Bank loan of $5.5m to Barnard, of which $2m had already been used to pay off his Victorian creditors. The Government was also paying premium prices for land associated with the raceway and to develop nearby recreation facilities amounting already to some $15m.

In February 1990 Carr claimed that the costs to the taxpayer had ballooned to more than $53m. Greiner responded by stressing the additional recreational benefits for what were Labor electorates. He also produced a Treasury estimate that over 20 years the return should be $478m at about twice more than the costs, while the guarantees were considerably lower than those Labor provided for the Sydney Entertainment Centre and the Sydney Football Stadium. Greiner had "absolutely no doubt in saying that the investment is absolutely first class".[58] The costs to the taxpayers in fact just kept mounting, and the Opposition constantly reminded Greiner in his first term of the unfolding disaster, which the floundering of Robert Rowland-Smith, the Minister for Sport, in the Legislative Council did nothing to avert.

Greiner later acknowledged that Eastern Creek was a mistake. It was a mistake in two parts: he was "sold a pup" by John Harvey, his minder during the 1988 election, who had "morphed" into his chief of staff and become the Premier's representative in making the deals and running the project; and the "pup" could be sold because Greiner had not been true to his own principles. It was one thing to allow a manager to manage– Greiner kept to that principle, as he did with Metherell – but he now accepts he should have looked more closely at Harvey's complicated business and employment record.[59] A graduate of the Harvard Business School, and the Managing Director of NSW Inc., should have avoided making deals with the first private entrepreneurs to come up with an idea, and have looked more carefully at the costs and ramifications of the arrangement.

## Aboriginal affairs

Growing up in a household where his father was dismissive of Aboriginal people, and where great value was placed on assimilating into Australian society, it is not surprising that Greiner did not favour special privileges let alone separate rights for particular ethnic groups. When Leader of the Opposition he accepted that historic disadvantages ought to be confronted, but said no Aborigines in NSW had "a special affinity with particular land"; therefore, "a logical basis for special rights . . . does not exist".[60] Greiner entered government with the intention of repealing Wran's *Aboriginal Land Rights Act 1983*. He immediately abolished the Department of Aboriginal Affairs and created an Office of Aboriginal Affairs within the Premier's Department. In September 1988 and April 1989 the Government produced papers which proposed the formation of smaller and self-managing community councils, the "mainstreaming" of all State Aboriginal services to the relevant government departments, and placing a priority on economic development and social improvement. The proposals embodied Greiner's concerns about separatism, financial mismanagement, poor living standards and the failure of self-advancement in Aboriginal communities.

The Government launched an extensive consultation process, and appointed Charles Perkins, the former Secretary of the Commonwealth Department of Aboriginal Affairs, to prepare an independent report. Early in October 1989, while Wal Murray was overseas, Greiner told representatives of the NSW Aboriginal Land Council (NSWALC) – including one he had previously accused of rorting the system – that the Government intended to amend rather than repeal the Wran legislation and to focus on accountability and improved services. The outcome of further consultation was the *Aboriginal Land Rights (Amendment) Act 1990* which passed with bi-partisan support in September 1990. In its final form, the legislation extended the powers and functions of the NSWALC, reduced the powers of regional Land Councils and expanded the functions of Local Aboriginal Land Councils. It also provided for the participation of the Electoral Commissioner in Council elections, the audit of annual financial statements and the investigation of Council affairs and appointment of administrators. A person elected to an office under the Act had to disclose any direct or indirect pecuniary interest if it might conflict with the proper performance of the duties of the office. Speaking earlier in the year, Greiner said the amendments "flow from two years of extensive debate and consultation" and acknowledged they represented "a significant departure from the Government's pre-election policy regarding Aboriginal affairs".[61]

Greiner had dropped his opposition to what he had criticised as separatism to focus on accountability and management, on applying code of conduct principles to elected officials, and on socio-economic development. For someone with supposedly "bad political instincts", he was acutely aware that politics was about what was possible.

## Senator Kathryn Greiner?

When Senator Peter Baume signalled his intention to resign his seat, Ted Pickering called Kathryn in mid-October 1990 to ask her to nominate for the vacancy. A number of leading contenders, all from the Group, were expected to withdraw in her favour. Her pre-selection seemed assured. Kathryn was tempted but, after talking with family and friends over a weekend, decided against putting her name forward because her children (Justin was then aged 18 and about to finish school and Kara was nearly 16) would have been left "with no parent at all". Much later she said, "I knew in my heart of hearts what the decision would be": the children were still teenagers and Nick could not have managed during her long absences from Sydney. When questioned before Kathryn made the decision, her husband was at best lukewarm. "The question is whether, on her merits, she would be good at it. I think the answer to that is probably yes." He called Kathryn "a great asset politically", thought that an already "harum-scarum private life" would become "a bit more so", and recalled how she had "traditionally said one politician in the family is enough". Pickering thought that Greiner in fact stopped her from going ahead. If he did so, it was only in the sense that Kathryn made her decision with the family circumstances in mind.[62]

After her decision became public, Greiner said it was his "preferred option". He thought Kathryn now needed to find something fulfilling and satisfying and "more compatible with her variety of other responsibilities to myself and the family". Greiner's political instinct told him that the "great asset" was indispensable to his premiership.

### Endnotes

[1]   Interview: Greiner, 30 May 2012.

[2]   Interview: Pickering, 13 July 2012.

[3]   An example of the latter was the failed attempt in 1988 to remove Labor's "Johnno" Johnson as President of the Legislative Council. It was a "lapse of political judgment . . . a hasty move . . . hard to fathom": Clune and Griffith, *Decision and Deliberation,* pp. 568 and 590-1.

[4]   Interview: Greiner, 30 September 2011.

[5]   Interview: Carr, 30 January 2012.

[6]   Asked in 1988 whether she could do the job of Premier, Kathryn said she could do it better because she was tougher than her husband and "a real shit". *Australian,* 13 April 1994.

[7]   Interview: Greiner, 30 March 2011.

[8]   Interview: Allan, 14 September 2011.

[9]   Anne Susskind, *SMH,* 6 June 1988; interview: Malcolm Kerr, 24 April 2012.

[10]   Stirton to Greiner, 14 March 1989, Research Material, Various Matters, Greiner Papers.

[11]   *NSWPD,* Third Series, vol. 205, p. 4341, 1 December 1988.

[12]   Two NP backbenchers were not so restrained. See *Northern Daily Leader,* 17 and 19 August 1988.

[13]   Terry Metherell, Autobiography. Terry Metherell generously gave me access to his unpublished Autobiography when I was doing research on the NSW Liberals.

[14] Interview, Pickering: 13 July 2011.

[15] *DT* and *SMH*, 21 July 1990.

[16] *SMH*, 11 September 1990.

[17] Interview: Sturgess, 22 June 2011.

[18] Seaton Papers.

[19] *NSWPD*, Third Series, vol. 203, pp. 1138-9.

[20] The above three paragraphs are mainly based on interviews with Sturgess on 22 June and Greiner on 7 Sepember 2011; for Murray's summary of his conversation with Singleton, see Davey, *The Nationals*, pp. 318-9, and for Greiner's comments and the general reportage in *SMH*, 25 January 1989.

[21] *DT*, 17 January 1989.

[22] *NSWPD*, Third Series, vol. 206, pp. 4919-24.

[23] *Ibid.*, vol. 213, pp. 856-67.

[24] For a brief account of this affair, see Ernest Chaples and Barbara Page, "The New South Wales Independent Commission against Corruption", in Laffin and Painter, *Reform and Reversal*, pp. 58-62. For the Roden Report, see ICAC, *Report on Investigation into North Coast Land Development*, July 1990, pp. xiii-xxvi and pp. 1-670.

[25] Page has represented Ballina since 1988, and is currently the Minister for Local Government and for the North Coast in the O'Farrell Government.

[26] Davey, *The Nationals*, pp. 331-2.

[27] Personal Diary, quoted in Sturgess, "Guarding the Polity", pp. 12-13.

[28] For reactions to the ICAC *Report*, see *SMH*, 12 and 14 July and *DT*, 12-13 July 1990.

[29] An extreme example of what Sayers and Baird, Minister for Transport, inherited was reproduced in the *Financial Times* (London), 6 June 1990.

[30] *NSWPD*, Third Series, vol. 213, p. 981; Interview: Sturgess, 22 June 2012.

[31] *SMH*, 6 and 23 June 1990; *NSWPD*, Third Series, vol. 217, 13 September 1990, pp. 7159-65.

[32] *DT*, 28 July 1988.

[33] *Australian* and *SMH*, 1-3 August 1988; Paul Kelly, *The End of Certainty: Power, Politics and Business in Australia*, rev.ed., Allen & Unwin, St Leonards, 1994, pp. 420-8; John Howard, *Lazarus Rising: A Personal and Political Biography*, HarperCollins, Sydney, 2010. pp. 173-5.

[34] *DT*, 11 August and 10 December; *SMH*, 29 August 1988.

[35] Interview: Howard, 21 December 2011.

[36] State Director to State President, 22 April 1988, Alphabetical Correspondence, LPA, ML, MSS 7205/36.

[37] Interview: Sturgess, 27 September 2004.

[38] The official responsible under the Act was Fergus Hynes of the Secretariat: personal communication.

[39] Starr Papers.

[40] Undated note, written after his resignation, Starr Papers.

[41] Interview: Starr, 28 July 2004.

[42] *NSWPD*, Third Series, vol. 204, pp. 2583-4.

[43] For the dismissal of Geoff Cahill, see Marian Wilkinson, *The Fixer: the Untold Story of Graham Richardson,* Heinemann, Melbourne, 1996, pp. 76-8; for the removal of Starr, see Hancock, *Liberals,* pp. 269-71.

[44] *SMH,* 26 Oct. 1988.

[45] Telephone Messages Book, 26 October 1988-12 October 1990, Greiner Papers.

[46] Minutes of the State Executive, 4 November 1988, LPA, ML, MSS 7205/11.

[47] *Sun-Herald,* 6 November 1988.

[48] Interviews: Greiner, 22 November 2010 and Puplick, 13 December 2011.

[49] Minutes of State Council, 26 November 1988, LPA, ML, MSS 7205/5; Hancock, *Liberals,* p. 274.

[50] Interview: Howard, 21 December 2011.

[51] *Daily Mirror,* 11 May 1989.

[52] Interview: Kortlang, 12 July 2011.

[53] Interview: Howard, 21 December 2011.

[54] For Labor's queries on the subject, see Jack Hallam in *NSWPD,* Third Series, vol. 208, p. 8039.

[55] Puplick: personal communication, 18 December 2011.

[56] Except where otherwise stated, the above two paragraphs draw upon *Australian, Daily Mirror, DT* and *SMH,* 11-12 May 1989. Howard mentioned Greiner's name just twice and only in passing in his autobiography. He did not refer to their disagreements over immigration or the "Starr wars", or to Kortlang's involvement in the May 1989 coup.

[57] Mike Kable, "All Stops Out For Eastern Creek", *Revs Motorcycle News,* 7-20 February 1990, pp. 20-1.

58  *NSWPD*, Third Series, vol. 213, 22 February 1990, pp. 52-9; vol. 219, 21 November 1990, pp. 10167-9.

59  Interview: Greiner 30 March 2011; for a less than laudatory article on Harvey's record, see Ben Hills, *SMH*, 20 September 1997.

60  *NSWPD*, Third Series, vol. 181, p. 143.

61  *SMH*, 7 September 1988 and 5-6 October 1989; *NSWPD*, Third Series, vol. 207, 20 April 1989, pp. 6956-8 and vol. 214, 10 May 1990, pp. 2948-9 ; NSW Department of Aboriginal Affairs, *Background Paper, Review of the Aboriginal Land Rights Act 1983*, Sydney, 2000, pp. 13-20.

62  Interviews: Kathryn Greiner, 14 September 2010 and 29 March 2011; Justin Greiner, 18 April; Nick Greiner, 30 March; Pickering 13 July 2011. See esp. *Australian*, 19 and 23 October; *SMH*, 19-20 and 23 October 1990. John Tierney was eventually selected for the Senate vacancy.

# 12

# "New Federalism"

Dick Humphry believes that Nick Greiner "wasn't just a State politician . . . he could transcend State politics". Humphry, who served several ministers in his public service career, the majority of them Labor, considers Greiner to be "the outstanding one in terms of vision", a vision which extended beyond the borders of NSW.[1] In 1990 Greiner demonstrated this wider field of interest by enthusiastically supporting Bob Hawke's attempts to promote a more co-operative federal relationship while simultaneously challenging the Liberal Party to abandon its habit of always trumpeting, invoking or defending "States' rights".

In one respect, however, he was no different from the other State Premiers – his predecessors and contemporaries – in complaining about Canberra's control and manipulation of the financial relationship. Unlike most State Liberals, however, his objections were not accompanied by ritual denunciations of centralism. A clause in the 1948 Federal Platform committed Liberals to "the maintenance unimpaired of the Federal system of government". Menzies and Holt had always genuflected before this command, even as they presided over a steady accumulation of Commonwealth power. John Gorton angered the Liberal State Premiers Robin Askin and Henry Bolte by arguing that the Party should amend the rhetoric to match the reality. They reacted to his "centralism" by joining the campaign which led to his downfall as Prime Minister in March 1971. Malcolm Fraser's brand of "New Federalism",[2] projected as co-operative and anti-centralist in contrast to the Gorton and Gough Whitlam approach, failed to impress Liberals such as Sir Charles Court, the Premier of Western Australia. He believed that the Commonwealth continued to deprive the States of sufficient funds and kept attacking Canberra in the name of "States' rights". By not taking the Askin-Bolte-Court position Greiner demonstrated once again how little he had inherited from what Pickering called the Liberal "gene pool".

Greiner operated on two levels in his approach to Commonwealth-State issues. First, as Premier and Treasurer he played his part in the annual ritual of the Premiers' Conference; that is, he arrived with many demands and few expectations, received the Commonwealth's take-it-or-leave package, and returned to Sydney blaming the Commonwealth for subsequent reductions in services and increases in taxes and charges. Early in May 1988, before attending his first Conference, he referred to these occasions as "a circus of monumental proportions". Prompted by Robin Gray, the Liberal Premier of Tasmania, he proposed an immediate adjournment when the Conference convened because there was no point "slinking off to the Cabinet room" when the Government's offer was not "the basis for getting anywhere productive". Hawke growled: "You're entitled in your initial appearance here to use stupid language."[3] It looked like an unpropitious beginning, but everyone present knew the roles being played and there was no damage to the Greiner-Hawke relationship.

Greiner closely followed the script in the May 1989 Conference. In advance he warned of increases in taxes and charges and cuts to essential services, and blamed the Treasurer, Paul Keating. He expressed surprise when the Commonwealth slashed the funding grant to NSW by $287m in real terms and said the decision was "impossible to justify". Returning to Sydney, Greiner announced immediate cuts in services and imposed an even tighter squeeze on public service employment. The ritual did vary slightly in 1989. Hawke and Keating called the Conference the "most docile and cooperative" for some years, and the Premier of NSW, who wanted the Commonwealth to slash the States' global borrowing limit, praised the Commonwealth for slicing off $1bn, even though he wanted a greater reduction.

Greiner's second level of approach was to focus on reform. Specifically, he wanted to address the problems of vertical fiscal imbalance and special purpose grants. The imbalance occurred because the Commonwealth collected revenue far in excess of its needs and the revenue the States could raise was not nearly sufficient to meet their expenditure requirements. Greiner wanted the States to have greater access to sources of revenue. He also wanted to reduce the number of Commonwealth special purpose grants to the States made under s96 of the Constitution. Regarding them as tied grants, Greiner argued that the Commonwealth used them to trespass on the States' independence and that the grants became expenditure as well as revenue items. More broadly, to advance the cause of micro-economic reform, Greiner called for a reduction in the duplication of activity and responsibilities within the Federation, and for the establishment of national infrastructures – especially in electricity and transport – the absence of which he considered grossly inefficient.

For Greiner it was just common sense. As he argued at the end 1991, Australia could no longer think of itself as an island cut off from world markets and indulge in the luxury of isolation. Countries across the world, irrespective "of badge or ideology", had been "mugged by reality". There was now "an international market for smaller, more efficient government", and governments were privatising and deregulating in the quest for financial capital in circumstances where investors could move at will in and out of any jurisdiction. Globalisation had forced governments to compete with each other over the costs and services they offered business. Instead, therefore, of becoming involved as investors like the Labor Governments of Victoria and Western Australia, or second-guessing movements in the market, governments should – preferably in cooperation – be addressing the excessive costs and regulations affecting Australian business and reforming uncompetitive government trading enterprises.[4]

## The Premiers' Conference of June 1990

At the end of May 1990 Greiner left Sydney to visit the United States, Britain and Europe. He wanted to help restore Australia's financial reputation which had been trashed by the behaviour of "corporate cowboys". There was a real fear that overseas investors would not renew their NSW Treasury bonds. After concluding his official business Greiner planned to have a brief holiday in Europe with Kathryn. The situation was so serious that he accepted Percy Allan's advice to visit banks in Amsterdam, Frankfurt and Zurich. There were some welcome interludes: he had two meetings in Washington with Vice-President Dan Quayle, attended the five-yearly reunion of the Harvard Class of 1970, and spent an hour with Margaret Thatcher at No. 10 Downing Street. Less welcome was the London *Financial Times* survey of NSW which was published on 5 June. Declaring that "Mr Greiner is looking like a one-term Premier", the paper said his boast about NSW becoming one of the "Tiger Economies" of the Asia/Pacific region in the 1990s was sounding "a little hollow". Greiner dismissed the survey as itself "hollow". But the budgetary situation continued to preoccupy him. He announced while abroad that he would not follow Keating's command to cut services by reducing funding for the priority areas of education, health and law and order. Nor would he raise taxes and charges above the rate of inflation. Instead, he would increase borrowings – which would have an "infinitesimal" impact on debt reduction – and reduce capital works expenditure.[5]

The Hawke Government had its own problems in the lead-up to the 1990 Premiers' Conference. Faced with a ten per cent fall in his projected budget surplus, Keating needed the States to follow the Commonwealth and cut their spending. He reminded them that Australia continued to live beyond its means.[6] For his part, Hawke needed a sense of purpose to define his fourth term. He had barely won the election of March 1990, scraping back via deals with the Democrats and the Greens and helped by the Coalition's poor performance in NSW and Queensland.

Hawke grasped an unlikely source for revitalization. Whereas in his Boyer Lectures of 1979 he supported abolition of the States and strengthening of local government, he made no attempt to promote this ideal in government, except for maintaining the Commonwealth's financial hold. Three weeks before the scheduled Premiers' Conference opened on 28 June Hawke told the Premiers he wanted to widen the agenda to cover micro-economic reform. On the eve of the Conference he announced his intention of calling a special meeting to review the whole area of Federal-State relations, and to address the questions of how to provide the best services and how to "co-operate to deliver a competitive, efficient economy".[7] During the Conference he said that a Special Premiers' Conference, to be held later in the year, would start the process of creating a real partnership, and look to new issues like environmental protection alongside the familiar ones of finance and the allocation of functions.[8]

Notionally, Hawke went into the June meeting surrounded by allies. Five of the six Premiers were Labor. Three of them – Wayne Goss (Queensland), Carmen Lawrence (Western Australia) and Michael Field (Tasmania) – were newcomers, and John Cain (Victoria) and John Bannon (South Australia) were veterans. It hardly mattered that the Chief Ministers of the ACT and the Northern Territory were, respectively, Liberal and Country Liberal. The Liberal Premier of NSW did matter, and he proved to be Hawke's closest and most effective ally. The two men were genuine micro-economic reformers and had a high regard for each other's intelligence.[9] But their commitment to a genuine partnership had to be placed on hold in mid-1990. The conventions of warfare took precedence because the States were more than usually angry about their treatment. Greiner's markedly deteriorating budgetary situation in NSW meant that he went to Canberra determined to engage with the Commonwealth in what proved to be one of the most acrimonious of the post-war Premiers' Conferences.

Greiner's preliminary manoeuvres aroused Paul Keating by

challenging the Commonwealth on its home ground. In the lead-up to the Conference the NSW Government placed full-page advertisements in the national and Sydney newspapers. They included graphs designed to show how, since the advent of the Hawke Government in 1983, the Commonwealth had increased its spending and derived more revenue in real terms by a greater margin than had occurred in the States. Moreover, while increasing its own spending in real terms by 32.4 per cent, it had reduced payments to the States by 5.3 per cent. In other words, the Commonwealth should be addressing its own actions instead of lecturing the States on cutting back.[10] Keating accused Greiner of a "blatantly dishonest presentation of public statistics" and of using a "tricky fudged up table" in relation to revenues. The figures looked better by using the starting-point of 1985 instead of 1983 when Hawke came to power. Greiner stood his ground. Keating had selected a starting-point half way through the Hawke years to suit himself, which was "nonsense".[11]

Although he was prepared to fight the Commonwealth for the sake of financial justice, Greiner's overriding concern remained one of rationalising and reforming the relationship. Tactically and strategically it suited his cause to forge a link between Hawke's interest in micro-economic reform and a redistribution of responsibilities and a fairer financial relationship within the Federation. To this end, Sturgess and the Cabinet Office provided Greiner with a 42-page document – "Micro-economic reform of Commonwealth-State relations" – which called for the coherent, rational division of functions and responsibilities, an agreement on allocating responsibilities, and the introduction of modern management practices to shared programs. The paper underscored more of the problems arising from tied grants, including a loss of flexibility, onerous reporting responsibilities, inadequate consultation and skewed State priorities. It also noted how the Commonwealth practice of annual appropriations created uncertainty and inhibited forward planning.[12]

So, in addition to taking on the Commonwealth over specific financial arrangements, Greiner went to Canberra in June 1990 with three objectives. First, he wanted a more sensible distribution of powers and functions between the Commonwealth and the States. He raised the possibility of ceding power to the Commonwealth over industrial relations and control over consumer, health and food standards while retaining a role for the States in the general areas of health and education. To facilitate movement, Greiner recommended forming a task force of officials to work on means of implementing change. Secondly, Greiner wanted the States to have greater power to determine their own spending priorities. Keating's pre-Conference claim of an intention to increase overall funding for the States was "about 70-80 per cent a con job" because the money consisted mainly of tied grants. Thirdly, Greiner wanted a commitment from all governments to a uniform presentation of their accounts to ensure more rational decision-making on public policy.[13]

Greiner was not alone. Bannon, who had also been Federal President of the Labor Party since 1988, had long advocated a review of overlap and duplication. Greiner and Bannon each devised 11-point plans for the Conference, and all the Premiers came together with a statement of principles, worked out beforehand by the State Treasurers. These principles included a commitment to a rolling three-year forward funding program, to Commonwealth-State co-operation on the implementation of micro-economic reform, and to a rationalisation of functions.[14] This broad consensus among the Premiers did not, however, extend to the abandonment of party politics. On arriving in Canberra, Greiner was surprised to find himself excluded when the Labor Premiers caucused on the evening before the opening session.

For all of Hawke's talk of co-operation, the Commonwealth did not modify what had become its traditional lack of consideration. The Premiers and Chief Ministers received their offer in the usual way; that is, a package was slipped under the door of their hotel rooms before breakfast. In sum, the overall general purpose grant was to be reduced by $400m or two per cent in real terms (by $150m for NSW or about

$80 per family), to be offset by an increase in tied grants. The Premiers and Chief Ministers declared the offer a "farce". They were warned. Should they reject the package – which they had no real power to do – the Commonwealth would withdraw its sweetener, namely, to maintain, an albeit-reduced, general purpose grant in real terms for three years. At one stage Hawke told the Premiers and Chief Ministers to "bugger off". But they remained united in their outrage, and announced their rejection of the package at a press conference. Excluded overnight from the Labor caucus, and now sitting between Lawrence and Bannon at the press conference, Greiner remarked that his personal hygiene had clearly improved.

The Premiers had forced the Conference, for the first time in 20 years, to reconvene for a second day. They made a last-minute attempt to secure a trade-off – the States would cut their borrowings by $300m if the general purpose grant was reduced by just $200m – which the Commonwealth brusquely rejected. Bannon described Keating as "obdurate" and called it a "non-negotiable conference". At least Greiner could continue to blame the Commonwealth for further hardships inflicted on his constituency, while giving an assurance there would be little impact on average families.[15] More importantly, he had in Canberra established a good rapport with the Labor Premiers and had made a further mark as someone with a constructive interest in reforming Federal-State relations.

### Hawke and Greiner look to the future

On 19 July, three weeks after the Premiers' Conference, Hawke addressed the National Press Club in Canberra on the subject of "Towards a Closer Partnership". He spoke of seeking "better co-operation" between the Commonwealth and the States within the existing constitutional framework, and identified six areas requiring immediate attention: micro-economic reform, the financial relationship, the delivery of services, social justice, industrial relations and the environment. He announced that a high-level bureaucratic committee, chaired by Mike Codd, the Secretary of the Department of the Prime Minister and Cabinet (PM&C), would prepare its agenda for the Special Premiers' Conference in October. Hawke offered the States a number of inducements to secure their co-operation. He agreed to transfer power to the States to collect the bank accounts debits tax worth about $400m a year. Although an equivalent amount would be deducted from the annual funding grant, the tax would widen the States' revenue base and enable them to determine the level at which it would be levied. The Commonwealth was also prepared to reduce the proportion of tied grants. The States might not get more money but would have greater autonomy in deciding how their funds would be spent. While stressing the need for Commonwealth control of macro-economic policy – all the Premiers and, with alacrity, Greiner, accepted this proposition – Hawke offered an additional incentive: changes to the Federal-State financial arrangements could take place within that framework.

Hawke defined his approach in words Greiner might himself have chosen: the process would follow "sensible, predictable and practical steps". At one level, the Prime Minister had little choice. He had to work with the States because the majority of major utilities and regulatory jurisdictions lay in their domain.[16] Hawke wanted to hold a separate conference to consider constitutional reform but, as Greiner pointed out, much could be done through "co-operative federalism" without taking on the harder task of trying to amend the Constitution. He agreed with the general sense of Hawke's speech and expected NSW "to take a lead and be very helpful in the whole process of reform".[17] Three Labor Premiers also responded favourably and so did John Hewson who became Leader of the Opposition after the 1990 Federal election.

The NSW Premier had been booked to speak at the National Press Club on 25 July. The subject matter and the title of his address – "Physician, Heal Thyself: Micro-Economic Reform of Australian Government" – was chosen in advance of Hawke's speech.[18] He seized the moment, however, to give what in essence became the States' response to Hawke's "New Federalism".

Greiner's starting-point was that governments had long been telling all branches of industry to restructure so Australia could compete successfully in world markets. It was now the turn of governments to do the same. It was time to create "a truly national economy", and a national policy for dealing with social welfare and environmental problems. It was time, too, "for Australian politicians – Federal and State – to grow up, to rise above their parochialism, their desire to score cheap political points, and to act – for once – as a nation". Greiner clearly felt he could speak with moral authority:

> my Government has overhauled the education system, substantially rebuilt the State Rail Authority and Electricity Commission, closed down and contracted out grossly uneconomic government services such as the printing office and the government warehouse. Established a real senior executive service, with rigorous performance assessment, overhauled the State's accounting system . . . The list goes on.

Greiner observed how this restructuring involved a political cost and was undertaken "in the face of massive opposition from vested interests". Yet there was now a "unique opportunity" because of the coincidence of factors: with Europe coming together following the break-up of the Soviet bloc, the obstructions to unity in Australia seemed petty; Australia could not afford inefficient industries in the face of increasing international competitiveness; Australia was approaching the centenary of federation; and the Prime Minister and several State Premiers were committed to reform.

Greiner nonetheless entered important caveats. The reform had to be structural, and heads of government should agree on a set of principles to guide the division of functions rather than leave it to bureaucrats to organise trade-offs. The process should not be treated as one requiring constitutional change because there were no major constitutional impediments to a transfer of powers and functions or standing in the way of remedying vertical fiscal imbalance. The current difficulties "have more to do with the parochialism of State politicians and bureaucrats and the vote-buying and empire-building tendencies of Commonwealth politicians and bureaucrats". The Commonwealth needed to moderate the arrogance and condescension which characterised its dealings with the States. There was a wealth of talent, for instance, in the NSW administration. State and Federal politicians must accept a self-denying ordinance to stay out of each other's territory. The political and bureaucratic involvement should remain at the highest level. Greiner recommended the example of NSW where a committee, chaired by Sturgess, would represent the Government. Finally, drawing upon the advice of Roger Douglas, the key to success for sweeping reform lay in operating on a broad front where there could be winners on both sides. Undertaking small changes in a few areas allowed discontent to focus on specific issues and to obstruct reform. Hawke's offer of a very broad program of reform was, therefore, essential to its success.

Re-iterating his point about first reaching an accord on principles, Greiner foresaw "broad areas of almost universal agreement", starting with the acceptance of the Commonwealth having all the powers necessary for managing the national economy. He favoured a single regulatory regime for Australian business, with uniformity in commercial laws, manufacturing standards, consumer laws, food standards and public health regulation. He also advocated a single, integrated transmission grid for the eastern States, and the development of a trade in water rights across State boundaries. The States should vacate the fields of social welfare policy and industrial relations. Acknowledging he might be in a minority of one within his own Cabinet over withdrawal from industrial relations, he pointed out that the proposed NSW legislation went "considerably further – and faster – towards true enterprise bargaining, voluntary unionism and overall workplace freedom" than Labor governments could presently accept. But it was "a two-way street".

The States were better equipped to deal with service delivery and so, apart from determining macro-economic and social welfare policy, the Commonwealth should largely vacate the fields of education, health and housing. He favoured a "competitive federalism" in service delivery to encourage diversity, quoting Mao Tse-Tung in support: "Let a hundred flowers bloom."

The card-carrying Liberal was not above making a political point within the framework of micro-economic reform. "It is a matter of national shame" that Labor administrations were still debating whether to sell government trading enterprises. The days of government-owned airlines, banks and insurance offices were numbered everywhere. Greiner predicted that all three would, because of "the brutal reality of capital requirements", cease to be in public ownership in Australia by the end of the century. Not one of them had a social purpose. They were commercial organisations which paid dividends and tax equivalents to their owners. In circumstances of monopoly, they should be restructured to introduce competition or, as in the case of GrainCorp in NSW, sold to the users. The Federal Government and the Labor Premiers should understand that the real priorities were, first, micro-economic reform and, secondly, getting macro-economic policy right by bringing interest rates down and making Australia internationally competitive. The Federal Government should not be diverted from pursuing these objectives by giving too much attention to Federal-State relations and constitutional change.

## The Special Premiers' Conference

The steering committee of senior Commonwealth and State public servants – tagged the "Piglets", as the offspring of the "HOG" (Heads of Government) – took control of the preparations for the SPC. Professor Patrick Weller, commissioned by PM&C to undertake a management review, reported in 1995 that the Department was central and pivotal to the whole process.[19] A commissioned report from NSW or Queensland would almost certainly have concluded that the involvement of State officials was critical. Wayne Goss thought so. He singled out Gary Sturgess and his own chief policy adviser, Kevin Rudd. Sturgess added Marcelle Anderson, the Secretary of the Department of Premier and Cabinet in Western Australia. Writing for the *Australian Financial Review,* Prue Anderson thought that this "troika" could, because of a shared party political background with their Premiers, synchronise "bureaucratic action with the ministerial arm of government". She referred to Sturgess having a "rampant visionary style" and said he was "in the mind of the Premier (Greiner)". Anderson may not have appreciated that co-operative – and competitive – federalism was more a Greiner than a Sturgess preoccupation.[20] Either way, Sturgess proved to be such a forceful contributor that Hawke's most recent biographer referred to complaints by Premiers about his "arrogance, condescending airs and self-appointed role as policy savant". Canberra's public servants probably felt the same way, judging by Codd's efforts to circumvent the Sturgess-Rudd (no doubt more advanced and definitive) model of Commonwealth-State relations. Possibly, some Canberra officials felt at once superior and threatened, and behaved in a manner which justified Greiner's concerns about arrogant and condescending attitudes.[21]

Greiner made a brief trip to Brisbane in the week before the Special Premiers' Conference to address a meeting of the Liberal Party's Federal Council. To attend such a gathering of the elite faithful was, for him, a distraction from the real business of government. On the other hand, the Council provided a forum where he could exploit his status as Australia's sole Liberal Premier. John Hewson could not match Greiner in prestige because the Federal Liberals had now lost four elections in a row. According to polling in late October, Greiner appeared to have emerged well from the dark days of Metherell and the North Coast investigation. He stood before the Council assured of an attentive hearing.

Earlier speakers had regurgitated the traditional positions on socialism and States' rights. Greiner quickly amended his prepared speech and questioned the shibboleths which were so much part of the history and the pre-history of the modern Liberal Party:

> I always cringe when I come to these meetings and we tell the
> world 'don't vote for (the) Labor Party, they are socialists; we are
> for free enterprise – please vote for us'. . . . that message is too
> simple and is not a message that will sell to the Australian public in
> the 1990s and the next century.

No one was better placed in the Liberal Party to make the point that
traditional political ties were continuing to break up: more people, he
said, were prepared to cast their vote on the basis of leadership and
performance. The Liberals could now take large chunks of the blue
collar vote from Labor yet risked losing some of their own white collar
support to independents and the Greens. More voters wanted national
responsibility in management, including that of the environment, and
lower costs and a higher standard of living. They were not persuaded by
outdated rhetoric.

Greiner reminded the Party that the electorate was not interested in
"arid jurisdictional arguments" about Commonwealth-State relations.
Liberals had to abandon their obsession with "extreme versions of
States' rights", and pay more attention to "peoples' rights". Some of
the Party's heavyweights – notably Valder, John Elliott (the outgoing
Federal President, who called Greiner "visionary") and Michael Kroger
(the Victorian State President) – liked what they heard. They had just
witnessed Council's decision to defer a sensible proposal to give the
Federal Executive some modest powers to intervene in the affairs of
the State Divisions. The Liberal Party at the Federal level was itself
a federation of State Divisions where the Executive and the Council
depended totally upon the goodwill of the individual components.[22] The
smaller Divisions insisted upon preserving their autonomy, even to the
point where a former, failed West Australian Parliamentary Leader could
talk of a split should federal intervention ever take place. It was this sort
of attitude which prompted Greiner to let loose on what he saw as the
troglodyte wing of the Liberal Party.

Greiner was equally critical of those who had spoken disparagingly about the Special Premiers' Conference: "we do not do ourselves any credit at all" by calling it a "sham" and "a waste of time" and a "grab" for more central power. Greiner defended Hawke and Keating; they were "fair dinkum" in their intentions to remove the duplication of functions for the sake of the national interest. He agreed with Hawke that Europe would soon be more integrated than the Australian Commonwealth. If France and Germany, Turkey and Greece could establish a single market, then Australia ought to be capable of moving towards "a single market, a single economy, indeed a single nation". This was not an argument for greater centralisation. Rather, it was a typical Greiner plea for common sense and rationality; in this case for working out what to do when Australia was falling far short of a sensible distribution of responsibilities between governments. His argument was about advancing efficiency.

The NSW Premier did not spare the Liberal Party's traditional opponents. He attacked ministers such as John Dawkins (Education) and Brian Howe (Health) who used tied grants to direct State policies. He also applied pressure to the Prime Minister by listing six tests which had to be passed before the Conference could be regarded as a success: there should be an agreement to address the problems of vertical fiscal imbalance; an agreement to reduce tied grants; progress towards regulatory uniformity; progress towards national environmental standards; progress in the removal of duplication; and acceptance of more micro-economic reform. In outlining these "tests" Greiner brought together what he had been talking about for a decade, starting with his comments soon after he first won Ku-ring-gai. He had spoken then about wanting to reduce the duplication of services, to give the States unfettered control over health and education, to abolish specific purpose grants, and for the Federal Government to take the lead.[23] More recently, he had raised these issues in the lead-up to the June Premiers' Conference, during the Conference itself, and in his July address to the National Press Club. Hitherto, his comments had not received much notice outside official circles. Greiner's challenge to the Liberal Party to grow up so enlivened the annual meeting of the Federal Council that a normally boring event attracted a full round of media attention.[24]

Hawke met the Premiers privately on the eve of the Conference and nudged them towards acceptance of the proposed communiqué prepared by PM&C. Next day he opened the Conference by thanking the Premiers for their "positive" response to his call in July for a closer and more effective partnership. He stressed the need for greater cooperation within the existing Federal framework and explained that the object of the meeting was to secure a broad agreement on a set of principles to guide action on the key areas: the general financial arrangements, micro-economic reform, duplication of services, the environment, and industrial relations. He also made a commitment: the Commonwealth would work with the States to achieve a substantial reduction in tied grants.

Following convention, the Premier of NSW spoke immediately after Hawke. He described the Conference as unique because it was about shared purposes and principles and not about deals and confrontation. It was also unique because no election was expected anywhere for 18 months. Here was an opportunity and an imperative to act at a time of revenue and economic difficulties. Greiner shared the Prime Minister's hope for "some clear-cut agreement on principles – on riding instructions" at the highest political level. He did not want to see "an exercise in good intentions"; rather, he looked for "some very finite time-frames for achieving real change". The issues – inter-governmental relations, micro-economic reform and duplication – were not new but all States were now converted to the cause, though he was not sure "we are quite so converted as to exactly how we get ourselves to the church". NSW was pleased to be involved in the process, and was not approaching it as a grab for more power or in an attitude of "them and us". Its approach was co-operative. He was looking forward to contributing to what he hoped would be "an historic process of reform".[25]

Greiner said after the first day that "(w)e are at least closer to getting under the sheets". But he remained cautious; it would be easier to achieve micro-economic and regulatory reform than to secure changes in the financial relationship or in dealing with duplication. He also acknowledged that agreement over the general direction did not eliminate different emphases. There were also some delicate side-issues. Bannon had heard that "green-eyed Greiner" was trying to steal South Australia's contract to hold the Formula One Grand Prix, just as NSW had taken the motorcycle race from Victoria. The NSW Premier assured him that a bid would not be made until the present contract expired. Bannon accepted his assurance: "Mr Greiner is an honest man, he looks you straight in the eye and speaks the truth, so what else could I do?" One photograph in the press carried a warning. Sitting on Hawke's right at the final press conference – Greiner was on his left – Paul Keating did not look at all pleased with the outcome. Joan Kirner, who had replaced Cain as the Premier of Victoria in the previous August, might have claimed that "even" the Treasurer was all peace and light. Within 12 months, as part of his second attempt to win the Labor leadership, he effectively smashed Hawke's "New Federalism".

The agreed communiqué, issued after the second day, began with a general statement: "past inefficiencies can no longer be tolerated" and an "integral part of any micro economic reform strategy is a more effective public sector". The aim was to make the best of cooperation, avoid duplication "and achieve significant progress towards increasing Australian competitiveness".[26] It was agreed that senior expert officials should undertake a fundamental review of Commonwealth-State financial arrangements with the aim of reducing vertical fiscal imbalance while recognising the Commonwealth's need for adequate means to discharge its responsibility for macro-economic management. The Conference adopted a uniform, national approach to interstate road haulage, agreed to establish a national rail freight corporation, and to consider the need for a national electricity grid and a national environment code. It was decided to hold special conferences in Sydney or Canberra in May 1991 and in Perth the following November.

Greiner could reasonably conclude that his six tests had been more or less met. In explaining the success of the Conference, Kirner said "the preparedness of Nick Greiner to take a non-political approach . . . was very important". Goss thought all the participants were due some credit but singled out the NSW Premier: "it would have been very easy for him to score a political point . . . and he's chosen not to do that." Most of the commentators also emphasised Greiner's role, with Michelle Grattan in the *Age* calling it "Nick Greiner's conference". Greiner was certainly not carried away by the euphoria and the pleasantries. He knew that the next stages were not "likely to be easy" because "the empires will strike back", and some of these empires included ministers, bureaucracies and vested interests. But he had no intention of giving ground to them in NSW and he was confident that other heads of government would take the same attitude. [27]

In the event, the empires did strike back in the form of an internal revolt against Hawke's prime ministership. Within 20 months of the Special Premiers' Conference of 1990 the two key figures in the whole operation – Hawke and Greiner – were both out of office, and any chance of implementing the most constructive version of "New Federalism" was lost.

# Endnotes

1    Interview: Humphry, 26 September 2011.

2    Marcus Haward and Graham Smith, "What's New about the 'New Federalism'?", *Australian Journal of Political Science*, vol. 27, Special Issue, 1992, pp. 39-51.

3    *SMH*, 13 May 1988; interview: Greiner, 10 Septembert 2012.

4    Nick Greiner, "That 'Obstructive Spirit of Provincialism' has been Curbed", Federalism Research Centre in Canberra, 1991. Sir George Dibbs, Premier of NSW, had claimed in 1894 that the "obstructive spirit of provincialism can be curbed". Sturgess provided the text for the Greiner paper.

5    *Daily Mirror*, 31 May, 1 and 4 June; *DT*, 28 May, 5 and 7 June; *SMH*, 2 and 4-5 June; *Sunday Telegraph*, 3 June 1990.

6    *Australian*, 28 June 1990.

7    *Ibid.*

8    *SMH*, 29 June 1990.

9    Interview: Greiner, 10 September 2012.

10   *Australian, AFR*, and *SMH*, 21 June 1990.

11   For an edited text of Keating's address, see *Australian*, 29 June 1990. See also the articles by Matthew Moore and Milton Cockburn in *SMH*, 29 June 1990.

12   Brian Galligan, *A Federal Republic: Australia's Constitutional System of Government*, CUP, Melbourne, 1995, pp. 196 and 204.

13   *SMH*, 27 June and *AFR*, 28 June 1990.

14   For Bannon, see Andrew Parkin and Vern Marshall, "Federal Relations", in Andrew Parkin and Allan Patience (eds), *The Bannon Decade: The Politics of Restraint in South Australia*, Allen & Unwin, St Leonards, 1992, ch. 8. For the plans, see *SMH*, 27 June 1990.

15   *Australian*, 30 June-1 July; and *SMH*, 30 June 1990.

16   Brian Galligan, "Australian Federalism: Rethinking and Restructuring", *Australian Journal of Political Science*, vol. 27, Special Issue, 1992, p. 2.

17   For Hawke's speech and Greiner's immediate response, see *Canberra Times*, 20 July 1990.

18   Sturgess, *Greinerism*.

19   Patrick Weller, *Commonwealth-State Reform Processes: A Policy Management Review*, prepared for the Department of the Prime Minister and Cabinet, June 1995.

[20]  Interview; Greiner, 2012.

[21]  The above paragraph draws upon Weller, *Commonwealth-State Reform Processes*, p. 15; interview: Sturgess, 21 June 2011; Roy Eccleston, "Queensland Politics", *Australian*, 18 March 1992; Prue Anderson, *AFR*, 20 August 1993; Robert Macklin, *Kevin Rudd: The Biography*, Viking, Camberwell, 2007, p. 91; Blanche D'Alpuget, *Hawke: The Prime Minister*, MUP, Carlton, 2010, p. 318-20.

[22]  John Carrick to Fred Osborne (NSW State President), 13 March 1968, Osborne Papers, NLA, MS 3662/13/16.

[23]  See Chapter Five.

[24]  For press accounts of the meeting, see *Australian* and *Courier-Mail*, 25 October; *SMH*, 25-7 October; *Sun-Herald*, 28 October 1990.

[25]  Special Premiers' Conference, Brisbane, October 1990. For press reports see *AFR*, *The Age*, *Australian*, *DT*, and *SMH*, 31 October-1 November 1990.

[26]  Communiqué, Special Premiers' Conference – Brisbane, 30/31 October 1990.

[27]  *SMH*, 31 October 1990. For a later academic view of the "Greiner-Goss-Bannon-Hawke new federalism initiative" which made micro-economic reform "the centrepiece of intergovernmental relations", and stressed the role of Sturgess and Rudd, see Cliff Walsh, "The Economics of Federalism and Federal Reform", *University of NSW Law Journal*, vol. 31, no. 2, 2008, p. 553.

# 13

# "Leadership that's working"

Rumours of an early poll in NSW were circulating within weeks of Greiner telling the Special Premiers' Conference that no election was scheduled anywhere in Australia in the next 18 months. Greiner already had an election strategy committee in place by the end of 1990, and the Liberal Party Organisation had established a Campaign Unit as early as the previous May. Preparations could not be properly set in motion, however, until the Electoral Districts Commission completed its work in March 1991. The Commission removed the severe anti-Coalition bias of the old boundaries without providing the Liberal and National parties the expected rewards for being in government. Greiner had unintentionally disadvantaged several of his backbenchers by keeping his promise to reduce the size of the Legislative Assembly to 99 seats. Either they had to find new seats or make themselves known to voters in rearranged ones. An early poll gave them little time to reap the benefits of incumbency or to become known.

It was, as Greiner put it, "pretty much" his decision to call an election for May 1991, a year before it was due. He acted after Michael Lambert, Deputy Secretary of the Treasury, advised him in a private note of the difficulties of proceeding with a reform agenda in the face of the deepening recession. His standing as an economic manager could take a battering in 1992 and the electorate might not then be prepared to blame all its woes on the Commonwealth or reject State Labor's plans for recovery.[1]

Labor's attempts to question his managerial credentials did not trouble him. Greiner "took no notice of Bob",[2] except occasionally to ridicule his ignorance of economics. Carr found it hard to unsettle him in debate[3] while the attack on "waste and mismanagement", whether focussed on Eastern Creek or the cost and size of the Senior Executive Service, had not dented the Government's clear lead in the polls. The Leader of the Opposition did receive some useful ammunition when, a few days before Greiner called the early election, Bob Walker, the Professor of Accounting at Sydney University, questioned the Premier's proud claim to have delivered two genuine budget surpluses. Greiner liked to contrast his record with that of the Labor States, and especially Victoria which had a deficit of around $1.2bn. Walker argued that Greiner had a narrow view of what constituted relevant figures. By applying the basis of Victoria's calculations to NSW, Walker found that the actual deficit of both States was roughly comparable. He accused Greiner of not meeting his own demand that the States provide "uniform, timely and accurate information" about their finances. Walker also criticised the Government for taking a $400,000 advance from Elcom to fund current expenditure, a decision Greiner stoutly defended as one commonly taken by governments throughout Australia. Percy Allan felt that Walker was "stalking" Treasury, and the professor certainly became a persistent and irritating critic. But it hardly mattered whether he had a good case. An argument about the true deficit was just too esoteric to influence an election result.[4]

### "Not a good look"

Charges of providing "jobs for the boys or girls", on the other hand, did damage Greiner's standing in the lead-up to the election and, according to received wisdom, eventually cost him votes.

Within three months of Kathryn Greiner declining Senate pre-selection in October 1990 Neil Pickard, the Minister for Minerals and Energy, announced her appointment to the board of Elcom, a government trading enterprise, at a fee of $24,000 pa. Pickard explained she had "experience in a business capacity", while her understanding of community needs gave her "considerable insight into consumer interests". The *Australian Financial Review* was forthright.[5] A lengthy editorial argued that the issue was one of credentials, not nepotism: Kathryn did not meet Greiner's prerequisite for appointment to the boards of GTEs, namely, of possession of "business expertise and/or special knowledge". The *AFR* argued that consumer advocacy by itself was no longer an adequate qualification for GTE managers. The appointment endangered the Premier's "solid record for running his administration with integrity", and undermined his program "to improve the quality of GTE management by setting up a commercial meritocracy". If Kathryn Greiner became the Elcom board's "community spokesperson", the Government would have "thrown three years of hard-won reform down the drain". The editorial concluded that "this job is inappropriate. She should turn it down."

Callers to talkback radio questioned the Premier's ethics and accused him of "hypocrisy". Carr was uncertain how to respond because Kathryn Greiner was seen to be popular. He then decided she had "talked herself into trouble", principally by admitting to having no knowledge of Elcom and saying she would never have been offered the position had she not been the Premier's wife. It was now safe to express outrage. Not only, Carr said, did the Premier's wife have her hand in the taxpayer's pocket, her attendance fee for ten half-day meetings a year was greater than the annual wage packet of many families in the Western Suburbs. Kathryn's husband, pleased because the job met the requirement of being fulfilling, satisfying and compatible, said he was not responsible for the appointment. Reminded of his promise not to stack government boards with party acolytes, Greiner insisted his wife was not one of the "party faithful". He cited her sharp questioning of ministers on Radio 2UE, where she had been a guest commentator, as evidence of her capacity to ask hard questions. It was reasonable to ask that Kathryn be judged on her merits. None of the arguments seemed to mollify the public anger.

As Kathryn said later, "it was not a good look." Her many skills did not in 1991 include management or commercial qualifications. Greiner, in hindsight, agreed. He acknowledged the validity of the *AFR*'s criticisms and said he should have vetoed the appointment because his wife did not meet the selection criteria.[6]

On 29 March, two weeks after a brief corridor conversation with him, Greiner announced Pickard's appointment as the NSW Agent-General in London. Pickard's seat of Hornsby, which he had held since 1973, was abolished in the 1991 redistribution. Although a large part of Hornsby was absorbed in Greiner's seat of Ku-ring-gai, it was inconceivable Pickard would challenge the Premier for pre-selection, let alone defeat him. Nevertheless, to avoid a potentially messy situation, the Premier found him alternative employment. For being what the *DTM* called "such a decent bloke over Hornsby", Pickard would receive, in addition to his handsome superannuation package, an annual income of $87,000, live in a luxury apartment and have a chauffeur-driven limousine at his disposal.

Pickard would be replacing Norman Brunsden in a post Greiner originally intended to abolish as "a ceremonial vestige of colonial days". The former chairman of Price Waterhouse succeeded the former Labor minister, Kevin Stewart, the most recent beneficiary – as Greiner put it – of the Labor Party's pension scheme. The Premier's approach to media questioning about the Pickard appointment was straightforward. He admitted making a "U-turn". It was "an entirely transparent decision: I don't seek to duck it or obfuscate it", and there was "an element of consolation" because Pickard was left without a seat. Unwisely, Greiner said he would rule out only for the "foreseeable future" any consideration for two other Liberal MPs whose seats had also been abolished.

No one was surprised by Pickard's claim to be "a person with tremendous skills" who had more to give than the mere businessman he was succeeding. But the commentators who were generally sceptical about Pickard's ability were surprised when Greiner genuinely praised Pickard's achievements as a minister. He amplified his feelings in a letter to one of his backbenchers who had protested about the appointment. Greiner said he had always believed that senior government appointments should be made on merit. Pickard was a very experienced minister and, during his tenure, Elcom had achieved a 58 per cent increase in productivity, kept price rises below the rate of inflation, and negotiated large coal contracts with overseas governments. Pickard had made "a substantial contribution to the management of the State".[7]

Carr promptly attacked the Pickard appointment as another example of Greiner providing "jobs for the boys". He also said many voters would see the move to London as somehow linked to Pickard's appointment of Kathryn Greiner to the Elcom board. Labor, on winning government, would recall Pickard and abolish the post. Some on Greiner's side of politics were stunned by the "arrogance" of his decision.[8] A commonly-expressed view in the media was that the Premier had conceded some of the moral ground to the Labor Party by not applying the high standards he so often espoused. Greiner later conceded that he had been "a bit arrogant" in making the appointment though Pickard had been "a surprisingly good minister". He did not like the man; he just wanted some peace and quiet. It was, nonetheless, "a bad political judgment".[9]

Three days before Greiner was expected to call an early election John Dowd announced his intention to leave politics. Although he had been re-endorsed for Lane Cove, Dowd had already informed Greiner of his doubts about serving another four-year term. He now decided against doing "a fraud" on the electorate by quitting before his term expired. Press speculation linked Dowd's departure to a proposal to create super-ministries and to split the work of the Attorney-General's Department. Dowd did not like the proposal but he had more pressing personal issues on his mind. Seriously in debt, separated from his wife and still required to support a family, Dowd needed to establish an earning capacity for the longer term. The Premier had previously promised Peter Collins that he would be Attorney-General for the expected second term. If Dowd left Parliament at a later date but not as Attorney-General, he might have difficulty getting sufficient work at the Bar. As senior counsel (he took silk at the end of 1990), he would be expensive to hire and considered an unknown quantity. Greiner referred obliquely to Dowd's need to deal with "a range of personal matters" as the explanation for his sudden departure, denied there was any falling-out, and expressed a concern felt by many about the Attorney-General's well-being because he overloaded himself with work. Dowd, in return, hinted at residual bitterness. Asked if he liked the Premier, Dowd replied that, after knowing him for 20 years, "I do not know that I know him yet. There are aspects . . . I find immensely admirable and there are aspects that, in certain respects, I do not think he is as good as I am."[10]

The Group wanted John Hannaford, MLC, to replace Dowd in Lane Cove, and planned to endorse him without having to undergo a formal pre-selection. Greiner openly backed Hannaford, regarding him as one of the more able ministers and a potential Leader. All the plans fell through, however, because the local Lane Cove Liberals insisted on their right to hold a pre-selection. Kerry Chikarovski, daughter of a former General Secretary, Greg Bartels, and a future Leader, triumphed. Hannaford's leadership prospects were permanently damaged while John Booth, the member for Wakehurst who had lost his own pre-selection and was the Group's choice to replace Hannaford in the Council, ceased to have a parliamentary career. Greiner appeared, as ever, unfazed by what he could not control. He publicly welcomed the arrival of the newly-anointed candidate for Lane Cove. It was neither his business nor his problem if the Group failed to get its way on matters which did not directly touch him.

## The Campaign

On 3 May 1991 Nick Greiner announced on that an election would be held on Saturday 25 May. A headline in the *SMH* fairly described the Premier's intentions: "Greiner makes a dash for it." Greiner justified an early election on the ground that Labor and the Australian Democrats had repeatedly blocked industrial relations reform in the Legislative Council. Conceding that the Government "had not been perfect", it was – "on any reasonable assessment" – the one credible contender to lead NSW in the 1990s. He asked for a "clear and powerful mandate" to proceed with reform and to pass industrial relations legislation.

Some commentators believed there was no compelling reason for Greiner to go to the polls.[11] Of the Government's five industrial relations reforms, the Legislative Council had accepted two, rejected two and not yet voted on the fifth. It was argued that the Premier still had options to exploit. Yet Greiner could reasonably argue that the linchpin of the legislation – voluntary unionism – would never pass through the present Council. He could, with the expected support of two Call to Australia MPs (Fred and Elaine Nile), achieve his legislative goal in the next Parliament.[12]

Virtually everyone expected the Government to be returned with a clear majority, if not an even bigger one. Publicly, Greiner was one of very few Liberals to enter a caveat. He had seen enough of politics, horse races and football matches to know that "favourites are not certainties". Privately, he was very confident. He thought he had done enough to deserve re-election and that the Opposition had done little to merit being returned to the government benches. Asked if he would attempt to beat Wran's record of ten years as Premier, Greiner replied: "I'm certainly not looking for a lifetime tenure."[13] He already had a retirement date in mind. After winning control of both Houses, and implementing the bulk of his reforms, he would leave politics around November 1993 to give his successor 18 months to prepare for the next election.[14]

It was hard not to be complacent. Greg Daniel of the Liberal Party's advertising agency told a briefing of MPs and candidates that "this will be the mother of all elections".[15] A Saulwick poll, conducted on the night before the election was called, recorded a 15-point lead for the Government over the Opposition, the one disturbing finding being that nearly 14 per cent said they would vote for Independents. The major print media outlets and most economics commentators thought Greiner deserved to win. Alan Wood in the *Australian* thought it was important for Greiner to secure a second term, and that he increased the pace of reform because "his model of government is crucial to Australia in the 1990s".[16] The *SMH* editorial of 4 May, headed "The NSW Inc [sic] State Election", saw "management" as the principal issue, but felt that Greiner need not feel embarrassed about a possible blow-out in the deficit as a result of the recession. By contrast with Victorian Labor, Greiner's "careful financial management" of NSW since 1988 meant his Government could "easily cope with a bad year".[17]

The one sour note emanated from a source he could afford to ignore. Whereas Labor criticised him for pushing too hard and too fast, Des Moore of the Institute of Public Affairs (IPA) in Victoria and a former Deputy Secretary of the Commonwealth Treasury demanded he move harder and faster. Greiner would have to lift his performance if he wanted to claim a record as a reformer because he had failed to cut the cost of government, had allowed outlays to grow above the rate needed to maintain services, and kept NSW as a higher taxed State than Victoria while maintaining a roughly comparable budget deficit. Greiner was unimpressed by what he called the "ideologically pure"; some parts of the IPA findings were "stupid" and others "extreme".[18]

On the day after Greiner made his poll announcement the *Daily Telegraph Mirror* carried a full page Liberal Party advertisement. Over a photograph of the Premier sitting at the desk in his office, at once serious-looking yet with a hint of a smile, there appeared the words: "Nick Greiner. Leadership that's working". The next page expanded upon the simple message: leadership was a rare thing in politics; it was about solving problems, taking tough decisions and shouldering criticism; Greiner had sought "to create and manage a better, more honest New South Wales"; he had confronted and dealt with neglected, vital issues; NSW was now seen to be the best managed State in Australia; there was still much to do and Labor could not do it; "your support for Nick Greiner will help him finish the job".

This advertisement neatly encapsulated the essence of the campaign for re-election: the almost exclusive focus on Greiner; the stress on his leadership, decision-making and management skills; the dual themes of achieving reform and of pressing ahead with more of the same; the pre-eminence of NSW which was so far ahead of the Labor-run States. The Liberals set out to run what the media called "a Presidential-style campaign". The Premier himself was the sole issue. To avoid any other issues emerging or taking over, there was a deliberate decision to forgo a negative campaign directed at the Labor Party. Commentators were convinced that Greiner and his advisers wanted a campaign free of issues.[19] The one exception was the attempt to exploit Labor's well-documented economic mismanagement in Victoria and Western Australia. An advertisement inserted in the *Sunday Telegraph* for 12 May read: "And if you're wondering what life would be like under Labor, just ask a Victorian".

Carr was potentially embarrassed by another Labor connection. Brian Burke, the former Labor Premier of Western Australia, whom Greiner had once admired, announced in late April that he would resign in July as Ambassador to Ireland and the Holy See. Burke was due to appear before the Royal Commission into the activities of "WA Inc.", the sobriquet for what originated as Burke's sleazy deals with disreputable and failed Perth business figures. Burke tried to resign on 9 May but, because he was appointed by the Governor-General, could not do so. Further discomforted by Burke's earlier claims to be protected by Labor "mates" in Canberra, the Hawke Government, on the same day, effectively sacked him, 16 days before NSW went to the polls. Surprisingly, to some, the Greiner Government and the Liberal Party made no concerted effort to link Labor in NSW to its dubious or bungling interstate comrades. "Leadership that's working" was about being constructive.

Nick Greiner delivered his policy speech on Mother's Day, 12 May, in the Riverside Theatre, Parramatta. He stood near the centre-point of a marginal Liberal-held seat which had become notionally Labor after the redistribution. The central theme of the policy speech was the promise from the CEO of "NSW Inc." of "more gain for your pain". While he was not going to engage in the "lunacy" of promising large new programs in an unfavourable economic environment, there would be extra funding on health, education and law and order, all financed by asset sales. The Government would keep its own expenditure under control and continue to reduce State debt, but it was "plain stupid" to suppose that "management and compassion are contradictory". The one major new proposal involved breaking Elcom into three smaller companies.

Unlike the audience at the Rockdale Town Hall in 1988, this one was carefully screened. There were no Labor interlopers. The audience proved to be so keen on standing ovations it rose as one when the ministers were invited to take a bow. There was much colour and movement with a jazz pianist and a master of ceremonies to warm things up. John Hewson was there, prompting Nick Greiner to remark, "how nice it is to be leading a party in NSW where you can be proud of your federal leader". Murray and Carr were not accompanied by Federal counterparts at their respective launches.

Mark Coultan remarked of the Liberal Party launch that a new Nick Greiner was on display: not the politician with the "lopsided grin" talking economics but "an athlete, a champion". Interspersed with film of winners in action – Bradman attacking the bowling, Phar Lap victorious in the Melbourne Cup, Allan Border reclaiming the Ashes, Wally Lewis scoring for Australia and Craig Johnston for Liverpool – were shots of another winner, of Greiner jogging in a South Sydney jumper or playing tennis. Coultan called it "the most self-assured function" the Liberals had put together in a generation. He also observed how the Party itself was different. There was not a blue rinse in sight. Instead, ethnic groups held signs proclaiming "Hungarians for Greiner", "Russians for Greiner", "Greeks for Greiner" and "Chinese for Greiner". As for the Premier, he "has never looked to be more in control of his party, his job or himself".[20] Whether he or anyone else in the family felt comfortable is another matter. All four smiling members of the family stood, joined hands, and held them aloft.

Greiner's campaign headquarters had been established on two floors in the Regent Hotel in George Street. (Carr made a point of highlighting his own modest surrounds and travel arrangements.) Greiner emerged each morning to sweep into and out of electorates. Sometimes he arrived and left by helicopter, always accompanied by the media. Sometimes the local candidate learnt of a "presidential visit" after it had taken place. For a candidate to be included, it helped to be fit, important and under threat. Early one morning Greiner and Michael Yabsley (thought to be in trouble in Vaucluse) emerged from a limousine at Bondi Beach in running gear and set off for a jog, accompanied by television cameras and trailed by the Premier's principal press officer dressed in a pin-stripe suit. On occasions, a special effort was needed. Four executive jets took the Greiner-Murray entourage to Tamworth for the NP campaign launch. The accompanying journalists did not complain about the free beer and sandwiches served on board.

The style and theme of the Greiner campaign left a huge opening for the Opposition. Bob Carr exploited it brilliantly. Speaking immediately after the election announcement, Carr said Labor would highlight the Government's "waste and mismanagement". It was a shrewd strategy because the more "waste" Carr could uncover and promise to eliminate, the more his spending pledges could be recouped by cutting Greiner's budget. He could also cast doubt on Greiner's claims to be an efficient manager. On 11 May Carr produced a 35-page document prepared by two former Treasury officials backing his plans for cuts of $1.2bn which included abolition of the Chief Secretary's Department, sacking half the Senior Executive Service, selling 500 executive service cars and reducing ministerial staff and departmental travel. Within a week, Carr offered relief for struggling families with promises to cut car registration fees, electricity charges and local government rates. He conducted stunts for the benefit of journalists and television crews. To expose "waste", Carr led an unauthorised tour of the unoccupied upper floors of the McKell Building in George Street vacated by the Health Department's head office staff. In his policy speech Carr pledged to cut his own and other ministerial salaries, a saving of about $100,000. The gifted speech writer, Graham Freudeberg, gave him some telling lines: "Fellow citizens, NSW is not a corporation. We are a community"; NSW under Greiner had become a "harsher, meaner, less caring, less fair society".

Carr grabbed attention with a clever scare campaign over a consumption tax. Nick Greiner had been ambushed on television by Laurie Oakes of Channel Nine with a leaked Treasury document on the first Sunday of the campaign. The Treasury paper had canvassed the possibility of introducing such a tax, a subject of special interest to Percy Allan who had raised the question with Chris Higgins, the Secretary to the Commonwealth Treasury. Greiner described the document as "theoretical" and said it had been prepared with the next Premiers' Conference in mind. He pointed out that such a tax would need prior Federal Government approval and could not realistically come into operation until 1995 or 1996. He added: "The reality is you neither can nor should have a tax like this without a mandate from the people. I am not seeking a mandate."[21] Next day he sought to make light of the matter: there was as much chance of a consumption tax being introduced in NSW as last-placed Parramatta had of winning the 1991 Rugby League premiership.[22] Carr was not to be diverted by an unequivocal "No". Moving among shoppers he warned them that Greiner's "supermarket tax" was on the way.[23] Near the end of the second week of the campaign Labor ran an advertisement highlighting Greiner's "secret plan" for a consumption tax and asked voters whether they were prepared to gamble 15 cents of every dollar they earned "on another one of Mr Greiner's promises".[24]

If Greiner appeared to stutter over the consumption tax during the first week of the campaign,[25] Carr had to deal with sabotage from his own side at the beginning of the last week. Ralph Willis, the Federal

Minister for Finance, effectively dismissed the Opposition's claims that Greiner would impose a consumption tax. Willis told Channel Nine's *Sunday* program that the constitutional and political difficulties made it unlikely any government in NSW would impose such a tax. Willis later issued a statement saying he had understood from the documents that the Greiner Government was pursuing the tax option. By then, Greiner had taken charge of the issue: the Willis admission "had blown Mr Carr out of the water".[26]

In general, however, Greiner kept to the script which required others to do the jousting. He believed that many of Carr's claims were simply too silly to deserve serious attention. When he did speak out, he spoke briefly.[27] He was pleased, for example, when a *Sydney Morning Herald* investigation found that his Government had actually spent just $500m of the $1.5bn the Opposition claimed had been wasted. Yet, apart from commenting that another of Carr's allegations had been exposed as gross exaggeration, Greiner steered clear of engaging in debate over the matter.[28]

## Coalition tremors

In February 1991 the Liberal Party resolved to contest all the Assembly seats except for those currently held by the National Party. The Liberals' Management Committee had decided in March to field a candidate in Tamworth which had become "vacant" because the sitting NP member had decided to retire. The State Executive subsequently rejected a decision to reverse the decision, and then rejected its refusal to reverse the Management Committee's decision. It left the matter in the hands of the State President. Eventually, the Liberals reached an agreement with the Nationals whereby the Liberal Party would not nominate for three rural seats, including Tamworth, in return for the NP's Robert Webster standing aside for John Fahey in Southern Highlands. Webster, the self-styled "sacrificial lamb", was rewarded with a winnable position on the joint ticket for the Legislative Council.[29]

Tamworth figured significantly for Greiner during and especially after the May election. It was the NP's second-safest seat in NSW. After a ten-week and often nasty pre-selection battle, David Briggs, who managed the Tamworth Base Hospital and was backed by local businessmen as a "new breed" National, won the nomination. But he had been supported by just one of the nine local NP branches whereas Tony Windsor, a Werris Creek farmer, had seven behind him. A photograph in the local paper showed a smiling Windsor congratulating Briggs on his victory. Pressed by local Nationals and well-wishers, Windsor soon broke his undertaking freely given at the pre-selection not to stand as an independent or for another party. Nominating as an Independent, Windsor declared himself "The People's choice". Having sought National Party endorsement he discovered that, after 40 years of one-party domination of Tamworth's politics, "Enough is Enough".

Greiner may have been the only Liberal present when he attended the official National Party campaign launch in Tamworth on 9 May. No member of the local Liberal Party was invited. Greiner nevertheless lauded the unity of the two parties when he spoke. He also had some good news to deliver. New figures showed that, whereas the national unemployment rate had risen by 0.5 per cent to 9.9 per cent, the rate in NSW had fallen from 8.8 to 8.6 per cent. In Opposition he used to say the States could do little to influence the economic cycle; as Premier he took some of the credit for this windfall. The Liberal Party did the same. A newspaper advertisement listed the unemployment figures for each State and explained why NSW had the lowest figure: "Our leadership *is* working" [emphasis in the original].[30]

Greiner's good news for Tamworth was somewhat overshadowed when a local poll found that Briggs was not assured of victory. Moreover, four of the nine NP branches in the electorate withdrew their support for Briggs. It would never have occurred to Greiner, however, as he watched local Nationals in raptures over Murray, that he would need to negotiate with an Independent member from Tamworth in order to retain government. Nor did it appear to matter that the Tamworth branch of his Party was urging fellow Liberals to vote Independent. Fortunately, the strong language followed his visit. The branch press release declared that Briggs was being promoted by those who had appeared before ICAC, had presented the "vintage political vaudeville – the Joh for PM Show", and had recently conducted "the extended season of the Grand Tamworth Pre-selection Pantomime". The release also referred to the "blatant political thuggery" which prevented the Liberals from offering their own candidate. Liberal voters were tired "of being compelled to vote for whoever the National Party puts up as 'our' representative". Greiner's "Coalition first" approach – one he shared with Howard – continued to upset many country Liberals.[31]

## Results

At the end of the campaign a *Herald* editorial declared that Greiner would, and should, "be easily re-elected". Malcolm Mackerras, the election expert, predicted an easy victory, with the Coalition taking 60 of the 99 Assembly seats. Robert Maher, State Director of the Liberal Party, and John Stirton, who looked after much of the polling, did raise the alarm. They realised in the last few days of the campaign, and they passed on their findings, that an easy victory was a false hope.

It was quickly apparent on election night that things were going very wrong. Seats which the Coalition thought it might take from Labor were confirmed as safe for the Opposition, and Labor had won back seats taken by Independents in 1988. More seriously, a number of Coalition seats were plainly sliding away. The Greiners watched the results on television in the Regent Hotel before arriving at the tally room soon after 11.00 pm. It was a subdued, unemotional Premier who described his reaction as "a little surprised and a little disappointed". He and Kathryn remained for a short time before heading to a Liberal Party gathering at the Inter-Continental Hotel where he repeated the comment, and where most of the champagne remained corked. One journalist noted how, when Greiner was in difficulty, his face became "set in a strange grin": at the tally room, "it was set in Araldite". Gary Sturgess, who was not involved in the 1991 election and who talked just once to the Premier during the campaign, regarded the result as a "complete shock". He joined the crowd in the Inter-Continental Hotel to watch the results. At one point, Greiner said the situation looked "tough" and that it was hard to push through reform and win re-election. He told Sturgess he was "sorry" for what had happened because Sturgess had been part of the exercise – "inextricably so".[32] On election night, "Leadership that's working" looked distinctly out of place.

Next day Greiner consoled himself with one thought: "this is a hard time to be in government anywhere in Australia." On the Monday he told a brief media conference he accepted responsibility for the Government's performance: "the buck clearly stops with me and it ought to stay there." He later informed a meeting of Liberal ministers he did not intend to resign as Leader, even if he could not form a government. Greiner was typically candid and down-to-earth. The Party had run

> in a technical sense an excellent campaign. The criticism goes to strategy and I think I'm responsible for the strategy, ultimately. If I'd said run a much more negative campaign, kick the proverbial out of these blokes, they would have done it.

The Premier accepted he was perceived as arrogant, yet "(i)n many ways arrogance and strong leadership are pretty much matters of perception; they are two sides of the (same) coin".[33] He might easily have added that within the Liberal Party arrogance is acceptable when the Leader takes the faithful to the Promised Land, and resented only when he fails to do so.

The figures were not as bad as first appeared. The Coalition had won 52.7 per cent of the two-party preferred vote; and the Liberal share of the primary vote had fallen by only 1.6 per cent. It seemed fairly certain by Monday that the Liberal Party had lost five seats to Labor (Bathurst,

Cessnock, Hurstville, Parramatta and Penrith) and one (David Hay's seat of Manly) to an Independent while Tony Windsor took Tamworth from the Nationals. Ironically, the Coalition won seven of the 15 vacancies in the Council and, with the support of Call to Australia, could now control the Upper House. At this stage, the Government had 47 confirmed seats in the Legislative Assembly, Labor 46 and the Independents 4. Two Liberal-held seats – Maitland and The Entrance – remained in doubt. A victory for either of the major parties would not alter the fact of a hung parliament. Two of the Independents – John Hatton, the member for South Coast since 1973, and Clover Moore – were already talking about using their enhanced importance to demand reform of parliamentary procedures. They kept expanding their wish list as the week advanced while Dr Peter Macdonald, who was careful not to claim victory in Manly before the result was confirmed, joined them to work out a plan, which included seeking advice from constitutional lawyers.

Nick Greiner had phoned Hatton on the Sunday to float the idea of him accepting the speakership. If Hatton accepted the offer, Greiner intended to offer Kevin Rozzoli, the incumbent, the dubious consolation prize of Corrective Services. For days, Hatton never seemed available to take calls from the Premier or his office. He did, however, talk over the speakership with his wife, and with Moore, Macdonald and the press. According to his authorised biographer, Hatton took the proposal very seriously, believing the job would give him some power to clean up the Bear Pit as well as providing him with a larger office. Rozzoli thought Hatton's public musings about bringing "democracy" to the Bear Pit, changing standing orders and hoping, with assurances of bi-partisan support, "we can have a disciplined House", showed how he misunderstood the role and was very naive. In the event, Moore and Macdonald persuaded Hatton to reject Greiner's offer. They argued that their proposed Charter of Reform would not be signed if he occupied the Chair. The battle had to be fought on the floor of the Parliament.[34]

By Thursday it was clear that the Liberals would hold Maitland and

The Entrance, though Labor intended to challenge both results. Greiner, however, could now form a minority government once he had locked Tony Windsor into an agreement. Windsor had described himself as "conservative" who leant "towards the Coalition". A compact was sealed early in June, the full details of which were not published until the middle of the month. The Government made two kinds of commitment. On the more general issues, Greiner agreed there would be no increase in land or payroll tax (indeed, the aim would be to reduce both), "Just terms" legislation would be introduced in the next Parliament, the sale of GrainCorp would require the approval of the major users, and rail freight charges were to be reviewed to ensure more equitable treatment of wheat exports in relation to passenger charges. The Government agreed to a raft of specific concessions for Windsor's electorate. They included a promise to build a new court house-police station complex in Tamworth city, to give serious consideration to a tender by a local company for State Transit Authority buses, and to second an experienced officer to the Tamworth Development Corporation to draft an economic development plan consistent with the Government's approach. In return, Windsor signed a letter promising to support the Coalition as "an independent conservative" on motions relating to Supply and to no-confidence except, in the case of the latter, where corruption or "gross maladministration" was involved.

Tamworth's daily newspaper trumpeted Windsor's achievement: "Windsor v Greiner. Round 1 – Tamworth." Another headline read, "Deals snare a bagful of promises". Windsor rejected any suggestion of having sold out to Greiner. For the Independents to hold the balance of power, he said, was the best thing that could have happened to Tamworth. Besides, "I will be voting with this electorate in mind". He was not bound to support the Coalition on matters which would have a detrimental effect on Tamworth or country people.[35] No doubt a number of NP MPs envied Windsor's success. He had wrested more concessions from a city-based Liberal Leader than they could hope to secure, and it was all the more irksome when an ex-National achieved what the Nationals had always set out to do. The price, from Greiner's point of view, was a small one. Some principles had to be compromised and the Labor Party could claim that the special projects in Tamworth alone would cost up to $10 million. Given that everything looked so grim on election night, the future looked a lot brighter ten days later.

But Greiner and the Liberals had to wear days and weeks of recriminations and gratuitous advice. John Hewson counselled the NSW Liberals to learn how to sell messages properly. A Federal Victorian front bencher said it was about time the NSW Liberals learnt how to campaign. Even Howard, who was more balanced than some of his Federal colleagues, said "Mr Greiner's campaign . . . was not forward enough". Wal Murray blamed the Liberals for the 14.5 per cent drop in the NP vote in country NSW. Graeme Starr thought the Government "may have lost an unlosable election" and said the Liberal Party must "get rid of the spivs". While Liberal critics attacked the Secretariat and the Secretariat attacked the critics, and nearly everyone attacked the campaign strategy, the State Director pointed out how right up until 7.00 pm on election-day everyone thought the campaign was "excellent".[36] Robert Maher launched himself at the Party's self-serving office-bearers and at the "amateurish" attitudes of a Party which was too accustomed to losing badly or winning reasonably well. He would later admit to Greiner that the central campaign had erred in not confronting Labor and fighting for votes.[37] Peter King, the Group-aligned State President, defended the Secretariat and blamed, instead, poor on-the-ground campaigning and organisation for what happened. King immediately set up an investigative Task Force representing "all sections of the Liberal Party" but excluding parliamentarians and the State Director.

Several State MPs wrote to Greiner. Sixty-nine year-old Beryl Evans, MLC, told him "you all may be good managers, but are poor salesmen". There was no compassion when things were tough and no attempt to soften the blows. She thought the Government – and Greiner himself – gave the impression of saying: "This is for your good and the good of the State, so lump it." Liz Kernohan, who won Camden in 1991, sent Greiner a long letter attacking "American hoo ha" (sic) campaigning as "un-Australian" and reported how using the Regent Hotel as the campaign headquarters was not appreciated by those who were hurting. Paul Zammit also wrote a long letter claiming that "the perceived arrogance and ego" of many ministers "played a major part in the Saturday night debacle". Metherell's "Thatcherism" also did "irreparable damage". Zammit reported a much earlier conversation with an unidentified minister who said the Government was losing 50,000 Year 12 students every year, along with their teachers and parents. The minister had no intention of doing anything about it because Metherell was Greiner's friend and the minister wanted to keep his job. Zammit concluded by repeating comments he had previously made to Greiner, namely, the Premier needed people in Cabinet who had a feel for the battlers. It was a fair point, even if it looked like a job application from someone with a grievance: Greiner had neglected his obvious talent.[38]

Maher had to keep reminding everyone that the election had not been lost. The Coalition was still in government. Sir Charles Court told Greiner how he and David Brand had managed to govern Western Australia for six years with a majority of one. Court urged Greiner and his colleagues not to "shy at every shadow" but to build up a score sheet for positive and effective action.[39] The NSW Premier publicly declared his intention to do just that. He told a lunch meeting of the Institute of Company Directors at the Regent Hotel on 30 May that micro-economic reform was to be pursued "with even greater enthusiasm". He specifically referred to industrial relations reform, tollways and privatisation of the Government Insurance Office, the State Bank and GrainCorp. "There will be no deviation, whatsoever, absolutely none, from the agenda that has been very clearly laid down".[40]

# Endnotes

1   Interviews: Greiner, 24 September and 2 November 2005; 30 March 2011; 24 December 2012.

2   Interview: Greiner 30 March 2011.

3   Interview: Carr, 30 January 2012.

4   Bob Walker, "How NSW managed to hide a $1.2bn deficit", *New Accountant*, 2 May 1991. For Carr and Greiner on the subject on 30 April see *NSWPD*, Third Series, vol. 222, pp. 2690-3, 2699-2705. Interview: Allen, 14 September 2011. For Walker's overall criticism of Greiner's financial management, see his chapter in Laffin and Painter, *Reform and Reversal*.

5   *AFR*, 21 January 1991.

6   *AFR*, 21 January; *SMH*, 22-4, 26 January, and 15 March; *Daily Telegraph Mirror (DTM)*, 22-3 January1991; interviews: Kathryn Greiner, 29 March, Nick Greiner, 30 March 2011 and Carr, 30 January 2012. Kathryn agreed to donate her fee to the Save the Children Fund and in July decided not to seek re-appointment when the board was corporatised. Greiner called it "a correct political decision basically to stop me being belted up" and she deserved "a break" from all the flak she had copped. *Australian*, 17 July 1991.

7   Greiner to Andrew Tink, 17 April 1991, Correspondence with Members, Greiner Papers.

8   For published material on the Pickard appointment, see *SMH*, 29-31 March, *DTM*, 30 March and 9 May 1991; Collins, *Bear Pit*, p. 172.

9   Interview: Greiner 30 March 2011.

10  *SMH* and *DTM*, 1 May 1991; interview: Greiner, 30 March 2011; Dowd, 22 November 2011.

11  Malcolm Farr in *DTM*, 4 May 1991.

12  Greiner also called a simultaneous referendum to reform the Council itself by reducing the membership from 45 to 42 and terms from twelve to eight years. For the complicated story of Legislative Council reform in 1991 and of the vote to approve a referendum, see Clune and Griffith, *Decision and Deliberation*, pp. 587-9.

13  *DTM*, 4 May 1991.

14  Interview: Greiner, 30 September 2011.

15  Interview: Michael Yabsley, 10 March 2005.

16  *Australian*, 4-5 May 1991.

17  For this favourable editorial comment and accounts of the Greiner election date announcement, see *SMH*, 4 May 1991.

18  *AFR* and *SMH*, 6 May 1991.

19  See Malcolm Farr in *DTM*, 11 May 1991.

20  *SMH*, 13 May 1991.

21  *Australian* and *SMH*, 6 May 1991.

22  *DTM*, 7 May 1991.

23  *SMH*, 7 May 1991.

24  *DTM*, 16 May 1991.

25  Sue Quinn, *Sunday Telegraph*, 12 May 1991.

26  *DTM*, 20 May 1991.

27  Interview: Percy Allan, 14 September 2011.

28  *SMH*, 6 and 8 May 1991; interview: Greiner, 30 March 2011. Metherell went one step further. The Teachers' Federation wanted to invoke memories of him but he kept such a low profile his Labor opponent felt he was reduced to shadow boxing. *SMH*, 16 May 1991.

29  Minutes of Management Committee, LPA, ML, MSS 7205/13; Minutes of State Executive, *ibid.*, /10; Coalition Relations Agreement, 1983-1989, *ibid.*, /186; Press Release, 25 May 1992, National Party – Southern NSW, *ibid.*, /187. Interview: Webster, 15 Sep. 2011.

30  *DTM*, 11 May 1991.

31  For the above three paragraphs, see the *Northern Daily Leader*, 9-11 and from 15 April; *Tamworth City Times*, 17 April, 1, 8, 15, 22 and 29 May; *DTM*, 11 May 1991; Davey, *Nationals*, pp. 342-4.

32  Interview: Sturgess, 22 June 2011.

33  *SMH*, 28 May 1991.

34  Ruth Richmond, *The Stench in this Parliament: The Authorised Biography of John Hatton AO*, published by Ruth Richmond, Malwala, 2009, pp. 176-7; Kevin Rozzoli, *Gavel to Gavel: An Insider's View of Parliament*, UNSW Press, Sydney, 2006, pp. 4-7.

35  *Northern Daily Leader* 5 June and *SMH*, 14 June 1991.

36  For Maher's criticisms of the Party Organisation, see State Election Report, 31 May 1991, LPA, ML, MSS 7205/51.

37  Maher to Greiner, 24 June 1991, *ibid.*

38  Correspondence with Members, Greiner Papers. One former minister recalled Greiner saying to Zammit: "Paul, your prospects are about as good as a crab in a tank in a Chinese restaurant." Interview, Yabsley, 29 November 2011. Zammit explained his failure to be promoted to Cabinet because, compared to Greiner and Michael Photios, he was "too ethnic". See interview (Barry York): Zammit, NLA, ORAL TRC 3847.

39  Court to Greiner, 31 May 1991, Correspondence with Members, Greiner Papers.

40  *SMH*, 31 May 1992.

# 14

# "A minority Government today, a minority Government tomorrow"

For all the strong language of his address to the Institute of Company Directors, the Premier had – according to his closest confidante in government – "lost his nerve". He had been "shaken quite strongly" by the election result. Sturgess tried to persuade him that, while he had lost a lot of men in the battle, he had still won.[1] On the other hand, another close observer thought Greiner remained resolute in his commitment to the reform agenda.[2] Either way, the Premier had a clear understanding of what happened on 25 May 1991. He told Paul Zammit in the immediate aftermath of the election that claims of the Government being arrogant and out of touch with the electorate had little bearing on the result. He pointed to the figures for the Legislative Council, where the Coalition vote had fallen by just 0.8 per cent since 1988 while Labor's vote dropped by 0.2 per cent.[3] Greiner's reading of the Legislative Council vote can be questioned but the important point is that the Premier was ruling out a change of direction. He did not accept that the electorate had rejected his reform agenda. The problem was essentially one of "style" and "marketing".

The Liberal Party's Task Force report, in effect, accepted this argument but had a different starting point and a different approach.[4] Consciously or otherwise, the Task Force settled some scores on behalf of those who felt they had been derided or disregarded by the managers of the 1991 campaign. Many members of the NSW Division of the Liberal Party, in large part a voluntary organisation, did not appreciate either being or feeling sidelined by paid officials and parliamentary representatives.

The original version of the report, drafted by the campaign manager for a Newcastle seat, was considered too angry and not well composed. Joe Hockey, the President of the NSW Young Liberals and a banking and finance lawyer with Corr Chambers Westgarth in Sydney, re-drafted the report in his employer's offices. Hockey and Jan Kleinig, the Task Force chair, had a problem. Greiner kept calling for frankness and honesty but the authors felt they had to pull their punches in relation to the Premier to ensure that the report was politically acceptable. As Hockey explained, "we had to speak in a coded language". The Task Force also had to be careful in using the evidence before it. Hockey has a vivid memory of Greg Daniel being "most scathing" about Nick Greiner. Daniel had mapped out a negative advertising campaign to counter Carr's effective if misleading attacks on the Government. Greiner refused to countenance it.[5] His standard response to Carr was an unwillingness to take him, and his "nonsense", seriously.

The coded language of the Task Force is not difficult to crack. The central message was that Nick Greiner, directly or indirectly, was responsible for much that had gone wrong. Nevertheless, the Premier remained "[o]ne of the greatest assets of the Party in NSW". Instead, therefore, of always accusing Greiner or his Government of arrogance, the Task Force sometimes referred to "perceived arrogance", even to "so-called arrogance and complacency". It was impossible, however, to hide the guilty party when listing examples of arrogance and mismanagement: the decision to call an early election without adequately explaining the broken promise not to do so; the appointments of Kathryn Greiner and Neil Pickard; the use of the Regent Hotel as campaign headquarters; and the presidential-style election campaign. The Premier was immediately or ultimately responsible for all of them.

Even so, it was better to pounce on the courtiers rather than the king. "They" did not understand "political marketing" and yet "they" exercised "excessive influence". But who were "they"? The Task Force did not identify them, either by rank or by name. There were vague references to "key" advisers in Greiner's office and to ministers and ministerial advisers, to "some elements" in the Campaign Committee and to some of the professional staff of the Organisation. Perhaps the "key" advisers were not identified because members of the Task Force knew they included senior public servants who were offering "policy" advice which ignored "political" implications. Curiously, the Task Force did not consider another possibility, namely, that Nick Greiner was never desperate for advice. Or perhaps it thought it was better not to say so.

To counter the role of those who did not understand "political marketing", and to assert the Organisation's rightful and valuable place in the NSW Liberal Party, the Task Force recommended the appointment of a political strategy unit within the Premier's Office which should "have practical structural links with the Party machine". In future, campaign strategy "should be undertaken by the party organisation together with the parliamentary leader and his advisers". Election planning should also involve Liberal Party branch members who were closer to the electorates while the Campaign Committee "should have substantial membership from the State Executive and (newly-appointed) experts at the Secretariat".

The Task Force claimed that the election "was not lost in the three weeks before 25 May". The process began soon after 19 March 1988 when the Government neglected "the need for political wisdom". From this point, major issues were "politically mishandled" and decisions "taken at the highest level ignored the individual qualities of the electorate and concentrated almost exclusively on a management level". Evidently, the deficiencies in "style" and "marketing" were more profound than the Leader seemed to appreciate. They would not be overcome by a "meet and greet" campaign, or by going head-to-head with the Opposition, modifying the "presidential" approach and showing more sympathy for the battlers. The underlying message to the Premier was that he should think seriously about his "NSW Inc." approach to politics. He and his advisers should, in the words of the revered Sir Robert Menzies, be more "politics conscious", and not merely management-oriented.

But commitment was one thing; reality – which to the Harvard graduate was always critical – was another. From June 1991 Greiner had to contend with three factors he could not change: he did not have full control of the Assembly (and by January 1992 he was even more dependent); his authority within Cabinet was no longer absolute; and the immediate priority was to mitigate the effects of the recession and to preserve the State's triple-A rating in the face of a rising deficit and falling revenue.

## Cabinet changes

In the midst of fielding criticisms of the campaign strategy, recovering from the shock of near-defeat, and negotiating with Windsor, Nick Greiner began considering the make-up of his Cabinet. Three Liberal Party vacancies, caused by Dowd's retirement, Pickard's translation and Hay's election defeat, had to be filled. The National Party intended to dump Rowland-Smith for George Souris so there would be a fourth new face. Greiner decided to promote Anne Cohen, Terry Griffiths and Ron Phillips, and he appointed three assistant ministers: Smiles (Treasury), Zammit (Office of Aboriginal Affairs) and the NP's Don Page (Roads and Transport).

Three significant decisions underpinned the composition and structure of the new Cabinet. First, Metherell was not included. The former minister believed he and the Premier had reached "a clear understanding" during talks in September 1990 about his reinstatement following the next election. They had a telephone conversation on 27 May, two days after the poll, which Metherell found "reassuring". There was nothing in Greiner's demeanour "to suggest the slightest reservation about my promised return". Friends and colleagues – notably, Moore and Hannaford – were also confident Metherell would come back. Convinced he would get an economic portfolio, probably Minerals and Energy, Metherell became agitated when he read an obviously inspired leak in the *SMH* on Saturday 1 June. Bernard Lagan correctly predicted the inclusion of Cohen and Phillips in the ministry and referred to "many" in the Cabinet believing that the close election result had rendered Metherell "too much of a political liability". On information supplied by Hannaford, Metherell believed the alleged detractors were Collins and Fahey, though he knew there was little or no support from the Nationals. His friends had probably done Metherell a disservice by boosting his hopes. Ted Pickering brought him closer to reality. Metherell telephoned him to learn that Greiner had not consulted the Group's leader and that Pickering considered it entirely appropriate for the Premier not to consult anyone. In Pickering's view, the election had left the Premier with little political capital which he was unlikely to risk on Metherell while the tax issue remained a mark against the former minister in the minds of some (unnamed) people.

Greiner does not recall speaking to Metherell on 27 May. He has a clear recollection, however, of having no intention of returning him to Cabinet. He might have hinted previously at a possible return to the ministry but for Metherell to believe he could come back after the election result was simply "delusional". The best Greiner could do was to appoint Metherell Parliamentary Secretary to the Premier, with special responsibility for urban affairs. Metherell thought Greiner had committed "an outright act of disloyalty".[6] He would deliver retribution in the following October.

The second decision involved a rearrangement of portfolios with the objective of separating the policy and management functions of government. Greiner started by splitting the Health and the Attorney-General's Departments into two bodies. Hannaford became Minister for Health and Community Services and was responsible for policy while Phillips took the new ministry of Health Services Management. Collins took over the Attorney-General's Department but its management functions for courts and administration were transferred, along with the Department of Corrective Services, to what became the Justice Department headed by Terry Griffiths. When announcing these arrangements, Greiner acknowledged he was moving into untried territory. There were risks attached to this new approach yet "we go into it with good will, with a clear philosophy direction and I think it makes a great deal of sense". The Premier also said he did not know of any precedents (there were, in fact, many). Sturgess was very aware of one. Towards the end of her prime ministership Margaret Thatcher embarked on the radical reform of the civil service in line with the "Next Steps" program which presupposed the separation of policy-making and administration.[7]

The third decision addressed the questions of "style" and "marketing". Two of the three assistant ministers would take some of his workload and free him "to be a lot more political, a lot more people-orientated". He could now get out among the voters and not have to spend "an extraordinary amount of time on meetings which are of no political significance". Of all the criticism he had heard during the previous two weeks, the one which struck home was that he had to become "a better salesman of the Government". Whether he wanted Bruce Baird to sell the Government, or simply be free to concentrate on substantive transport issues, Greiner had a good argument for giving him an assistant. Baird had signed 16,000 letters during the last year: "If anyone thinks that's a good idea then I am a monkey's uncle."[8]

## The Independents

After Windsor was locked in, Greiner sought further stability by reaching agreement with the other three Independents. The problem was that two of them – Hatton and Clover Moore – were not conservative, while Macdonald appeared to be far more "green" than everyone in the Coalition except, possibly, Tim Moore and Metherell. The three Independents did have their individual interests. Hatton had been a long-term campaigner against corruption in the police force and the Public Service; Moore's support base in the diverse inner city seat of Bligh included its numerically-strong gay community and she had a special interest in community participation in decision-making; Macdonald fought the middle-class seat of Manly largely to protect its environment. But the three of them had many things in common, including a desire to redress the balance between the executive and the legislature and to make government more open and accountable.[9]

Greiner had long espoused some of the views they put together in their "Charter of Reform" which they presented to the Premier on 12 June. Their specific demands were notable for the following: fixed-term parliaments; an expanded *Freedom of Information Act*; wider powers for the Ombudsman and the Auditor-General; a review of parliamentary procedures and standing orders to allow greater participation by private members; introduction of estimates committees and better budget scrutiny processes; legislation to protect public service whistle-blowers; wider powers for parliamentary committees; and restrictions placed on defamation laws. In return, the three Independents would support the Government on money bills and no-confidence motions, except in cases involving "corruption or gross maladministration".

Greiner met them for more than an hour on 13 June. He agreed to hand the Charter to a Cabinet sub-committee though, as Hatton commented after the meeting, the Premier had warned them "in no uncertain terms" their bargaining position had weakened as a result of the Windsor deal. Yet Greiner was well aware of how an unforeseen absence from the Assembly or, worse still, a by-election loss would affect the Government's survival. So, although he was in no hurry, he appointed Tim Moore, the Leader of the House, and Garry West of the NP, the Minister for Conservation and Land Management, to negotiate some form of agreement with the three Independents.

There was little immediate movement and by the end of July the Independents felt so frustrated they issued an ultimatum: the Government should agree to their proposals for legal and parliamentary reform or face the prospect of their supporting a no-confidence motion. A *SMH* editorial on 5 August wondered whether the "studied casualness" in the approach of the Cabinet sub-committee reflected the Premier's "misguided attitude" that, in the event of a face-off, the Independents would not risk losing their seats by forcing the Government to the polls. As Greiner now faced an Opposition "that looks and behaves as if it is the next Government", he should win the goodwill of the Independents by agreeing to most of their proposals. On 6 August Greiner handed a document to the three Independents saying that the Government would agree in principle to a number of their demands, including four-year fixed terms, a requirement for MPs to disclose political donations, and wide-ranging changes to Freedom of Information laws. There were some sticking points. The Government had no intention of giving the NSW Ombudsman full access to Cabinet documents. Nevertheless, Hatton acknowledged the Government had been more forthcoming than in the past and assured Greiner he had no reason to worry in the short term about "us" opposing Supply or supporting a no-confidence motion.[10]

The negotiations continued over matters both of principle and of detail but, at the end of September, Hatton claimed that the differences between the Government and the Independents remained "quite considerable".[11] A decision to gag debate on industrial relations legislation had especially irked the Independents who, while not ready to abandon talks, called on the Government to be "fair dinkum". Greiner did not regard the dispute as too serious and spoke of the two sides agreeing to a cooling-off period. He still had the numbers, and Labor's challenge to the results in Maitland and The Entrance remained in the hands of the Court of Disputed Returns. Hatton raised the prospect of an adverse decision in the more vulnerable seat of The Entrance. Bob Graham, a former butcher, had retained the seat in the May election by just 116 votes, and the Liberal Party had moved immediately into election mode once Labor appealed.[12] For the moment, however, Nick Greiner had no great reason for concern.

### "An appalling act of betrayal"

On 2 October Terry Metherell announced his resignation from the Liberal Party "live" on the ABC's *7.30 Report*. Henceforth, he would sit as an Independent, reducing the Coalition's numbers to 48. Should Labor take The Entrance, the Government and the Opposition would each hold 47 seats.

The former Minister for Education had recorded in his diary in late May that, if he were not offered a major portfolio, he would "most probably become an Independent Liberal – moving to the cross benches". He saw himself as a Liberal, not as a creature *of* the Liberal Party. Metherell cited examples of the Government's increasing conservatism and the greater influence of the National Party to explain his increasing disillusionment. But his decision to resign was primarily a delayed reaction to Greiner's failure to reinstate him. The timing and manner of the resignation became an act of "pay-back",[13] designed to inflict maximum damage. Metherell had contacted Quentin Dempster of the ABC, and made arrangements a week in advance of 2 October to announce his departure on the *7.30 Report*. He gambled against an early disclosure which would have allowed Greiner and his office either to try and dissuade him or to attack him ahead of the announcement, thus reducing his television appearance to an anti-climax and to a reaction to their criticism. No word slipped out. Metherell actually sat next to the Premier at a two-hour urban planning meeting on the afternoon of 2 October. Greiner's first inkling of trouble ahead was the message he received just prior to the *7.30 Report* going to air when he was preparing to attend a business engagement at the Sheraton Wentworth.

Metherell did not hold back. Special leadership qualities, he said, were required in times of great economic and social stress. Barton, Deakin, Curtin and Menzies had such qualities. Greiner did not. His Government had lost its way, he seemed unable to reach out and take the community into his confidence, and the Government had ceased to be "warm and green". The Premier offered no clear vision to lift the people of NSW in this time of deep recession, and his Government was dividing the community because of its obsession with cost-cutting. Metherell levelled a number of specific charges, highlighting sins of commission and omission. Notably, the economic "dry" of yesteryear now wanted Greiner to borrow more, to increase the budget deficit to pay for more capital works and social welfare programs, and return to "a more balanced liberalism" where free enterprise would be matched by "strong environmental safeguards" and "compassion" for the low income families of Western Sydney and the Central and North Coast.

Nick Greiner seemed unconcerned: "A minority Government today, a minority Government tomorrow". The Government's policies and their direction would remain the same. At most, the Premier acknowledged his hurt: he had given Metherell "personal and professional loyalty of the highest order" (he could have added how he had paid a heavy personal and political price in doing so). He was "stupefied" by Metherell's criticisms, and wondered whether, having journeyed from the far Left to the far Right, the former Minister had retraced his steps. "I'm buggered if I know." Without access to Metherell's diaries Greiner was unaware of what triggered the resignation. In any case, he was "not in the business of psychoanalysing Dr Metherell", though he suspected it would be "a tough job".[14]

Other Liberals were more outspoken. Branch members, the Secretariat, backbenchers and ministers all railed against what Michael Yabsley called "an appalling act of betrayal". Maher accused Metherell of "gross disloyalty", of "deceit, treachery and cowardice", and of engaging in "a night of self-indulgence" and a "night of infamy". Inevitably, some Liberals invoked the dastardly parallel of Judas Iscariot. Yet no one in October 1991 could plausibly claim that Metherell's denunciations on the *7.30 Report* had more than wounded Nick Greiner or that his reward was the modern equivalent of thirty pieces of silver. Besides, the real impact of Metherell's actions on 2 October was not apparent until six months later when Greiner approved his appointment to a job in the

NSW Public Service. When Greiner needed his Party to applaud or just accept the decision, many Liberals thought that rewarding a traitor was too high a price to pay for retrieving his seat.

## The Memorandum of Understanding

The immediate effect of the Metherell resignation was to strengthen the bargaining position of the three Independents. They expanded their demands to include changes in government policies relating to the environment, industrial relations and casinos. Hatton observed how the Independents could now secure their Charter of Reform without the support of the conservative parties. He found it "disturbing" that the Premier had lost none of his "arrogance" in refusing to change direction. Although Greiner still had the most seats in the Assembly and, therefore, had the right to govern, Greiner did not have the right "to force his policies on the people of NSW". (Apparently, three non-aligned Independents, with a combined primary vote of less than two per cent, did have such a right.) Hatton issued a warning: if Carr obtained a majority of votes in the Assembly, the more "humane" Opposition Leader should be given the opportunity to form a government. A "baton change" would preserve the stable government the Independents assured everyone was what they wanted, and without forcing them to face another election. Although Clover Moore and Dr Macdonald were not so blunt, they remained no less determined to secure what the former called "a different style, real consultation and amending legislation".[15]

The Metherell resignation had so increased the pressure on the Government to reach an agreement that, within three weeks, the press could report signatures were imminent. Hatton declared that the Government "is sincere in this matter" and Clover Moore spoke of a spirit of "enthusiastic co-operation" which had previously been absent.[16] Yet Nick Greiner was not without bargaining power. Hatton admitted there was a degree of self-preservation in the decision to sign an agreement with the Premier. The Independents did not want to be seen as responsible for the Government "lurching from crisis to crisis", unable to deal with the very real problems of the day. Moreover, the Greiner Government deserved the Independents' support: it had been commissioned to govern and had won over half of the two-party preferred vote. Moody's, the international credit ratings agency, injected a further note of urgency on 28 October when it announced it was reviewing the State's triple-A rating. Speaking in the Assembly, the Premier quoted the managing director of the Sydney office of Moody's who said the decision was not a criticism of the State Government's record.[17] Rather, Moody's had "some concerns" because of the impact of "exogenous factors" – as Greiner described them, "the impact of the current Federal Government and its disastrous economic policies", including the cuts in Commonwealth spending in NSW – which had caused the deterioration in the State's revenue base. Moody's identified "the large degree of political uncertainty in the State" as one of the main reasons for its review, and Greiner accused the Opposition of "assiduously" promoting "a climate of artificial instability".

On 31 October Greiner, flanked by Macdonald and Hatton, and with Clover Moore sitting next to the latter, signed a Memorandum of Understanding. The starting proposition was that the balance of power between the Parliament and the Executive had shifted too far towards the Executive. The Independents agreed to vote with the Government on all Appropriation and Supply bills and on motions of no confidence except where matters of corruption or gross maladministration were involved. They were also free to move a vote of no confidence if the Government (including Windsor) had fewer numbers than the Opposition and was not providing "satisfactory government". For its part, the Government agreed to the introduction of fixed four-year terms and of improvements to parliamentary procedures to enable ordinary members to render the Government more accountable, and to provide wider opportunities for community scrutiny of legislation on significant matters of public interest. The Government also agreed to overhaul electoral funding legislation, to strengthen the *Freedom of Information Act*, and extend the range of information provided by statutory authorities. It would ensure greater protection for whistle-blowers, amend defamation legislation by removing restrictions presently operating against "full and fair media reporting", introduce a system of external scrutiny of the legal profession, strengthen the roles of the Auditor-General and the Ombudsman, and extend the rights of third parties in some cases and particularly in relation to environmental matters. The Government further agreed to meet with the Independents on a monthly basis "to ensure that the spirit and intent of the Independent Members' proposals are accommodated in the most practical and cost-effective manner". Timetables were set for implementing the agreement which was to be interpreted "according to the spirit . . . not the letter".[18]

In the Assembly, the Premier described the agreement as "historic" in providing "stability of government and substantial parliamentary, constitutional and legal reform". He also observed that the agreement represented "the most far-reaching change in the governance of New South Wales".[19] Hatton later spoke warmly of the early months following the election, attributing much of the success of the negotiations to the approach taken by Tim Moore and Garry West and to Greiner's good-will. The resistance, Hatton said, emanated particularly from the National Party. Hatton wrote privately to Greiner on 4 November.[20] He expected there would be "areas of sharp disagreement" for the remainder of the Parliament but "the integrity and intention of the process which led up to the agreement, and the agreement itself, is not one of them".

> We wish to reaffirm our trust in the spirit and intent of the agreement. Any attempts by the Labor Party to drive wedges of discontent will fail as far as the agreement is concerned.

### The business of governing

Nick Greiner had two good reasons for leaving Tim Moore in charge of the negotiations with the Independents; he did not become Premier of NSW in order to spend a lot of time talking to the member for the South

Coast, and there were more pressing matters requiring his attention than
John Hatton's expanding number of causes.

Besides, he had acquired one of his own. Greiner played a critical
role at the beginning in bringing the Olympic Games to Sydney in 2000.
Despite opposition from senior bureaucrats and some ministers, he
promised the full backing of the NSW Government to the proposed
bid for the Games. Early in 1991 he spoke to media representatives
in his office and told them bluntly that taxpayer dollars would not be
forthcoming, and the bid would not succeed, if the media played its usual
"knocking role". News Ltd, Fairfax and the electronic media accepted
his admonition. Greiner was largely responsible for tipping the vote in
favour of Rod McGeoch as the CEO of the bid, in a decision taken
after the State election because he liked the idea of someone reputedly
abrasive as the strong man to preside over conflicting interests and egos.[21]

Greiner maintained a primary interest in supporting Hawke's "New
Federalism", and he figured prominently at the second Special Premiers'
Conference held in Sydney on 30 July. This meeting approved a number
of proposals previously thrashed out by officials: removal of trade
barriers between the States; national recognition of trade and professional
qualifications; establishment of a national rail freight scheme, a national
system for heavy vehicle registration and an eastern Australia electricity
grid; the introduction of national performance criteria for GTEs;
creation of national environmental standards; and development of
uniform food standards. The commentators spoke of "a new Australian
common market" which some saw as the offspring of a "Greiner-Hawke
love affair". Greiner said the decisions taken at Sydney were about "jobs,
people and the wealth of the consumer" while Hawke called it "the most
important meeting since World War II". The tough decisions on financial
relations had yet to be made but, late in 1991, Greiner felt sufficiently
confident to deliver the previously-mentioned paper to the Federalism
Research Centre, and hoped that the next Special Premiers' Conference,
scheduled for Perth in November, would take reform of the financial
relationship to the next stage.

The meeting never took place. Keating, who had lost his first-round challenge to Hawke's leadership in June 1991 and moved to the backbench, used a speech to the National Press Club on 22 October to open a new front in the battle.[22] He called Hawke's plan to give the States more taxing powers "a disaster" and a repudiation of Labor values. Keating visualised the dismembering of the national government and cited Greiner and faceless Federal and State bureaucrats as the driving forces behind this "New Federalism". The former Treasurer campaigned in Caucus to build opposition to two proposals. One, put forward by the bureaucrats, would allow the States to levy a 5 per cent income tax or a 22 per cent surcharge on tax paid, a gain of $10bn for State revenues. The other, proposed by the Premiers to meet the objection that the States would thereby acquire income tax powers, was a compromise scheme for a national income tax sharing arrangement whereby up to 6 per cent of income tax revenue (again, around $10bn) collected by the Commonwealth would be handed to the States. Greiner accused Keating of conducting a "totally selfish and totally hypocritical" campaign against "New Federalism" and said the opportunity for substantial progress had been "hurt by the Labor leadership fracas".

When Federal Cabinet rejected the States' compromise plan as a State income tax under another name the Premiers decided to boycott the Perth meeting, claiming that Hawke had broken his undertaking to redress vertical fiscal imbalance. The Prime Minister's "New Federalism" had been, as Greiner put it, "derailed" by Keating's leadership ambitions. He did not think it fit to mention Hawke's decision to abandon his dream of a fourth term legacy in order to hold onto power.[23] Greiner left it to the Labor Premiers – principally, Lawrence, Bannon and Goss – to fulminate publicly about Hawke's "betrayal". But he readily joined them in Adelaide for an alternative conference of Premiers and Territory leaders, to which the Commonwealth was not invited, where the States confirmed their commitment to a fixed share of income tax revenue, to micro-economic reform and to the formation of a Council of the Federation (with Hawke in the chair).

Greiner's principal concern in the second half of 1991, however, was the $1bn hole in the budget caused by the collapse of the property market and the cutbacks in Commonwealth grants. A mini-budget on 2 July 1991 left no doubt why he had called an early poll. The measures introduced were designed to cut debt by $2.5bn in real terms over three years. Greiner planned to sell the GIO and the State Bank and to collect special dividends from statutory authorities to raise $3.5bn. Public Service numbers were to be cut by 12,500 over two years, and by sackings if necessary, and jobs would be cut from the SES and SES salaries were to be frozen. Spending on capital works was to be slashed, more government services were to be contracted out, and subsidies for users of the SRA's freight service would be reduced. The Government also intended to address the vexed question of the school transport scheme which could cost $330m by 1993-4. It took one very familiar step by raising the price of tobacco.

The Premier described the mini-budget as "people painless"; that is, unlike the June statement of 1988, fewer individuals and families would be affected. He could also report some good news. NSW had retained its triple-A rating, had been protected from the worst of the recession, was best placed to protect job opportunities and living standards, and had led Australia in micro-economic reform, public sector reform and financial management. Greiner's problem was that even the cleverest of marketing would not excite or win the gratitude of those who could not think of themselves as "clients" or "shareholders".[24]

The next step was the 1991-2 Budget of 24 September, Greiner's fourth and, as it turned out, his last.[25] Greiner said it was framed "in the most difficult circumstances since 1931". As he did in the July mini-budget, he outlined the Government's relative success in dealing with an environment far removed from Labor's "charmed life" of expanding revenues in the 1980s and its consequent "spending spree". Faced now with what Percy Allan said was a possible deficit of $2bn, he proposed to save up to half that amount by cutting back capital works programs in health, roads, and law and order, and by shedding 1,300 staff from the Road Transport Authority. He attempted to ease some of the pain with a $10m Recession Support Program directed mainly at existing charities and community-based organisations, and there were to be exemptions from land tax and land tax rebates for some groups. But there were no major tax cuts, nor could there be. Even after savage reductions in spending, the budgeted deficit for 1991-2 stood at $1,089m, and the projected deficit for 1992-3 would also exceed $1bn, falling to $885m in 1993-4.

The brave new world was not abandoned: "New South Wales has the most comprehensive and exciting financial management and micro-economic reform program in Australia." Moreover, while to some, the term "bottom line" was one of the most dreaded and irritating inventions of "management speak", in this instance Greiner gave it a warmer connotation, perhaps marking an improvement in "style" and "marketing":

> Our bottom line is simply to create an efficient, effective, low
>
> cost, low debt public sector which can produce the best results for consumers and the best results for taxpayers.
>
> The final results will be lower taxes, lower charges, more jobs and higher living standards for the people of New South Wales.

Delivering reform in the economic and political environment of 1991 was not going to be easy, even for one who remained committed. There was, however, one matter on which the Government was determined to proceed. Greiner had long favoured industrial relations reform. He was fortunate in coming into office at a time when the Labor Council of NSW, which had enjoyed considerable power under Wran and Unsworth and was potentially a formidable opponent, was to an extent hamstrung by the falling numbers of its union base, by the Federal Labor Government's support for deregulation of the labour market, and even by the previous State Labor Government's market-oriented approach as evident in its occupational health and safety legislation.

John Fahey piloted industrial relations reform through both Houses. The legislation was designed to foster enterprise bargaining agreements between employers and employees. It established a new Industrial Relations Commission and an Industrial Court to interpret and enforce awards. Critically, from a union viewpoint, the legislation outlawed payments to workers on strike, restricted access of union officials to work sites, and ended the closed shop in favour of voluntary unionism.

Greiner spoke in the second reading debate on 10 September 1991.[26] He attacked Carr for wanting to preserve the "protected and fostered position" of trade unions. Greiner said his entire time as a political leader was "about getting rid of vested interests and about governing in the public interest". Union preference, he argued, amounted in practice to compulsory unionism, to the closed shop. Carr was in effect defending a small vested interest exercising a privileged monopoly position to serve its own ends. Greiner had long wanted to get rid of "the most serious intrusions on individual freedoms" and the "greatest obstacle to economic progress in New South Wales". This legislation amounted to "the single most important thing that we, as a Parliament, can do for the well-being of the men and women, and particularly the children, of New South Wales". Greiner could also claim he had a mandate for reform. He might be heading a minority government but, as he reminded the Assembly, he had fought the election in part over industrial relations reform and obtained nearly 53 per cent of the two-party preferred vote.

The Labor Council called a general strike for 23 October 1991, the first of its kind since the dark days of 1917. Hitherto, Greiner had been complimentary about the Council, saying it was "generally . . . quite responsible in the way it . . . co-operated with the microeconomic reforms that this Government has instituted."[27] On 22 October he introduced a motion condemning the Council for defying a NSW Industrial Commission ruling that participation by the public sector unions would be illegal. Greiner accused the Council of causing a massive disruption of the NSW economy at a time when workers were suffering under the current recession caused by Federal Labor. It would cost $100 for a family on average earnings and would change nothing and achieve nothing.[28] He did not hold back in what became a highly charged debate. The strike was "the greatest act of industrial bastardry in the past 50 years", constituted "absolute unadulterated madness" and was "an unmitigated act of treachery". It was a case of "mob rule by union leaders and industrial thugs".

Greiner's central purpose was to force Carr and the Labor Party to say whether or not they supported the general strike. He stressed how the issue was not the proposed legislation but whether the strike was an appropriate form of response. Carr flailed about brilliantly, as only he could. There were taunts and sharp jibes and clever insults. He made one constructive and substantive point: the need to establish a framework for industrial co-operation while preserving union rights and minimum wage awards. The speech was more notable, however, for what he did not say; he refused to condemn or support the strike. In fact, only three Labor backbenchers in the Assembly, and then only by way of interjection, supported it. After rejecting amendments the Assembly carried the Greiner motion by 51 votes to 45. All five Independents voted with the Government.

The Premier planned to use his official car to pick up workers, and ordered his ministers and backbenchers to help out. The Labor Council expected about one million of the State's work force of 2.6 million to strike. Some 600,000 probably did so, and public transport, factories, docks, offices and schools were seriously affected. Yet the strike proved to be the futile gesture Greiner said it would be. The Parliament finally approved the legislation on 31 October and the Greiner Government could claim to be a pioneer in instigating comprehensive legislation to encourage non-union and enterprise agreements.[29]

## An Independent Report Card

The Government commissioned Don Nicholls who, it will be recalled, had written most of the Curran Report, to review its financial performance since taking office. He was also asked to review progress made in addressing issues raised by the Commission of Audit in 1988. Specifically, he was asked to report on the growth of the public sector, changes in debt levels, the financial performance of the budget and non-budget sectors, the financial performance of NSW compared with other States, and the requirements to retain its triple-A rating. Nicholls began his review on 2 October 1991 and submitted his findings on 29 November.[30] He described his report as "a wide-ranging study of the finances of New South Wales during the first term of the present government", and he thought it the first time "an Australian government has commissioned a report of this kind". Nicholls said his emphasis was on relative change and not on absolute values. For example, he sought to know whether NSW was spending relatively more or less in 1991 than in 1987-8 on education, whether NSW was spending relatively more or less on education than the other States, and whether the gap had widened or narrowed.

Nicholls' main conclusion was that:

> In the past three years the financial management of the state has been transformed, with debt abating and with the improvement in the financial operations of government trading enterprises probably unmatched in any other state and in any other period at least since World War II.

He added one serious rider: "On the other hand the government has had difficulty in restraining the growth of general government services (health etc.) and has not achieved its own targets for this sector."[31] Significantly, Nicholls also concluded that, while the period from 1987-8 to 1991 was marked by major initiatives to improve financial management, there were – taking just a few areas – other substantial changes: the reorganisation of the mission and objectives of education, the commitment to more open government, and a changed emphasis in law and order with the introduction of truth in sentencing and of ICAC. "In fact it is surprising that the period 1987-88 to 1990-91 has sometimes been portrayed as sterile, dominated by an emphasis on money management."

Chapter Two of the report summarised in 12 pages Nicholls' "Findings and Suggestions". Nick Greiner had every reason to be pleased. For example, Nicholls found that the NSW economy had held up better than Victoria's and, to a lesser extent, better than the economies of most other States. The NSW public sector had shrunk over the three years, mainly in the non-budget sector. There had been substantial gains in the productivity of GTEs with the most significant gains occurring in the last three years. NSW had implemented a comprehensive program placing it ahead of all the other States in promoting commercialisation and sound management, though only two GTEs had so far been corporatised. NSW had led the way over the last three years in national micro-economic reform and had changed the culture of the NSW public sector. Ninety per cent of the Commission of Audit's proposals were accepted and virtually all had been or were being implemented. The Commission's proposed budget strategy of tax reductions, asset sales and improved transport operating costs had been or would be shortly achieved, even if progress was slow in some other areas.

Nicholls' list of suggestions ranged through budgeting and accounting (he stressed need for full accrual accounting to be implemented in the public sector), to a series of recommendations relating to GTEs (including the full costing of services) and setting target ratios for State liabilities. There was nothing about his suggestions to bother Greiner, notwithstanding a nudge about following up those Commission of Audit proposals still marked "under consideration" or "deferred". One set of recommendations would have been especially welcome. Nicholls endorsed Greiner's priority of maintaining the State's triple-A rating and urged the Government to resist expenditure initiatives which could not be met from present allocations and to reject any financing of "make work" or "pump priming" programs.

After obtaining such a good report card at the end of November Greiner received an inconvenient reminder of his tenuous hold on government. On 11 December Justice Slattery, sitting as the Court of Disputed Returns, rejected Labor's challenge over Maitland but ruled Bob Graham's election in The Entrance invalid. An official error had caused some 230 votes to be wrongly cast in other electorates. Properly recorded, they might have affected the outcome. Michael Yabsley provided ministerial oversight for the Liberal Party's campaign for a by-election set down for 18 January 1991 and which the Government knew it could not win.

Greiner's limited involvement ceased altogether when his mother died three days before the poll. Her death was unexpected, and unrelated to the cancer which had cost her a leg. Clare Greiner had entered hospital for tests for a possible heart condition and died from a heart attack after what had been a normal procedure.[32] A Requiem Mass was celebrated at St Mary's Church, North Sydney, on 17 January, followed by an interment at French's Forest Cemetery. St Mary's was ministered by Jesuits and the Australian Jesuit Mission in India was one of the many charities Clare had supported. Kara Greiner once described her grandmother as "a force of nature",[33] and it was this drive and determination which helped ensure that Kara's father fitted into an environment far removed from his birthplace.

The margin of the predicted defeat in The Entrance was at least reassuring. Greiner could point out how the anti-government swing of 4.9 per cent was well below the average of 9.7 per cent during the previous decade. He conceded that the result was "the sort of kick in the pants" expected in a by-election. Governing, he observed, had become slightly more difficult: the consultation process "will have to be perhaps even better". He could also say how the campaign itself was "technically, well, if not perfect then close to it". Bob Graham had focussed on local issues. No one in The Entrance heard anything about "Leadership that's working". There were no presidential sweeps through the electorate. Lessons had been learnt, and the Liberals could take further solace from the spirit of on-the-ground campaigning.

With the Coalition and Labor each holding 47 seats, the Government now needed the votes of two Independents, in addition to Windsor's support, to pass its legislation in the Legislative Assembly. Clearly, the Government could not afford to lose another seat. The journalist Mark Coultan speculated that such an eventuality might see the Premier contemplating Paul Keating's "Paris option" of just walking away from politics; in Greiner's case, taking company directorships or a job in the international finance community.[34] In the prevailing circumstances, it would be immensely helpful if Terry Metherell either re-joined the Liberal Party or resigned his safe North Shore seat of Davidson. Yet neither possibility appeared to be on the horizon in January 1992.

After personal and political setbacks, it was a good time to get away. The Greiners set off early in February for a family skiing holiday in Europe.


## Endnotes

[1]  Interview: Sturgess, 22 June 2011.

[2]  Interview: Allan, 14 Sepember 2011.

[3]  Correspondence with Members, Greiner Papers.

[4]  Liberal Party of Australia (NSW Division), 1991 State Election Campaign: Task Force Report, 5 July 1991. The Task Force interviewed some 150 people, received around 200 written submissions, and made 57 recommendations.

[5]  Interview: Hockey, 29 October 2012.

[6]  The above two paragraphs draw principally upon an interview with Metherell on 15 June 2006 and with Greiner on 7 February 2010 as well as Terry Metherell, Autobiography.

[7]  Margaret Thatcher, *The Downing Street Years*, HarperCollins, London, 1993, p. 49.

[8]  For the above two paragraphs, see *SMH*, 7 June 1991.

[9]  For an analysis of the Independents' positions, see Steven Reynolds, "Minority government from the other side of the fence: Policy outcomes for the NSW Independents 1991-95 and the Tasmanian Greens 1989-92", *Legislative Studies*, vol. 13, no. 1, 1998, pp. 17-39; Rodney Smith, *Against the Machines: Minor Parties and Independents in New South Wales, 1910-2006*, Federation Press, Leichhardt, 2006, esp. pp. 62-8, 155-9.

[10] *SMH*, 31 July, 5 and 7 August 1991.

[11] *SMH*, 28 September 1991.

[12] Management Committee Minutes, LPA, ML, MSS 7205/13.

[13] Interview: Metherell, 15 June 2006.

[14] For the above paragraphs, see *SMH*, 3-4 Oct. 1991 and Hancock, *Liberals*, pp. 293-5.

[15] *SMH*, 4 October 1991.

[16] *SMH*, 25 October 1991.

[17] *NSWPD*, Third Series, vol. 225, pp. 3792-5; *SMH*, 29 October 1991.

[18] Clune and Griffith, *Decision and Deliberation*, pp. 541-2.

[19] *NSWPD*, Third Series, vol. 225, pp. 4004-5. For Moore's favourable view of the outcome, see T. J. Moore, "Balancing reform and survival", *The Parliamentarian*, April 1994, pp. 114, 117-18.

[20] Letters from members, Greiner Papers.

[21] Rod McGeoch with Glenda Korporaal, *The Bid: How Australia Won the 2000 Games*, William Heinemann, Australia, 1993, esp. p. 23; *Australian*, 19 October 1993.

[22] *Australian*, 23 October 1991.

[23] For Greiner's comments on Keating, see *SMH*, 8 November 1991.

[24] *NSWPD*, Third Series, vol. 223, p. 46. For the mixed reactions, see also *SMH*, 3 July 1991.

[25] For Greiner's speech, see *NSWPD*, Third Series, vol. 223, pp. 1587-601.

[26] *Ibid.*, vol. 223, pp. 909-14.

[27] *Ibid.*, vol. 222, p. 2503, 18 April 1991.

[28] For the debate and divisions, see *ibid.*, vol. 224, pp. 2954-83.

[29] Suzanne Jamieson, "Industrial Relations" in Laffin and Painter, *Reform and Reversal*, p. 153.

[30] *How the Government Has Performed: An Independent Review of the Financial Performance of the New South Wales Government 1988 to 1991*, November 1991.

[31] On p. 115 of his chapter on "State Finances and Financial Management" in Laffin and Painter, *Reform and Reversal*, Professor Walker quoted Nicholls' rider while removing the words, "On the other hand", and omitting altogether the sentence setting out Nicholls' main conclusion.

[32] Interview: Chris Greiner, 13 November 2011.

[33] Interview: Kara Greiner, 19 April 2011.

[34] For post by-election comments, see *Sunday Telegraph*, 19 January and *SMH*, 20 January 1992. For the Liberal Party's assessment of the campaign, see Minutes of State Executive, 31 January 1992, LPA, ML, MSS 7205/10.

# 15

# "The public will draw
its own conclusions"

Nick Greiner returned to Australia in mid-February refreshed and confident. Gary Sturgess had been working on a vision statement which would make the Government appear warmer and greener. Legislation was ready to be introduced to advance the reform program. A Royal Visit was imminent and, closet republican that he was, the Premier of NSW was not going to gainsay the goodwill and euphoria. The polls were unhealthy though well short of terminal. A *Bulletin* poll published on 11 February showed that Greiner and Carr were level on the question of preferred Premier; 33 per cent approved of Greiner's performance compared to a figure of 39 per cent for Carr; and Labor led the Coalition 46-43 per cent on primary figures. Recovery from the recession was slow yet there were some good economic signs. The "Nervous Nellies" in the Liberal Party were clearly worrying about the future, and a few Nationals were daring to question the Government's direction. Peter Cochran, the NP member for Monaro, wrote to the Premier early in February to express his doubts about aspects of the reform program and to attack Tim Moore, the Minister for the Environment, for pandering to the Green movement and for his philosophical allegiance to the left-wing of the Labor Party. Cochran wanted Greiner to review Moore's continued membership of the Cabinet. Greiner could afford to do nothing. Cochran was really Wal Murray's problem, and even then Cochran was little more than an irritant on the margins of the National Party.[1]

Taking everything into account Nick Greiner could look forward to a productive year in government.

## The "Metherell Affair": Part One

While the Greiners were in Europe Terry Metherell was entertaining doubts about his role on the cross-benches.[2] He never fitted in with the other Independents and was thinking about leaving politics altogether. His four private member's Bills relating to the environment were stalled in the Legislative Assembly and his wife, Louise, was pregnant with their first child. On Friday 7 February 1992 Metherell talked with Brad Hazzard, the Liberal MP for Wakehurst, in a car park after both had attended a breakfast meeting at the Warringah Shire Council. Metherell and Hazzard were close friends, with the former helping the latter to defeat the sitting member, John Booth, in the Wakehurst pre-selection for the 1991 election. During this car park encounter Metherell spoke of his desire to make a contribution to public life outside of politics, and expressed an interest in the four senior jobs being advertised in the newly-established Environmental Protection Authority (EPA). Hazzard alerted Tim Moore, Metherell's other close friend in Macquarie Street. Moore pointed out that applications for those jobs had already closed. The Metherells, the Hazzards and the Moores dined together at the Metherell home on the following Sunday; the subject discussed in the car park was not mentioned.

When Greiner returned to Sydney, Hazzard arranged for Moore and himself to meet the Premier at his home on 16 February at around 6.00 pm. Greiner turned up late for the meeting. He had forgotten about the arrangement, and Kathryn had to contact him on his car phone. Greiner learnt for the first time of Metherell's interest in leaving politics. There was a brief discussion about whether Metherell might return to Cabinet. It was quickly agreed this was not an option. Wal Murray was intransigent, and Greiner was worried about the response of his backbench to any reward handed to Metherell. Moore explained how applications for all four director jobs had closed but raised the possibility of creating a fifth position. Greiner said he was prepared to consider such a proposal, and asked Moore to prepare one. He insisted on two conditions: Metherell must be able to do any job on his merits, and no additional funds must be involved.  If these two conditions were met he "would not stand in [Metherell's] way". Greiner also authorised Hazzard to hold further talks with Metherell while keeping Moore informed. As for any political advantage to the Government, the Premier later informed ICAC in his sworn statement that Hazzard made the sole explicit reference to this possibility during the meeting. No one really needed to spell out the obvious.

After the others left, Greiner informed his wife of what had transpired. Kathryn told him in no uncertain terms to have nothing to do with Terry Metherell. She had been "shocked beyond belief" by Metherell's action in walking out of the Liberal Party, and was at her "angriest" after all the support given to him when he was Minister for Education. Kathryn had no difficulty in maintaining her rage. Greiner's first mistake over what became the "Metherell affair" was not to take his wife's advice.

### Royal Visit

The Queen and the Duke of Edinburgh arrived in Australia on 18 February with the main purpose of celebrating the 150th anniversary of the founding of the City of Sydney. The press noted how Kathryn Greiner curtsied when she greeted the Queen at Sydney airport while Annita Keating, the Prime Minister's wife, just delivered a warm handshake. Some British tabloids described Mrs Keating's action as a "snub" even though a Palace official had said the curtsey was no longer obligatory. Local monarchists took further umbrage when five Labor MLCs boycotted an afternoon tea with the Queen at Parliament House – one National Party MP wanted them charged with treason – although their republican principles did not require absence when the Queen opened Parliament on 20 February. The Premier was circumspect: "You can call me 'not-a-republican'." Out of general earshot, Prince Philip, observing a sign hanging out of a building in Macquarie Street reading "Poms Go Home", turned to the Premier and said, "if you are going to kick us out, why not do it quickly".[3]

The Speech which the Queen delivered on Greiner's behalf contained a notable change from the one she had made to the State Parliament in 1954. On this earlier occasion, she spoke of "the contentment and prosperity of *my people in New South Wales*" [emphasis added]. The possessive was missing in 1991 when she referred to the "aspirations of your fellow Australians" and "the welfare of New South Wales and its people". Continuity was maintained when the Queen's sentences began, like those delivered by successive Governors, with the words "My Government" and "My Ministers". For the most part, the Speech was unexceptional. There were references to "the people of many nations" who had recently "rejected authoritarian rule and embraced democracy" in Eastern and Central Europe, to straitened economic times and drought and flooding in NSW, and to the NSW Government being "a willing partner" with all the governments of Australia "towards developing a more efficient and competitive economy". No legislative proposals were outlined.[4]

Instead, the Premier used his Address in Reply speech on 5 March to set out a program which he did not survive in office to fulfil. He began with the Charter of Reform, reiterating his personal commitment to major parliamentary and constitutional change. He spoke of bringing in wide-ranging legislation to further the attack on official corruption by protecting whistle-blowers and preventing corrupt officials from receiving government-funded superannuation. Public sector accountability was to be enhanced by changes to the *Freedom of Information Act*. There was to be an independent tribunal to oversee the prices charged for government monopoly services, and legislation to deregulate solicitors' fees subject to appropriate safeguards and to end the legal profession's monopoly over conveyancing services. The Government planned to give greater autonomy to local councils while making them more accountable to the communities they represented, to create a natural resources management council and establish long-term protection of endangered species of flora and fauna, and to permit legal casino gaming whilst ensuring it was devoid of corrupt influences. There were also proposals to deal with matters ranging from regulation of co-operatives and retirement villages to the use of audio-visual links in certain legal proceedings and the outlawing of age discrimination.

As Greiner acknowledged, "the finely balanced nature of the Parliament" required the Government to adopt a different strategy, but his list of proposed new laws showed how it was "still setting the lead with its agenda for change and for positive reform". The list is also notable for what was missing: the pursuit of root and branch change. Nor was Greiner's reticence early in 1992 to be explained solely in terms of a "finely balanced" Parliament. He had to carry ministers, a number of whom did not share his interpretation of the May election result. Yet, even if Nick Greiner still had a majority in his own right, he would have been lapped in the reform stakes by the headstrong Jeff Kennett who came to power in Victoria in October 1992. As ever rational and pragmatic, Greiner's priority in the New Year was to keep the budget under control. He kept making the point that it behoved all sides of politics to be conscious of the impact of the current recession on the State's revenues. Although NSW had retained its triple-A rating with two international agencies (Standard and Poors and Moody's), its status was at risk if the Government engaged in improvident spending when facing a reduced revenue base. Everyone should support restraint.

Nevertheless, continuing structural reform was essential to ensure greater public sector efficiency and the proceeds from selling GTEs were needed to reduce debt and lower interest rate costs. The Premier denied, as he had often done, that his Government had "an ideological commitment to privatisation" but he turned on the Labor Party for its opposition to the sale of the State Bank and the GIO. Governments

– State and Federal – should see that the future lay in "the creation of real wealth-generating jobs and not in the protection of make-work or pretend jobs".[5] Greiner was not going to "shy at every shadow".

## Internal Problems

Greiner was not blessed by some of those who sat behind him in the Assembly. During February-March, one of his MPs was facing bankruptcy, another was charged with tax fraud, and a third was being investigated by ICAC.

Tony Packard, who was born in England and had migrated to Australia in 1967, owned a car dealership on the Windsor Road, Baulkham Hills. Famed for his showiness, and for his advertisements – "let me do the right thing for you" – Packard was one of the brashest of a generally brash breed. The Liberal Party selected him ahead of eight other candidates (including Jim Cameron, who had returned to fold) to succeed the gentlemanly Fred Caterson in a by-election for The Hills in 1990. Packard won with the backing of the Group. Many older members wondered whether a car salesman was a bridge too far for a Party which could barely accommodate real estate agents. Early in 1992 Packard was being pursued by the Australian Taxation Office and several major creditors led by Westpac. The Labor Party joined the hunt when Parliament moved to ordinary business on 25 February. Greiner faced several questions to which he responded with the Wran approach of toughing things out and accusing the Opposition of getting into the gutter. He simply denied there was evidence of impropriety and adopted the inventive approach of blaming Packard's financial problems on a Labor-generated recession.[6]

Phillip Smiles presented Greiner with a more immediate problem. The one-time rock music promoter and later a management consultant had won Mosman in 1984. The redistribution obliged a move to the seat of North Shore in 1991, where he defeated a Ted Mack-supported Independent after running a brilliant on-the-ground campaign. Greiner's contacts with Smiles since university days had not brought them any closer, and they drew further apart when Smiles organised a media stunt to protest against the financial arrangements for the Harbour tunnel. Smiles had kept pushing for elevation to the front bench. One version of a conversation with Greiner on the subject, repeated enthusiastically around Macquarie Street, had Greiner telling Smiles that if a Cabinet position became vacant, and there were only two people left on earth, he would miss out.[7] Greiner relented to the extent of appointing him chairman of an important committee of investigation and, in February 1991, made him Assistant Treasurer while leaving him outside the ministry. In October 1991 Smiles was being called to account for misleading Parliament over the question of whether he did or did not send out a letter declaring that the Eastern Creek raceway was a "black hole". His action annoyed Greiner but, while acknowledging that Smiles had many times differed from him publicly and in the Party Room, the Premier said he had never known him to tell a lie during the 25 years of their acquaintance.[8] Smiles stood aside from his position as Assistant Treasurer in February 1992 when he was charged with four counts of tax fraud. He remained in Parliament, a continuing embarrassment to a government which did not want to face a by-election.[9].

The Hills did not present a problem – Packard had a margin of 23 per cent – and North Shore might well return an Independent but Maitland presented the greater concern. Peter Blackmore's margin was a mere 0.4 per cent. It emerged in March that the former service station owner was under investigation by ICAC over an allegation that, as Mayor of Maitland, he had accepted the gift of a boat from a property developer. Following a six-month investigation, and two weeks after Greiner left politics, ICAC found the accusation to be false.

Amidst all these troubles there were whispers that Paul Zammit was contemplating early retirement. According to John Hatton, Zammit was considering another option. He approached Hatton in the underground car park of Parliament House after the Metherell resignation from the

Liberal Party to talk about becoming an Independent. Although "we did not recognise people as being Independents if they were fugitives from other political parties . . . we talked to him about it". Nothing came of the approach.[10] Zammit remained an assistant minister and remained unhappy about his lack of promotion.

## Challenges to the Premier's authority

In February-March Greiner faced the prospect of a revolt over property conveyancing, as well as the possibility of Hatton withdrawing his support on confidence motions.

Solicitors currently held a monopoly over conveyancing which they were determined to protect against cut-price operators. Two Australian States and the Thatcher Government in the UK had already removed the monopoly in their respective jurisdictions. Peter Collins, the Attorney-General, wanted to follow suit, and the Law Society fiercely lobbied the Government against him. John Fahey, a solicitor, stood up for the profession while the National Party, concerned for solicitors operating in small country towns, argued strongly against deregulation. Nick Greiner supported Collins – he thought lawyers should not be exempt from micro-economic reform – yet did not speak in Cabinet. Even Gary Sturgess, as Collins reported his reaction, was bewildered by the Premier's refusal to take a stand. Collins was outraged by his silence. "The trust that existed between Leader and Deputy Leader was gone."[11]

Greiner was shrewder than the Attorney-General imagined. This supposedly clumsy or naive politician accepted that Cabinet was overwhelmingly against the Collins proposal. There was a time before the May election when Greiner could get his way despite having numbers of nineteen-to-one against him. After May 1991 he saw no point in risking humiliation. Instead, soon after returning from overseas in February, the Premier took the issue into the public arena. He said the wrong signal had been sent in November because it indicated "the public interest was being sacrificed to a vested interest". Greiner announced that Cabinet would be asked to review the earlier decision "in a calm and reasoned way". As the *SMH* pointed out, the Government could hardly preach efficiency and reform to unions and the public sector while protecting a powerful interest group. Indeed, the Premier's credibility, and therefore his authority, was now truly on the line, all the more so given Labor's intention to introduce its own deregulation legislation.[12]

Greiner persuaded Cabinet to review its earlier decision. A committee was appointed to find a compromise, its membership consisting of Collins (in favour of deregulation), Fahey (against deregulation and a friend of John Marsden who was President of the Law Society) and Garry West (representing the National Party). The outcome was a compromise which allowed outsiders to engage in conveyancing though under a scheme regulated by solicitors. From their different perspectives, both Collins and John Marsden saw the final legislation as a move against the Attorney-General. Marsden claimed that Greiner and Fahey "capitulated" on conveyancing as a first move to promote Fahey ahead of Collins as the next Premier.[13]

Hatton was becoming even more of a troublemaker. In mid-February he wanted the Premier to understand that "Mr Nice Guy is not around anymore". He had done his best to co-operate but Stephen Mutch, a Liberal MLC, had been criticising him around the South Coast for allegedly neglecting his electorate. Hatton was also unhappy about the direction of the Government's policies, especially its support for privatisation of hospitals.[14] By the beginning of March he was not sure the Independents would stand by their agreement with the Government. Should Greiner lose another seat in a by-election, his concern about the Government's policies might lead him to withdraw his support. The Charter of Reform contained a provision allowing the Independents to bring Greiner down if he failed to provide "satisfactory government". Hatton had seemingly broadened the definition of this term to include the direction of policy.[15] On 18 March Hatton attacked Greiner's support for the private ownership and management of hospitals and community health services, and in particular the Government's plans for a hospital in Port Macquarie. He said the privatisation of public health threatened to alienate him from the Greiner Government".[16] Not that Hatton was consistently "difficult". When his own political survival was at stake he could shift the definition of high moral ground. The timber industry was a major employer on the South Coast and, to protect jobs in his electorate, Hatton detached himself from his two greener parliamentary colleagues to vote with the Government – as will be shown later – on controversial legislation on 10 March.

Hatton clearly irritated Greiner. Addressing a gathering on 24 April 1992 to mark the start of the fifth year of the Greiner Government, the Premier spoke of how the Liberal Party, the media and the people of NSW said he had not been sufficiently "political" during the last election. Now, to retain government, he had to play "hard politics", and that meant dealing with Hatton's threat, every second week, to bring the Government down "over some new initiative which he has discovered . . . he doesn't like".[17]

## "The vision thing"[18]

On 23 March, at a packed Journalists' Club in Sydney, which served an unappetising lunch of roast lamb and gravy, Nick Greiner launched *Facing the World*, his 70-page vision statement.

*Facing the World* consisted of five sets of proposals: to take full advantage of changes in technology and the world economy; to assist in creating real and sustainable jobs by reducing the costs to business of government regulation and public utilities; to make sure the NSW Government "is serving the people as customers"; to obtain better information about the environment so sound decisions could be made in balancing conservation and the use of resources; and to provide one of the best physical environments for the people of Sydney and its surrounding urban areas through the "environmentally sound management of future growth".

There were some specific items. The Government planned to introduce an annual $200 tax on owners of non-residential parking places in Sydney with the money to be spent on parking stations or bike storage at railway stations. Hunter Water was to be privatised and $100m was to be spent on an audit of natural resources. Minor offenders and fine defaulters were to be kept out of jail. Several education initiatives included allowing early school leavers to continue working while taking their HSC part-time, a commitment that half of all students taking a language for their HSC would choose from priority Asian-Pacific languages, and the creation of an Advanced Technology Park for three Sydney universities. There was to be a Guarantee of Service: public servants, including police, were to wear name tags so they could be identified by those they served, and public service office hours would be extended.

Predictably, the *Herald* journalists sneered. Mark Coultan said Greiner had taken his "NSW Inc. Government" to a hospitality school and returned with a "Have a Nice Day Government". He focussed on the change of language. The people of NSW were once "shareholders". Now they were to be "customers". Coultan conceded that Greiner "is an extremely reasonable man, a bright person in command of himself and his government – but visionary? Martin Luther King he ain't." Mike Steketee decided Greiner was not offering a vision so much as "an image transplant". It was a case of welcome to "user-friendly government". The *SMH* editorial was kinder. Greiner had delivered "a powerful restatement of objectives" with economic growth and a better quality of life highlighted ahead of public service efficiency, which nonetheless remained necessary to achieve a faster-growing and more competitive economy.

A journalist in the *DTM* spotted similarities between some of the wording in *Facing the World* and John Major's *Citizen's Charter* released in the United Kingdom in July 1991. Carr also seized on the similarities and suggested that, when casting about for a new vision, the visionaries had reached out to the British Tories. A spokesman for Greiner made the obvious point: "No one's got a mortgage on a good idea." Not that any attempt was made to hide the fact Sturgess had worked on *Facing the World* after observing the *Charter* at first hand on a visit to Britain. Major's objectives in formulating the *Citizen's Charter* were to improve the quality and the standing of the British Civil Service.[19] *Facing the World* picked up on the quality aspect by offering a choice of government services, by giving the public adequate information and listening to its needs, expressing policies in plain English, and extending opening hours. The Greiner document, however, was less concerned with the diminution of respect for the Public Service which Major saw as one effect of privatisation. Importantly, *Facing the World* was a direct outcome of the election of May 1991. If the Government had achieved a majority of three in its own right, Greiner would not have gone down the track of *Facing the World*. He would have kept to his original agenda and immediately privatised energy, Hunter Water and the buses.[20]

### The "Metherell Affair": Part Two

While dealing with the multiple and diverse matters of government and politics Nick Greiner was engaged in something to which he gave intermittent attention. Out of media sight, Brad Hazzard had arranged a late evening meeting at Parliament House for 26 February where Greiner talked to Metherell for the first time since Metherell walked out on his Leader.[21] (Greiner thought this meeting occurred on 17 March, an error which became important in the ICAC investigation.) The two had earlier exchanged notes over a Budapest newspaper article about Greiner who had suggested having a chat over "a glass of water" after Parliament resumed.

Metherell's diary provides an account of the meeting. Hazzard was present "partly to keep Nick honest; partly to 'mediate' if necessary". Mediation was not necessary: "from the first mineral water we were back on old terms." Although Greiner wanted to proceed with an appointment he was anxious to buy time. Any "overnight rapprochement" would not be convincing, and Wal Murray would not accept it. Both men discounted a job with the EPA, because the advertised positions had already been filled, and they did not want a position with a public profile which would receive constant media attention. A job in the Cabinet Office seemed the best option. It would be focussed on policy, and be constructive, creative and intellectually demanding. The Sturgess appointment had introduced the notion of a "political" job, and a position there would be "proper" while bringing Metherell close to the Premier and to the key priorities of the Government. Although "there would be 2 or 3 days of heavy media flak, led by the *Herald*", appointing Metherell would be seen as a change in direction towards a middle path as signified by Greiner's forthcoming "vision" statement. The meeting concluded with the two men agreeing to talk regularly, and the former minister was to send the Premier his four environmental Bills for closer examination.

Greiner had not committed himself but Metherell thought the Premier was well aware of the options: do nothing; create a Cabinet Office-type job with a specific purpose; or appoint Metherell to a "dead end" job running a commission of inquiry. The former minister, confident he "understood" Greiner, detected two things about him. First, "Nick is still hurt and bamboozled" by the furore over the appointments of former Liberal politicians and by the media's double standards in dealing, or not dealing, with Labor's exercises of patronage. Secondly, the "apparent confidence" Greiner displayed at the meeting "came from that unusual blend of tight self-control, complacency, assurance, fatalism and a shyness that insulated him from alternative and challenging viewpoints". For all the certainty of diagnosis, Metherell remained puzzled. Did Greiner really believe he was not in deep political trouble, and did this belief explain why he appeared to think he could choose the time when to act on the Metherell matter? Why was there no haste or panic to shore up his parliamentary majority, and why was there no display of anger or irritation during such a long and calm meeting? Perhaps in asking these questions Metherell demonstrated he had not "understood" all of Nick Greiner.

Hazzard and Metherell had a de-briefing session where they decided that the Premier "wasn't a politician's bootlaces", while agreeing he was still "head and shoulders above the rest". Askin, Menzies and Wran, they decided, would have shifted Metherell out within minutes of him declaring a wish to leave politics, or probably even tried to induce him to resign. They may have been abysmally ignorant of Menzies' character but they had given Greiner what he would regard as a glowing reference.

Five days after the "glass of water" meeting, Tim Moore told Metherell about the possibility of creating a fifth position within the EPA concerned with strategic planning and thinking about the future directions of environmental protection. It remains unclear whether Moore consulted the Premier before raising this matter. Metherell thought the proposal was – literally – "tailor made" for him, and was immediately interested. He insisted, however, that the passage of his wilderness protection and environmental education Bills were his immediate priority. He was also intimately involved in discussions about the environmental implications of logging. At the end of 1991 Metherell had supported Labor's Endangered Fauna (Interim Protection) Bill which required that an application for a logging licence be accompanied by a Fauna Impact Statement. Spurred on by the timber industry, which claimed its viability was threatened by this requirement, the Greiner Government introduced the Timber Industry (Interim Protection) Bill, a complicated piece of legislation which sought a compromise between conservationists and timber workers. An amended Bill passed the Assembly – Metherell voted against it – and the Niles supported the Government in returning a re-worked Bill to the Lower House. The Assembly was recalled on 10 March to deal with the legislation. Clover Moore and Dr Macdonald intended to vote with Labor to oppose the amended Bill, and Hatton was committed to supporting it. Metherell's vote, therefore, was crucial.

Moore and Metherell had continued to talk about various environmental issues. On the eve of the Assembly vote, Moore spoke again to Metherell about the proposal to create a fifth directorate in the

EPA. The Minister suggested to Greiner he might speak to Metherell after the Government had considered and approved further amendments to the timber legislation in line with Metherell's position. Greiner rang Metherell late that afternoon. What was said in this call, and what was meant by what was said, would also become key concerns at the ICAC hearing.

To the surprise of everyone except those privileged to know, Metherell supported the Government in the seven divisions called during the Bill's passage through the Assembly. The vote in each case was 44-all after which the Chairman of Committees or the Speaker cast a vote for the Government. Two days after the vote Moore, Hazzard and Metherell held further discussions at Metherell's home. On the same day Dick Humphry decided to create two new Senior Executive Service positions within the Premier's Department. Newspaper advertisements appeared soon afterwards while, on an unrelated matter, Moore began drafting a firm proposal for a fifth senior position to head a small strategic planning unit within the EPA. After looking over Moore's draft the Premier asked him to provide a stronger justification for this position, which Moore completed in a four-page letter to the Premier on 18 March.

Moore's letter made the case for creating an additional job in the EPA and for meeting Greiner's requirement that no extra costs be incurred.[22] He had previously argued for the establishment of a small, long-term strategy unit. That proposal was set aside because of budgetary considerations and Opposition attacks on the number of SES posts being created. Moore said he was reviving the idea because the economic restraints no longer applied. Greiner had said he would increase the EPA's forward budget beyond 1993, and Dr Neil Shepherd, the Director-General of EPA, had found savings within the organisation. A "helmsperson" was now needed to engage in long-term planning, one who was familiar with environmental education and would be acceptable to both industry and conservation groups. The unit itself should consist of a senior officer of an equivalent level to the other four directors, a personal assistant and one or two research staff at an approximate cost of $266,000pa.

No one reading Moore's letter on the day it was written – other than the author, Metherell, Hazzard and Greiner – would have known that a particular individual was in mind for the job. Another was actually mentioned. The Minister's apparently serious preference was to appoint Barry Jones, Australia's loquacious and best-known polymath. Unfortunately, Jones was unavailable because he remained a member of the Federal Parliament.

At this point the operation was gathering speed. On 20 March Greiner warned the Liberal Party's State Director of the prospect of "some movement in Davidson and we should be ready if that occurs". He did not tell Maher anything about the discussions with Metherell.[23] Three days later Greiner released his "Vision" statement which Metherell guardedly welcomed as "hanging out the lantern" and as a sign of the Government becoming "a little greener, a little warmer". He could not resist a barb: "anyone who knows Nick Greiner . . . [will realise that] this was a very difficult thing for him to do.  He didn't think before about providing visionary leadership."[24] (It will be recalled that 18 months earlier Metherell had spoken publicly about Greiner's "remarkable courage and vision, both personally and politically".) The press seized on Metherell's comments as an outward sign of a truce but the extent and purpose of the reconciliation remained unknown.

On the day Metherell made his comments about the "Vision" statement the Premier formally approved of the Moore proposal for an extra SES position within the EPA. Next day, 25 March, Greiner briefly met members of the Davidson State Electorate Conference who approved his request for an early pre-selection to be held in late April or early May. Greiner denied to the press there had been any deal involved in the rapprochement between Metherell and himself.[25] The Premier said he had not discussed the possibility of Metherell returning to the Liberal Party and was not negotiating a Windsor-like agreement.

He did agree there had been "a warming of relations" between the two men and pointed out how Metherell had been talking to other ministers on several matters. Referring to the "glass of water" meeting, Greiner said he could not remember who had initiated it, "and I don't think it matters". He did say that Metherell had earlier passed on some private correspondence from Hungary and suggested the two might have a chat. Greiner had informed a meeting of the Coalition parties of his contacts with Metherell and no one present had objected. Labor, at this stage, never doubted that Metherell would vote for the Government in a no-confidence motion.

On 26 March the Premier talked some more to Metherell and Hazzard in Parliament House, after which the three men lunched in the Parliament House Dining Room, an event which even the most somnolent would have noticed. After lunch, when Greiner rose in the Assembly to answer a Metherell question relating to a world heritage listing, Paul Gibson from the Labor benches, and one of Greiner's regular squash partners, interjected: "Love is in the air."[26] Pickering, who had been lunching in the Dining Room with members of the Police Union, told them they were witnessing history. He assumed that Metherell was returning to the fold so, when Maher rang him to say the Premier had authorised a call for nominations for Davidson, the Group's leader told the State Director a pre-selection was the last thing anyone needed.[27]

There was further movement when Humphry wrote to Moore on 1 April to inform him that the Premier had approved a fifth director's post in the EPA. Unconnected to this approval, applications for the SES positions in the Premier's Department closed on 3 April. By now there were rumours about Metherell resigning from Parliament and possibly taking a government job. Confronted by journalists, Metherell denied everything. Greiner himself was keen to maintain secrecy because an early exposure would almost certainly have sabotaged the arrangement. Indeed, possibly with sabotage in mind, Kathryn Greiner contacted Ken Hooper – as he believed, because of his journalistic connections – to tell him what was in the wind and whether anything could be done to forestall it.[28] A leak to the *DTM*, followed by an immediate outcry from every side of politics, a quiet word from Pickering and Sturgess, and objections from some senior bureaucrats, and the plan would have been stone dead.

Moore informed Dr Shepherd on 8 April of the intention to appoint Metherell to the EPA. He admitted to Shepherd he had not been open when he had spoken to the Director-General earlier about a new position in the EPA. Shepherd was so angry he contemplated resignation. He pointed out that, apart from being unacceptable to the EPA, the appointment would be illegal because the post had not been advertised and the merit selection process had not been followed as the *Public Sector Management Act* required. Late that evening, Moore told Greiner about the problem – Temby would label it a "snag" – whereupon the Premier rang Humphry to set up a meeting for 7.30 am on 9 April to consider the options. Up to this stage Greiner had never given any thought to the method of appointment. In the morning Humphry advised Greiner and Moore of a way out: Metherell could legitimately be appointed to the advertised position in the Premier's Department, and then seconded at ministerial direction to the EPA. Two conditions would have to be met: Metherell must resign from Parliament before being appointed to the Premier's Department, and he must apply in writing for appointment to one of the advertised positions in the Premier's Department. So far as Humphry was concerned the appointment was unorthodox though not unlawful. He was surprised, not shocked. In hindsight, he feels it would have been better to have paused and taken the time to give his advice in writing.[29]

Shepherd, consulted later in the day, laid down his own pre-conditions, twice offered Moore his resignation and, in Temby's words, had an hour-long "distinctly unpleasant meeting" with Metherell. Further meetings followed. By the end of the day Shepherd had reconciled himself to Metherell's arrival in the EPA. Greiner was never part of the discussions which took place after he left the early morning meeting with Moore and Humphry. He continued to see himself as a secondary player. Those driving the exercise were Metherell, who wanted a worthwhile job, Hazzard, who wanted to help a good friend, and Moore, who wanted to help a good friend secure a worthwhile job. Yet Greiner was critical to meeting Metherell's pre-condition: he would resign when, and only when, a job was available. Clearly, Metherell was feeling insecure. He met Greiner briefly on the evening of 9 April to report on his conversations with Shepherd and to seek Greiner's assurance that he would have a job in the Premier's Department if the EPA experiment did not work. The Premier told Metherell it was the normal practice to retain a senior public servant if a job ceased to be effective or justifiable.

At 4.00 pm on 9 April the Premier informed the Director-General of the Cabinet Office of what was about to occur. Sturgess placed some exclamation marks next to the entry he wrote in his notebook. His other reaction was that the Government would be savaged but in time the appointment would be regarded as a clever move. He now believes that Greiner wanted a quick approval from Humphry to avoid a situation where Humphry sought the advice of the Cabinet Office whose lawyers might have presented a problem.[30] At around 4.40 pm a reassured Metherell formally submitted an application for a position in the Premier's Department and handed in his resignation to Speaker Rozzoli just after the Legislative Assembly had risen. His three-sentence application was taken to the Executive Council where, some 35 minutes later, the Governor and Moore approved his appointment to the Premier's Department as a Policy Director on a five-year contract worth $110,000 pa. He would be transferred to the EPA after he and Louise returned from a holiday in Vanuatu. Moore, with Metherell standing beside him, announced the appointment at a hastily-summoned press conference on the following Saturday morning.

Nick Greiner was not present. There were some important phone calls to make. He started to ring ministers and was helped by Collins who, who after being informed of the Metherell appointment, offered to share the load. Greiner contacted Wal Murray who was about to leave New Zealand to return home. The Deputy Premier recalled saying that Greiner was "taking a chance", only to be told it was "all sorted out" and that there was "not a worry in the world".[31] No minister, it seems, raised objections although Fahey apparently spent some time ruminating. Yabsley congratulated Greiner. Even Hatton thought it "a brilliant political move", with the qualification that the public reaction could not be predicted.[32]

Greiner spoke briefly to the press on North Steyne Beach at Manly on the Saturday afternoon. He described the appointment as "good" for the electors of Davidson who had been disenfranchised by Metherell's defection, "good" for the stability of the Government, "good" for the Independents (presumably because it removed an unpredictable element from among their number), and "good" for the environment because Metherell was "committed to it and knows a helluva lot about it". He stressed how Metherell had taken the initiative, and how his own "input" had been limited to an insistence that Metherell must be qualified for any job offered to him. He added: "Of course it's political. It would be silly to say otherwise. The public will draw its own conclusions."[33]

# Endnotes

[1] *Bulletin*, 11 February 1992; Cochran to Greiner, 9 February 1992, Correspondence with Members, Greiner Papers.

[2] The following account draws upon interviews: Metherell 15 June 2006, Greiner 17 February 2010 and Kathryn Greiner, 29 March 2011; Metherell's Autobiography; LPA, ML, MSS 7205/62; ICAC, *Report on Investigation into the Metherell Resignation and Appointment*, June 1992; Michael Gleeson, Toni Allen, Michael Wilkins, *An Act of Corruption?*, ABC Books, Sydney, 2001 edition, ch. 11ff.

[3] Interview: Greiner, 30 March 2010.

[4] *NSWPD*, Third Series, vol. 228, pp. 1-2.

[5] *Ibid*, pp. 524-33.

[6] *Ibid.*, pp. 786-7. See the article on Packard by Mark Coultan, *SMH*, 7 March 1992. Packard resigned his seat on 27 July 1993 following his conviction on charges of unlawfully using listening devices in his car dealership.

[7] For two published versions, see *SMH*, 10 June 1989, and *Australian*, 22 December 1993. Greiner recalled this conversation in an interview on 30 March 2011.

[8] *NSWPD*, Third Series, vol. 225, p. 3620.

[9] Smiles resigned from Parliament in December 1993 when he was convicted of tax charges.

[10] Interview (John Farquharson): John Hatton, 16-17 December 2008, NLA, ORAL, TRC, 6048, pp. 54-5.

[11] For Collins' account of the November meeting, see *Bear Pit*, 179-80.

[12] *SMH*, 18-21 February 1992.

[13] Collins, *Bear Pit*, pp. 185-6; John Marsden, *I am what I am: My Life and Curious Times*, Penguin, Camberwell, 2004, p. 113.

[14] *SMH*, 19 February 1992.

[15] *SMH*, 3 March 1992.

[16] *NSWPD*, Third Series, vol. 228, p. 1242.

[17] Address in Parliament House to celebrate the fifth year of the Greiner Government, "The Death of Politics", 24 April 1992, Seaton Papers.

[18] Peter Bowers, *SMH*, 23 March 1992.

[19] For the *Citizen's Charter*, see John Major, *John Major: The Autobiography*, HarperCollins, London, 1999, ch.11.

[20] Interview: Greiner, 17 February 2010.

[21] ICAC, *Report,* pp. 19-20, 21.

[22] For a copy of Moore's letter to Greiner, see *ibid.*, Appendix 5.

[23] Maher's pre-hearing statement to ICAC, 7 May 1992, LPA, ML, MSS 7205/62.

[24] *SMH,* 25 March 1992.

[25] *SMH,* 26 March 1992.

[26] *NSWPD,* Third Series, vol. 229, p. 2120.

[27] Interview: Pickering, 13 July 2011.

[28] Interviews: Hooper, 20 April and 15 September 2011. Greiner was unaware of this approach to Hooper, and Kathryn Greiner does not recollect the occasion. Interviews: Greiner, 22 November 2011 and Kathryn Greiner, 14 May 2012.

[29] Interview: Humphry, 26 September 2011.

[30] Interview: Sturgess, 22 June 2011.

[31] Davey, *Nationals,* p. 348.

[32] Gleeson *et al.*, *An Act of Corruption?*, p. 129.

[33] *Sun-Herald* and *Sunday Telegraph,* 12 April 1992.

# 16

# "All Hell Breaks Loose"[1]

Greiner and Metherell had predicted a "media barrage" but no one directly involved in the episode foresaw what happened after the appointment was announced. A spontaneous public outcry, eagerly reported and encouraged by the media, exploited by the Opposition, and used to sanctify another crusade by what Tony Windsor called the "Independent Party" or the "Hatton Faction", led to the intervention of ICAC and to a successful censure motion against the Premier in the Legislative Assembly. Several factors explain the furore: a lull in political news in a non-sitting parliamentary period; a fourth estate eager to exercise its unelected power; a Government more vulnerable after the by-election for The Entrance; the popularity of talkback radio; the fact it was Metherell who had secured an easy passage into a job; the photos of the beneficiary and his wife luxuriating in Vanuatu; and Nick Greiner's promise not to follow Labor in providing "jobs for the boys".

Dick Humphry thought it would be all over in a week. It actually took three weeks before some calm was restored, and then only after ICAC had intervened and the censure motion was passed. Throughout this time Nick Greiner continued to conduct business as usual. Yet he was uncommonly defensive on a matter he thought had acquired attention well beyond its intrinsic significance. Obliged to change tack several times he nonetheless remained convinced of his own rectitude and continued to insist that the appointment was justified on the grounds of Metherell's qualifications.

## The first week

Bob Carr was quick off the mark. He had witnessed a few dubious transactions by Labor colleagues in his time, and had been himself accused of orchestrating one as a minister in 1986. Unabashed, he called the Metherell appointment a "sleazy deal". The Secretary of the NSW Public Service Professional Officers' Association was "appalled", and Professor Niland, the Chairman of the EPA Board, expressed his displeasure "quite forthrightly" to Tim Moore about the failure to observe due process.

When journalists turned on Greiner in the first week it was as if he had personally affronted them. Having taken the believers up the mountain he had proved unworthy of their trust. Matthew Moore of the *SMH*, who had written so approvingly of Greiner when he introduced the ICAC legislation in 1988, described the Metherell appointment as "breathtakingly arrogant". Greiner had learnt nothing from the hammering he took in the 1991 election or from the outcry over the Kathryn Greiner and Pickard appointments. He was, like all the others, prepared to "sell his grandmother" to stay in power.[2] Quentin Dempster of the ABC's *7.30 Report*, who had a regular column in the *Sun-Herald*, wrote on 19 April that "Greinerism" – once seen as a series of "hard management decisions" in favour of efficiency and debt reduction for the sake of our children's prosperity – "may soon be seen as just another big party, snout down, bare bum out". The editorials were marginally more restrained. The *SMH* thought the deal was at once "outrageous" and "audacious". On 14 April it acknowledged the sound politics of retrieving a Liberal seat, especially because of ICAC's investigation into Peter Blackmore. But Greiner "had breached the high standard of political propriety" he had set for his Government, while the "shabbiness" of the deal "may undermine its political usefulness". Although the *Sunday Telegraph* on 12 April announced that Greiner had "scored a major political coup" with the appointment of Metherell, and the *DTM*, the following day, thought that Greiner would welcome the stability he would acquire, the latter on 14 April called it an "outrageous deal", accused Greiner of running "an employment agency for Liberals", and said he had violated what he once stood for.

The media appeared to react to the public reaction. Letters to the editor, comments on talk-back radio, callers to MPs – all save a handful were hostile. The indignation, in about equal measure, was directed at "Tricky Nicky" for his alleged cynicism and debasement of political life and at the whole notion of "jobs for the boys", and at Terry Metherell for grasping a "sinecure" and daring to have fun in Vanuatu. One letter writer thought Greiner had "dived from the gutter to the sewer" and another saw him taking politics "out of the gutter and into the pits". The images and the metaphors were so unflattering, and the anger so widespread, that the media had no option but to follow suit.[3] The jokes – banal and mostly third-rate – began to circulate:

> Question: "What do you get if you cross Nick Greiner with a cash register?"
> Answer: "A politician who hands out money when you knife him in the back."[4]

There was a broad public consensus on two matters. First, Metherell should not have been appointed. The Government should cancel the appointment, or Metherell should voluntarily resign or, as the Labor Party proposed with the support of Windsor and the non-aligned Independents, special legislation should overturn the appointment and deny Metherell any compensation. Secondly, nearly everyone who spoke out agreed that, whether or not the appointment stood, Greiner was wounded, possibly fatally.

Some of the fiercest critics were Coalition MPs. Alby Schultz was amazed; there had not been "a great deal of thought for the principles of what we are doing". Peter Cochran said wartime traitors "are not treated as kindly". He consoled himself with the knowledge that Metherell had left the Parliament and with the thought that Metherell and the EPA "will have a happy marriage". Schultz and Cochran focussed their attack on Tim Moore rather than Greiner, and called for the Environment Minister to be sacked from Cabinet. The official minutes and separate handwritten notes indicate that members of the Liberal Party's Management Committee also expressed opposition to the appointment. At its scheduled meeting on 13 April Bevan Bradbury, a future State President and a former managing director and chairman of G.J. Coles, alone praised Greiner for his pragmatic policies and for being "a strong political animal". All the other recorded comments were critical. To avoid embarrassing the Premier, the Committee passed a seemingly innocuous resolution: "It was further decided that the President [Peter King] was to convey to the Premier confidentially and personally the views of the meeting." King met Greiner the next day and had what the President called a "frank discussion". Ron Phillips, Greiner's representative on the Committee, said at a subsequent meeting that it was difficult to call for solidarity with the Premier because of the comments leaked to the media after the meeting on 13 April.[5]

Ten days after the story broke, and ignoring Cabinet's unanimous endorsement of the appointment, Peter Collins pointed out how ministers had not been told of the pending appointment and said the whole issue "needs to be thrashed out finally in Cabinet".[6] Right on both counts, such a public statement simply fuelled media speculation about rifts within the Government and some idle gossip about a possible move against Greiner's leadership. The Federal Liberals were plainly unhappy. Hewson tried to be tactful, saying that the Metherell affair might be damaging the Party's chances of winning NSW seats. John Howard had no inhibitions. He said he had never disguised his contempt for Terry Metherell, and it was a pity for all the good work of the Greiner Government to be "overshadowed by a lack of finesse in some other matters".[7]

By the time Collins spoke out the Premier's own public posture had changed considerably. On the Tuesday after the announcement he remarked testily during a luncheon at the Hilton Hotel:

It is a political appointment and a political decision which any one
of you [the media] or Mr Carr or indeed anyone else who is waxing
lyrical in the same circumstances . . . would have clearly made . . .
Anyone who doesn't accept that is simply lying.[8]

He was still spruiking the deal on the Wednesday morning. Pressed by
John Laws on Radio 2UE, Greiner vigorously defended himself against
the charge of clumsiness and of lacking common sense. Laws said he
must have known what would happen. Greiner insisted he had looked
at the costs and the benefits and believed "absolutely, absolutely, the
benefits are greater" for the people of NSW through providing stable
government.[9] By the same evening he was beginning to retreat. After
talking to Fred Nile, whose Call to Australia votes he needed in the
Legislative Council, the Premier spoke of reviewing the options in
relation to the Metherell appointment. Yet he remained adamant on
two points: Terry Metherell was eminently qualified for the job; and the
Government would not be cancelling his contract.

On Saturday 18 April Greiner telephoned Metherell in Vanuatu to
tell him the EPA position would now be advertised. Metherell, he said,
appeared to be neither angry nor bitter. After all, the former Minister
for Education had promoted the concept of merit and achievement in
the school system. It was reasonable for him to be treated the same way,
"and he accepts that". The Premier added that Metherell was likely to
secure the job "on his merits". If he did not, "he'll be out". If, however,
Metherell failed to secure the EPA position or any other post in the
Public Service, Greiner said he could apply for compensation valued at
a year's salary of $110,000. The Premier now admitted it was a mistake
not to have advertised the EPA position in the first place: "I'd like to
think I'm big enough to own up to that mistake." (He could hardly own
up to the fact that the entire operation was predicated on the absence of
an advertisement.) Next day, Greiner said that all politicians applying for
public service positions would have to wait six months after resigning
their seats and would face independent panels.[10]

Few who commented were prepared to give Greiner credit for what was seen as "a complete somersault", an "about-face".[11] Labor was caught slightly on the hop but Carr still called the new arrangement "outrageous" because Metherell could work elsewhere in the Public Service or take a large compensation package.[12] Acknowledging that the Premier had done "the only thing he could do", Matthew Moore considered Metherell remained a "human hand grenade" for Greiner. The *SMH* advised the Premier to honour the agreement while making Metherell apply for the job, and buy him out if he failed to get it.[13] Confusion set in when the Premier's press officer, David Jones, answered a journalist's question by volunteering the information Metherell had actually applied for an advertised job – the one in the Premier's Department – for which there had been 60 applicants. The *SMH* misunderstood the message and assumed, as applications had closed on 3 April, Metherell made the application while he was still an MP.[14] Greiner immediately ordered documents to be released to confirm that Metherell had applied after handing in his resignation on 10 April.

Clearing up the confusion had only exacerbated Greiner's difficulties. It was now even plainer Metherell had applied for a job after applications had closed and been parachuted into it without a formal interview and ahead of other aspirants who had followed due process. Two of the applicants claimed they had never even received a reply to their applications. Carr called the operation a "total fix", a "total fiction". The Premier was upfront: "I have made no bones about it. It was clearly a political appointment. Therefore, there is nothing surprising that it was all done on the same day. We deliberately have not created any fictitious process about it." Greiner pointed out he had said many times that the position in the Premier's Department was the "legal vehicle" to enable Metherell's secondment to the EPA, and Humphry had advised that the appointment met all the requirements of the *Public Sector Management Act*. He repeated: "at no stage has there been any secret of the political nature of the appointment."[15]

The *SMH* asked ministers it could contact whether they would accept Metherell as a senior executive within their portfolio, whether they thought the Premier received good advice during the Metherell affair, and whether they still had confidence in the Premier given his handling of the matter. Tim Moore was the only minister to reply "Yes" to all three questions. The others avoided the first two altogether, and all save one expressed their confidence in Greiner as Leader. All Webster could offer was his confidence that Greiner would resolve the Metherell matter "satisfactorily".[16]

Early in the afternoon of 23 April Greiner, accompanied by Tim Moore, Hazzard and Humphry, met Macdonald and Clover Moore in the State Office Block. The two Independents were surprised by Hazzard's presence. Expecting a show of humility, they were also surprised by what they saw as his arrogance. The Premier acknowledged that his Government could go down over the Metherell affair. He sought to avoid this possibility by setting up a bi-partisan parliamentary inquiry in return for an agreement by the non-aligned Independents to hold off supporting a no-confidence motion until the inquiry's findings were released in two weeks. The *DTM* declared it would not give Greiner a similar breathing space.[17] The *SMH* was more accommodating but warned the Premier that Metherell would have to be paid out if he refused to resign. In this way the Premier could minimise the effects if not undo the damage caused by his "political stunt".[18] On 25 April the *SMH* elevated the "stunt" to a "monumental political blunder" – the word "audacious" had not survived beyond its first editorial on the subject. It concluded, probably correctly, that if the Premier had acted swiftly and sacked Metherell, or persuaded him to resign, the matter would not have gone out of control.

Greiner left the meeting with the Independents fully expecting to set up a bi-partisan parliamentary inquiry. By the end of the day he felt obliged to accept an ICAC investigation. There had already been a discussion within ICAC which decided to wait and see. When it became

clear there would be no neat parliamentary solution, Ian Temby phoned
Sturgess around 3.00 pm and then, accompanied by Deborah Sweeney,
later a judge of the District Court, met Greiner and Sturgess at 5.00 pm.
Temby brought with him a prepared press release and the proposition
that ICAC was the appropriate body to undertake a fact-finding inquiry
into allegations of corruption. Temby found the atmosphere in Greiner's
office "extremely tense . . . although Greiner remained superficially civil".
Either Greiner or Sturgess suggested that it would be better to proceed
by way of a parliamentary reference to ICAC to avoid a suggestion that
minds had been made up. Temby agreed and went off to see Carr.[19]

Greiner and Metherell met on the morning of 24 April. The Premier
put forward three options: Parliament could sack Metherell, Metherell
could resign, or Greiner could sack him and Metherell might pursue
compensation. Metherell offered another approach: he should step
aside until after the ICAC inquiry was completed. Greiner accepted this
suggestion later in the day and announced at a press conference that
ICAC would be investigating the "Metherell affair". Challenged at the
conference to say whether Metherell had been offered an inducement
to quit Parliament, Greiner replied, "at absolutely no time did I do so".[20]
He was equally firm in dismissing the Opposition's demand that he
follow Neville Wran's example and step aside while ICAC conducted
its investigation. Greiner pointed out how specific allegations had been
levelled against Wran and not one had been directed at him. On this
question the *SMH* decided that Greiner's stance was totally correct.[21]
Terry Metherell also spoke to the press. He was "sorry" his friends had
been crucified; by friends he meant Moore and Hazzard. He and Greiner
were "close political associates", not "close friends", though he was sorry
that the career of his close political associate had been ruined.[22]

Nick Greiner had another duty to perform on 24 April. He addressed
a special gathering in Parliament House on the theme of "The Death
of Politics", to mark the beginning of the fifth year of the Greiner
Government. It was a speech which revealed how much he had been

affected by the tumult of the previous two weeks. His calm and rational side was still evident but so was a sense of being unjustly pilloried. He had done no more than what politicians normally do, and what everyone had been telling him to do. In this speech he struck back at the fourth estate and its double standards, at what he saw as the increasingly insufferable John Hatton (as mentioned in the previous chapter), and at Bob Carr whom he regarded as a hypocrite and a lightweight opportunist.

Greiner began by saying he was stunned by the media reaction to what was a bold political act and hardly without precedent in NSW or in the rest of Australia. He acknowledged there had been a number of objections to the Metherell appointment, the strongest of them coming from within the Liberal Party. Greiner had not realised how antagonistic Liberals were towards the former minister, though he could fairly say no one had been more betrayed by Metherell than himself. Given the widespread antipathy towards Metherell it was clear he could not do the job despite having great ability and much to offer. Greiner said the Government had delivered on its promise to clean up NSW and "I won't depart from those high standards of integrity and probity in public office". Nor, however, was he "going to play the mug's game" and meet the media's requirement to "abide by a Playschool version of politics dreamed up by undergraduate political science students". He described the Metherell appointment as "hard" and "honest" politics. Everyone had accused him of not being political enough when fighting the last election. Now, to hold government, he had to play hard politics and deal with Hatton's latest obsession. Greiner told the audience he intended to continue with hard politics, and concluded with a warning: if the rules of politics have changed, if a "naive, kindergarten view" of making appointments were to apply, then it must be applied across the board. The Labor Party would be placed on notice and Carr would be called to account for his "devious interventions".[23]

Nick Greiner did not have to carry the full load or watch his back in this period. It helped when, on 23 April, Tim Moore publicly accepted responsibility for the Metherell appointment and apologised to the Premier for the damage caused to the Government. Moore also acknowledged that the appointment was a political mistake, even if it was legal and proper.[24] Cabinet met on Monday 27 April – Greiner's 45th birthday – after which the Premier said that reports of his political death were "extraordinarily premature". He could announce that the Cabinet and the two Coalition parties were supporting him while Chris Hartcher, the Liberal Whip, said the Party was "101 per cent" behind the Premier.

One recalcitrant, Alby Schultz, would not be silenced, even if his anger was mainly directed at Tim Moore. He blamed him for the episode and said he had not ruled out calling for Moore's resignation at the next Party Room meeting. Schultz also wondered how politically astute "some of these people" were, implying he had doubts about Greiner's political nous.[25] Zammit had written to Greiner on the same day referring to the anger felt on the backbench about the lack of consultation and information on important matters. It was now more than two weeks since the story of the Metherell appointment had broken but, amidst all the claims and counter-claims, there had not been a single word from the Premier or from Cabinet to say what was fact and what was fiction. Zammit had no doubt the Party Room would give the Premier strong support, and it would be stronger still if, in future, he gave an assurance of "detailed and on-going briefings" to the backbench. The assistant minister urged Greiner to consider appointing a Cabinet secretary to fulfil that role. Zammit's letter reads like yet another job application.[26]

## Censured

When Greiner entered the Legislative Assembly on Tuesday 28 April he expected a beating. At least he could start the day by taking the initiative. The Premier moved that the House request ICAC to investigate "the facts and circumstances" relating to Metherell's resignation from Parliament and to his public service appointment to determine:

(a) whether any corrupt conduct has occurred, is occurring or is about to occur; and

(b) whether any laws governing any public authority or public official need to be changed for the purpose of reducing the likelihood of the occurrence of corrupt conduct; and

(c) whether any methods of work, practices or procedures of any public authority or public official did or could allow, encourage or cause the occurrence of corrupt conduct.

These terms of reference had been devised by Temby and ICAC staff. Greiner proposed to add one more: "In particular, the commission is to consider whether it is desirable to proscribe or regulate the appointment of persons who have ceased to be members of Parliament to positions in the public sector." Notwithstanding his agreement with the Independents, the Premier could now say that Parliament was not, in the current atmosphere, the appropriate body to investigate what had become known as the "Metherell affair". Speaking further to the motion, Greiner said ICAC was established "precisely because it was necessary to have a body with the forensic expertise and the independence to examine impartially allegations of corruption". It was all the more important to have such a body in circumstances where the allegations were made "in a highly political atmosphere". As for the outcome, he felt sure a full and balanced investigation would vindicate his conduct.

The Opposition supported the motion but, understandably, could not resist delivering speeches in tones of both confected and genuine outrage. Bob Carr gave what Greiner called a "theatrical performance" as he re-defined the central issue: it was not so much a question of "jobs for the boys" – though the "political jobbery" in this case was "breathtaking in its arrogance and dishonesty" – but one of "a seat for a job". Seen in that light, and armed with favourable legal advice, Carr could, in effect, accuse Greiner of criminal bribery, and did so by insisting that the Premier was central to the entire operation. Greiner was adamant in response. He and his Government would be vindicated, there was no illegality, impropriety or corruption on his part, and Carr, a "hypocritical and cowardly liar", would "choke on his words".[27]

These exchanges between Greiner and Carr merely constituted the prologue to the main event. Carr moved an omnibus motion on the same day, declaring that Greiner and Moore deserved to be censured and should stand aside while ICAC conducted its inquiry, and that the Government should forthwith rescind the Metherell appointment and legislate to make any Metherell claim for compensation unlawful.

Greiner, in response, adopted two approaches.[28] First, he pointed out how Labor had behaved in government. It operated a "cradle-to-the grave employment service"; and many of its beneficiaries were "no-hopers", a description which could not be applied to Metherell. There might not be an exact parallel with the Metherell case, Greiner added, but there were many instances where Labor had traded seats for jobs. Turning towards Hatton, he observed how Labor would never have set up ICAC and, if either Wran or Unsworth had remained in office, there would be no Ministerial Code of Conduct and no *Freedom of Information Act*.

Greiner's case against Labor was unanswerable in terms of relative guilt even though most Opposition MPs were either comfortable about the past or brazen in spite of it. The Premier knew, however, that comparative innocence did not constitute a sufficient defence. His second approach was to argue that he was guilty of bad judgment, not of illegality or immorality. "What we have done in the eyes of the electorate is wrong, I accept that, but it was not illegal, it was not immoral, it was not corrupt." He admitted misreading the public mood, and not understanding the "deep-seated resentment in the community about political manoeuvres". The trouble was that Greiner had himself raised the bar of expectations. He might warn that if what he and Moore had done was considered "corrupt", then every political appointment made in NSW was equally tainted, and if what they did was deemed unlawful by "entirely new standards", it would mean "the death of politics in this State". It looked like a case of wanting it both ways: to be credited with cleaning up a corrupt polity, and justifying his actions as consistent with the standards of that polity. He did have a better and less complicated argument. On grounds of fairness he should not be judged before ICAC had reached its verdict. Yet he could not expect fair treatment from a Labor Party bent on gaining political advantage and hoping for a baton change, nor a "fair go" from three "sea-green incorruptibles" who were on a mission.

The censure motion was carried by 50 votes to 45, with Windsor joining the non-aligned Independents in voting with the Opposition. Clover Moore, Macdonald and Windsor supported the Government in a 49-46 vote rejecting the call for Greiner and Tim Moore to stand aside and the demand to rescind the Metherell appointment and withhold compensation. Four days after the censure motion was passed Andrew Humpherson, the Deputy President of the Warringah Shire Council and the area business manager for the Shell Company, won the by-election for Davidson. He had previously secured Liberal pre-selection by defeating Greiner's preferred candidate, Deborah Klika, who was supported by the Group. Davidson was the Liberals' eighth safest seat and there were fears in the Party, and excited anticipation in the media, that the seat might go to an Independent. Labor stayed out of the fight though a former member of the Party – Greiner described her as a "Labor stooge" – was expected to poll well. Despite a fall of 16 per cent in the Liberal primary vote, Humpherson won easily enough, defeating 13 other candidates, of whom 10 were Independents.

The original objective had been achieved. Greiner now had 48 reliable votes in the Assembly, although he still needed a non-aligned Independent in addition to Windsor to pass his legislation. There was good news on another front. A Herald Saulwick poll recorded that 34 per cent of respondents preferred Greiner as Liberal Leader; 24 per cent opted for Chadwick, 13 per cent for Collins and 6 per cent for Baird. John Fahey was not included in the poll.[29] Nick Greiner may have been wounded by the end of April but he remained, as the post-election Task Force had described him ten months earlier, as one of the Liberal Party's "greatest assets" in NSW.

# Endnotes

1 ICAC, *Report*, p. 18.

2 *SMH*, 13 Apr. 1992.

3 For some of the popular reaction, see *Sun-Herald*, 12 and 19 April and *DTM* and *SMH*, 13-17 April 1992.

4 *SMH*, 17 April 1992.

5 Minutes of Management Committee, 13 April 1992, LPA, ML, MSS 7205/13 and 18.

6 *SMH*, 22 April 1992.

7 *SMH*, 24 April 1992.

8 *Australian*, 14 April 1992.

9 Gleeson *et al.*, *An Act of Corruption?*, p. 133.

10 *Sunday Telegraph*, 19 April 1992.

11 *SMH*, 20 April 1992.

12 *Sunday Telegraph*, 19 April 1992.

13 *SMH*, 20 April 1992.

14 *DTM* and *SMH*, 22 April 1992.

15 *DTM*, 22-3, April 1992.

16 *SMH*, 22 April 1992.

17 *DTM*, 24 April 1992.

18 *DTM* and *SMH*, 24 April 1992; Gleeson *et al.*, *An Act of Corruption?*, p. 142.

19 The account in this paragraph draws mainly on an interview (Chris Cunneen) with Temby, May-June 1995, NLA, TRC, 3258, pp. 256-8, and interview: Temby, 23 November 2011.

20 Gleeson *et al.*, *An Act of Corruption?*, pp. 147-8.

21 *SMH*, 25 April 1992.

22 *DTM*, 25 April 1992.

23 Seaton Papers.

24 *SMH*, 24 April 1992.

25 *Sunday Telegraph*, 26 April 1992.

26 Letters from Members, Greiner Papers.

27 *NSWPD*, Third Series, vol. 229, pp. 2794-2801, 2839-42.

28 *Ibid.*, pp. 2848-61.

29 *SMH*, 4 May 1992.

# 17

# Hearings

Ian Temby opened proceedings at the Commission headquarters in
Redfern on 11 May. Peter Clark, QC, a Melbourne-based barrister,
had been appointed Counsel Assisting the Commission. The principal
parties to appear before ICAC were represented by leading figures of the
NSW Bar: Greiner by Roger Gyles, QC, Moore by Chester Porter, QC,
and Metherell by David Rofe, QC. Cabinet had agreed to fund Greiner's
and Moore's legal costs but Peter Collins, as Attorney-General, decided
against any funding for Metherell and Hazzard.

Moore chose the first day of hearings to announce his intention
to resign from Parliament after the sittings ended for the year. He had
endured enough of the criticism from those who said he went too far,
and from those who thought he did not go far enough.[1] But the media
was more interested in the obvious discrepancy between the Greiner
and Metherell sworn statements forwarded in advance of the hearings.
Whereas Metherell employed notes and diary entries composed at or
near the relevant time, the Premier's statement relied upon references "to
the best of my recollection" and included occasional acknowledgements
of his lack of recall. Seen alongside Metherell's assured, detailed and
professional statement, Greiner's looked thin and inadequate. Worse
still, one glaring error – Greiner said he first met Metherell on 17 March
when he was referring to a meeting which took place on 26 February –
was used at the hearing and in the press to imply that Greiner deliberately
provided a later date to minimise his role in the Metherell appointment.
Added to this error, the genuine lapses in memory looked, to some, to
have a sinister purpose.

Metherell's diaries became a principal talking point during the Commission's proceedings. In a much-criticised decision the Commissioner allowed publication of substantial portions. The principal effect was to expose Metherell to derision for his overweening self-regard and dismissive or wounding comments about everybody with whom he came into contact.[2] Metherell, understandably, felt hurt. In his Autobiography he described Temby's publication of his diaries as a "grave error of judgment" and as "unnecessary, willful [sic] and irresponsible".

Greiner escaped fairly mildly. In addition to the "politician's bootlaces" reference quoted earlier, another Metherell-Hazzard assessment described the Premier as having "no subtlety or guile – talked of 'vision' instead of showing it . . . talk instead of giving leadership" [sic]. As pressure mounted on the Premier, Metherell wrote on 22 April that "Greiner ducks, weaves, evades and qualifies himself out of existence as a strong leader, preferring . . . managed solutions to 'manageable' problems". The ABC's Quentin Dempster had reason to be embarrassed. Metherell recorded Dempster's advice to him on 18 April: "never trust the Hungarian." Of Metherell's friends, Hazzard sometimes took himself too seriously and Tim Moore had handed Metherell "a stinging, a returning throbbing hurt", having twice let down a good cause. Among the others, Chadwick was lazy and Collins a leaker.

## Metherell's evidence[3]

Greiner did not fare well when Metherell was cross-examined between 11 and 13 May. Metherell said he once had a good working relationship with the Premier. They saw each other on a daily basis when the Assembly was sitting and once a week in Cabinet, and had occasional meetings at other times. Metherell stressed he did not have a personal relationship with Greiner like his rapport with Moore and Hazzard, and did not discuss his private references to Greiner as a "brother". Replying to a Temby question, Metherell said Greiner was supportive of him "[t]o a point as a minister and over the tax case" but "less supportive than he should have been" during the education controversy. The low point was what Metherell saw as a breach of trust in not restoring him to the ministry after the May 1991 election. When questioned by the relentless Chester Porter, Metherell denied that his resignation from the Liberal Party, and his decision not to forewarn Greiner, were acts of malice. Porter was not alone in suspending belief. (It will be recalled that, long after the event, Metherell called his decision "pay-back".)

One of the key issues arising out of the Metherell diaries, and of his turn in the witness stand, involved Metherell's vote on the Timber Industry (Interim Protection) Bill on 10 March 1992. It will be recalled that Metherell appeared to change sides, thereby enabling the Government to pass its legislation. According to Metherell's diary, the Premier rang him around 5.00 pm on 9 March to say he had met with Tim Moore and Garry West and that the Government was moving towards Metherell's position on the timber legislation. The diary entry then read: "it would be helpful if I supported a compromise tomorrow: & [Greiner] couldn't resist adding that it would be 'helpful' in resolving 'the other matter' we'd been discussing (ie the job)." Cross-examined by his own counsel, Metherell said he had voted on the timber legislation solely in accordance with his conscience. He had not been influenced by any "improper" matters and, apart from the Premier's telephone call, had received "no such improper approach".

The implication was clear. Metherell believed that the Premier had asked him to vote for the amended Bill and, in return, would support his appointment to the Public Service. Porter challenged Metherell to be explicit:

> So if you are to be believed, you interpreted that as being a nasty suggestion by the premier? - - - I took it as being a reference to the position that we had been discussing.
>
> You took it as being an improper suggestion, didn't you? - - - Well, I took it as – I don't know that I took it as improper but I took it at as something in the – not to the premier's credit, I think would be the way I would put it.

At this point Temby intervened to suggest the words "sufficiently untoward to warrant noting". Metherell responded: "That's right." Not to be denied, Porter observed how Metherell did not enter any protest in his diary and further suggested that either Greiner never used the words in the first place or the diarist had misinterpreted them. No, he did not protest because the Premier had not made the suggestion in blunt terms. Metherell admitted telling just one person – his wife – about the phone call.

Porter had uncovered something unusual. Metherell's vote had supposedly been solicited, an action sufficiently important to relate to his wife but not significant enough to warrant a protest in his diary or to tell his close friend, Tim Moore. When Metherell said he simply ignored what he saw as Greiner's proposition, Porter pointed out he did not ignore it. He wrote it down, albeit some hours later and probably "ie the job" even later. Metherell emphatically denied the idea. He did, however, tell the Commission that, in making the diary note, he thought Greiner's statement "was in keeping with a trait that was in the premier's character or personality". Was he perhaps "scared" of Greiner?: "certainly not". He agreed it was reasonable to say he would not worry about hurting the Premier's feelings.

This particular section of Metherell's evidence helped to focus Greiner's mind. He learnt of the diary entry after emerging from the Special Premiers' Conference he was attending in Canberra. Greiner ordered an inquiry about the phone call of which he had no recollection. A switchboard operator alone recalled it. On the basis of her confirmation of a call being made, and drawing on the evidence of his own appointments book, Greiner pieced together a memorandum for his counsel.[4]

Greiner began by saying that after he came back from overseas in February the Government had decided to focus on jobs and job security issues and not worry too much about losing votes in the Legislative Assembly. Hence it would oppose the Opposition's amendments to the Timber Industry Bill, leaving it to face the outrage of the timber workers.

But a meeting involving Greiner, Moore and officials on the afternoon of 9 March decided to back the compromise which Metherell had proposed; that is, to transfer responsibility for the Environment Impact Statement from the Forestry Commission to the Director of Planning, and approve, with one major possible exception, the protection of formal wilderness and national park nominations. The Government would then either get what it wanted "clear and clean", or cancel the lot. It was also decided that Garry West, who was due to speak on the ABC's *7.30 Report,* should refer to conciliatory indications from the Independents.

When the meeting concluded, Moore suggested to the Premier he might telephone Metherell who had previously asked to speak to Greiner. It was now around 5.00 pm. Returning to his office, and before shaving, he asked the switchboard operator to call Metherell. He then left to speak to the Institute of Public Administration (he was due there at 5.15 pm), after which he launched the Red Cross Appeal at 6.00 pm, attended a cocktail party at Sydney University at 7.30 pm and a dinner in East Sydney at 8.15 pm. Already that day he had attended a quarterly State Bank meeting, launched a Jewish Charity Appeal, held other meetings, addressed a business lunch, visited Moorefield Girls High School and launched the new St George Private Hospital. Greiner told Gyles it was "[p]robably [my] busiest day ever".

It is hardly surprising that the phone call did not register in Greiner's mind, especially because the subject was of no particular moment. As he told Gyles, there was no need for additional pressure. He did not need Metherell to change his vote because the Government had already changed its stand to meet his requirements. The Premier also noted three oddities in the Metherell account of the phone call: Greiner did not speak to West before making the call and would not, therefore, have said he did so; the phrase, "other matter", was not his form of speech; and, as for the "the job", he had done "<u>nothing</u>" [Greiner's emphasis] about it since the meeting on 26 February and had no intention of doing anything because he had left it all to Moore. If the word "helpful" was used, Greiner concluded, he was employing a throw-away line to state the obvious, both in relation to the outcome and for the Government's attitude towards Metherell. There was nothing "important" or "vital" at stake. The Premier thought it significant that Moore made no mention of the phone call the next day, implying that the minister understood its insignificance. Finally, for him, horse-trading was "totally out of character". His notes to Gyles read: "I don't horse-trade, stick to merits. Approach is completely alien to my character and style."

### Greiner's evidence

Nick Greiner gave his evidence to the Commission on Thursday 21 May, 28 years to the day after he first met Kathryn Callaghan. In their reports, the ABC and much of the press fastened on those aspects of his deportment and replies where they could scoff and demean. An actor appearing as Greiner on the *7.30 Report* depicted him as nervous, shifty and uneasy, highlighting his failure on some 20 occasions to recall the details of conversations or of meetings. The Premier confessed to being "dumbfounded" when he heard Metherell's evidence about the telephone conversation of 9 March. He could not remember "one thing" about it. But, in response to a Temby question, he said he had never to his knowledge "made any improper or corrupt suggestion to anyone, much less to a Member of Parliament", adding, "one has a shrewd suspicion if one did, one would remember it". Nevertheless, Greiner's failure to recall so many of what the Commissioner called "primary facts" left him open to ridicule and raised suspicions of deliberate deceit.

To read the 117-page transcript of his evidence is to appreciate the extent to which, by focussing on the memory lapses, the media distorted or ignored so much of what Greiner had to say. Questioned by Gyles, he took the opportunity to correct the errors in his statement to the Commission: he accepted that there was a conversation on 26 February, that he had made a phone call on 9 March, and that his statement about a conversation occurring on 17 March actually took place on 26 February.

He made a point which escaped general media notice: he reckoned to work 15-16 hours a day for at least six days a week, starting at 6.00 am and lasting until 10-11 o'clock at night. As for the call on 9 March, Greiner summarised for the hearing what had been one of his busiest days as Premier; he had attended eight formal functions, held three meetings and conducted a variety of phone calls and conversations. Metherell, learned counsel, Commissioner Temby and journalists may have worked long hours, but they were not required to deal in any one day with such a wide range of disconnected substantial and minor issues. Given Greiner's view that the Metherell affair was really Moore's business, it is hardly surprising that the details were never fixed in his mind.

Peter Clark, Counsel Assisting, tried several approaches. He sought Greiner's agreement that the connection between Metherell's resignation from Parliament and his appointment to the job were not just sequential but consequential. Greiner in response kept firmly to his line that he had to be assured the job was a proper one which Metherell could do on his merits. Clark also sought to link the appointment to speculation about the future of some of Greiner's MPs and speculation about his own leadership. The reply on this occasion was there would always be speculation but that he never felt under threat.

There were two critical moments in Clark's cross-examination. First, he pressed Greiner on his personal assessment of Metherell, in effect raising the question of how the Premier, holding such a low opinion of him in many respects, could then appoint him to a well-paid, senior position in the Public Service. The exchange went as follows:

> Mr Greiner, when Dr Metherell resigned from the Liberal Party, did you believe that that was an act of gross disloyalty? ----Yes.
>
> An act of gross disloyalty both to you and to the Liberal Party? ----Yes.
>
> Did you believe it was the act of a deceitful man? ----Yes.
>
> Both to you and to the Liberal Party? ----Yes.
>
> Did you believe it was the act of a man who was capable of

treachery? ----Yes.

Both, again to you, and to the Liberal Party. ----Yes.

Refusing to be drawn on his views about Metherell's mental state, Greiner could not recall any comment he might have made about it at the time. He acknowledged that reading the transcript of Metherell's evidence and part of his diaries reinforced his view of him as someone capable of political treachery, personal disloyalty and deceitfulness. Clark then asked:

> And this was the man that you were prepared to have work as a policy director in your department? ----In my judgment he would have done that task admirably and indeed he was being appointed to my department only as a means of being put in another position.

If the questions were designed to expose inconsistencies or lapses in judgment they produced answers which could be justified in any setting. Greiner's views of Metherell's personal failings related solely to how they affected the Liberal Party and himself, and did not relate at all to his capacity to work in the Premier's Department or the EPA. No one could reasonably conclude that Greiner had approved an appointment against his better judgment and which had no justification other than to obtain a parliamentary seat. When Temby suggested he was "not a particularly good hater", Greiner replied: "I think that's correct sir."

Clark's other objective was to establish that Greiner was the effective "decision-maker" in the Metherell appointment. To this end, Clark led him through the sequence of events from 16 February. Clark highlighted nine specific occasions to show how Greiner was present from start to finish, and asked him whether he would accept he was "the person in charge throughout these proceedings, throughout the events as they unfolded". Greiner said he was not, "other than in the sense that the premier is obviously the premier and I suppose had the blackball". The most Greiner would concede as Clark kept pressing his case was that he held a blackball, did not stand in the way of further discussions, and had approved the creation of a position in the EPA. Counsel Assisting then ordered a video showing Greiner's statement at Manly on 11 April that his only input was to say any job offered had to be one for which Metherell was qualified. Clark, and Temby, sought to use this comment to raise questions about the Premier's credibility. Greiner said his input claim was related to the one area where he had taken an initiative, namely, his requirement that Metherell had the necessary qualifications for any job offered. Apart from this initiative, he was "simply responding" to situations and "not standing in the way of what had gone on".[5]

Gyles objected when Clark raised the question of whether Greiner had deliberately played down his role during the interview at Manly. Temby overruled Gyles; the issue went to the "general questions of credit". Obliged to answer, Greiner said he had given many thousands of interviews where it was important to have a simple view and his simple view of his role was not to exercise a blackball, "and then to facilitate". There was no playing up or playing down of his role. Tim Moore had made it clear in his press release he was the person who negotiated the detail, and Greiner did not see his own comment on 11 April as "an unreasonable approach to take to that press conference". Nor did he accept that the error in claiming the meeting on 26 February took place on 17 March was a deliberate attempt to give the impression of him being involved at a later date. Nor was he trying to distance himself from the phone call of 9 March and the events surrounding the timber legislation of 9-10 March. Temby agreed: there was no intention to mislead.

Clark also pursued Greiner over the pre-selection and the by-election for the seat of Davidson. He implied that Greiner's leadership was in question. Clark wanted the Premier to agree that a victory in Davidson would have enhanced his reputation in the Liberal Party by enabling him to say he had restored the numbers in the Assembly. Greiner replied: "I might have been able to say that, sir, I wouldn't have, and it wouldn't have been particularly exciting." Clark then referred to Greiner's Ministerial Code of Conduct, and focussed on the section requiring ministers to perform their tasks "impartially, disinterestedly and in the best interests" of the people of NSW. Greiner confirmed that the Metherell appointment met the test of "best interests". It was a view he had held all along. Temby asked him whether he would say "there's no difficulty about something being in the best interests of the state also being in the best interests of [his] political party". Greiner was consistent and open: "Absolutely, and of the government which I lead."

Temby raised the question of "trading" in politics. He said it was not unknown to offer support for legislation in the hope of support returning later for something you want. Greiner replied that in general terms the observation was correct but he had been "widely criticised – probably correctly – for not being a horse trader and for not exercising the pressure or power that I'm able to do". He agreed with Temby that, in politics, there often had to be a compromise to get results, and politicians did things which were inconsistent with their principles. Once again he emphasised his reliance on "the power of argument" rather than horse-trading. No doubt others, and others on his behalf, engaged in horse-trading "but it's very much not me". Metherell's counsel would have none of this: surely the agreement with Windsor amounted to horse-trading? Greiner answered: Windsor had put up a number of propositions none of which was unacceptable, all of them had been made public, and Windsor derived no personal gain except in a broad political sense.

It is possible, reading the full transcript of his evidence twenty years later, to draw two contradictory conclusions about Greiner's failure to recollect dates, events and the substance of conversations. Either he had convenient memory lapses which enabled him to avoid lying, or he really did have a problem remembering all the details of a very busy existence. A clue lies in his responses to questioning about the role he played in the Metherell appointment. Clark, Temby and Rofe believed he was consistently central to the whole operation. Greiner believed he was not. He has never understood how anyone could assume, on the evidence presented, that he was a principal player throughout the entire exercise and was on a par with Tim Moore and Metherell. If

Greiner's understanding of his role is accepted as genuine, then it is hardly surprising that the details disappeared from a mind dealing with so much at once, and that he could not recollect matters which were more important to others. A fair reading might focus more on the consistency and steadfastness of Greiner's answers, on his conviction that the Metherell appointment was justified even though he saw him to be treacherous, on his openness about the political nature of the appointment, and his sheer intelligence under cross-examination. Temby was struck at various times by the latter. He said later in an interview how he had "a lot of respect for Greiner's intelligence. He was a good example of a decently educated man, he really was intelligent."[6]

Greiner was bothered by what happened at the hearings. On the day after his appearance he sent a note to his legal team.[7] The rational and sharp-minded Greiner saw things his lawyers might have missed. He noted inconsistencies between what Metherell said outside the Commission and what he said at the hearings. In Metherell's diary entry he treated Greiner's mixing up of the dates of 26 February and 17 March as an honest error but, through his counsel, suggested in the hearings it was deliberate or sinister. Why did he change his mind? In relation to the phone call of 9 March, Metherell had said in his press statement of 24 April and to Quentin Dempster on the *7.30 Report* that all the participants will come through with total integrity. Why did he change his mind with a different story at ICAC?

Metherell had claimed that Greiner said virtually nothing about the amendments in their telephone conversation of 9 March, but would get back to him about it. Given that the Government had just agreed to the amendments, and discussed Greiner's support for this compromise, this aspect of the Metherell record was "inconceivable". In the context of the compromise which had been worked out, and the agreed desire to have a warming of relations, "the 'helpful' statement, if made, could only be seen as a statement of the glaringly obvious". Greiner also pointed out that on 10 March, when the vote was taken on the timber legislation and he was "paired", he felt so uninvolved after the compromise was agreed that he did not discover the outcome until the following day. This fact "was hardly consistent with sinister action or intent. Presumably if I felt it worthwhile to attempt to 'buy' a vote I would have followed up, monitored the debate etc". His actions were "totally consistent" with believing that the compromise would pass and, if it did not, the Coalition would still gain politically. Greiner also wanted his legal team to grasp that his role was a minor one while his discussions over the Davidson pre-selection hardly qualified as involvement in the negotiation.

## Other evidence and final submissions

On the day after Greiner's appearance Dr Shepherd made it very clear what he thought of the Metherell appointment. He accepted its legality but was totally opposed: the position was not needed, the level of appointment was too high, and he had misgivings about Metherell's integrity and loyalty, believed he was unable to work in a team, would create a credibility problem for the EPA, and would cause internal tensions. Humphry's pre-hearing statement and oral testimony statement were remarkable for his strong defence of his ability to weigh up matters during the course of a 20-minute meeting in the Premier's office. He was trained to make up his mind quickly while knowing he could not re-visit issues, and he was certain that Metherell was better than the other three candidates. Pickering agreed he had told a Labor MLC at Sydney airport, just before he boarded an international flight, something to the effect that Metherell "would not be with us much longer". He claimed not to be privy to more information than the Greiner request to Robert Maher to prepare for a pre-selection. His experience and observation told him that a by-election was imminent.

Temby's decision to hear final submissions behind closed doors undoubtedly helped Greiner because Clark's submission was damning. Heard in public, and seized upon by the media, his request for prosecution might well have finished the Premier before the final report was delivered.

Clark argued that the conduct of Greiner, Moore, Metherell, Hazzard and Humphry amounted to corruption and that of Greiner, Moore and Metherell could constitute the common law offence of bribery to which Hazzard and Humphry were accessories. Should the Commissioner reject these arguments, Clark suggested a lesser alternative: the actions of Greiner and Moore constituted reasonable grounds for their removal from office while the Commissioner might recommend Metherell's dismissal from the Public Service.

## Outside and after the Hearing

The media was transfixed by the hearings. The *SMH* provided extensive coverage, published excerpts from the Metherell diaries on 16 May and kept watch for any sign of anti-Greiner feeling within the Coalition ranks. Not that Greiner lacked vocal supporters. Kathryn told a luncheon on 12 May that she knew Terry Metherell "very well. And I've known both his wives." He was a "drama queen" who could not resist public attention. Just two politicians escaped getting a serve: her husband was "honest" and had "a great sense of purpose", and Bob Carr had "the finest mind in the ALP, particularly in NSW – but there is not a lot to beat". Next morning Alan Jones attacked ICAC on Radio 2UE for making the Metherell diaries public and said the whole inquiry was "totally discredited" by this action. Jones said he could not "give two hoots about what Mr Temby or his mob come up with now their methods have proven themselves unworthy of public trust."[8]   Prompted by Metherell's counsel, the Commissioner issued warnings to outsiders; they should respect the dignity of the proceedings and desist from personal abuse. Arguably, the Commissioner had himself contributed to public vilification by the very act of making Metherell's diaries publicly available.

Peta Seaton of his office staff kept the Premier informed of proceedings at the Commission while Nick Greiner spent most of the hearing days and the following weeks engaged in what he regarded as the important business; that is, governing NSW and, critically, dealing with a deteriorating budgetary situation.

Greiner went to the Special Premiers' Conference of 11 May in the hope of obtaining a good working relationship with Prime Minister Keating as a step towards a better funding outcome at the financial Premiers' Conference in June. He recognised there was no likelihood in the short term of reforming the Commonwealth-State financial relationship. But it was essential for NSW to be given a funding boost over and above the rate of inflation because of a looming crisis in its health system.

Greiner believed that Keating recognised the plight of the States and wanted "an agreed position" rather than a resumption of hostilities. He was at one, however, with the other Premiers who detected a centralist agenda in Keating's stimulus package launched as the "One Nation" program in February 1992 and designed in part to deal with the recession.[9] Specifically, the Premiers objected to the Commonwealth proposal to take over spending on vocational education and training. They sought to counter "a major shift in constitutional responsibility" and a significant increase in tied grants. Their alternative was a "national partnership" to be achieved within a new "Council of the Australian Federation". This body would review spending proposals which involved both the Commonwealth and the States. It would, like the Special Premiers' Conference, include an advisory group of senior officials. In addition to increased funding, Greiner and the other Premiers kept to their previous line by seeking a fixed share of the Commonwealth's total tax revenue and a reduction of specific purpose grants.

A blow-out in the Federal Budget – a predicted deficit of $4.7bn had risen to $9.3bn – ended any prospect of the States securing more funds. Greiner warned of cuts in basic services. There was also little progress at the Conference on a range of issues, though he was pleased because Keating was ready to discuss a more predictable system for Commonwealth grants and because the meeting itself was conducted in a friendly atmosphere. The major, long-term outcome was an agreement to establish an institution – the Council of Australian Governments

(COAG) – to be chaired by the Prime Minister and serviced by a secretariat. COAG would meet twice annually at venues rotated among the States to deal with non-financial matters such as health and education. The States had wanted a decision-making body with functions including revenue and expenditure. Greiner had certainly hoped for more, and continues to believe that an opportunity was lost when Hawke and himself were ousted from power.[10]

The regular Premiers' Conference was held in Canberra on Friday 12 June, one week before Temby handed down his report. Greiner observed that the proposed Federal grant, which amounted to a fall of two per cent for 1992-3 and was based on a formula which provided the smaller States with a higher per capita grant, meant that NSW and Victoria had been "screwed for years". He said there was "no way" NSW would accept an increase lower than the rate of inflation. Bob Carr spoke out in support and suggested that the two biggest States might seek redress in the High Court.

NSW and Victoria had in fact gone to the Conference with pre-planned tax increases which Greiner and Kirner announced at the press conference following the meeting. They caught the Prime Minister and the Treasurer, John Dawkins, by surprise, both of whom worried about the effect on the rate of inflation. Greiner announced rises in taxes and charges applying to tobacco, alcohol, bank account debits, car stamp duty, public transport and car registration. The expected return of $262m would cost families around another $350 a year. Next day the Greiner Government placed full-page advertisements in the *SMH* and the *DTM*. They had clearly been prepared in advance of the Conference. Headed, "Mr Keating dumps the people of his own State", the four graphics were designed to show how NSW (and Victoria) lost out to the other States, how Commonwealth funding to NSW had declined by $1bn in real terms since 1987-8 and how Keating had done nothing to correct the effects of "his recession" on property revenue which had fallen by $800m in real terms since 1988-9. On Sunday 14 June Greiner promised there would be no further rises in the next Budget. Instead, pensioners could expect a tax cut, young people would be helped to get jobs and more money would be spent on health.

While Greiner was talking to Canberra, trying to preserve the State's triple-A rating, and preparing what he assumed would be his fifth Budget, a myriad of other matters occupied his attention. On 8 May, Roger Gyles, in an earlier guise, submitted his final Royal Commission report on the building industry. The revelations about the malpractices of builders as well as of the unions obliged Greiner to cut all contact with the Master Builders' Association and the Australian Federation of Construction Contractors until they cleaned up their act.[11] Another issue brought Greiner into conflict with the three non-aligned Independents. The Government had previously signed a contract for a private company to build and operate a 160-bed public hospital and lease 70 per cent back to the Government on a 20-year contract. The three non-aligned Independents decided on 10 June that they would join with the Labor Party to pass legislation to prevent the privatisation of Port Macquarie Hospital. The Premier called the decision "a straight case of ideological stupidity". He knew that, with the support of the Niles, the Bill would be defeated in the Legislative Council. In that event the Government would proceed with the privatisation proposal. On 16 June two of the non-aligned Independents said such an action would be deemed "provocative".[12]

Throughout the period from the end of April until the ICAC Report was released some on his side of politics felt a need to express their unhappiness. On 10 May John Howard said he could neither defend nor explain the Premier's decision to appoint Metherell to a position in the Public Service. It had damaged the Liberal Party in NSW. The former Leader of the Federal Opposition would not give public advice to State colleagues yet he would not "dissemble and pretend something's not a problem when it is". A Federal shadow minister reportedly said that Greiner had been "sucked in by the Left of the party", apparently referring to Pickering and Tim Moore; "senior sources" in the Federal

Organisation said Greiner had "picked up the vibes" of its reaction; and
Hewson had apparently referred to the NSW "problem" at a recent Party
Room meeting.[13] Elements of the National Party were likewise displeased,
though for quite different reasons. Ray Chappell, MP for the Northern
Tablelands, sent Greiner a three-page fax on 29 May saying he had ceased
to be a proud member of the Government and wondered how long
he could remain loyal to it. He had accepted the need for reform, and
supported it, but his communities were in open revolt because they could
take only so much change at once.[14]

## Preparing for the best and the worst

Despite the poor press he received during the Commission hearings, and
despite Clark's final submission calling for criminal charges, Nick Greiner
remained outwardly and inwardly confident about the outcome.[15] Ken
Hooper, too, was reasonably optimistic. He wrote an undated ten-page
paper examining three possible scenarios following the publication of
the Temby Report.[16]

Scenario One assumed that Greiner would receive an "all clear". He
could then go to a Party meeting, secure a quick unanimous endorsement,
and hold a media conference in the State Office Block where he would
call on Carr to eat his words and declare he would get on with governing
NSW. He should avoid belting the media and might have to sit back
and be "screwed" over what to do about Metherell and his job. But the
Premier should do interviews with the very acceptable Alan Jones, John
Laws and Jim Whaley, keep attacking Carr while turning the media's
attention to the "Vision statement" and, by Day Four after the Report
arrived, use Parliament to attack the Labor Party and its practice of
providing "jobs for the boys".

Under Scenario Two – "The Grey Area" – the Commissioner might
clear the Premier of corruption and inducement yet criticise both the
fact and the process of the Metherell appointment, comment adversely
on the Premier's lapses in memory, and decide that Humphry acted too

hastily. There would be too many "unknowns" if Temby followed this line. The key, however, was for Greiner to secure Party Room support for sacking Metherell and refusing any compensation. He might then persuade the Independents not to support a Labor no-confidence motion. There were other possibilities and considerations. Humphry might offer to resign though he would be portrayed as the scapegoat and the Premier would suffer in the fall-out. Greiner could allow a conscience vote in the Assembly on the Metherell issue although there were risks of a field day for the media and for increased Party Room pressure on Greiner and/ or Moore to resign. Moore and Hazzard might resign from Parliament, with the Independents holding back from a no-confidence motion until after the by-elections because one of their like-minded souls could win Hazzard's seat.

At least Scenario Three – "The Doomsday Option" – offered certainty. Greiner, Moore and Hazzard would resign in the face of adverse findings, it would now be up to the Governor to make a decision about commissioning a new Premier, and Greiner should hold a press conference and thereafter have no further media contacts. "By that stage, the weather will be perfect in Fiji." Greiner's handwritten note, referring to what he called this "Black" scenario, reads, "Announce resignation effective 24/6."

Peter Collins had his own concerns. His decision not to approve funding for Hazzard angered many Liberal backbenchers while his ministerial colleagues, after supporting his stand in Cabinet, allegedly left Collins isolated over the issue.[17] Whereas the Attorney-General thought his decision was principled and independent, evidence of "a fearless first law officer", others saw him courting public opinion to suit his own ends. He was pleased, therefore, when the *Sydney Morning Herald* suggested a feature article to allow him to tell his side of the story.[18]

Mike Steketee's long piece appeared on Saturday 6 June. Under the headline – "THE MINISTER FOR PETER COLLINS" – Steketee relayed an assessment remarkably similar to the one held in Greiner's office and whispered by several ministers. Collins was described as overly ambitious, disloyal, bent on running his own race, and failing to fulfil any of the normal functions of a Deputy Leader. His "professional, let alone social, relationship with Greiner" was "virtually . . . non-existent". In one telling passage, Steketee explained why the two men operated so differently.

> Greiner's starting point is policy – what needs to be done, particularly the economic reform to make the public sector more efficient. Collins begins with politics – what is achievable, what looks good, and what makes him look good.

Greiner was "so little interested in the combat of politics" he had endangered both his Government and his reforms. Collins, who "lives and breathes politics", applied many of his skills to advancing his own ambitions. Either, Steketee suggested, someone should knock their heads together or, failing that, a new deputy might be found.

Collins thought briefly of resigning when he read the Steketee article. In the week after it appeared some of the views expressed were incorporated in a document – apparently written by a person or persons in Greiner's office – and prepared on the assumption that Temby would exonerate Greiner completely. The real purpose was to plan for some post-ICAC triumphalism and for the Premier to reclaim the political agenda.[19]

Once cleared by Temby, Greiner should go onto the front foot. Taking the example of Neville Wran, who used Sir Laurence Street's findings to make an angry attack on the press and the Opposition, the author(s) urged Greiner to hold a "fiery and dramatic" press conference immediately after the Report's release. He should resurrect Carr's comments on his alleged criminality, launch into the ABC and the *SMH,* announce the possibility of taking legal action, and forgo his traditional rational approach – "the reality is", "this is a nonsense" – and adopt a wholly emotional tone. He should also foreshadow, minus the details, a reshuffle and a radical legislative program, suggest a willingness to amend the *Public Sector Management Act* to limit political appointments, and propose that ICAC hearings should be held in-camera to protect the innocent from kangaroo courts and trial by media. The advice included some family involvement for the Sunday papers and women's magazines, with the Premier expressing anger about his wife carrying the hurt of the family. The plan also envisaged a king-hit for Quentin Dempster in the course of an in-studio interview.

A vindicated Greiner could then demonstrate his new resolve with an exercise in leadership by shifting senior ministers about, dealing with the problem areas of Police and Housing (meaning to sack Pickering and Schipp?), bringing more women into the Cabinet (Wendy Machin and Kerry Chikarovski were mentioned), recalling Pickard from London, promoting Fahey to replace Moore as Leader of the House and, perhaps above all, finding a new Deputy Leader. Greiner needed a Deputy who played the "traditional" supportive role. Peter Collins might repeatedly protest his total loyalty, and insist he would never challenge Nick Greiner. But Collins was persistently criticised within the Government, and by Greiner, for not performing the normal functions of advising and supporting his Leader and being a sounding board for him with the backbench. Moving Collins to Treasury might keep him fully occupied.

The author(s) suggested Greiner make several internal changes: notably, sacking some of his personal and press staff, bringing in some of the ministerial staffers, and replacing his Chief of Staff[20] with someone more authoritative and influential like Nick Minchin or Ian Kortlang. It appears Hooper had not effectively defined jobs, allocated responsibilities or conducted regular staff meetings. Nor had he exercised sufficient control over ministers' agendas and the operations of ministerial staffs or organised and supervised a more aggressive and systematic attack on the Opposition (too much, apparently, was left to the Premier). Finally, as a mark of decisive leadership, all international trips should be cancelled and all interstate trips should be personally approved by the Premier.

The document did not stop there. Drawing this time on Paul Keating's practice, it suggested that Greiner should create an agenda removed from the current difficulties. He could push items such as limiting the number of terms a politician might sit in parliament, citizen-initiated referenda, opening up appointments to statutory bodies to inspection, and introducing a code of conduct for politicians. All ministers should provide the Premier with three initiatives, a special group should be formed to work on them, and the Premier could raise them and run them for weeks. The Government would thus be seen to have moved beyond "the ICAC malaise".

Greiner added some handwritten notes to this section, listing more than a dozen possible initiatives, including voluntary voting, and placing a question mark against the proposal to recall Pickard. He also noted that Murray and Moore might retire, and clearly had in mind replacing Gerry Peacocke (NP) and Schipp. Greiner also wondered whether Collins might accept a change of portfolios in return for an assurance he would not be challenged as Deputy Leader. In handwritten notes on a shorter version of the second paper, Greiner wrote: "No one has ever questioned my honesty/integrity . . . bitterly resent . . . totally unfounded". On the media, he commented: "disgusting; irresponsibility; sleazy; & malice" and referred to its "easy defamation of public figures". Quentin Dempster "rehearsed live crosses", was a "player not [an] observer", did "gloating skits", and allegedly gloated about devouring the Premier; his contract should be "terminated".[21]

The days before Temby handed down his Report were typically busy for Greiner. The media was diverted by other matters: the artist Brett Whiteley was found dead in a motel room, the singer Peter Allen died of an AIDS-related illness, Princess Diana was plainly miserable, and Brian Burke, the former Premier of Western Australia, made a court appearance. Nick Greiner dealt with the aftermath of the Premiers' Conference and with the consequences of the proposed new

Commonwealth superannuation scheme which he said would take an additional $70-80m from the State budget next year and $1.5bn by the year 2000. He held a 90-minute Cabinet meeting on Thursday 18 June, the day before the Report was to be delivered to the Speaker of the Legislative Assembly and the President of the Legislative Council. It was necessary to discuss tactics for the release and consider the approach to Parliament when it met the following Wednesday to discuss the Report. The Coalition partners were absent, having left for Port Macquarie for the NP's State Conference. Greiner was not at all apprehensive. He told ministers he would quit if Temby found he had acted corruptly but there was not the slightest doubt in his mind he would be cleared of any wrongdoing. Ministers agreed to meet again at 2.00 pm the following day after Greiner, Moore and their legal teams had time to digest the findings which would be delivered to them some two hours before the public release.

Greiner was so confident of the outcome that he excused Roger Gyles from attending the planned meeting with the lawyers to examine Temby's findings. It is a measure of that confidence and, equally, a reflection of his imperfect political antennae, that he saw nothing significant, let alone troublesome, in a message Kevin Rozzoli passed onto him a day or two earlier. Temby had mentioned to the Speaker that his Report was "not inconsequential".[22]

# Endnotes

1. *SMH*, 12 May 1992.

2. The ABC radio station in Canberra ran a competition for an appropriate title for the Metherell dairies. *Withering Hates* was the winner. For the published diaries, see *SMH*, 16 May 1992.

3. For the following account of the hearings, see ICAC, *Transcript of Proceedings*, 5-25 May 1992, State Parliamentary Library.

4. Seaton Papers.

5. Metherell's counsel also wanted to establish Greiner's "fairly substantial" role in the appointment and suggested Greiner was dissembling in claiming his role was limited to the blackball and the requirement for Metherell to meet the job qualifications. Judging by Rofe's questions, the earlier rapprochement with Metherell now counted for very little.

6. Interview (Cunneen): Temby, p. 283.

7. Notes for Counsel, Greiner to David Ferguson/Roger Gyles, 22 May 1992, Seaton Papers.

8. *SMH*, 13-14 May 1992; Gleeson *et al.*, *An Act of Corruption?*, pp. 163-4.

9. Paul Kelly, *The March of Patriots: The Struggle for Modern Australia*, MUP, Carlton, 2009, ch. 3.

10. *Australian, AFR, DT* and *SMH*, 11-12 May 1992; Interview: Greiner, 12 September 2012; Martin Painter, *Collaborative Federalism: Economic Reform in Australia in the 1990s*, CUP, Melbourne, 1998, ch. 3.

11. *SMH*, 3 June 1992; Jamieson, "Industrial Relations", in Laffin and Painter, *Reform and Reversal*, pp. 151-2.

12. *SMH*, 11 and 17 June 1992.

13. *Australian*, 11 May 1992.

14. Letters from Members, Greiner Papers.

15. Interview: Greiner, 17 February 2010.

16. Possible Scenarios Post ICAC, ICAC, Greiner Papers.

17. For Collins' account of this episode, see *Bear Pit*, pp. 189-93.

18. *Ibid.*, pp. 194-5.

19. Post-ICAC Strategy, ICAC, Greiner Papers.

20  Curiously the paper referred by name to John Harvey, not Ken Hooper. Harvey had been pushed out the door in mid-1990.

21  ICAC, Greiner Papers.

22  Interviews: Greiner, 17 February 2010 and 7 January 2013.

# 18

# Verdicts and Resignations

Greiner, Tim Moore and their legal teams began poring over the Temby Report[1] around noon on Friday 19 June. It took just a few moments to fasten onto its stark message. The fourth paragraph of the Preface read:

> The conclusion reached is that the conduct of Mr Greiner and Mr Moore – respectively the Premier and the Minister for the Environment – was corrupt within the meaning of the Independent Commission Against Corruption Act 1988 (the ICAC Act) in that it involved the partial exercise of official functions, it also involved a breach of public trust, and could involve reasonable grounds for dismissing them from their official Ministerial positions.

Temby had decided that Greiner's and Moore's actions fell within the definition of corrupt conduct in section 8 (1) of the *ICAC Act*. Section 8 (1) defined corrupt conduct in four parts, of which Temby considered three to be relevant, namely:

> (a) any conduct of any person (whether or not a public official) that adversely affects, or that could adversely affect, either directly or indirectly, the honest or impartial exercise of official functions by any public official, any group or body of public officials, or any public authority; or
>
> (b) any conduct of a public official that constitutes or involves the dishonest or partial exercise of any of his or her official functions; or
>
> (c) any conduct of a public official or former public official that constitutes or involves a breach of public trust. . . .

The Commissioner found "not much difficulty about s8". Greiner and Moore "could have adversely affected, at least indirectly, the impartial exercise of official functions by Humphry". Greiner and Moore, as well as Humphry, had, as public officials, shown partiality to Metherell over all other applicants who had not received equal or similar consideration. Greiner and Moore had been involved in a breach of public trust in that Metherell was given a job for "extraneous reasons", namely, his friendship with Moore, the advantage accruing to the Liberal Party, and the advantage to Greiner and Moore by enhancing their prospects of remaining in government. Metherell, incidentally, "was knowingly concerned in the consequential breach of public trust".[2]

For conduct to be deemed corrupt under the Act, it also had to meet one of the conditions set out in section 9 (1):

> Despite section 8, conduct does not amount to corruption unless it could constitute or involve:
>
> (a) a criminal offence; or
>
> (b) a disciplinary offence; or
>
> (c) reasonable grounds for dismissing, dispensing with the services of or otherwise terminating the services of a public official.

Temby decided that neither (a) nor (b) applied to Greiner and Moore. Ministers were not subject to discipline which ruled out (b). In the case of (a) their conduct did not constitute the common law offence of bribery because the offer to Metherell was not made to influence his actions in public office or to act contrary to the known standards of honesty and integrity. In rejecting the arguments of Counsel Assisting, Temby did not endorse Metherell's interpretation of Greiner's use of the phrase, "the other matter", when the Premier telephoned Metherell on 9 March. While accepting Metherell's belief he had been offered an improper inducement, Temby also accepted that Greiner's reference to "the other matter" might have meant something quite different. The Premier saw how Metherell's resignation and his taking of a public service position "must be done in a credible manner". There had to be a "warming" of the Greiner-Metherell relationship. So, the Premier might have been suggesting that a principled shift to the Government's position on the Bill could assist in making such a "warming" public and be regarded as a precursor to the lunch Metherell and Greiner had together on 27 March. Taking this possibility into account, Temby concluded he could not find against Greiner for corruptly soliciting Metherell's vote during the telephone call of 9 March.[3]

The Commissioner did, however, decide that (c) applied to Greiner and Moore. Although they believed they were not doing anything corrupt, "viewed objectively, in terms of the ICAC Act, their conduct must be so categorised".[4] It was "simply misleading" for the Premier to claim he played a minor role in the whole affair. That is: Greiner gave the go-ahead to Moore and Hazzard on 16 February; discussed the matter with Metherell and in Hazzard's presence on 26 February; had various discussions with Moore; approved the fifth position after 18 March with Metherell being the preferred choice; met Metherell and Hazzard on 27 March; instructed Humphry to create the fifth position; arranged for a pre-selection for Metherell's seat; and was involved in meetings on 8-9 April to sort out some difficulties. There were, therefore, "reasonable grounds" for Greiner's dismissal because he "played a major role in the negotiations". These negotiations led to Metherell resigning his seat in exchange for an SES post assigned to him by a process which was not impartial. Greiner knew of Moore's desire to help a friend, and the outcome politically advantaged the Government and Greiner personally, and involved filling a senior public service position other than on a competitive merit basis and in a manner which favoured Metherell over other applicants.[5]

ICAC was not required to decide whether the Governor should or should not dismiss the Premier. Temby's task was to determine whether there were reasonable grounds for taking action under section 9 (c) of the Act. According to the "political realities", the Governor would act only on the advice of the Premier or the Executive Council or in the event of Parliament passing a vote of no confidence in an individual or in the Government. Temby left it to Parliament, therefore, to decide what to do, and in "deference" to the institution declined to suggest what course it might follow.[6]

## A frenetic Friday afternoon

After reading the Preface a "shell-shocked" Premier came very close to throwing in the towel.[7] He sent a message to Ted Pickering to come immediately to the State Office Block. When Pickering arrived he had to wait outside the Premier's office while the lawyers continued to read quickly through the Report. A sentence on p. 73 captured their attention:

> As with Metherell, I do not think that it can be concluded that Greiner saw himself, or would be seen by a notional jury, as conducting himself contrary to known and recognised standards of honesty and integrity.

His "honesty and integrity" seemingly intact, the Premier could counter-attack: he was guilty only of a technical offence and should not be judged according to a higher moral standard than the current community standards. By 2.00 pm the lawyers were convinced there were grounds for appeal. They urged Greiner not to resign because, if he did so, he would never be able to clear his name. Greiner was already deciding to do what came naturally. He would stand firm.

Pickering and Collins, who had joined the Police Minister, were called into the room and given a quick oral briefing. The rest of the ministry – minus the NP ministers who were in Port Macquarie – assembled in the Cabinet Room and received the same message: Temby had found that Greiner and Moore had committed a technical breach of the Act but, on legal advice and encouragement, both men would appeal to the Supreme Court. They would stay in office and tough it out. No one in the Cabinet Room openly demurred.

As mid-afternoon approached, Greiner made two fateful decisions, one by default and the other with resolve. First, he would not stand aside while an appeal went ahead: "I don't think it occurred to me." In retrospect, he acknowledges that the "sensible, correct and entirely obvious" action would have been to "do a Wran": step aside, install Wal Murray as Acting Premier, and wait for the Court to pass judgment. This action would have established a breathing space, made clear he accepted there was a case to answer, protected the Government by separating its future from his own fate, and rendered it difficult for the non-aligned Independents to join Labor in pursuing him. Instead, Greiner focussed on what was uppermost in his mind, namely, the decision not to resign. He would put up with talking to the non-aligned Independents which, on reflection, "was not the best way to handle [the situation] in terms of my longevity". There was no discussion with others about the possible options. It was "not my style" to do so; "I was inclined to get on and do things", was "too independent", and liked "to operate so much on my own".[8]

Secondly, Greiner decided to issue a statement and face a media conference in the State Office Block at 3.00 pm. Once he issued his statement, and defended himself in the manner he did, the pressure to resign outright simply intensified.

In the press release Greiner emphasised how Temby found he had acted according to known standards of honesty and integrity, did not think he was doing anything corrupt, and had not engaged in criminal conduct. Greiner said he had relied on Humphry's professional advice and believed what he did was lawful. Temby had found that the Metherell appointment amounted – technically – to corrupt conduct because it was contrary to the merit provisions of the *Public Service Management Act*, and because Metherell was shown favouritism. But the Commissioner also said Parliament must determine the seriousness of the breach. On a fair reading of the Report, Greiner believed Parliament should conclude no more than it did in the April censure motion, adding that he had, and expected to retain, the full confidence of Coalition ministers. Temby, he said, had specifically declined to recommend consideration be given to dismissal, and had found that Greiner had always acted in the matter "with complete integrity".[9]

The heated press conference was a disaster.[10] The Premier kept reiterating the favourable elements of Temby's Report and presenting a favourable spin on everything else. The journalists who asked questions, spoke, interrupted or merely shouted, were not interested in Greiner's interpretation. They were especially dismissive – even outraged – by his distinction between conduct deemed corrupt within the meaning of the Act and him not being personally corrupt. He was "a corrupt Premier" who should resign. Indeed, why had he not done so already? Greiner kept stressing it was now up to Parliament. He refused to speculate about what the Independents might do, and refused to comment on the question of whether Metherell would keep his job. When Greiner insisted he should not be judged by a future set of standards, one artful questioner wanted to know whether "jobs for the boys" amounted, therefore, to a currently acceptable standard. Greiner replied that there would be a new set of standards where "jobs for the boys" would not be acceptable. Stressing his unanimous support from ministers, he noted how the NP State Conference in Port Macquarie had just expressed its complete confidence in him, and in his continuing role as Premier of NSW.

Wal Murray had interrupted a business session at Port Macquarie to give an abbreviated account of the findings. Dismissing the Report as a "mishmash", and accusing Temby of having "two bob each way", Murray described Greiner's offence as no more serious than doing 70kms in a 60km zone. Like the Premier, Murray extended Temby's words beyond what the Commissioner actually said: "I fully support the statement in the report that nothing had been found to affect Mr Greiner's integrity." Murray later told journalists that Greiner's integrity "shines through" the Report.[11]

Some ministers in Sydney who listened to the press conference were either confused or appalled. Four of them met afterwards in the basement car park of the Parliament. Baird, Chadwick, Cohen and Collins agreed that Greiner was finished as Premier. When Pickering joined them he urged them to hold fast and not to move against the Premier, though he would later claim to have known since first learning of Temby's findings that Greiner's time was up. He was not prepared, however, to tap him on the shoulder. A young man with a family, who would be hurt by the label of corrupt conduct and who had made a great contribution to the governance of NSW, was entitled to his day in court and to "go out with dignity". Virginia Chadwick spoke to Greiner later that afternoon but denied a press claim she told him to resign.[12] The encounter in the car park had one important ramification. Senior ministers told a journalist from the *Sydney Morning Herald* that the Premier should resign. Greiner believed Baird was one of them and, when the prospect of his resignation moved from possible to probable to certain, decided that Baird's "disloyalty" should not be rewarded with the Party leadership.[13]

One minister stood totally and very publicly on Greiner's side. Speaking on the ABC's *7.30 Report* on Friday, Michael Yabsley accused the media of emphasising a small part of the ICAC findings. Temby's "honesty and integrity" sentence was now central to the defence, and Yabsley managed to cite it without distorting the meaning. Yabsley also launched into Quentin Dempster on the program, questioning his impartiality given his many contacts with Metherell and calling him "pious and sanctimonious". Two days after confronting Dempster, Yabsley said the Government had created "a monster" in ICAC. He declared Greiner to be "absolutely untainted" and vowed to resign should he be forced out. Whereas a few ministers were clearly unimpressed by Yabsley's performance, Baird would later regret he had not publicly stood by Greiner as the junior minister had done.[14]

## The ups and downs of the weekend

The Saturday press in Sydney bore similar messages. It was "a tragedy" that Greiner's position should be on the line. The *DTM* was just more emphatic about what should happen, if not thoroughly cognisant with what was possible: the Premier should tender his resignation and call an election. The *SMH* wanted Greiner to resign if he believed in the integrity of ICAC, even though he was not corrupt and his actions over the Metherell affair did not amount to corruption as most would understand the term. A number of journalists wrote about the "irony" of Greiner being found corrupt by his own creation, excoriated him for not living up to his stated principles (and, by implication, theirs), and ridiculed or abused him for persisting to claim his admitted error of judgment amounted to nothing more than technical corruption. The Melbourne *Age* exercised its mortgage on moral outrage. Its editorial described Greiner as "a man of withered personal and political judgment and bloated self-delusion" who was guilty of "Olympian hypocrisy" and "ethical blindness", and had engaged in a "desperate and devious ploy" which was either "brazen, ludicrous or pathetic".

There were better things to do on a Saturday than sit at home. The Greiners made an unscheduled trip to Port Macquarie where Greiner addressed the NP's State Conference.[15] He asked: "Where's the fairness? Where's the commonsense in dismissing an avowedly honest Premier and an avowedly honest Government because of a partial appointment to a relatively junior position, a non-chief executive position in the Public Service?" (Metherell's salary was well above average male earnings.) He repeated points made on the previous day, and said nothing new or additional had emerged from the Temby inquiry. He had "owned up", "copped it sweet", and "I daresay I have paid a price, both personally and in a political sense". Yet the best legal advice said the Commissioner was wrong in law. Besides, every political decision is "partial" and all political leaders seek political advantage in decisions they make. Although Metherell had initiated the whole process and Humphry had formally appointed him, neither was found to be corrupt. Greiner was happy for them but he and Moore had been treated differently and were subjected to a different moral standard. As for suggestions that his situation had its parallels in the dismissals of Lang and Whitlam, Greiner rightly said it was a comparison "with no legs at all".

It was a well-aimed speech. Greiner carefully highlighted the contribution of individual NP ministers when referring to the Government's "long list of landmark achievements". After what happened in the North Coast case, a National Party audience could be relied upon to see "unfairness" in any ICAC finding. Such an audience was unlikely to ask who brought in the *Public Service Management Act* or to know or care about the tradition whereby ministers played no role in lower-level appointments. It was also an emotional speech. Greiner was close to tears as he referred to the "hurt" for himself, Kathryn and the children. "It would have been easy to walk away. It would also have been wrong." Acknowledging that no one was indispensable, the Premier said he believed his continuing leadership was in the interests of the people of NSW and proposed to continue in the job. What he now asked was to be given "a fair go". The Conference gave him three standing ovations. As one National MP correctly remarked, Greiner received the sort of reception "he wouldn't get from his own party".[16]

Kathryn also spoke out at Port Macquarie. "The family", she said, "has rallied behind him 100 per cent simply because . . . he's basically a very honest, straightforward economic manager". She described how Justin had decorated the upstairs part of their house on the Friday afternoon with signs declaring support and urging him to "keep going". The children were "shocked", like everyone else. After all, "this is their father". Kathryn said it "really makes my Irish blood absolutely boil" at the concept of Nick and of Tim Moore engaging in a breach of public trust. "If their behaviour is flawed, then stand up Neville Wran and, by God, John Bannon."[17]

Wal Murray thought he had better news for Greiner. Spencer Ferrier, a member of the NP's Central Executive and a Sydney-based lawyer who acted for National MPs called before ICAC,[18] had faxed him two pieces of advice. The first was intriguing if hardly helpful. Ferrier argued that because the Act at no point dealt with the question of whether a person was "corrupt" – it dealt only with "corrupt conduct" – a person who engaged in such conduct was not necessarily morally corrupt. "There can be innocent corrupt conduct." The next piece offered more hope. Ferrier reminded Murray that conduct deemed corrupt under section 8 could not be corrupt unless there were reasonable grounds for dismissal. The Governor alone had the power to dismiss the Premier but could not do so because, as Temby found, the Premier had acted in accordance with recognised standards of honesty and integrity. If the Governor cannot dismiss him because of the absence of reasonable grounds then the Commissioner cannot find him guilty of "corrupt conduct" and therefore had nothing to refer to the Parliament.[19] Murray passed on this advice to Greiner and to the assembled media in Port Macquarie.

The press on the Sunday morning carried two critical stories. In one, Hatton said that the ICAC findings touched the entire Government and thereby "triggered" the clause in their agreement allowing the Independents to withdraw their support on a no-confidence motion. He expected that the Independents would be holding talks with the Government in the coming days.

In the other story, a number of senior Liberals had clearly raised the possibility of dumping the Premier if the Opposition and the Independents threatened to bring down the Government. One Liberal reportedly commented that, if the Independents could not give a "cast-iron guarantee" against supporting such a motion, Nick Greiner would be "tapped on the shoulder". Someone described as a "senior strategist" claimed the Liberal Party was "totally reassessing" its position on the leadership and was definitely talking about the shoulder tap. If, according to an unnamed minister, a general motion of no confidence looked certain to pass, the Premier would be approached "with sorrow" and told his leadership was "no longer viable". A "senior State Government figure" applied an inapposite analogy by likening the ICAC findings against the Premier to the discovery that a close member of the family had cancer: the loyalty and respect remained but the subject could not be avoided.[20]

By now Greiner knew that the Liberal Party's State President and the Federal Liberals were not allies. In Port Macquarie, Peter King said he did not agree with Wal Murray that Temby had got everything completely wrong. Later, while speaking of the Party "sticking 100 per cent behind the Premier", he said several senior ministers had the experience and skills to replace him if necessary.[21] Hewson had talked to Greiner and reported how "Mr Greiner has accepted the position of Mr Temby, and that it's a matter for the Parliament and these processes are going to run their course". He conceded there had been damage to the Party's standing in NSW by the adverse publicity of the preceding ten weeks, beginning with the announcement of the Metherell appointment. Andrew Robb, the Federal Director of the Party, said he was confident the Premier would act in the best interests of the Liberal Party. Decoded, the message was that Greiner should resign.

The next day Greiner was the Swans' guest of honour for its AFL match against Geelong at the Sydney Cricket Ground. Before the game he spoke at a luncheon of the "loyalty and support" which was important to the Swans in a city still coming to terms with the invasion of a southern code. He hoped, he said, to be "a good-luck omen" for what was expected to be a difficult game against a top side. Greiner then joined a crowd of more than 11,000 to see the Swans thrashed by 75 points in what was their fifth successive defeat. On the bright side, there was evidence of "loyalty and support" for the AFL: the crowd in attendance was larger than those of all but two Rugby League games that weekend, even if it was smaller than five of the other six AFL matches which drew numbers of between 21,000 and 68,000.[22]

One Sunday appointment was cancelled. Greiner had a longstanding commitment to attend the black-tie official opening of the Newcastle Entertainment Centre which preceded a sell-out John Denver concert. The organisers were told around noon the Premier had cancelled the appointment because he was very busy in the aftermath of the ICAC findings. Chadwick took his place. According to the press report, "the people of Newcastle, probably renowned as being among his sternest critics", applauded when an official said the Premier had been vital in ensuring the facility was built.[23] Instead of the flying visit to Newcastle after the football, the Greiners attended a hastily-arranged dinner at the BBQ King restaurant in Goulburn Street, Chinatown. Organised by Ron Phillips, the gathering expanded from an original twenty to near fifty. At Pickering's suggestion, or insistence, all three of the undeclared contenders for Greiner's job – Baird, Collins and Fahey – were present. Collins thought the "dynamics of the evening were horrendous, with everybody trying to outdo the other with bonhomie and bravado". Another report offered a different angle: "everyone revelled in it" and all were "liberated" by their "open carelessness".[24]

## Mad Monday

Greiner formally instructed his solicitors, Minter Ellison, on Monday morning to apply to the Supreme Court to quash all or part of the ICAC Report as it saw fit, or to make other orders as appropriate. Although at this stage no decision had been made on the entirety of the grounds for appeal, the solicitors were focussing on the argument that the Commission was wrong in law and had exceeded its jurisdiction. Minter Ellison expected a single judge to hear the application immediately and refer the matter directly to the Court of Appeal which might hear argument one day next week and hand down a judgment shortly afterwards. The solicitors felt that the entire proceedings could be completed within a fortnight.[25]

Tim Moore faxed Greiner a three-page message at 10.30 am. He had come up with a range of complex legal manoeuvres and possibilities, but said he would not be disappointed if the Premier chose not to act on his musings. Greiner simply filed them.[26] He was happy for the lawyers to deal with the legal matters, and concentrated instead on trying to persuade the non-aligned Independents to give him time.

He began on the Monday morning with public appeals and assurances. He told Radio 2UE he would step down if the court upheld the Temby Report. There would be no alternative "in terms of the reality of both the wellbeing of the Government and of the party". Speaking on the Monday afternoon at the Queen Victoria Building, where he launched the Government's float of its principal asset, the GIO, the Premier chose his words carefully. He was not going to lash Temby and ICAC. He would only say "Mr Temby might have made a mistake. I made a mistake. I make them regularly." All he wanted was the same right given to crooks and thugs: to have his day in court to make sure that the law was "right".

Greiner issued a press statement late on the Monday saying how he and Moore wanted the ICAC Report reviewed as a matter of urgency and by the State's highest court. Their legal advice said the Report was "fundamentally flawed" and the two men would seek orders exonerating them both. It would be "a total denial of natural justice" for Parliament to resolve this matter before the Report was confirmed as legally correct or had one or more of its key findings substantially altered. The matter should be dealt with quickly, though only on the basis of a legally-correct document, and any motion which the Opposition and the Independents wanted to move could be debated soon after the court made a determination.[27]

Greiner's "kitchen cabinet" – consisting of Pickering and Fahey – had the task of pushing the case for delay with the non-aligned Independents. Accounts of different meetings on Monday between the two ministers and Clover Moore and Peter Macdonald vary considerably. As a result, there is some confusion about what was resolved, if anything, before Hatton arrived from the South Coast on Tuesday. The one certainty, in the minds of the Greiner camp, was that his hope for political survival lay with Clover Moore. His chances were diminishing, however, because all three non-aligned Independents felt they had further grounds for taking an uncompromising line. They noted the Murray and Yabsley comments about Temby and ICAC, heard Valder refer on ABC radio to Temby's one-time Labor candidature which should have debarred him from the inquiry, and knew of Bronwyn Bishop's support for Valder's "valid point". Peter Macdonald was now claiming that the Government had become complicit because of the campaign being waged against Temby and ICAC. The Premier's friends had given the non-aligned Independents a rationale for exercising power without responsibility.

Throughout a day of various encounters, phone conversations, ignored phone calls and misunderstandings, the senselessness of the whole affair became apparent when Metherell issued a public statement saying he would not take up his position in the Premier's Department nor seek compensation. It was the right time to resign because ICAC had cleared his name and accepted his integrity. He wanted to prevent his family life from being disrupted by continuing controversy, and knew he could not play the creative role ICAC had acknowledged was his motivation and which others might deliberately and maliciously misinterpret.[28] Greiner told talkback radio in the afternoon that Metherell had made the right choice and probably had "a good case" for compensation. It may be wondered whether another Premier in a similar situation would have responded with a rational reference to an employee's rights in law.

Late on the Monday afternoon Greiner met members of the Liberal Party's Management Committee and received stronger support than the State President had offered. After Greiner spoke of being "flabbergasted" by the "wrong and unfair" Report, Ron Phillips said the "vast majority" of the Government were trying to find ways to back him. Another committee member described Greiner as the "sentimental favourite" and asked how it would be possible "politically" to solve the matter and suggested that public statements of support would not hurt.

Pointing out how Greiner was still a young man, Bevan Bradbury said it would be a serious mistake for the stigma of corruption to remain on him.[29]

## The Ultimatum

On Tuesday morning the Greiners attended a breakfast Yabsley had arranged at the Inter-Continental Hotel. Cabinet ministers, backbenchers and staffers joined high profile figures such as Rodney Adler, the CEO of FAI Insurance, Nick Farr-Jones, the captain of the Wallabies, and Sir Ron Brierley, the New Zealand entrepreneur and a one-time shareholder of the White River Corporation. John Farnham's arresting hit song, "You're the Voice", greeted the Greiners on their arrival: "We're all someone's daughter/ We're all someone's son/How long can we look at each other/ Down the barrel of a gun?" Collins saw the seating plan as critical to understanding the entire exercise. He was placed near the staff entrance; Baird was located near the toilets.[30] Unlike Baird, whom Greiner had momentarily misjudged, Collins had no real ground for complaint. It was an occasion for the loyalists to be seated front and centre.

The non-aligned Independents and their advisers met in an Oxford Street motel and agreed on an ultimatum: Greiner and Tim Moore had 24 hours to resign; if they did not, the "Hatton Party" would support a motion of no-confidence in the Government. It appears that the two recent arrivals in the Legislative Assembly respected and willingly deferred to the man of multiple principles from the South Coast. Clover Moore confirmed her commitment with a press statement, a copy of which she faxed to the Premier just before 2.00 pm. The non-aligned Independents – Hatton described them as being "rock solid" – then marched together in a public display of solidarity and moral purpose to the State Office Block in response to Greiner's request for a meeting. Those present were Greiner, Tim Moore, Pickering, Fahey, Hatton, Macdonald and Clover Moore as well as three advisers to the Independents. Ken Hooper was also present.[31]

The key exchange occurred very early in the proceedings. Greiner asked if it was fair to dismiss Tim Moore and himself three days before a court might find they were not corrupt. Hatton said no court could alter the facts as found by Temby, and those facts, as Greiner and Moore both agreed, were not in dispute. Hatton acknowledged that the Greiner Government was the most honest in his experience and he was saddened by what had happened, but the Premier himself had established the guidelines, while the Government's attacks on Temby and ICAC had crystallised his own decision. Sensing the importance of these attacks, Fahey pointed out how Greiner had spoken to those who had made unauthorised statements, ensured that Yabsley and Valder did not appear on the *7.30 Report* the previous evening, and had publicly supported ICAC and not criticised Temby personally. Peter King, he added, had written to the *SMH* disassociating the Party from Valder's comments, and Pickering assured everybody that the Liberal Party machine had not criticised ICAC. The Independents remained unmoved.

The fact that they could regard the Murray-Valder-Yabsley involvement as extending the "stain of corruption", and allow those attacks to crystallise thinking, suggests that an appeal to commonsense and rationality would get nowhere. The argument for a "fair go" was similarly doomed. Even if the Independents had not delivered their ultimatum at a press conference an hour earlier and so could not be seen – yet again – to vacillate, Hatton was beyond persuasion and the other two, in his company, were immovable. Hatton was as certain of the Premier's guilt as Greiner was of his innocence. As he explained after the event, Hatton was armed with the findings of a computer into which Hilton Jones, his adviser and a Coral Sea veteran, had fed weeks of research. The computer had communicated a finding of misconduct.[32]

Greiner tried another option, the one which might have worked on the previous Friday. He offered, with Tim Moore, to stand aside until the court made its decision. When Clover Moore asked why he simply did not resign when the Report was handed down, Greiner replied that, with all the legal advice telling him the Report was "a piece of shit", he could not in conscience do this to himself. Hardened criminals had a right of appeal: why couldn't he and Tim Moore have the same right? Would the Independents or their families, placed in a similar situation, give up without a fight? Hatton said he would not, yet if he knew he was in the wrong he would temper his predilection to act. The reply missed the point. Nick Greiner "knew" he was not in the wrong. But, as Hatton and the other two had decided "the facts" were against him, they viewed any legal challenge as a delaying tactic relevant only to the process of dismissal and not to the Report's findings of corrupt conduct.

As the meeting neared its end, Clover Moore and Macdonald asked the Premier to consider resigning, thereby removing the need for a no-confidence motion against the Government. Greiner said he would consider the idea. In turn, the Independents agreed to give their final answer early next morning.

Greiner told the assembled media after the meeting how neither he nor Tim Moore would be resigning that evening. Soon afterwards, the Independents made it clear to every news service and television program they were sticking to their decision. Hatton called it "an awesome responsibility" and told *A Current Affair* about the weeks of research and the "independent" assessment (it was unclear whether he was referring to Hilton Jones or the computer) that helped him make up his mind prior to Temby's use of the word "corrupt". He also told the *7.30 Report* that the Greiner Government "is the cleanest Government I have seen in my 19 years [in Parliament]".[33]

Pickering felt sure Greiner was all but finished. He sought and obtained the Premier's authority to muster the numbers for Fahey. While it went against the grain for Greiner to endorse a successor, the "disloyal" behaviour of Baird and Collins justified a change of attitude. Fahey was a beer-drinking Catholic and was, therefore, like Askin and himself, though in a different way, a "non-typical Liberal", an essential attribute in Greiner's view for capturing what was really a Labor State. Greiner did not tell Pickering, however, he would have preferred Virginia Chadwick, if she had been prepared to nominate. He had a high estimate of her abilities and "you couldn't get a more non-typical Liberal than a woman from Newcastle".[34] Yet Chadwick always rejected his promptings about the leadership, possibly influenced by her habitual reaction to stress.

Greiner returned to Wahroonga, and Pickering and John Marsden worked the phones late into the night speaking directly to MPs or to those who might win them over. Fahey and his wife, Colleen, were also present. Pickering's master-stroke was to speak to Michael Photios who was on his way home from parliamentary business in Paris. The young MP, a former companion of one of Pickering's daughters, remained a key organiser within the Group and a Baird supporter. Pickering told Photios when he reached Singapore airport that Fahey and not Baird was the Group's preferred candidate. Photios was to do and say nothing. He was taken from Sydney airport in Pickering's car and kept out of contact until it was too late for him to influence or be influenced. Even before Photios arrived in Sydney, however, Pickering could tell the Minister for Industrial Relations he would be the next Premier of NSW.[35]

### The best speech he never gave

On the evening of 23 June Greiner wrote five pages of notes for a speech he never delivered.

The Premier planned to begin with a reference to Hatton's statement on the *7.30 Report* about the Greiner Government being the cleanest he had known. He intended to speak warmly about ICAC and the Commissioner. Greiner saw ICAC – his Government's creation – as central to changing the culture of NSW. Although the legislation was criticised by lawyers and civil libertarians, he was prepared for overkill and taking risks. ICAC would have its wins, make mistakes and lose in the courts, but Greiner thought it would evolve over time and dramatically change attitudes for the better. It had embarrassed the Government more than Labor and had chosen not to look into Labor's past, yet he remained a supporter of ICAC as an institution. He had appointed Temby as a person of integrity and as a competent criminal lawyer and did not believe he was politically biased, despite criticisms of the Commissioner emanating from colleagues, journalists and lawyers.

ICAC and its Commissioner were not, however, omnipotent. The Commission had the same standing as other tribunals, and its opinions were just that – opinions – and were properly subject to criticisms from those who disagreed. If it made errors in law it would expect to have them tested and, if appropriate, corrected. "Mr Temby would expect nothing less." So, there should be no "nonsense" about accepting the umpire's decision, even if it was wrong. While the fact-finding "has been thoroughly and professionally done", he "categorically" rejected "the heart and soul of its findings" of there being corrupt conduct within the meaning of the Act. Nor did Greiner accept much of Temby's commentary and analysis. As he said in 1988, ICAC was not intended to be "a tribunal of morals". So, while he supported ICAC and the Commissioner, he found serious fault with the Report, and was entitled to do so, entitled to test it in law, and entitled to acknowledgement from Labor and the Independents for his "huge personal effort" to promote accountability, and for the honesty and integrity recognised by every media commentator.

Greiner was now ready for the direct assault. The Opposition was engaging in self-serving "nonsense" in claiming that the ICAC Report had to be accepted for fear of harming the Commission. Hatton was fiercely critical of royal commissions – and ICAC was really a standing royal commission – yet would deny Greiner the right to do the same. Carr's own record hardly qualified him to demand Greiner's prosecution. Clover Moore was being hypocritical in view of her involvement in another case concerning ICAC. She had written to the Premier on 13 April 1992 on behalf of town planners who believed that a recently-released ICAC Report into South Sydney Council's Planning Department was biased, inaccurate, sensationalist and flippant. On the basis of the findings, the Council had dismissed a planner and Moore wanted a review of ICAC procedures to give persons being investigated a right of appeal. Sturgess and Greiner had decided that Moore's letter should be referred to the Parliamentary Committee on ICAC. Greiner's point was that Moore, rightly as it turned out, had not accepted an ICAC determination and thought it important to allow an appeal. While the facts were not in dispute in the Metherell affair, Greiner felt entitled to ask why Clover Moore was unwilling to wait in his case for the appeal to be heard before taking action.[36]

Temby on p. 74 of his Report had identified six "facts" which warranted his conclusion that there were reasonable and justifiable grounds for dismissing the Premier. Greiner planned to respond to each in turn.

1. Temby said he had played "a major role" in the negotiations with Metherell. Tim Moore had that role. Greiner conceded he held a blackball but he never negotiated with Metherell other than talking over his legislative proposals, a matter on which the Commissioner placed no weight.

2. Temby said the negotiations "led to Metherell resigning his seat in exchange for an SES position". Greiner acknowledged this point in the censure debate.

3. Temby said the process was not impartial but the notion of partial decisions being wrong is "absolutely ridiculous". A colleague counted 60 such decisions in the past week; every capital works decision is partial. The Government made partial decisions "galore" in The Entrance campaign, and Labor does the same in every marginal seat.

4. and 5. Temby said Greiner knew that the Metherell appointment was, with Greiner's knowledge, made to help Tim Moore's friend and to advantage the Government. Yes, Moore wanted to help a friend and said so. Greiner wanted political advantage – "WOW – I did and so does every political leader and so they should. I said so [at] the time."

6. Temby said the appointment was not made on competitive

merit and Metherell was favoured. That was true, but many appointments are made without interview, and provision exists for the practice in the guidelines. "True of CEOs, true of ICAC Commissioner, true of judges".

Greiner planned to argue that these six facts would not be sufficient to hang "the proverbial dog, much less a Premier". His preferred defence had always been to deny he had committed a "mortal sin", to admit an error of judgment while downplaying its significance, and to stress how Metherell was well qualified for a position in the EPA. This part of the speech would have varied the emphasis by reminding his Labor opponents of the basic requirements of being in government, and by informing the Independents of some basic realities. Very simply, ministers regularly had to make, and did make, "partial" decisions, and regularly they had to spend, and did spend, public money for political advantage.

At the same time, Greiner wanted one last shot at "the great advocates of natural justice" who sat opposite and on the side who would sentence him before he could fully exercise his right of appeal. It was not just that seven QCs, five senior litigation solicitors and the Solicitor-General all said his legal position was very strong. To charge ahead before the Court made its findings was "a gross travesty of justice". The appeal was not intended as a delay. The issue was not marginal: it went to the core of the Report in saying it was fundamentally flawed. And no Parliament and no jury of the people of NSW "would dismiss anyone much less a Premier whose record of achievement and integrity is second to none".

Clearly, Greiner intended to go out with "both barrels blazing" as Kathryn had threatened to do during the hearings. And he would deliver his own epitaph. He had collected quotations from editorials and commentators praising his time in government, and he listed his achievements in reforming government and promoting accountability, and advances made in the economy, education, health, the environment, and justice. Greiner's peroration would include a saying by former

American President Theodore Roosevelt which Sturgess had passed on to him. It was not the critic who counted, the one who pointed out how the strong man had stumbled, but the one

> whose face is marred by dust and sweat and blood; who strives valiantly; who errs, who comes short again and again, because there is no effort without error and shortcoming; but who does actually strive to do the deeds . . . who at the best knows in the end the triumph of high achievement, and who at the worst, if he fails, at least fails while daring greatly.

## Dumped

On the morning of 24 June Peter King sent a handwritten note to Greiner after trying without success to contact him by telephone. King said he was aware the Independents had not changed their "obstinate" position overnight. In these circumstances Greiner should consider the appointment of a caretaker government led by Wal Murray. The Court could then complete its work and the Party would have time "to cool off". In any event, "unless the Independents see sense . . . you must resign as Premier". He was "sorry for the tough call".[37] It is unclear just when Greiner saw this note though he certainly had King in mind when he spoke later about the lack of support from senior members of the Party.

After two of the Independents told the media in the early morning they had not changed their minds – Hatton, being decent, told the Premier directly – phone calls with the three of them confirmed the position. Pickering then told Greiner in his office it was time to resign. Asked why, "my logic was as clear as a bell".[38] He pointed out that if he, Pickering, was Leader of the Opposition he would go into the House and say that the Opposition would not be moving a motion of no-confidence in the Premier until after he had his day in court, effectively placing the Government in the hands of the Court of Appeal. Now the advice from the lawyers was that the chances were 50-50. In other words, the Government would have a 50-50 chance of survival. Pickering thought the risk was too great. Greiner, he recalled, agreed "wholeheartedly" with this analysis, and said he would resign. And there was no point in that situation taking up Greiner's last minute thought of postponing a no-confidence vote with a filibuster on a motion to take note of the Report while waiting for the Court to hand down its verdict. The Court would still be the arbiter of the Government's fate. The two men went straight into the Cabinet Room where Greiner broke the news of his intended resignation. Many ministers were "upset"; Yabsley spoke defiantly and emotionally in support of Greiner remaining in office, but most senior Liberals kept their peace.

Greiner and Pickering returned to the Premier's office where Greiner said he was going to tell the Party Room of his support for Fahey and to say that neither Baird nor Collins should, under any circumstances, be elected Leader. Pickering told him that this approach was "not on". Pickering had been fielding calls and comments from backbenchers who were "cranky" about Greiner's "absolute bloody stupidity" over Metherell. Any statement of support for Fahey or attack on Baird or Collins would have the opposite effect. Greiner flew at him, saying it was the harshest thing ever said to him in his entire political career. Pickering responded that he had been loyal to Greiner since the beginning and done everything "to protect him from himself". Greiner proceeded to announce his resignation decision to the Party Room, said the meeting would adjourn for an hour and then reassemble to elect his replacement. He would, at the reconvened meeting, nominate John Fahey as his successor. Baird and Collins had been effectively ambushed. In an emotionally charged atmosphere, with loyalty as much as political judgment on trial, they had no time to counter Greiner's implicit final demand for support. Pickering had to work hard during the hour he had available.

The Premier began the hour by confronting Baird for his acts of "disloyalty" over the previous days in putting himself forward for the leadership. Collins recalled how a shaken Baird told him of the exchange soon after 10.00 am and reported Greiner as saying that he would sit on the cross-benches and, if necessary, vote with the Independents if Collins won the leadership.[39] At 10.15 Nick Greiner met the press. Fortunately, Ian Kortlang had arrived from Washington DC that morning with Sue Cato, a former Greiner staffer. The two of them walked into Parliament House and took over the arrangements for the press conference. Military planning and order were imposed on something approaching chaos, and ensured that Greiner was provided with a "level of dignity".[40] The Kortlang of 1986-8 had returned to make a brief and final contribution.

Greiner began the proceedings with a brief statement. He said his preferred course was to stand aside for Wal Murray as caretaker Premier while the Supreme Court made its decision. But three "totally illegitimate" Independents had rejected "that most reasonable, most fair and most sensible option". He acknowledged that a majority of Liberal ministers and MPs were also not prepared to take the risk of standing firm. Given the Party's loyalty to him over a decade it would be churlish and "not on" for him to back his judgment against the Party's. Greiner spoke of his "outrage" at "being shot a couple of days before the trial". Although this press conference would be his last as Premier, he had no intention of reviewing his record at length.

> Suffice to say that we have set and I have set new standards of integrity, new standards of honesty and that on any reasonable assessment we'll be judged by history as the most successful reformist Government this State has ever had.

Greiner concluded by thanking his wife, who stood by his side throughout the conference, his family, staff, Wal Murray, the National Party and the Liberal Party – and referred to Kathryn's support as being "beyond compare".

Asked about who was his chosen successor, Greiner said he believed there were three candidates and, of them, "Mr Fahey is clearly the best candidate. I think for practical purposes he is the only candidate." (In the event, nearly half the Party Room disagreed with him.) A question which implied he had not made the decision himself drew a sharp response in vintage Greiner language: "I mean, as you would all know, the nonsense you all write about 'taps on shoulders' and things has been nonsense from the start and remains nonsense." A Channel 7 reporter asked if he still disagreed with the ICAC Report. Greiner described the question as "offensively stupid". He remained publicly gracious about Temby while insisting that his Report was wrong in law and wrong in many of his conclusions and commentary. He also told the assembled journalists he continued to support ICAC as an institution.[41]

Returning to the Party Room, Greiner provided one of the 23 votes out of the available 44 which elected Fahey on the first ballot. Collins received 11 and Baird 10. Collins opted out at this point and Baird easily defeated Terry Griffiths for the deputy leadership.[42] Once again, and for the last time, Pickering had delivered for Nick Greiner. Whether he could have done so if Greiner had put his own leadership to the test is another matter.

### The end of the day

Many at the end of the Party Room meeting wanted to express their anger or sadness but Greiner went quickly back to his office to address the distraught staff. He then saw the Governor, Peter Sinclair, to hand in his and his Government's resignation. He decided against attending Parliament in the afternoon. Very properly, Greiner stepped well back to allow Fahey to take centre stage. His press secretary later revealed that the former Premier cried on "that awful Wednesday". When interviewed after the Court of Appeal delivered its verdict, Greiner confirmed that he did.[43] It was an event remarkable for being unusual. But Greiner was not alone; a number of ministers and office staff were similarly moved. When Percy Allan ran into Kathryn Greiner he, too, broke into tears. He knew it would be back to "politics as normal": "we had all been spoilt" and it had been "the most exciting time in our lives".[44]

Kathryn recalled that Paul Keating was the first person to contact her husband when his resignation became public. The second was Alan

Jones. Later that evening Jones hosted a dinner at the Park Hyatt in Sydney. The Greiners were joined there by the Kaldors, the Websters and the Yabsleys for what became a bacchanalian feast. It was such a good night that those who attended have different recollections of who was actually there. Kathryn collected the table napkins as they all left and, probably wisely, has not made them available. The comments scrawled upon them caused great hilarity because they were highly defamatory.[45]

# Endnotes

1  ICAC, *Report*.

2  *Ibid.*, pp. 53-4. See chs 7 and 9 for his consideration and rejection of any proceedings against Metherell, Humphry and Hazzard.

3  *Ibid.*, ch. 4.

4  *Ibid.*, p. v.

5  *Ibid.*, pp. 74-6. For Temby's findings regarding Moore, see p. 79.

6  *Ibid.*, pp. 63-4.

7  For Kathryn's account of his reaction, see *Sunday Telegraph*, 21 June 1992.

8  Interview: Greiner, 17 February 2010.

9  Transcript, ICAC, Greiner Papers.

10  Transcript, ICAC, Greiner Papers. For newspaper coverage, see esp. *SMH*, 20 June 1992.

11  *Port Macquarie News*, 22 June 1992.

12  *SMH*, 23 June 1992. Greiner does not recall them having a conversation, let alone what was said. Interview: Greiner 17 February 2010.

13  Baird was able to prove he was not one of the ministers who contacted the journalist. Interview: Baird, 3 January 2012.

14  *DTM*, 20 June and *SMH*, 22 June 1992; Interview: Baird, 3 January 2012. Commenting on the Yabsley statement – "If Nick Greiner goes, I go too" – Collins (*Bear Pit*, p. 201) wrote: "[u]nkind souls quipped that this was too good an offer to refuse."

15  Transcript, ICAC, Greiner Papers; *Port Macquarie News*, 22 June 1992.

16  *Sun-Herald*, 21 June 1992.

17  For Kathryn's comments to journalists, see *Sunday Telegraph*, 21 June 1992 and Gleeson *et al.*, *An Act of Corruption?*, pp. 190-1. Bannon had bolstered his minority government by giving two Labor Independents jobs as Speaker and Chairman of Committees respectively.

18  Davey, *Nationals*, p. 320.

19  ICAC, Greiner Papers. For Murray's rendition of this advice, see Gleeson *et al.*, *An Act of Corruption?*, pp. 191-2.

20  *Sun-Herald* and *Sunday Telegraph*, 21 June and *SMH*, 22 June 1992.

21  *Sunday Telegraph* and *Sun-Herald*, 21 June and *SMH*, 22 June 1992.

22  *AFR*, *Age*, and *SMH*, 22 June 1992.

23  *Newcastle Herald*, 22 June 1992.

[24] Collins, *Bear Pit*, p. 202; Gleeson *et al.*, *An Act of Corruption?*, pp. 194-5. Malcolm Kerr agreed with the Collins interpretation. Interview: Kerr, 24 April 2012. It may, or may not be important, but the evening is not fixed in the memory of two of the significant participants. Interviews: Pickering, 13 July 2011; Baird, 3 January 2012.

[25] Minter Ellison to Premier, 22 June 1992, ICAC, Greiner Papers.

[26] ICAC, Greiner Papers.

[27] *Ibid.*

[28] For the text of Metherell's statement, see *SMH*, 23 June 1992.

[29] Minutes of Management Committee (handwritten version), 22 June 1992, LPA, ML, MSS 7205/18.

[30] Collins, *Bear Pit*, p. 203.

[31] Conference Report, 23 June 1992, ICAC, Greiner Papers. For another account of the meeting and of its immediate aftermath, see Gleeson *et al.*, *An Act of Corruption?*, pp. 207-12.

[32] *DTM*, 27 June 1992.

[33] ICAC, Greiner Papers.

[34] Interview: Greiner, 17 February 2010.

[35] Interviews: Photios, 21 April 2006 and Pickering, 13 July 2011; Collins, *Bear Pit*, pp. 206-7.

[36] ICAC, Greiner Papers. The planner was reinstated by the Industrial Relations Commission which criticised ICAC for reaching conclusions based on insufficient evidence and for getting the facts wrong.

[37] ICAC, Greiner Papers.

[38] Interview: Pickering, 13 July 2011.

[39] Collins, *Bear Pit*, p. 207. Baird does not remember this conversation with Greiner or Collins but has since said that his wife does recall him telling her the story Collins recounted. Personal communication: Baird, 9 January 2012.

[40] Interview: Kortlang, 12 July 2011; Gleeson *et al.*, *An Act of Corruption?*, pp. 217-18.

[41] For a transcript of the press conference, see *SMH*, 25 June 1992.

[42] For Collins' account of the events of 24 June, see *Bear Pit*, pp. 204-9.

[43] *DTM*, 11 July and *Sunday Telegraph*, 23 August 1992.

[44] Interview: Allan 14 September 2011.

[45] Interviews: Kathryn Greiner, 29 March 2011, and Robert Webster, 15 September 2011; personal communications: Michael Yabsley, 28 June and 2 July and Alan Jones, 12 December 2012.

# 19

# Vindicated

The ABC had arranged a live telecast of proceedings in the Legislative Assembly on Wednesday afternoon 24 June. Greiner's resignation in the morning had turned the occasion into an anti-climax. Yet for a week, Greiner, ICAC and Fahey's new ministry and its outlook remained a subject of discussion on radio, television and in the press, overshadowed as a news item only by the accidental death of a young Penrith rugby league player. In those seven days, bordered at each end by two parliamentary debates, the motives and actions of all the main participants in the Metherell affair were thoroughly dissected and assessed according to political perspective or notions of what seemed important.

The sitting of the Legislative Assembly on the afternoon of 24 June provided the opportunity for some of the key figures to vent their feelings and rehearse their arguments which they repeated, elaborated and refined in the following days.[1] The Government speakers were sombre – Fahey called it "the saddest day of my life" – and angry, though necessarily restrained by the need to keep the Independents onside. Michael Yabsley, however, having honoured his promise to resign from the ministry, was unmuzzled: the Independents were "political offal", "a new form of political scum", "pious sanctimonious individuals", and "the political dregs"; Clover Moore "comes cheap" and was a "feral cat" who had struck a deal over fixed-term parliaments so that she could "stick her greasy little paw into the superannuation till".

The Opposition exploded in righteous indignation, partly out of frustration because the Greiner resignation had averted a baton change. Carr and his Deputy Leader, Dr Andrew Refshauge, brazenly cast the first stone as they laid into "jobs for the boys". The Independents had so much to say each required an extension of time. Clover Moore responded angrily to Yabsley's slurs and, of the three, was by far the most coherent. All were at once "comfortable" (Hatton's word) about what they had done and yet very defensive. Hatton surprised many by asserting that attacks on Temby and ICAC amounted to attacks on Hatton himself. Macdonald surprised no one by saying it had been left to the Independents "to act as the conscience of this place".

The fourth Independent made an intriguing speech. Tony Windsor said he continued to believe that Greiner and Tim Moore had been "morally wrong", and would eventually have to resign. He had rung Greiner on the Tuesday morning to urge him to stand aside during the Court hearing. While the Premier remained uncertain about how the other Independents would react to this action, Windsor said he knew "those people". They would see the fairness of such a proposal and not support a no-confidence motion if the Premier stood aside while the Court heard his application. Windsor now recognised his knowledge of them "was seriously deficient". For him, "Hatton the hypocrite" had "lost all credibility in relation to justice and corruption", Macdonald and Clover Moore had been driven by the media, and all three members of the "Independent party" had breached the "fair go" principle. Their actions were also "morally wrong". Windsor posed a question which was worrying him. Given the Temby decision, had he, Windsor, been guilty of corrupt conduct in using his position to secure concessions from the Greiner Government?

Next day, 25 June, it was the turn of the commentators and the editorialists. Two words – "irony" and "tragedy" – were popular in describing or explaining what had happened. "Irony", because Greiner had been brought down by his own creation; and "tragedy", because he was obviously not personally corrupt, had run a clean government and, in the words of the *Sydney Morning Herald,* was "the most competent Premier NSW (was) likely to have for a very long time". It was tempting to invoke Greek or Shakespearean tragedy. The play had come to its inevitable end because of the leading man's fatal flaw. Either he was an "unpolitician politician" who was insensitive to political reality, or was so convinced of his own virtue he assumed that honourable ends justified dodgy means.[2] The more prosaic focussed on the former Premier's own responsibility for his fall and the consequences of compromising his own high standards. The *SMH* shared out the responsibility. Greiner may have "blundered into a form of technical corruption" but, to "their great discredit", the Independents had cut him down before Temby's "technical point" could be tested in the courts.[3]

Journalists with an interest in the economy and financial management generally regretted Greiner's demise. Ross Gittins said he "should be remembered as the best economic manager this State has had". The former Premier had challenged the assumption of his predecessors that "good economic management meant letting sleeping inefficiencies lie". He had also saved NSW from the financial disasters of the Labor States and of Robin Gray in Tasmania. The critics had made so much of his rare lapse with the Eastern Creek fiasco – "a modest waste of money . . . compared with the populist stunts his predecessors got up to" – because everyone now expected so much better of him.[4] Paddy McGuinness described Greiner as "the best failed premier NSW has ever had, and a far better Premier than any of those who retired voluntarily".[5] McGuinness listed many of Greiner's achievements: the reforms in the education system which were "necessary and desirable" for all of Metherell's "blundering"; the reforms of the public sector, in industrial relations, and in financial management; and his commitment to co-operative federalism and, after the 1991 election, to the most radical reforms of the system of government in NSW since 1856. McGuinness concluded by suggesting that Greiner's "greatest gift" to NSW was to ensure that the next State Labor Government "will be the first really honest one in our history".

Friends rallied behind the former Premier. Tony Berg, his Sydney University and Harvard contemporary and, in 1992, the Managing Director of Macquarie Bank, noted how NSW was leading Australia in micro-economic reform. Rodney Adler of FAI said the Greiner Government was very competent and visionary. Nick Farr-Jones and John Quayle, the general manager of the NSW Rugby League, both spoke out, with Quayle commenting that Metherell and not the Premier had "let the team down". Kortlang said that, whereas Greiner had been brought down by "three non-entities which history will give no names . . . history will see him as a great premier". Even the acting head of the NSW Aboriginal Land Council, who admitted having had "moments" with the former Premier, said "we had no problems with him" at the time of his departure. Others were less well-disposed. Harry Herbert of the NSW Council of Social Services spoke of too many cuts; Pam Simons of the Women's Electoral Lobby said Greiner had not done much for women; and Jeff Angel of the Total Environment Centre claimed that Greiner's final act on the environment – the Resource Management Package – amounted to a complete surrender to the National Party's anti-environment approach.

Greiner's side of politics was understandably distraught, angry or effusive, stressing his role as a reformer and a pacesetter. John Hewson described Greiner's premiership as "one of extraordinary achievement", though Hewson was obviously relieved by his departure. Jeff Kennett, expecting to defeat the discredited Kirner Government at the imminent Victorian election and looking forward to working with Greiner, called his resignation "an absolute tragedy" and declared Greiner "is not corrupt, has never been corrupt and will never be corrupt." Ray Groom, the Premier of Tasmania, stressed how Greiner had introduced much-needed reforms which had since been adopted throughout Australia. Peter King expected Greiner to be vindicated by the Court of Appeal while his reputation as a reformer and as a first-class administrator would stay untarnished.

Many on the other side of politics also spoke warmly of the fallen

Premier. The former Labor Prime Minister, Bob Hawke, joined the current one, Paul Keating, in sending a message of sympathy. Both men spoke out publicly in Greiner's support. Hawke wrote a piece for the *Sun-Herald* on 28 June to say: "Nick Greiner is not a corrupt man . . . the application of this word to this man is nothing less than a tragedy". He also suggested that Australia had "reached a remarkably parlous condition" if an act of political stupidity could attract "the tag of corruption". Joan Kirner said Greiner had run a clean and "reasonably efficient" Government and that history would regard him as a good leader. Although she disagreed with him on a number of privatisation and social justice issues, "on the national level Nick Greiner made a major contribution to treating this country as a country that should be governed nationally". Wayne Goss called Greiner's resignation "a real loss to Australian politics". He later told a luncheon in Brisbane on 15 July that "Nick Greiner is not corrupt", and his "forced resignation is a loss to NSW and I think also to Australian politics". The country has "a serious problem" if political leaders of such ability and integrity "are driven from office by lowest common denominator public debate". In effect, Goss had criticised ICAC, his Labor counterpart, Bob Carr, the three Independent MPs and the media. He also aligned himself firmly with one of Greiner's principal arguments. In seeking what Temby had condemned as "dark and self-interested" party advantage, Greiner was doing no more than "what politicians do each day at the office".[6]

Both Houses revisited the issue on 30 June and 1 July. Carr moved a vote of no-confidence in the Government, a principal effect of which was to enable the three non-aligned Independents to ascend yet another moral peak. By rejecting options which would have caused chaos, by rescuing the Greiner Government from its self-created crisis, and by now preserving the Fahey Government, the Independents were seeking to maintain the stability of government. Macdonald came closest to spelling out the implication: the three Independents had saved the triple-A rating. As Hatton would later tell the hundreds of letter writers who sent him mixed responses to his actions, to do nothing would have led to "havoc and instability".[7]

## Awaiting the final judgment

Chief Justice Gleeson and Justices Mahoney and Priestley of the Supreme Court, sitting as a Court of Appeal, began hearing the Greiner and Moore applications on 30 June. A "relaxed-looking" Greiner took a seat behind Roger Gyles, QC. The former Premier may have been in unfamiliar surroundings but he knew one face from his Riverview days. Murray Gleeson had adjudicated debates in which the young Nick was a participant, and Greiner remembered him as the one who had probably voted for his team when they lost the final of the GPS debating competition. Greiner heard Gyles and then Chester Porter, appearing for Tim Moore, contend that ICAC should not stamp conduct as "corrupt" when it would not be so found by any court of law. Gyles said the Temby finding was "odious", and Porter called it "ridiculous" and, employing a favourite Greiner word, "nonsense".[8] The former Premier left the court room confident of being cleared.

The graduate of the Harvard Business School was not about to sit at home and brood while waiting for the Court's decision. He was already considering his business options. Ms Moore of Cruikshank Management Resources, an executive employment agency, was pessimistic about his prospects. She thought Greiner would have to rely on "jobs for the boys" to find a suitable position in the private sector. His excellent tertiary qualifications and obvious suitability for a position as a CEO would not be sufficient. "Unless he's got well-placed friends he's going to find it extremely difficult to get a job." She knew of many who were losing positions in the $120,000 plus bracket and were not securing comparable re-employment. Reading this article, a less secure man might have thought he would be forever haunted by persons surnamed "Moore". Serenella Tonello of Drake Executive Services scoffed at the negativity of Cruikshank Management Resources. Greiner may be "a naive politician" but he was not afraid of hard work, he inspired loyalty which "is the true mark of a corporate leader", had proved "able to effect change and make decisions", and whichever company secured him would be better off for doing so.[9]

A first step was to acquire office accommodation in the City. Greiner moved into the tenth floor of 139 Macquarie Street. Previously occupied by Ted Pickering as Police Minister, his new suite of offices overlooked the Botanical Gardens and the Harbour and provided a clear view of the Sydney Heads. The next step was to open a file labelled "The Afterlife", and Greiner began filling it with a comprehensive assessment of expected earnings and outgoings. The file includes a legal document provided by the Premier's Department conferring entitlements for life: a taxpayer-funded office and two staff, a car and a driver, 12 first class domestic air trips each year for two, 12 air trips each year for two within NSW, and free national rail travel as well as postage and telephone expenses.[10] Greiner was well-positioned to launch a business career.

On 6 July he had lunch with Ervin Graf. Born and educated in Hungary, and holding an architecture degree, Graf had taken Miklós Greiner's route from Budapest to Bratislava and Vienna in 1949. The Greiners and the Grafs might well have done business in Budapest because Graf's father was a timber retailer. Ervin was initially rejected by the Australian migration authorities because they were looking for tradesmen, not architects. He re-defined himself as a bricklayer and arrived in Sydney in 1950, founded a company in 1952 which became Stocks and Holdings, and built homes, offices and shopping centres. Following a couple more meetings after 6 July – Graf thought Nick Greiner had "a very good mind" and was "wasted in politics" – the former Premier joined Graf's board as Deputy Chairman.[11] A second and more satisfying career in business was under way.

Janet Mahon had to white-out most of the entries in her employer's appointment diary for the weeks immediately following his resignation. The gaps were quickly filled. The entries included many games of squash,

as well as visits to the Opera House accompanied by Kathryn. Greiner
had meetings, lunches and dinners with business contacts, and with the
new Premier and former ministerial colleagues. He met frequently with
Sturgess, Allan and Humphry. Other engagements included sessions
with Rod McGeoch, the CEO of the Olympic Bid; a hastily-arranged
private dinner at Circular Quay with Jeff and Felicity Kennett; a lunch
with John Hewson at Machiavelli's in Clarence Street where the elite
could meet and be seen; two weekend trips to Coolangatta to stay in a
unit owned by Peter Charlton of the Liberal Party's 500 Club; a farewell
barbecue for his staff in Koora Avenue; and a farewell lunch for Ken
Hooper at Parliament House. Two days before his meeting with Graf,
and accompanied by his father, Kathryn and Justin, all guests of the
Chairman of the Trustees of the SCG, Greiner saw the Wallabies defeat
the All Blacks. In Brisbane a fortnight later he watched the Wallabies add
the Bledisloe Cup to the world crown they won the year before. On 24
July he flew to London. Neil Pickard, the NSW Agent-General, soon to
be summoned home by Fahey, sent a car to Heathrow to take Greiner to
the Dorchester Hotel. His principal destination, however, was Barcelona
and the Olympic Games where he was part of the team negotiating for
Sydney to host the Games in 2000. It was not quite the frenetic pace of
the Premier's Office but Greiner was fully occupied as he waited for the
Court's verdict.

**Cleared**

The Court of Appeal handed down its verdict on Friday 21 August. All
three judges agreed with the Commissioner that Greiner and Moore had
shown "partiality" over the Metherell appointment which constituted
corruption under section 8 of the Act. But Gleeson, CJ, and Priestley,
JA, determined that, because Temby had found that the two men had
acted within the known standards of honesty and integrity, he could not
possibly find grounds for dismissal under section 9. They could not,
therefore, have acted corruptly within the meaning of the Act. Temby's

finding was made "without or in excess of jurisdiction". Chief Justice
Gleeson said that Temby had approached the question of corruption as
a matter "to be determined by his personal and subjective opinion" when
he should have applied "objective standards established and recognised
by law", and he had failed to spell out his criteria for reasonable
grounds for dismissal. Justice Priestley observed how Temby had tried
to introduce new standards to justify dismissal, and drew attention
to Greiner's statement in introducing the ICAC legislation that it was
"intended to enforce only those standards established or recognised by
law". Mahoney, JA, dissented, arguing that the Commissioner had every
right to reach the conclusions he did and was not required to provide
the details of his reasoning. Mahoney added, however, that he would not
have concluded as Temby had done. Further,

> The description of the conduct of Mr Greiner and Mr Moore as
> corrupt is not a description which, in the ordinary and proper use
> of language, would be applied to it . . . The injustice arises because
> the Act applies corrupt conduct to conduct which, in the ordinary
> meaning of the word [,] is not corrupt.[12]

On the morning the Court delivered its judgment, the Greiners were
present at the Sydney Town Hall to see their daughter take out first prize
in the State finals of the Plain English Speaking Award valued at $500.
Kara's topic was "Coming back to Earth with a thud". The *SMH* had
sponsored the Award, prompting her mother to remark it was "quite the
best thing the *Herald* has ever done". Greiner briefly left the audience
to take the telephone call which gave him the news which he passed on
to Kara as she waited to give her presentation. The two embraced and
Greiner was later heard to remark that the "goodies have won". While
Kara left the Town Hall to celebrate at McDonald's, the Greiner parents
joined Neville Wran, among others, for a lunch hosted by Alan Jones.
Greiner was abrupt in the face of the media stampede which preceded
the lunch. He felt vindicated. The Court had found Temby's finding to
be "absolutely wrong", suggestions of corrupt conduct on his part were

"totally . . . nonsensical", and the Court had delivered "in legal terms what public opinion and common sense decided two months ago".[13]

Ian Temby held a press conference soon after the verdict was announced. He regretted the majority decision, understood it to mean that ministers were placed "in a specially privileged class as opposed to all others in the public sector", and was considering an appeal to the High Court, although he was concerned about the public expense. Temby thought it a matter of interpretation whether the Court had removed the label of "corruption" imposed on Greiner and Moore. He declined to offer them any apology. After all, they should be aware "that nothing we did was aimed at them personally". He had always found Mr Greiner to be "a very reasonable man" but would not be astonished to learn he was angry. The Commissioner hoped, disingenuously as it turned out, that any anger "won't last into perpetuity". Perhaps the Act should be amended to provide for a finding of "improper" actions which fell short of "corrupt" conduct. Perhaps, too, Parliament should require no more of ICAC than to reach a finding on the facts, and it may have been preferable for him to have said so in his Report. Temby was in no mood, however, to make too many concessions. Besides, he had already found a way of excusing or minimising his "error": "we were sailing in uncharted waters and the judges are saying that in a legal sense we took the wrong course."[14]

Two of the three Independents – Hatton and Macdonald – said they would take the same action again, insisting they had acted on the facts of the case and not on the ICAC Report. Greiner understood them to mean they would have demanded his resignation even if Temby had cleared him of any wrongdoing. This position was one of "unbridled arrogance" and "you have to be certifiable to take that line".[15] Either the former Premier did not know, or had forgotten about, Hatton's computer-assisted advice. Clover Moore said the Court decision had not changed the facts. The two men had to resign "because of their actions – whether labelled corrupt or improper".[16] The Opposition Leader was equally recalcitrant. Carr wanted the Court of Appeal's decision challenged in the High Court. In any event, no technical finding altered "the essential facts of the case": a job was created illegally to induce Metherell to quit Parliament. The Court of Appeal had upheld Temby's finding: "the former Premier acted corruptly in the Metherell affair."[17]

Wal Murray urged a major overhaul of ICAC, accused Temby of "crucifying" innocent people, savagely attacked "Mr Carr and his three stooges", and called on the non-aligned Independents to apologise and to consider resigning from Parliament. He especially singled out Hatton for his refusal to back down when he had been "proven wrong". Neville Wran refused to be drawn on how he felt about Greiner but said he had "very strong views about Mr Temby". Those who sent Greiner telegrams of congratulation included Philip Ruddock, a Liberal moderate and a Federal MP, Charles Blunt, the former Federal NP Leader, Virginia Chadwick's office, and George Souris of the State National Party.[18] The Sydney press was now firmly on his side. The *Herald* disagreed with Carr: the Court of Appeal had removed the stigma of corruption from Greiner and Moore. One editorial declared that two "good men" had "deserved better treatment" from the Independents. A second editorial announced that "(t)he public rightly considers Mr Greiner is not corrupt and should never have been labelled so". After unmercifully pursuing and excoriating Greiner, the *DTM* discovered that more safeguards were needed to protect individuals and to prevent "the bruting [sic] around of allegations" which might not withstand judicial questioning. Both the Sydney papers looked to the parliamentary oversight committee to press ahead with a review of ICAC, and most of the media seemed to think that the future of the Commission was now the issue.

Harry M. Miller had already signed the Greiners for speaking engagements, with Kathryn about to start an "exciting" career in radio and television. The Greiners agreed to speak without remuneration on Channel Nine's *60 Minutes* television program on Sunday.[19] The former Premier told the program that Temby's Report was "appalling" and "morally and intellectually bankrupt" and that ICAC and its Commissioner had suffered the most damage from the Metherell affair. Future commissioners would need to exercise "common sense" because if a finding "doesn't make sense to your average 15 year-old then you have to think twice about recommending it". Kathryn acknowledged that she had indeed advised her husband against appointing Metherell when first told of the plan (on Sunday 17 February), and regretted not having made more of a stand over the issue. Both asserted they had no plans hereafter to take up political careers. Asked if she had ever contemplated entering politics, Kara responded: "I might be dumb but I'm not insane."[20]

On the same day Greiner had an interview with Errol Simper of the *Australian*.[21] He felt vindicated and was unrepentant. Yes, he had committed "a major political error" which had hurt his party, his Government and himself, but he had nothing to apologise for "in a moral and ethical sense". Once again, and with feeling, he sought to place the episode in perspective. This time he directed his comments to the political stability which Wall Street bankers admired about NSW and which depended on the operations of the party system. That system would not work if "pedantic, legalistic things" were used to regulate everything in minute detail. He had, for party advantage and stability, returned the seat of Davidson to the voters. Wal Murray had got it right: at worst, he had been caught speeding. Temby and the Independents had, therefore, set a very low level for "mortal sins". Greiner thought Temby showed "a lack of grace" in his reaction to the Court's decision. The Independents had denied him natural justice and, although they carried on about the supremacy of Parliament, had declined to let Parliament deal with his case. Carr was continuing "to tell lies about me". But Greiner was not "bitter and twisted". Temby and Metherell were the only individuals to have suffered whereas the events of the last two months "had brought the family together". Yet, even as Greiner was speaking in "almost academic terms", Simper detected an inner tension. He saw "a burning in his brown eyes, which bespeaks of something approaching venom".

On Monday 24 August Greiner conducted an hour-long chat at a press conference held in the Premier's media room.[22] The journalists accepted he had either buried or moved on from most of the bitterness. In his own words, Greiner was "relaxed with the world". He would speak to Metherell if he met him in the street, though would not invite him home for dinner (someone should have asked the same question in relation to Temby). Greiner spent most of the time either talking about his achievements or expressing regrets about policy mistakes. His major achievements included raising the accountability and integrity of the main public institutions in NSW and his work with Bob Hawke on a new federalism. He had not followed Fraser and Wran in doing little except those things which lifted popularity ratings. Peter Collins received another serve for being the odd man out in his Government. Greiner regretted the failure to move further on health policy, especially in not establishing contracting arrangements for medical and non-medical services and reorganising health boards. He did acknowledge, however, that extensive and rapid change would have chewed up the political capital which Metherell was already spending in the Education portfolio. He wished the State Bank had been sold in 1988, he had changed the school bus pass system, and managed the Eastern Creek motorcycle track much better.

Some matters and some people still riled him: the positions taken by the three Independents and much of the media, the lack of support from the Liberal Party between 19 and 24 June, Carr's comments about him – and Ian Temby. Although he bore no grudges against the Liberal Party, he had hoped for more support and more robust responses from his parliamentary colleagues. He pointedly praised the National Party as "a pillar of strength for the Coalition". Referring to the Commissioner's comment that the Court of Appeal decision meant ICAC had to treat ministers differently, Greiner let fly at Temby:

> It is a cop-out to say I [Temby] might have stuffed it up but the legislation made me do it. . . . With the Act as it is Mr Temby

> should have produced a different report and the ICAC would be
> a much stronger organisation for it. It is obvious the legislation
> applied to ministers, and it ought to . . . and it would not have
> required someone of Mr Temby's legal nous to see that.

Greiner thought that ICAC might work more effectively if it focussed solely on being a fact-finding organisation, more like a royal commission. He also threatened to take legal action for defamation against Bob Carr for his remarks made in the wake of the Court decision.

Most published or reported statements shared Greiner's view that the Court of Appeal's majority decision amounted to a complete vindication. A few were not so sure. Although the *Canberra Times* thought the decision removed the "slur" of being "technically corrupt", it did not leave Greiner and Moore "without a stain upon their character or upon their judgment".[23] Some lawyers and law academics, especially those with an interest in administrative law, were bemused by the majority decision. They believed that tribunals normally exercised discretionary powers in the course of reaching decisions; they chose the standards to apply, and subjectivity was expected. One persistent critic noted how the Court required the Commissioner to apply legal objective standards yet itself failed to identify those standards. Indeed, the Court's own decision, in common with Temby's, was both objective and subjective.[24] Other commentators focussed on the issue of the former Premier's non-traditional involvement in a public service appointment. It was argued that a Public Service Board, similar in form to the one Greiner abolished in 1988, would have protected the Premier from himself, and Humphry from the Premier's instruction, by standing in the way of the Metherell appointment.[25]

One week after the Court of Appeal announced its decision, and on the day Temby said that ICAC would not appeal against the Court's ruling,[26] the Liberal Party hosted a "Dinner of Appreciation" in honour of the Greiners at the Sydney Convention Centre, Darling Harbour. The Party took bookings for some 1,000 guests, collected $61,000, and engaged afterwards in its customary bickering, this time about the cost of the tickets and whether it had sought to profit from the function.[27] Alan Jones was the principal speaker at the dinner. He called it the opportunity "to salute a class act, Nick and Kathryn Greiner". Quoting Greiner's oft-repeated comment about not being a political animal, Jones expressed his regret that people never saw enough of "the real Nick Greiner". Greiner had entered politics because "he simply thought he could run the show better than others". To prove that he could, and did, Jones gave an account of Greiner's achievements in managing the State, referring at the same time to "one of Nick Greiner's manifest political weaknesses", namely, "his unpreparedness . . . to constantly sell the story of his extraordinary reform and success". Jones also praised Kathryn Greiner for her passion, her formidable mind and for the way she touched people.

This was also an occasion to settle some scores. Jones launched into "the opportunism and rank abuse of power" by the three Independents who commanded a vote in the electorate of 1.2 per cent. He observed how some of Greiner's colleagues had "turned to jelly" instead of defying the Independents. At this point some at the dinner might have looked sideways or lowered their heads. But ICAC was the principal target. The Temby Report was "a prostitution of truth, a defiance of logic, a betrayal of consistent argument and good people". The Court of Appeal had endorsed what Jones and others had said at the outset: the ICAC judgment was "without foundation in law, grossly manipulative of public opinion and in the end unjustifiably destructive of the political careers of two men".[28]

## Tidying up

The Government had agreed to pay Greiner's and Moore's costs and the Court of Appeal had awarded some costs to the plaintiffs but arguments continued into 1994 over who should be paying what amounts. An exasperated Greiner referred to one note he received as "today's episode of Blue Hills" and, on a later occasion, to an "appalling breach of faith" by the Government. His appeal costs amounted to $306,386-84 ($85,685 for Gyles, $73,900 for junior counsel and $146, 801-84 for Minter Ellison). There was confusion when a bill in excess of $390,000 was presented until it was discovered that Gyles' fees had been double counted. There was a further delay because the solicitors representing both sides could not agree on just how much the Government and ICAC should each contribute to Greiner's costs. The two bodies sought to protect their share of the taxpayers' enforced benevolence.

Greiner had instructed his solicitors to demand a retraction and an apology from Carr, and a letter was sent to Carr's solicitors. While Minter Ellison agreed that the Opposition Leader's statements were false and defamatory, they cautioned against taking any further action. Carr would not eat humble pie and retract, the matter could take three years before it reached trial, the jury would be a lottery, the costs could be huge, and Carr might, if indemnified by the Labor Party, string it out to increase Greiner's costs. Heeding this advice, Greiner decided not to proceed.[29]

Meanwhile, the Parliamentary Joint Committee (PJC), which had reacted to the shocks and after-shocks of the Metherell Affair by undertaking a review of the ICAC legislation, had produced a discussion paper which identified ten issues for consideration. Of them, three were particularly important to Greiner: the definition of corrupt conduct; the labelling of conduct by individuals as corrupt; and the standards to be applied by the Commission. The PJC subsequently called for submissions, conducted hearings and interviews, and delivered a report with recommendations for change in May 1993.[30]

Malcolm Kerr, the Committee Chairman, had sent ICAC's 48-page submission[31] along with all the other principal documents to Greiner. Greiner did not respond with a formal submission nor did he appear before the PJC. Instead, he sent two letters to Kerr in November 1992.[32] In the first – dated 5 November – he attacked Temby's argument that it was "essential" for ICAC to have the power "to make findings of fact, state reasons for those findings, and where necessary describe the conduct in ordinary language", and for it to have the power "to state opinions that others consider prosecution, disciplinary action or dismissal". Greiner told Kerr that it was "perhaps unsurprising" he rejected ICAC's "amazing request for more (untrammelled) power to express its opinion *about past behaviour*" [emphases and brackets in the original]. ICAC's expressions of opinion, in his experience alone, made it dangerous to trust commissioners. They were human and therefore driven by prejudices and by the media. They should be restricted to making general recommendations and denied the right to make personal judgments which could not be appealed and were unrestrained by established law and practice. Temby was wrong in trying to set ICAC outside the law and to apply standards retrospectively as he did in the Metherell case. ICAC should find on questions of fact alone, and leave it to other authorities to take follow-up action. Further, commissioners should not be allowed to act as Temby had done in publishing parts of the Metherell diaries. Individuals – Greiner excluded himself – should not be defamed by releasing material irrelevant to the main investigation.

On the issue of partiality, Greiner said ministers in all governments allocated resources "on a 'political' basis that is inconsistent with the avowedly impartial, technical advice of the bureaucracy". Because the three judges of the Court of Appeal considered he had shown partiality over the Metherell appointment, thus meeting the definition of corrupt conduct as set out in section 8 of the *ICAC Act*, Greiner argued that the Parliament should decide whether any opprobrium – other than a "political" one – should attach to this process. If the answer was "No", which ought to be the case, then Parliament should consider amending section 8. It continued to annoy him that Temby had not only committed the fundamental legal mistake as identified by the Court of Appeal; he had made "a gross error of judgment and commonsense" on the issue of partiality.[33]

Before and soon after Greiner wrote this letter, Temby and Adrian

Roden (of the North Coast investigation), on behalf of ICAC, exchanged arguments with Athol Moffitt, a former Royal Commissioner and a retired judge of the NSW Supreme Court, and Justice Clarke of the current Supreme Court. Moffitt and Clarke wanted to restrict ICAC to findings of "primary facts". Roden and Temby wanted ICAC to have the power to express opinions in "ordinary language" about the conduct it was investigating. Although the transcript of the Temby-Roden appearance before the PJC highlights developing strains in the relationship between ICAC and both sides of the Parliament, all sides agreed about one thing: a satisfactory and working definition of "corrupt conduct" could not be achieved. There was even broad though not unanimous agreement in favour of repealing section 9. But the sticking point remained: should ICAC be expressing opinions or applying labels.[34]

Greiner was obviously familiar with the arguments when he wrote again to Kerr on 12 November. He accepted that the technical definition of corrupt conduct was unproductive, could not usefully be amended and should, therefore, be dumped. But ICAC's argument for more and unfettered power to express the Commissioner's personal views remained "totally unacceptable", and even putting the idea forward "demonstrates the delusions of the ICAC as to its role and standing". On the other hand, he now agreed that limiting ICAC to finding primary facts was "probably too restrictive". ICAC should be able to recommend changes in the law to apply in the future where, for example, it found there was no unlawful behaviour in a particular case. Such an outcome would be preferable to ICAC's preferred option of finding that, although there was no unlawful conduct, the conduct itself was "improper".[35] The PJC agreed with Greiner to the extent of recommending that ICAC be required to apply objective standards recognised by law in any findings made about named individuals. The parliamentary committee also confirmed that ICAC was a fact-finding investigative body and asked the NSW Law Reform Commission to advise on what was meant by "primary facts", and whether there should be a review mechanism for a finding on facts.[36]

Greiner next contributed to discussions about ICAC when he spoke out in May 1994 after the Independents and the Labor Opposition combined to call for a royal commission to investigate police corruption. The subsequent appointment of the Wood Royal Commission into the NSW Police Service has been described as one of John Hatton's "important achievements".[37] Yet ICAC, which Hatton had strongly defended in June 1992 in registering another "achievement" – the destruction of a Premier – and which he said in March 1994 had become the institution he "had longed to see established" in NSW,[38] had all the powers necessary to conduct such an investigation. Greiner could reasonably ask why Commissioner Temby never exercised these powers and never pursued a known and major example of corruption outside of the allegations that some police consorted with known criminals. In Greiner's view, Hatton and the Labor Party had compounded the damage caused by Temby's failures.[39]

Greiner had correctly predicted that ICAC and Temby himself would suffer as a result of the Metherell affair. The Fahey Government was in no hurry to make ICAC more effective. On 4 March 1994, at his final meeting with the PJC, Temby said it was "disappointing and frustrating" that the Act remained unchanged. At the previous meeting, held on 15 October 1993, Temby feared that the Committee was treating the Commission as "an adversary".[40] Already criticised for not acting in some areas or pushing too hard in others, for putting on "show trials", engaging in media stunts and allegedly for being at times incompetent, ICAC and Temby had become larger and easier targets after the Commissioner handed down his findings on Greiner and Moore. The Coalition MPs were not alone on the PJC in failing to hide hostility. Even though Temby could produce survey results confirming that ICAC had public recognition and support, which Greiner in 1988 had hoped would be the case, neither side of politics was enthusiastic about the institution, neither side rewarded its first Commissioner with a seat on the bench, and many Sydney lawyers and civil libertarians remained generally unwelcoming.

# Endnotes

[1]  For the debate on Fahey's motion to note the ICAC Report, see *NSWPD,* Third Series, vol. 230, pp. 4127-94. For the debate on the no-confidence motion on 30 June-1 July, see *ibid.,* vol. 231, pp. 4763-95; 4821-62; 5194-5231.

[2]  Shaun Carney, *Age,* and Paddy McGuinness, *Australian,* 25 June 1992.

[3]  *Age* and *SMH,* 25 June 1992.

[4]  *SMH,* 25 June 1992.

[5]  *Australian,* 25 June 1992.

[6]  *SMH,* 18 July 1992.

[7]  Hatton to Robert Vincin, 14 July 1992, ICAC, Greiner Papers.

[8]  *Australian,* 14-5 July 1992.

[9]  *DTM,* 25 June 1992.

[10]  Neville Wran and, later, Bob Carr received similar benefits. Barry O'Farrell, as Premier, made the fair point that former Premiers, who were already well paid in the private sector, did not need the taxpayer to meet the full cost of their expenses. Greiner had voluntarily reduced his legal entitlement but the continuation of other benefits remains in contention. *SMH,* 26 October 2011 and 27 March 2013.

[11]  *SMH,* 25 August 1992.

[12]  This passage was quoted by ICAC's former counsel: M. H. Tobias, "Corrupt Conduct under the ICAC Act – An Overview", Institute of Criminology Seminar, 8 October 1992.

[13]  *SMH,* 22 August; *Weekend Australian,* 22/23 August 1992.

[14]  *Weekend Australian,* 22/23 August; *SMH,* 22 August 1992.

[15]  *Australian,* 25 August 1992.

[16]  *SMH,* 25 August 1992.

[17]  *SMH,* 22 August 1992.

[18]  ICAC, Greiner Papers.

[19]  *Sunday Telegraph,* 23 August 1992.

[20]  *Sun-Herald,* 23 August and *SMH,* 24 August 1992.

[21]  *Australian,* 24 August 1992.

[22]  *SMH, 25 August 1992.*

[23]  *Canberra Times*, 22 August 1992.

[24]  Margaret Allars, "In Search of Legal Objective Standards: The Meaning of Greiner v Independent Commission Against Corruption", *Current Issues in Criminal Justice*, vol. 6, no. 1, 1994, pp. 107-135; and Margaret Allars, *Administrative Law: Cases and Commentary*, Butterworths, Sydney, 1997. See also Peter McClellan, "Administrative Law and the Independent Commission Against Corruption", *Australian Institute of Administrative Law Forum*, No. 4, 1995, pp. 21-34. Temby favours the Allars view. Interview: Temby, 23 November 2011.

[25]  Barbara Page, "The Metherell Affair: Patronage and the Public Service", *Current Affairs Bulletin*, vol. 69, no. 3, 1992, pp. 27-8. See also John Nethercote's articles, *Canberra Times*, 23 July and 25 August 1992.

[26]  Instead of an appeal, Temby published a 21-page document which, although entitled *Second Report on Investigation into the Metherell Resignation and Appointment*, amounted to ICAC's response to criticism of its activities and positions.

[27]  Report to Management Committee, 18 September 1992, Management Committee Meeting, 18 September 1992, LPA, ML, MSS 7205/18.

[28]  Address by Alan Jones, 28 August 1992, Greiner Papers. A "citizens' dinner" was held two days later where Fahey proposed a toast which was seconded by Charles Curran of the Commission of Audit.

[29]  Patrick George to Greiner, 4 September and Greiner to George, 14 September 1988, ICAC, Greiner Papers.

[30]  For the review and the follow-up, see Marie Swain, "The Independent Commission Against Corruption: An Overview", NSW Parliamentary Library, Briefing Note, 018/94, 1994, p. 18ff., and Summary of Conclusions, Parliamentary Joint Committee, *Review of the ICAC Act*, May 1993.

[31]  ICAC, Submission to the Committee on ICAC: *Review of the ICAC Act*, October 1992, ICAC, Greiner Papers.

[32]  ICAC, Greiner Papers.

[33]  Greiner to Malcolm Kerr, 5 November 1992, ICAC, Greiner Papers. A (so far, unidentified) fax consisting of several pages arrived in Greiner's office the day after he sent this note raising a number of questions about Temby's behaviour before and during the hearings. For example, why did he take charge of an inquiry he had initiated and, to an extent, pre-judged? Why did he not disclose his previous association with Counsel Assisting who was an assistant Commonwealth DPP when Temby was the Commonwealth DPP? Why did he talk privately with Counsel Assisting before Clark

made his final and damaging submission? Greiner did not pursue these matters in correspondence.

[34] For the transcript, see NSW Parliament, *Evidence taken before the Committee on ICAC*, 9 November 1992.

[35] Greiner to Malcolm Kerr, 12 November 1992, ICAC, Greiner Papers.

[36] Summary of Conclusions, Parliamentary Joint Committee, *Review of the ICAC Act*, May 1993.

[37] Clune and Griffith, *Decision and Deliberation*, p. 542.

[38] Parliament of NSW, *Collation of Evidence*, 4 March 1994, p. 97.

[39] *Manly Daily*, 4 June 1994.

[40] Parliament of NSW, *Collation of Evidence of the Commissioner of the ICAC Mr Ian Temby QC*, 15 October 1993, p. 3. On the same page he referred to the fact that it was now 14 months since the Court of Appeal decision and expressed his disappointment that little had changed in relation to ministers and other constitutional office-holders.

# 20

# "The Afterlife"

Nick Greiner slipped easily enough into what he called "The Afterlife". Being pursued by the business community certainly helped. Within six months of leaving the premiership, Greiner was Deputy Chairman of the Stockland Property Trust Group, a director of Australian Stationery Industries Pty Ltd, Defiance Mills Ltd, Brian McGuigan Wines Ltd and QBE Insurance. He was also a consultant with Clayton Utz and Coopers & Lybrand.[1]

Greiner took on many more responsibilities in the following four years. Alex Mitchell, in the *Sun-Herald* of 24 November 1996, claimed Greiner sat on 38 boards. But Mitchell failed to notice that twelve were subsidiaries of QBE Insurance, five were subsidiaries of McGuigan wines, and some were his father's or his own family companies. Mitchell was not alone, however, in raising questions about Greiner's many directorships. "Nobby" Clark, the former CEO of the National Australia Bank and the Chairman of Coles Myer (Greiner had joined the board in 1993), expressed his concern during the company's annual general meeting in November 1996: "My personal view is that he is on too many boards but that's not Nick's view." *Crikey* listed Greiner's "impressive tally" on 28 April 2004 as eleven chairs, three deputy chairs, five directorships and six consultancies, and commented on his wealth and taxpayer-funded pension. Greiner later acknowledged that he probably took on too much in the years immediately after resigning the premiership. He could, however, point out that he stayed with many companies for long periods (he was with Stockland for 18 years), made a real contribution and was not there for decoration, was always being asked to join boards, and was never invited to step down.[2]

The former Premier had plenty to do, but there were now fewer tasks he was obliged to perform. He upgraded his surroundings and lifestyle. In 1993 the family moved from the North Shore to the Eastern Suburbs. They bought a house with a pool in Ocean Street, Woollahra, valued at a little under $1m. The change made sense because both parents were working in the city, and because Justin and Kara were attending the University of Sydney. Kathryn said they lived much the same life as in Wahroonga without the same, constant pressure. There were now free weekends, the Greiners could walk to cinemas or their favourite restaurants,[3] and there were more opportunities for the pastimes they had always enjoyed, such as skiing holidays in Europe and the United States.

Like so many former heads of government, Greiner remained "on call" for the media. Sometimes he re-entered the political arena without an invitation. On other occasions he volunteered thoughts ranging from support for community-based institutions about centralised government to the condemnation of "risk-averse" politics.[4] Yet, unlike many recently-retired leaders, and especially those who had retirement thrust upon them, he neither felt the need to be noticed, nor suffered from a "relevance deprivation syndrome". He also had the saving grace of what Kara called his "absurdist sense of humour". It is hard to imagine Fraser, Hawke or Keating issuing the kind of invitation Greiner sent to friends and former staff members in June 1994 for a reunion to mark "the Second Anniversary of Liberation".[5] Greiner remained unhappy, if not bitter, about leaving unfinished business and about the manner of his departure (though he might disavow it), but he was, in two respects, very fortunate: he had never regarded politics as a long-term career, and he retained a capacity to laugh at himself and at most of those around him.

His opinions were always direct. The *Australian* invited Greiner to write an article after Hewson lost the "unlosable" Federal election in March 1993. Wrongly criticised in the past for being "ideological",

Greiner argued that the Liberal Party should be aiming for the "acceptable median" rather than the "theoretical optimum"; that is, for "a healthy dose of pragmatism". In his Barton lecture of 1984 Greiner had attacked governments for bending to sectional interests. Hewson, he wrote, had turned this notion on its head by deliberately offending interest groups – the more powerful the better. John Howard did not escape attention. His much-vaunted *Future Directions* of 1989 reflected "a society that was and will not be again, rather than one that is and must be changed for the better". He had another crack when Howard returned as Federal Liberal Leader in January 1995. The recycled Howard was susceptible to wooing voters "who would not vote Labor under any circumstances".[6]

Awards and honours arrived in many forms after 1992. One of the most welcome was Greiner's appointment as Companion of the Order of Australia in the Queen's Birthday Honours List for 1994. The citation read: "In recognition of service to public sector reform and management and to the community." Asked if he had received sufficient recognition and vindication, Greiner said he felt no need for either. Gratification for him was acceptance by the business and professional communities, and the knowledge that the reforms he introduced in NSW were being applied around Australia by governments of both persuasions. His one regret about leaving politics was not being Premier when Sydney won the Olympic bid. He was especially pleased to accept an Australian honour because he felt "largely responsible" for dropping the Imperial Honours List in NSW. Wran had suspended it but Greiner, despite opposition from Cabinet colleagues, was the one who ended the system altogether, after he had recommended a knighthood for the NSW Governor, Sir David Martin.[7]

## Taking a sabbatical

There was one major, though temporary, disruption in the early years of the "afterlife". The Greiners had travelled together in September 1993 to participate in Sydney's bid for the 2000 Olympic Games. Kathryn learnt, while in transit in Bangkok, that her father had died. She flew home immediately. Family friends were shocked when her husband went on to Monte Carlo with the rest of the bid team. There he met the much younger Greta Thomas who had gone to Monaco as part of her job in public relations. Rumours of marital problems surfaced when Greiner and Thomas were photographed together in August 1994. The following January the stories became more prevalent after Greiner was seen skiing with Thomas in Aspen, Colorado. Kathryn said her radio commitments with 2UE had kept her in Sydney. When, a month later, a *DTM* reporter asked if his marriage was in trouble, Greiner called it a "stupid question" and said he would not "glorify it with an answer".

On Saturday, 8 April 1995, Ken Hooper issued a statement on behalf of both the Greiners: "Nick and Kathryn Greiner announce that after long and careful consideration, Nick has chosen to leave the marriage and there will be a trial separation." Hooper said that Kathryn was "devastated by the decision". Both parties recognised the impact on their children, family and friends and asked the media to respect their privacy. Greiner was relaxed about it all. He intended to "start a new life". Kathryn, meanwhile, flew out of Sydney with a close friend, Liz Storey, to stay at the Sheraton Mirage Resort in Port Douglas.[8] She was more than angry: "I was enraged". Asked about the story of throwing her husband's clothes into the street, she replied: "No, I did worse. But I'm not going to tell you."[9]

A few mutual friends believe that none of this would have happened if Clare Greiner had still been alive. Chris Greiner thought that, while his mother would have been "a fearsome person to deal with", and her views would have been respected, his brother was strong enough to continue on his course.[10] A worried Miklós Greiner had asked a few of his son's friends to dissuade him from moving out. They included Clive Powell who had written references for Greiner for the 1977 and 1980 pre-selections. Some acted without any prompting. Apart from anything else, they were appalled by the timing. Greiner had walked out a few months before Kathryn would be contesting elections for the Sydney City Council. Heading the Sydney Alliance, which had replaced the moribund, Liberal-aligned Civic Reform group, she was at one stage considered a good chance to defeat the incumbent Mayor, Frank Sartor. Friends noted how, after years of receiving his wife's loyal and indispensable support, the former Premier was not standing by her side. Yet the break itself was neither clean nor final. The two of them, in Kathryn's words, "hadn't emotionally left this marriage". They met for dinner and visits to the theatre. Greiner sent her 25 roses (24 red, one yellow) to celebrate their silver wedding anniversary on 1 August 1995. He supported her in the latter stages of the election campaign in which the Alliance won three of the seven Council seats and Kathryn headed Sartor on the primary vote only to lose the mayoralty on Labor Party preferences.[11]

After living apart for several months Greiner told his wife he did not think he had made the right decision. They began what was "a bit like a courting ritual all over again". Greiner returned to Ocean Street late in 1995 and, in time, an unbroken friendship grew into an "enriched" relationship. Justin, who once had dinner with Greta and his father, found it easier than his sister to adjust both to the break-up and to the renewal. Kara took much longer to forgive. Nick Greiner said later of the estrangement: "I suppose it was a mid-life crisis". Kathryn called it his "sabbatical" from the marriage. The rapprochement did not come to pass without some straight talking. A counsellor had advised Kathryn not to see herself as "a victim". She had built on that advice. So her husband returned to a marriage where there were different rules of engagement, where his wife was even more determined to have a diverse and full career, and where Greiner became more in touch with his feelings even as he did not find that "an easy discussion to have with myself".[12]

## Business

Nick Greiner became a very wealthy man during his "afterlife", although not everything he touched turned into platinum. Some ventures – for example, the dot com company BMC Media and the on-line retailer dStore – were failures. Another, the multi-faceted IAMA Ltd, an agric-business company which was eventually taken over by Wesfarmers, was too complicated to make workable. Perhaps his biggest "mistake", however, was to join the board of Coles Myer.

By 1995 the giant conglomerate, which took about 20 cents of every retail dollar spent in Australia, was engulfed by controversy. The mercurial Melbourne businessman, Solomon Lew, attracted unfavourable publicity when the board approved his elevation from Chairman to Executive Chairman. Questions were raised about sales of goods to Coles Myer by private companies managed by Lew and by his fellow director, the transport magnate Lindsay Fox. Coles Myer lost $18m in 1993-4 when it indemnified a shell company which had helped Lew survive a difficult financial situation. While the media and institutional investors called for Lew's head, Greiner – now Deputy Chairman – found himself caught in the middle of warring factions as he tried to broker a compromise on the composition of the board in time for the annual general meeting on 21 November 1995. What he called his "previous life" had relevance. Having experienced the "winner-take-all" in internal Liberal Party politics, he argued there was "a need for a board that works, not one made up of mates on one side or another". Greiner's preferred candidate to replace Solomon Lew as board chairman was rejected by the institutional investors who installed "Nobby" Clark. On top of this rebuff, some 80 per cent of the 4,500 shareholders present at the meeting voted against Greiner remaining on the board. He was targeted because of anger about the group's financial performance and because he was perceived as a defender of Solomon Lew. It was only a minor setback. The proxy votes carried him through, and he and Lew were appointed deputy chairmen.

Greiner encountered further trouble at the 1996 annual general meeting. Major shareholders formed a unity ticket to re-elect seven directors, including Lew and Greiner. The Myer family broke ranks and used its 8.5 per cent share block to vote against Greiner's re-appointment, even though a member of the family had earlier asked him whether he would accept the chairmanship. Two-thirds of the shareholders who attended the testy six-and-a-half hour meeting also opposed Greiner's re-election. Questions were raised about his many directorships. Greiner was also called to account for past "misjudgements", including the Metherell appointment. Asked whether he was chastened by the size of his negative vote, Greiner replied: "Your humour is obviously undiminished at this hour of the afternoon."

Interviewed in 2002, three years after he left Coles Myer, Greiner acknowledged that there was not "the quintessence of harmony" on the board, and that he did not get on well with Solomon Lew. He found the board and the company "dysfunctional", there was evidence of corruption and kick-backs, and the public and private cultures were "discordant". Earlier, in October 1995, he referred to Solomon Lew's Central European background. Greiner saw Lew as an entrepreneur who did deals and was very good at it – much, he might have added, like his own father. But Lew was not a "classic" or a "natural" public company chairman. Coles Myer itself was "a failed merger" which would not have been permitted by regulators in the 1990s. The merger had never worked and could never work, and Greiner felt an increasing sense of frustration in associating with what should have been a great Australian institution.[13]

Greiner had another very public, controversial appointment as Chairman of British American Tobacco (BAT) from 1999 to 2004. He was "pleased" to be asked; very respectable figures like Sir Roden Cutler, VC, a former Governor of NSW, had sat on the board and BAT "was arguably the best-run company I've ever seen". BAT had to perform well because a large part of the community was hostile to its product. In government, Greiner's self-styled "contrarian streak" led him, a non-smoker, to give full support to a cigarette company's sponsorship of rugby league. Greiner said he favoured sensible and reasoned debate about legislative action, but retained concerns for individual rights and doubts about the practical effects of bans. While it was acceptable to ban a product or tax it out of existence, to condemn someone for being on the board of a legal company "is pretty stupid".

Greiner acknowledged that some of his closest friends were "upset" by his association with BAT, and he "copped a lot of flak" after becoming the honorary chairman of the Advisory Council of Sydney University's new Graduate School of Management. Other members of the Council included Bob Hawke, the journalist Paul Kelly, and two senior public servants from the Greiner reform years in government. About 20 students demonstrated at the launch of the Graduate School in July 2003 where the Premier, Bob Carr, commended Greiner's practical and theoretical experience. The University Senate subsequently voted 9-7 not to endorse his appointment; it had no power to sack him. Greiner resigned early in August to save the University from further controversy. He was not critical of those who campaigned against his presence on the Advisory Council – they were following their beliefs. But he remains critical of the "absolutely pusillanimous" response of the University's Chancellor, Vice-Chancellor and Senate in "capitulating to public health zealots"; "I don't like weakness." Nor did his wife. Kathryn resigned in protest from her University positions as chair of the Sydney Peace Foundation and council member of the Research Institute for Asia and the Pacific. "If they didn't want one Greiner they weren't getting any other." She also asked if the next step would be to ban children of tobacconists from enrolment.[14]

Greiner soon became aware of how much his "previous life" intruded into the business "afterlife". Political skills were sometimes as much in demand as economic and business know-how, and not just in the Coles Myer boardroom. In fact, the former Premier Greiner thought he was actually better at politics after leaving politics.[15] More importantly, there was an element of continuity in Greiner's approach to the two spheres.

He was always a strategist who was never much concerned about the detailed workings. The Chairman of Stockland remarked at a farewell for Greiner that there were three types of company director: those who wanted to know every detail; those who were half involved in the detail and half not; and Nick Greiner.[16] The Premier who wanted Terry Metherell to be appointed to a job in the Public Service but never bothered to ask how that might be done, or considered that there might be obstacles, became a company director who thought that boards should get the strategy right and let the managers implement it.

When Greiner arrived at Stockland he found there was no corporate governance policy or remuneration committee or a defined strategy. He chaired a committee on corporate governance soon after joining Coles Myer, and was at the forefront in the 1990s in arguing for improved performance in that field. By the turn of the century, he felt there was too much emphasis on governance and too little on doing the job for which companies existed, namely, to benefit their owners, the shareholders. In 2003 the Australian Securities Exchange (ASX) published ten principles which it considered essential for good governance.[17] Greiner said he had faith in the chief executive of ASX – Dick Humphry, the former head of the Premier's Department – but the principles should not be treated as the Ten Commandments. Directors, he said, must have the "intestinal fortitude" to resist intrusion and to act in the interests of shareholders. The problem was that directors were becoming risk averse. Company strategies focussed more on risk management than on getting the company to perform and enhance shareholder value. Greiner was now happier not sitting on boards of public companies where so much time was spent on writing the corporate governance section of the annual report.

In effect, he was saying, as he did when in government, process must not get in the way of outcomes. Traditional public service attitudes, Graeme Starr's approach as Liberal State Director, preoccupations with corporate governance: all were barriers to achieving change and desired results. In government, or in business, Greiner had a clear view of priorities. Governments had a primary duty to deliver better results for consumers and taxpayers; public companies had a primary duty to deliver better results for shareholders. To these ends, both should embrace change, refuse to stand still, and be prepared to take risks.

## Liberal Party politics in the "afterlife"

Since its foundation in 1945 the NSW Division of the Liberal Party had frequently visited the issue of candidate pre-selection. In the 1980s the quest for the perfect system was further complicated by factional struggles and became caught up in long, often cranky and always inconclusive internal reviews. Nick Greiner had generally managed to avoid a close involvement with the Liberal Party Organisation. In 1993, however, he agreed to sit as a "neutral" member of a committee of enquiry into pre-selection; the chairman and two other members were from the Group, two represented the Right. He had such a full diary that he missed the first meeting on 1 April, and attended only half of the remaining sessions. Chris Puplick of the Group appreciated his presence. He noted in his diary that meetings "were still being quite well driven by Nick Greiner" and spoke later of how Greiner took on the "Old Guard" (the Right) who probably did not understand his concept of what a modern political party should be about.[18] In the event, the committee agreed on a report, State Council approved some of it, and many more committees have since met and debated the same issues.

Greiner had another and, to him, a more important political engagement in 1993, one which removed him even further from John Howard. Paul Keating had re-ignited the republican debate soon after winning the Federal election of March 1993. Howard and other senior Liberals saw the issue as divisive for their Party and argued for standing aside. Privately, Greiner prepared notes on two questions, namely, whether the Liberals should participate in the debate, and what attitude they should take in the event of a referendum. On the first, he was adamant:

the Liberals had to take part; to do otherwise was a recipe for irrelevance. The Liberal Party needed to be more, not less, involved in an issue which most interested the two groups – the young and those of a non-English speaking background – which had largely rejected the Liberals in recent elections. To reassure the doubters, Greiner suggested the Party should make retention of the existing flag and continued membership of the Commonwealth as pre-conditions for considering the head of state issue. The "rational and politically astute course" would be to help fashion the most acceptable, or the least unacceptable, proposal for the creation of an Australian republic. The Liberal and National parties could then decide what position to take on a referendum. "That is how a sensible, pragmatic and relevant political party would deal with what is undoubtedly a difficult and divisive issue in its ranks."[19]

Greiner had no reservations about accepting the Prime Minister's invitation to join the Republic Advisory Committee chaired by Malcolm Turnbull. The Federal Liberals refused to participate but he wanted to be "sensible, pragmatic and relevant". He nonetheless regarded the republic, in the same way he regarded the Olympic Games or legalised homosexuality, as an issue to which he responded. Financial reform, on the other hand, was something he sought and actively pursued. Nevertheless, Greiner brought to republicanism an approach he applied across the board. He always favoured change, almost for its own sake. So, despite his earlier tactical position about retaining the flag, he joined Harold Scruby's campaign in support of a distinctively Australian ensign. Without developing a great passion, Greiner thought by the mid-1990s that a new flag was "the sensible way to go", especially with the Olympics coming to Sydney. He remained, however, a "minimalist" in relation to constitutional change, and was surprised by his misreading of public opinion when Australians voted overwhelmingly against a republic in the form presented in the referendum of 1999. Greiner had assumed the republic would pass because it was a "rational" step. A Jewish friend of the family and of Hungarian descent explained that to vote "No" was to support certainty and security. Miklós Greiner also voted for stability; the history of his country of birth was a sufficient argument to support a functioning constitutional monarchy. The referendum experience taught his elder son to recognise the importance of what he saw as an emotional response.[20]

Bob Carr believes that if Greiner had won the expected runaway victory in May 1991 the pressure on him to go Canberra would have been enormous.[21] During a luncheon in mid-1993, where Greiner was "roasted" by friends and former political opponents to raise money for charity, Bob Hawke injected a serious note into the proceedings. He urged the former Premier to have "a shot" at the Liberal Federal leadership "because, Christ, the country needs it". He also pointed out how "Nick and I are members of [a] very small and exclusive club". Both were "successful leaders . . . knocked off not by the electorate but by the machinations of others".[22] The possibility of a move into Federal politics re-appeared towards the end of 1994. Alexander Downer, who had replaced Hewson as Leader of the Opposition in the previous May, had made several gaffes and fallen badly in the polls. Ted Pickering talked to Valder and Greiner about the possibility of the former Premier moving to Canberra to take the Liberal leadership. According to Pickering, Greiner was prepared to pursue the idea. Robert Hill, Downer's factional rival from South Australia and Leader of the Opposition in the Senate, travelled to Sydney to see Greiner. The move stalled when the relationship with Greta Thomas started to become public knowledge. Greiner agrees with this account to the extent that he did meet Hill. He did not think his relationship with Thomas was an issue. In any case, he had no intention of entering Federal politics.[23]

Greiner's standing in the State Liberal Party derived in part from one very simple fact; until Barry O'Farrell won government in 2011, Greiner was the only NSW Liberal Leader to have won an election since 1973. Aspiring and actual parliamentary and organisational leaders sought his advice. At the end of 1998, John Hannaford and Ron Phillips (the latter had replaced the retired Pickering as head of the Group) used adverse polling figures to orchestrate a successful coup against the incumbent State Leader, Peter Collins. Kerry Chikarovski was installed in his place. Hannaford consulted many in the business community, including Greiner, before the "assassins" (as Collins called them) struck. Collins was convinced that the former Premier had been undermining him for some time, and thought Greiner must still have harboured a grudge against him. Greiner denies playing any role or bearing any grudge. Chikarovski did approach him in mid-1998 when her name was being touted as an alternative leader. "Nick was blunt, as usual. . . . he wasn't convinced that I would make a better Premier than Collins, but that I would make a better Leader of the Opposition." Greiner's comment was in character: someone who had been "a policy Premier" would have queried Chikarovski's credentials to manage NSW.[24]

Although Greiner was never a factional player, let alone a chieftain, he was prepared to help a friend drawn into a faction fight. His relationship with Bruce Baird had long been repaired by 1998 when Greiner provided him with a reference for pre-selection for the beach-side Federal seat of Cook in the southern suburbs of Sydney. Phillips had enlisted Baird as the "white knight" to challenge the sitting member and former Group supporter, Stephen Mutch. It will be recalled how, twelve years earlier, Mutch secured pre-selection for the Legislative Council by defeating the conservative candidate backed by Greiner in the interests of a more balanced team. In 1998, with Mutch now representing the Right, Greiner was again on the opposite side, though this time in the winning corner. If the former Premier ever bore political grudges – and Mutch was not one – he had occasion to invoke one five years later. Malcolm Turnbull had challenged the sitting Liberal, Peter King, for pre-selection for the Federal seat of Wentworth. Greiner had several reasons for supporting Turnbull; one was King's failure as State President to back the Premier when he was under siege in 1992.

In September 1999 Kathryn Greiner made her second attempt to win election as Lord Mayor of Sydney. Some weeks before polling day, Nick Greiner handed a file to Chikarovski as Leader of the State Parliamentary Liberal Party. The file consisted of unsubstantiated allegations of sexual harassment against Frank Sartor who was seeking re-election. Greiner also showed the material to other businessmen and talked openly about it. Malcolm Turnbull, for instance, read it in Greiner's office on 4 August. His wife, Lucy, a lawyer and daughter of the prominent barrister, Tom Hughes, QC, was Sartor's running mate. A few days before the poll on 11 September, four senior Liberals used parliamentary privilege to name Sartor as "a serial sexual harasser". The move badly misfired because there was no hard evidence. Chikarovski was humiliated, and Kathryn Greiner's cause was probably not helped. Sartor headed her in the primary vote and the Sydney Alliance was reduced to two councillors. Chikarovski came close in her memoirs to blaming Greiner for pressing her to use material which "seemed awfully thin". Kathryn agreed that her husband had passed on information to the Liberal Party but said she knew nothing about it: "Nick knew I would not have gone down that road".[25]

Addressing State Council in mid-March 2002, Greiner said that former leaders should not be telling the present ones how to do their job. A few days later he spoke out publicly on Liberal Party affairs for the first time in a decade. He supported John Brogden's challenge to Chikarovski's leadership, having previously backed him for Liberal pre-selection for Pittwater in 1996, arguing in a reference that Brogden "represents the future of the Party". (Some 20 years earlier many Liberals had seen Greiner as "the future".) In the lead-up to the vote in late March, Greiner hammered the point that Chikarovski could never deliver an election victory. Those who questioned his judgment, he said, should ask any Sydney taxi driver. After leading the Party to a huge defeat in March 1999, Chikarovski was failing to make inroads into the Carr Government. Greiner said Brogden "sounds right" and "looks right" and has "a better, newer image". Chikarovski felt Greiner had betrayed her, having once "forcefully promoted" her, and she felt especially aggrieved after having taken a "bath" for him over the Sartor allegations. It is uncertain whether Greiner's intervention changed or confirmed a single vote in an election which Brogden won 15-14.[26] Perhaps the more notable feature of his public stand was that, once again, he and Howard were on opposite sides. The Prime Minister had firmly endorsed Chikarovski's leadership a week before the vote.

On 14 March 2008 Nick Greiner gave the keynote address at a fund-raising dinner at the Westin Hotel, Sydney, marking the 20th anniversary of his election to government.[27] The context of this speech was critical: the Liberal Party had won only two State seats from Labor in the preceding 17 years, yet the NSW Labor Government had gone "from fair, to poor, to simply hopeless – the worst ever". Moves were underway to reform what Greiner called the Party's "dysfunctional organisational structure" as a first step to becoming "a genuine broad church able to take the middle ground of politics". In 2008 he was concerned that the now dominant Right faction in NSW had not only adopted the "winner-take-all" approach of the Group in the 1980s and 1990s. It was preventing the Liberal Party from being "the natural home for both social conservatives and progressives" and "a party of balance and moderation" which refused to insult the centre of Australian politics by rejecting its "warm and green concerns".

A rising star of the Right – like Greiner, with a migrant background – later described his speech as "damaging".[28] Most of the audience, however, clearly accepted his central theme: while the Liberal Party should take distinctive positions on questions such as privatisation and tax and labour market reform, and retain its traditional strengths in economic management, its focus should be on the community and not on itself, on a willingness to accept change, and on a passion for the environment and the less fortunate. Greiner had a telling message. In 1988:

> we were a united Coalition with stable, well-established leadership appealing to a broad-cross section of the community, with a clear

> focus on winning and a clear set of directions. People knew in a
> general sense . . . what sort of government they were getting and
> its key aspirations for reform, or to use our slogan, "change for
> the better".

He continued to speak out, taking positions which conservative
Liberals found unacceptable. No doubt even some of them were appalled
when, in March 2002, the NSW Senator, Bill Heffernan, one of Howard's
confidantes, made allegations under parliamentary privilege that Justice
Michael Kirby of the High Court had used a government car to pick
up adolescent male prostitutes. Greiner joined 34 long-term friends of
Kirby – a number, like Greiner himself, Kirby's contemporaries at Sydney
University – in signing an open letter affirming Kirby's moral integrity
and character, expressing anger at the besmirching of his reputation and
professing complete confidence in him. In 2011 Greiner touched a raw
conservative nerve when he backed same-sex marriage. Reminiscent of
his libertarian stance in supporting homosexual law reform in 1984, he
spoke of "natural justice" and "individual freedom" and of a change
which did not prevent organised religion or individuals "acting in accord
with conscientious views".[29]

## An Anniversary

The year 2013 marks the 25th anniversary of Nick Greiner's election
to government, and the 21st year since he entered his "afterlife".
The latter remains highly productive and fulfilling, though subject on
occasions to an external scrutiny no less relenting than in the case of the
former. Greiner is Chairman of Bradken Ltd, a global manufacturer and
supplier of differentiated capital and consumable products, most notably
to the mining industry. He is on the board of the Swiss-based, duty-
free retailer Nuance Group and the QBE Insurance Group Australia,
is Deputy Chairman of CHAMP Private Equity, sits on the Advisory
Council of Degremont, a water treatment company, and advises the
global and Australian arm of the Rothschild financial advice company.
His extensive business interests – past and present – give him one of the

longest entries in *Who's Who in Australia 2013* where he is identified as "Company Director and Consultant".

Greiner's current role and sense of purpose in the corporate world is best exemplified by his connection with CHAMP Private Equity.[30] CHAMP has been investing in companies and their management since 1987, effectively turning small entrepreneurial operations into large corporations and working on a global scale. Bradken is one of its success stories. For Greiner, the CHAMP connection is both personal and intellectual. He sits on the board alongside Bill Ferris, AC, the current Executive Chairman and a co-founder and, critically, a Baker Scholar with Greiner in the class of 1970. The former Premier fits in well with graduates of the Harvard Business School who think in terms of growth and who, adapting the words of the other co-founder, Joe Skrzynski, go "where others fear to tread". CHAMP appeals to Greiner on another count; it is committed to "responsible corporate citizenship" and encourages involvement in philanthropic activities. Greiner is a member of the advisory board of Opportunity Cambodia which seeks to provide opportunities through education and training for poor and vulnerable children from rural areas. Opportunity Cambodia established its first education facility in 2009. CHAMP is one of the corporate donors.

Greiner's many other commitments include two which have kept him in the headlines. Greiner, along with a former Victorian Labor Premier, John Brumby, and Bruce Carter, a managing partner of Ferrier Hodgson and an expert in corporate recovery, constituted the Federal Government's Review of GST Distribution. Appointed in March 2011, the panel was asked to advise the Government about sharing out the tax between the States. Acknowledging he was speaking outside the terms of reference, Greiner announced early in November 2012 that the inadequacy of the tax itself was the more pressing question; distribution of the tax funds was "a low-order issue". The panel's report, published at the end of the same month, called for the debate on the base and rate of the tax to be "unfrozen".[31] It was not the sort of debate politicians were keen to have.

Greiner's second commitment is to Infrastructure NSW (INSW). The new O'Farrell Government established INSW in July 2011 as a statutory body. A principal task was to prepare a 20-year State Infrastructure Strategy and five-year plans for its implementation. Nick Greiner was appointed Chairman and Paul Broad, formerly of the telecommunications company AAPT, was appointed CEO. There are representatives of the private sector on the board, as well as heads of government departments. In November 2011 Greiner described himself as "a leader and a doer; I don't want to sound immodest but I'm the ideal person, the natural pick." It became clear during 2012 that the Premier was unhappy because Greiner and Broad publicly argued that the Government must sell the electricity network to help fund infrastructure improvements and were critical of the Government's decision to release an unfunded draft transport master plan. Greiner could feel himself becoming sidelined as one of the Premier's important contacts.[32] It is possible that the "leader" and "doer", someone impatient for outcomes and exasperated by dilatoriness, who has a business experience and mentality, was not the right "pick" to work with a former ministerial staffer, Liberal Party apparatchik, and full-time professional politician.[33] At the same time, Greiner could be excused for looking enviously at O'Farrell's massive majority which guarantees him a second term, complicated only by what might eventuate in the next Legislative Council election.

Greiner's active life is also a varied one. He is a long-serving trustee of the Sydney Theatre Company Foundation, a Governor of the Committee for Economic Development of Australia and a life member of the South Sydney Rugby League Club (he had been a President of Soccer Australia). His *Who's Who* entry, which lists his recreations as "skiing, reading, spectator sport, theatre, opera, walking", speaks of a well-rounded "afterlife". Friends and family think he is less "unreconstructed" around the home. Justin and Kara have moved on from disenchantment about their father's "sabbatical", and speak warmly about his integrity, work ethic and sense of justice. They notice how what for them had been an "absent" parent has become a very present and devoted grandparent.

Justin and Kara followed their father as accomplished debaters; Justin took an MBA from Harvard, has had varied business experience and is now with the ANZ Bank; Kara, who once wrote scripts for *The Chaser* and worked for John Marsden, is a criminal and traffic law solicitor with interests in writing, music and the media. Kathryn retired from Sydney Council politics in 2004 but has taken leadership positions in public and private companies, and in government bodies and non-profit organisations. Recently, she was appointed Chair of the NSW Ministerial Advisory Committee on Ageing. Kathryn was made an Officer of the Order of Australia in 2001 for her contributions to social work, philanthropy awareness and local government. Noting her remark about being pleased to be so busy, "because it kept her out of Nick's way", Greiner commented:

> I think when you've been married a very long time it is not all that easy and I think there is some point in her comment that the only way it really works, in the sort of case of people like us, it works if there's a fairly large amount of space because otherwise it becomes more difficult.[34]

The family experienced an important milestone on 10 July 2004. Aged 96, Miklós Greiner died after mounting his exercise bike. He had planned another trip to Europe, accompanied by Eve Endrey, his companion. His elder son thought that the *SMH* heading fairly captured his father: "Gruff, tough and ever the patriarch". Nick Greiner found a form of escape in a political career but, even if that world removed him from the White River Corporation, he remained conscious of being a European-born son of a central European patriarch. He always had to prove himself to someone who believed you should work hard, take nothing for granted, "do not despair", "restart the fight which (is) called life", and regard the family as the cornerstone.[35]

Nick Greiner did experience one very dispiriting moment and, arguably, has never really got over it. Being forced out of office was not the problem. Greiner valued, above all, his integrity, and Temby's finding had called that integrity into question. He agreed that Temby's report "cut deep", but claims he recovered "very, very quickly" – basically, by the time he returned from the Barcelona Olympics and the Court of Appeal had made its decision. Ever-rational, however, Greiner does not doubt he could make a "plausible list" of the longer-term effects of the Temby decision on his life. That list might include his rapid accumulation of jobs and financial rewards, and a brief disruption to his married life. They could all be seen as attempts to forget, divert, obliterate, compensate or manage. Perhaps the clue to lasting scars lies in the survival of a grudge. Greiner bears no ill will to those in politics such as Wran, Sheahan and Walker who tried to wound or bring him down. They were simply doing their job. Greiner got on well with Wran until the latter's sad decline, and felt "quite moved" when an ailing Frank Walker rang to apologise for his personal attacks in the 1980s. Temby is different. It was not his job to crucify Greiner. He chose a conclusion which was "manifestly unfair", took no account of the reality of politics, and burdened Greiner with the taint of corruption which could never be entirely expunged.[36] While Temby was right in thinking that Greiner was "not a good hater", the former Premier goes close to allowing one exception.

Ironically, Temby, assisted by the three non-aligned Independents, actually liberated Greiner from what had become an uncomfortable, even unrewarding, time in Parliament. Thus emancipated, he returned to the career for which he had trained. Even so, he could look back on his life in politics as one of considerable achievement. Greiner may have been just a part of the reform process under way in Australia since the 1970s. The "driest" of the "dries" may have been disappointed by his "failure" to implement "their" program. Questions will continue to be asked, for example, about the value of contractual employment in the Public Service. Allowing for every qualification, it is unarguable that Greiner changed the mind-set of government in NSW and prepared the State for a world where the sovereign power of governments was diminishing.[37] Governments throughout Australia, irrespective of their party label, adopted and expanded upon Greiner's initiatives. It is a measure of his contribution that, far from wanting to put everything into reverse, Bob Carr stresses how, in so many instances, "I went further than Nick".[38] In this broad scheme of things, and taking account of some of the recent and current ICAC investigations, the case against him in 1992 looks risible.

The British politician, Enoch Powell, was probably right: "All political lives, unless they are cut off in midstream at a happy juncture, end in failure, because that is the nature of politics and of human affairs." Greiner's political life was cut off at a very unhappy juncture but his "political failure" did not diminish what he had achieved. And, even if he left behind some unfinished business, he did have another full life ahead of him and, being his father's and mother's son, he did not dwell too much on the past.

## Endnotes

[1] Of the other former politicians, Tim Moore has served as a Carr-appointed Commissioner of the NSW Land and Environment Court, Hazzard is a minister in the O'Farrell Government, and Metherell engaged in historical preservation in Manly but slipped so far out of sight that a former senior Greiner adviser assumed he was dead.

[2] Interview: Greiner, 22 November 2011.

[3] *Sun-Herald,* 3 April 1994.

[4] *Canberra Times,* 26 Nov. 1994: *Age,* 19 Aug. 1995. On the former, see also Nick Greiner, *Civic Capitalism: An Australian Agenda for Institutional Renewal,* Centre for Independent Studies, Marrickville, 1995.

[5] *Weekend Australian Magazine,* 16-17 July, 1994.

[6] *Weekend Australian,* 20-21 1993 and 28-29 January 1995.

[7] *Australian* and *SMH,* 13 June 1994.

[8] *Sun-Herald* and *Sunday Telegraph,* 9 April 1995.

[9] Craig McGregor, "What Katy did Next", *SMH,* 21 August 1999.

10  Interview: Chris Greiner, 13 November 2011.

11  *SMH*, 12 September 1995.

12  Craig McGregor, "What Katy did Next", *SMH*, 21 August 1999; interviews: Greiner, 2 November 2005; Kathryn Greiner, 29 March 2011 and 14 May 2012. See also, *SMH*, 10 April, *DTM*, 10 April and 13 April 1995 and 22 June 1996, *Sun-Herald*, 12 and 26 November 1995.

13  Transcript, Radio National, Background Briefing, 22 October 1995; transcript of ABC Interview with Adam Kohler, 15 September 2002; interview: Greiner 22 November 2011.

14  The above two paragraphs draw upon *NSWPD*, Third Series, vol. 221, 12 March 1991, pp. 705-7; *SMH*, 1 and 9 July, 5 and 12 August 2003; *AFR*, 18 November 2011; John Arbouw, "Looking through the hourglass", *Company Director*, vol. 19, no. 7, 2003, pp. 8-9; interview: Greiner, 22 November 2012.

15  Interview: Greiner, 24 September 2005.

16  Interview: Greiner, 24 December 2012.

17  ASX Corporate Governance Council, *Principles of Good Corporate Governance*, 31 March 2003.

18  Puplick, Diary, 13 May 1993 and personal communication, 19 December 2011.

19  Pre-selection inquiry, Greiner Papers. For the public airing of his views, see *SMH*, 19 June and *Australian*, 23 June 1993; Nick Greiner, "The Republic", *Sydney Papers*, vol. 6, no. 1, 1993.

20  Interviews: Greiner, 30 March and 22 November 2011. Greiner is presently the patron of Ausflag and Robert Webster, his former Cabinet colleague, chairs the organisation.

21  Interview: Carr, 31 January 2012.

22  *SMH*, 29 May and *Australian*, 29-30 May 1993. The "club" expanded when Morris Iemma and Kevin Rudd became members. Hawke also said in his speech that those who committed the "grotesque misuse and abuse of power and due process", and denied Greiner his rights in law, were the ones deserving "a supreme political roasting".

23  Interviews: Pickering, 13 July 2011; Greiner 10 September 2012.

24  Collins, *Bear Pit*, pp. 313-14; Kerry Chikarovski and Luis M. Garcia, *Chika*, Lothian Books, South Melbourne, 2004, pp. 84, 86 and 195; Interviews: Yabsley 7 April 2005; Hannaford, 19 January 2006; Greiner, 22 November 2011.

25  *NSWPD*, Third Series, pp. 65, 72, 86-7, 256-74; *SMH*, 9-11, 13-14, September and *Sunday Telegraph*, 19, September 1999; David Clune, 'New South Wales, July to December 1999', *Australian Journal of Politics and History*, vol. 46, no. 2, 2000, pp. 221-2; Chikarovski and Garcia, *Chika*, pp. 148-9; interview: Kathryn Greiner, 14 May 2012.

26  Pittwater SEC, LPA, ML, MSS 7205/65; *SMH*, 28 March 2002; Chikarovski and Garcia, *Chika*, ch. 14. Greiner heard later that Ian Glachan, the member for Albury, may have changed sides and voted for Brogden following Greiner's intervention. Interview: Greiner, 24 December 2012. Brogden proved not to be "the future". He lost the 2003 election, and in 2005 resigned the Liberal leadership, apparently attempted suicide and left Parliament after a story was leaked concerning earlier alleged sexist remarks and behaviour.

27  For an edited version, see *SMH*, 15-16 March 2008.

28  Private communication.

29  *SMH*, 13 April 2011.

30  For CHAMP, see http://www.champequity.com.au.

31  *AFR*, 3-4 Nov. and *Australian*, 1-2 December 2012.

32  For an account of a fracturing relationship, see Andrew Clennell, *DT*, 29 October 2012.

33  http://www.thepowerindex.com.au/sydney/nick-greiner, 15 November 2011.

34  *SMH*, 5 November 2011.

35  *SMH*, 3 August 2004: family papers, Greiner Papers.

36  Interview: Greiner, 26 March 2012.

37  Dick Humphry to Michael Osborne (Liberal Party State President), 30 April 1998, in reply to an invitation to attend a 10th anniversary dinner to mark the election of the Greiner Government. LPA, ML, MSS 7205/85.

38  Interview: Carr, 30 January 2012, and material subsequently delivered by Carr to the author. See also Laffin and Painter, *Reform and Reversal*, p. 280.

# Select Bibliography

## Official Publications

*Annual Reports, Statements, and Bulletins*, NSW Premier's Department and the Cabinet Office

Commission of Audit, *Focus on Reform*, Sydney, 1988

*How the Government Has Performed: An Independent Review of the Financial Performance of the New South Wales Government 1988 to 1991*, November 1991

*New South Wales Parliamentary Debates*

## Publications – ICAC

*Annual Reports*

*Transcript of Proceedings*, 5-25 May, 1992

*Report on Investigation into the Metherell Resignation and Appointment*, June 1992

*Second Report on Investigation into the Metherell Resignation and Appointment*, September, 1992

Parliamentary Joint Committee on ICAC, *Reports, Hearings and Collations of Evidence*

## Manuscripts – Liberal Party of Australia

Federal Secretariat, National Library of Australia, Canberra

New South Wales Division, Mitchell Library, Sydney

## Personal Papers (held in private hands)

Foot, Rosemary

Greiner family

Puplick, Chris

Seaton, Peta

Sturgess, Gary

Yabsley, Michael

## Personal Papers (held in the Mitchell Library)

Collins, Peter

Metherell, Terry

## Unpublished manuscripts

Barrington, John, The Leadership Style of the Hon. Nick Greiner, Australian Graduate School of Management, August 1994, Greiner Papers.

Metherell, Terry, Autobiography, n.d.

Sturgess, Gary, Warm and Dry: the Evolution of Greinerism, Sydney, 1992, ML.

Windsor, Gerard, Friends and Sometime Scholars: a History of St Ignatius' College, Riverview, 1977, NLA.

## Newspapers and Periodicals

*Age, Australian, Australian Financial Review, Bulletin, Daily Mirror, Daily Telegraph, Daily Telegraph Mirror, Economic Review, Honi Soit, National Times, Our Alma Mater, Sun-Herald, Sunday Telegraph, Sydney Morning Herald, The Aloysian, Union Recorder*

## Journals

*Australian Journal of Public Administration*

*Canberra Bulletin of Public Administration*

## Books

Boschken, Herman L., *Corporate Power and the Mismarketing of Urban Development: Boise Cascade Recreation Communities*, Praeger Publishers, New York, 1974.

Bramston, Troy (ed.), *The Wran Era*, Federation Press, Leichhardt, 2006.

Chaples, E., Nelson H., Turner, K. (eds), *The Wran Model: Electoral Politics in New South Wales 1981 and 1984*, OUP, Melbourne, 1985.

Chase, Steve, *You Didn't Get It From Me: A Reporter's Account of Political Life in New South Wales from 1988-2002*, ABC Books, Sydney, 2006.

Chikarovski, Kerry and Garcia, Luis, *Chika*, Thomas Lothian, South Melbourne, 2004.

Clune, David and Griffith, Gareth, *Decision and Deliberation: The Parliament of New South Wales 1856-2003*, Federation Press, Leichhardt, 2006.

Clune, David and Turner, Ken (eds), *The Premiers of New South Wales*, vol. 2, *1901-2005*, Federation Press, Leichhardt, 2006.

Clune, David and Smith Rodney, *From Carr to Keneally: Labor in Office 1995-2011*, Allen & Unwin, Sydney, 2012.

Cohen, Peter, *The Gospel According to the Harvard Business School*, Doubleday & Company, Inc., New York, 1973.

Collins, Peter, *The Bear Pit: A Life in Politics*, Allen & Unwin, Crows Nest, 2000.

Connell, W., Sherington, G. E., Fletcher, B. H., Turney, C., and Bygott, U., *Australia's First: A History of the University of Sydney Volume 2 1940-1990*, University of Sydney and Hale & Iremonger, Sydney, 1995.

Davey, Paul, *The Nationals: The Progressive, Country and National Party in New South Wales 1919 to 2006*, Federation Press, Leichhardt, 2006.

Dodkin, Marilyn, *Bob Carr: the Reluctant Leader*, UNSW Press, Sydney, 2003.

Galligan, Brian (ed.), *Australian State Politics*, Longman Cheshire, Melbourne, 1986.

Gleeson, Michael, Toni Allen, Michael Wilkins, *An Act of Corruption?* ABC Books, Sydney, 2001 edition.

Hancock, Ian, *The Liberals: A History of the NSW Division of the Liberal Party of Australia 1945-2000*, Federation Press, Leichhardt, 2007.

Henderson, Gerard, *Menzies' Child: The Liberal Party of Australia*, revised HarperCollins edition, Pymble, 1998.

Hogan, Michael and Clune, David (eds), *The People's Choice: Electoral Politics in 20th Century New South Wales*, vol. 3, Parliament of New South Wales and the University of Sydney, Sydney, 2001.

Howard, John, *Lazarus Rising: A Personal and Political Biography*, HarperCollins, Sydney, 2010.

Hughes, Colin A., *A Handbook of Australian Government and Politics 1975-1984*, ANU Press, Sydney, 1977.

-------*A Handbook of Australian Government and Politics 1985-1999*, Federation Press, Leichhardt, 2002.

Hyde, John, *Dry: In Defence of Economic Freedom*, IPA, Melbourne, 2002.

Laffin, Martin and Painter, Martin (eds), *Reform and Reversal: Lessons from the Coalition Government in New South Wales 1988-1995*, Macmillan, South Melbourne, 1995.

Lea-Scarlett, Errol, *Riverview: Aspects of the Story of Saint Ignatius' College & its Peninsula 1836-1988*, Hale & Iremonger, Sydney, 1989.

McMullin, Ross, *The Light on the Hill: The Australian Labor Party 1891-1991*, Oxford University Press, Melbourne, 1991.

Leser, David, *Bronwyn Bishop: A Woman in Pursuit of Power*, Text Publishing, Melbourne, 1994.

Margo, Jill, *Frank Lowy: pushing the limits*, HarperCollins, Pymble, 2001 edition.

Public Policy Forum, *The Campaign Managers: The 1988 New South Wales State Election – by the people who ran it*, Australian Graduate School of Management, Sydney, 1989.

Richmond, Ruth, *The Stench in this Parliament: The Authorised Biography of John Hatton AO*, published by Ruth Richmond, Malwala, 2009.

Robertson, Geoffrey, *Geoffrey Robertson's Hypotheticals: Dramatisations of the moral dilemmas of the 1980s*, North Ryde, 1986.

Rozzoli, Kevin, *Gavel to Gavel: An insider's view of Parliament*, UNSW Press, Sydney, 2006.

Starr, Graeme, *Carrick: Principles, Politics and Policy*, Connor Court, Ballan, 2012.

Smith, Rodney, *Against the Machines: Minor Parties and Independents in New South Wales, 1910-2006*, Federation Press, Leichhardt, 2006.

Steketee, Mike and Cockburn, Milton, *Wran: An Unauthorised Biography*, Allen & Unwin, Sydney, 1986.

Tiffen, Rodney, *Scandals: Media, Politics & Corruption in Contemporary Australia*, UNSW Press, Sydney, 1999.

Turner, Ken and Hogan, Michael (eds), *The Worldly Art of Politics*, Federation Press, Leichhardt, 2006.

West, Andrew and Morris, Rachel, *Bob Carr: A Self-Made Man*, HarperCollins, Pymble, 2003.

# Index